The Newly Industrializing Countries:
Trade and Adjustment

The Royal Institute of International Affairs is an unofficial body which promotes the scientific study of international questions and does not express opinions of its own. The opinions expressed in this publication are the responsibility of the authors.

The Institute and its Research Committee are grateful for the comments and suggestions made by Dr Wolfgang Hager, J. P. Hayes and Dr Geoffrey Shepherd, who were asked to review the manuscript of this book.

The Newly Industrializing Countries: Trade and Adjustment

Louis Turner and
Neil McMullen

with Colin I. Bradford, jr, Lawrence G. Franko,
Laura L. Megna, Sherry Stephenson and Stephen
Woolcock

Published for the Royal Institute of International Affairs
by George Allen & Unwin

George Allen & Unwin (Publishers) Ltd,
40 Museum Street, London WC1A 1LU, UK

George Allen & Unwin (Publishers) Ltd,
Park Lane, Hemel Hempstead, Herts HP2 4TE, UK

Allen & Unwin Inc.,
9 Winchester Terrace, Winchester, Mass 01890, USA

George Allen & Unwin Australia Pty Ltd,
8 Napier Street, North Sydney, NSW 2060, Australia

The Royal Institute of International Affairs,
Chatham House, 10 St James's Square, London SW1Y 4LE

Jacket by Colin Enskat Associates
based on a design by Peter Phillips.

First published in 1982

British Library Cataloguing in Publication Data

Turner, Louis
  The newly industrializing countries.
1. Commerce 2. Manufactures
I. Title II. McMullen, Neil
III. Royal Institute of International Affairs
338.9′ 009171′ 3   HD9720
ISBN 0-04-382036-0

Library of Congress Cataloging in Publication Data

  Turner, Louis, 1942–
The newly industrializing countries, trade and adjustment.
Bibliography: p.
Includes index.
1. Underdeveloped areas – Industries – Addresses, essays, lectures. 2. Under-
developed areas – Commercial policy – Addresses, essays, lectures. 3. Inter-
national economic relations – Addresses, essays, lectures. 4. Trade
adjustment assistance – Addresses, essays, lectures. I. McMullen, Neil. II.
Royal Institute of International Affairs. III. Title.
HC59.7.T87   338.09172′4   82-4006
ISBN 0-04-382036-0   AACR2

Set in 10 on 11 point Plantin by Typesetters (Birmingham) Ltd,
and printed in Great Britain
by Mackays of Chatham

Contents

In memory of

Sir Andrew Shonfield,

the originator of the project
from which this volume sprang,
and a constant inspiration
to those around him

Contributors

Colin I. Bradford, jr, is Associate Director of the Concilium on International and Area Studies, Yale University.

Lawrence G. Franko is Chief Economist for the Compagnie pour le financement et l'investissement, S.A. (FINVEST). He is also a Professor at the European Institute of Business Administration (INSEAD).

Neil McMullen is Executive Vice-President and Director of International Studies at the National Planning Association, Washington DC.

Laura Megna is a professional economist at the National Planning Association, Washington DC.

Sherry Stephenson is a doctoral candidate at the School of International Affairs, University of Geneva. Formerly an officer with GATT and UNCTAD.

Louis Turner is a Research Fellow at the Royal Institute of International Affairs, London.

Stephen Woolcock is a Research Fellow at the Royal Institute of International Affairs, London.

Abbreviations

AEG-Telefunken	A West German electronics company
AIC	Advanced industrialized country
AISI	American Iron and Steel Institute
AQL	Acceptable quality level
ASEAN	Association of South East Asian Nations
AT&T	American Telephone & Telegraph Company
BEFIEX	Comessão para Concessão da Beneficios Fiscais a Programas Especiais de Exportação (a Brazilian Commission which oversees a programme of export subsidies)
BF/BOF	Blast furnace/Basic oxygen furnace (steel processes)
BISPA	British Independent Steel Producers Association
BL	The British motor-car firm, formerly registered as the British Leyland Motor Company
BMFT	Bundesministerium für Forschung und Technologie
BMW	Bayerische Motorenwerke
BP	British Petroleum
BREMA	British Radio Equipment Manufacturers Association
BSC	British Steel Corporation
BTU	British Thermal Unit
CB	Citizens' Band (radio)
CBS	Columbia Broadcasting System
CEA	Council of Economic Advisers (USA)
CEFIC	European Council of Chemical Manufacturing Federations
CFP	Compagnie Française des Pétroles
CIRFS	Comité International de la Rayonne et des Fibres Synthétiques
COMITEXTIL	Coordination Committee for the Textile Industries in the European Economic Community
CPE	Centrally planned economies
CRT	Cathode ray tube
DGB	Deutscher Gewerkschaftsbund (German TUC)
DM	Deutschmark
DR/EF	Direct reduction/Electric arc furnace (steel processes)
EC	European Communities
ECE	Economic Commission for Europe
ECSC	European Coal and Steel Community
EFTA	European Free Trade Association
EIB	European Investment Bank
ENI	Ente Nazionale Idrocarburi
EPA	Environmental Protection Agency (USA)
FCO	Foreign and Commonwealth Office (UK)

FDP	Free Democratic Party (West Germany)
FRG	Federal Republic of Germany
FTC	Federal Trade Commission (USA)
GATT	General Agreement on Tariffs and Trade
GDP	Gross domestic product
GDR	German Democratic Republic
GE	General Electric Corporation (USA)
GEC	General Electric Company (UK)
GM	General Motors
GNP	Gross national product
G77	Group of 77 (a Third World economic forum with, in 1980, 119 members)
GSP	Generalized System of Preferences
GTE	General Telephone & Electronics
IBM	International Business Machines
ICI	Imperial Chemical Industries Ltd
ICL	International Computers Ltd (a British computer company)
IISI	International Iron and Steel Institute
IRC	Industrial Reorganization Corporation
JVC	Japan Victor Company (subsidiary of Matsushita)
LDCS	Less developed countries
LTA	Long-Term Arrangement (on cotton textiles)
MBB	Messerschmitt-Bölkow-Blohm
MCA	An American entertainments conglomerate
MFA	Multi-Fibre Arrangement
MFN	Most-favoured nation
MITI	Ministry of International Trade and Industry (Japan)
MMFS	Man-made fibres
mmt	Million metric tons
MNES	Multinational enterprises
MTNS	Multilateral Trade Negotiations
MVMA	Motor Vehicle Manufacturers Association (USA)
NEB	National Enterprise Board
NEDO	National Economic Development Office (UK)
NHTSA	National Highway Traffic Safety Administration (USA)
NIC	Newly industrializing country
NIEO	New International Economic Order
OECD	Organization for Economic Cooperation and Development
OMA	Orderly Marketing Agreement
OPEC	Organization of Petroleum Exporting Countries
PAL	A West European television-tube system
PIL	Precision In-Line (RCA television-tube technology)
PTT	Post, telephone and telecommunications utilities
R&D	Research and development
RCA	An American electronics company (originally: Radio Corporation of America)

SECAM	West European television-tube system
SIC	Standard Industrial Classification (USA)
SITC	Standard Industrial Trade Classification
SPD	Social Democratic Party (West Germany)
SVR	Sachverständigenrat zur Begutachen der gesamtwirtschaftlichen Entwicklung (West German advisory panel on macro-economic policy)
SWP	Sector Working Party (of NEDO)
TES	Temporary Employment Subsidy
TPM	Trigger-Price Mechanism
TSB	Textile Surveillance Body
UNCTAD	United Nations Conference on Trade and Development
UNICE	Union des Industries de la Communauté Européenne
UNIDO	United Nations Industrial Development Organization
VER	Voluntary Export Restraint
VFW	Vereinigte Flugtechnische Werke
VTR	Videotape-recorder
VW-Audi	Volkswagenwerk-Audi

Acknowledgements

It would be impracticable to thank everyone who has helped us write this book. Between us, we have visited India, Hong Kong, the Republic of Korea, Taiwan, Mexico and Brazil. In addition, we have carried out numerous interviews nearer home both in North America and Western Europe. Whether we were talking to government officials, businessmen, trade unionists, academics or journalists, we were consistently given the utmost help and advice, with the result that our book is immeasurably stronger than it would otherwise have been.

We must, however, single out for thanks the German Marshall Fund of the United States, as well as the Rockefeller Foundation, the Tinker Foundation and the General Electric Foundation, for providing the research grants which made this book possible.

October 1981

Louis Turner
Neil McMullen
Colin I. Bradford, jr
Lawrence G. Franko
Laura L. Megna
Sherry Stephenson
Stephen Woolcock

1
Introduction

Louis Turner

The world economy is in trouble. Not only has it failed to conquer the twin scourges of inflation and OPEC-determined oil prices, but it is drifting into a new protectionism, as key leaders lose their faith in the ability of the older industrialized economies to adjust to the economic challenges of the 1980s. The concept of 'Organized Trade' is gaining ground. The proportion of trade in manufactures which is thus 'organized' rose from 13 per cent in 1974 to 21 per cent by the end of the 1970s (Page, 1979, p. 172). Admittedly, some people are not overly worried by this slide away from the principles of free trade, but most would accept that the growing use of non-tariff devices, such as quotas, export subsidies or minimum selling prices, is a sign that all is not well with the international trading system.

Part of the problem, clearly, has been that world growth has slowed from the heady pace of the 1950s and 1960s. Slow growth makes importers feel vulnerable and thus more likely to call on governments for protection against foreign goods. However, a further strand in the importers' concern is a belief that the nature of the world trading system is rapidly changing. Competition is no longer seen to be coming from roughly similar countries with roughly similar factor endowments. Increasingly, it appears to be coming from countries like Japan and various 'mini-Japans' in the Third World, such as South Korea, Brazil or Taiwan. These are seen to be countries with very alien economic management systems, able to draw on labour forces whose discipline and cheapness give them a significant comparative advantage. The competition from Japan and these 'newly industralizing countries' (the NICs) is seen to pose fundamentally new problems for the longer-established trading nations. In the eyes of many, much of the trade from these newer exporters is seen to be somehow unfair. One clear expression of such worries is the current attempt by some advanced industrialized countries (the AICs) to loosen the terms of Article XIX of GATT to give broader international approval to selective actions against such exporters.

This book examines the interplay of political and economic forces in certain manufacturing industries, which are currently being (or likely to be) penetrated by the leading Third World exporters of manufactured goods – the NICs (the NICs are defined more precisely below). At one end of the spectrum the book looks at the relative ease with which the NICs will enter these industries; at the other end, it looks at issues such as the extent to which the NICs are a major new source of disruption to established interests: and the degree to which the old economies are coming to terms with the range of pressures bearing on them (of which the NICs may well only represent a small part). Where the AICs are clearly not coming to terms with new competitors, the book looks at what is happening at the level of trade politics.

There is a rapidly growing literature on the emergence of the NICs, the rise of the new protectionism, and the related question of the relative ease with which AIC economies can adjust to new challenges. Much of this work has been done round the OECD (Interfutures, 1979; OECD, 1979a, 1979b, 1979c), the World Bank (for example, Balassa, 1980; Keesing, 1979a; and Wolf, 1979), and GATT (primarily the work of Blackhurst, Marion and Tumlir, 1978). Some of this work (OECD, 1979a; FCO, 1979; Balassa, 1980) is primarily concerned with the integration of the NICs into the world economy. Its message generally is that these countries have actually had a limited impact, and that the potential problems look manageable at a macro-economic level. The adjustment debate is divided between the GATT authors (Blackhurst *et al.*, 1978), who mostly argue that governments should keep out of the adjustment process, and the OECD authors (OECD, 1979b) who are more concerned with the concept of 'positive adjustment' – the idea that AIC economies can be eased out of uncompetitive economic sectors and moved into more dynamic ones, on which the economic growth for the next decades can be built. There is also a growing literature on the political economy of protectionism (Cable and Rebelo, 1980; Glismann and Weiss, 1980; Hamilton, 1980; Helleiner, 1977; Pincus, 1975; Tharakan, 1980; Verreydt and Waelbroeck, 1980). This literature is decreasingly interested in explaining the variations in measurements of nominal and effective protection and instead, given the declining importance of tariffs, is concentrating on the pressures leading to the current increase in non-tariff interventions in trade.

These are all high-quality studies, almost universally written from a free-trading stance; however, while they may be winning the intellectual battles, they are not winning the war for the minds of practical decision-makers. As we write, the market-oriented Reagan administration has accepted the need to press Japanese automobile producers into accepting a voluntary-restraint agreement regarding their exports to the United States. Similarly, the Multi-Fibre Arrangement (MFA), which governs most of the trade in textiles and clothing between the Third World and the AICs, is up for renegotiation, and all the signs are that an already restrictive agreement will be made even more so. Elsewhere within GATT, there is the attempt, already mentioned, to relax the circumstances in which importers can take defensive actions against troublesome exporters. In these circumstances it seems as though policy is moving away from the free-trading intellectual tradition which has officially guided the international trading establishment since the end of the Second World War. The question is therefore whether policy-makers are really unthinkingly engaged in a lemming-like procession towards a world with much higher protective barriers, or whether there are aspects of today's world economy which are putting the traditional free-market philosophy under genuine political strain. Are the macro-economists, in other words, glossing over problems that cannot be left at the micro-level to the pure workings of economic forces?

The authors of this book would not claim to have all the answers to such questions, but the approach adopted is relatively distinctive, in that attention has been concentrated on the political and economic dynamics of five industrial sectors, very much chosen to provide insights into different aspects of the problems of old economies faced by actual and potential competition from non-traditional exporters of manufactured goods. This is not to say that the sectoral approach is unique as a way of gaining insights into the interplay of economic and political forces. After all, one thinks of the work of people like Vernon (1974) and Warnecke (1978), among others. However, much of this work aims at examining the development of industrial policies by AIC governments. There is much less sectoral work involving the less developed countries (LDCs) and, once one has noted Baranson's work (1967, 1969) on the automotive sector, one is primarily dealing with works on the textile and clothing sector (Keesing and Wolf, 1980; Cable, 1979), as befits the central role it plays in the Third World's exports of manufactured goods.

In contrast to these studies, this book offers conclusions drawn from a close scrutiny of developments within five contrasting industries – a scrutiny, moreover, which involves following these industries from the involvement (or lack of) of the leading LDCs, through the relevant trade politics, to the ultimate reactions of AIC economies to the mix of new pressures building up in each sector. It is this contrast of industries and geographical perspective which matters. It should avoid conclusions drawn from too close identification with a single industry or pressure group.

THE QUESTIONS

So, what are the problems with which this book is chiefly concerned?

First, we are concerned with adding nuances to the macro-economic work on the NICs carried out by bodies like the OECD and Britain's Foreign and Commonwealth Office (the FCO). Given that the general conclusion of such studies is that the NICs are a manageable problem, can we get a better understanding of why other industries are not as likely to encourage NIC participation on the scale found in the textile and clothing sector? How much of the differences between industries can be explained by the interplay of three factor inputs: physical capital, labour and human capital (taken as a measure of the skills and innovativeness of any given labour force)?[1] Can we point to other factors such as corporate structures and the dynamics of the international product cycle to help explain some of the variations found between sectors?

A second set of questions bears on how the new exporters relate to the established framework of international trade. Is the world faced with a change – from an expansion of intra-industry trade, within basically similar economies within specific regions, to an expansion of inter-industry trade between very dissimilar economies in different continents? To what extent are the new exporters forcing the process by using an array of devices which are essentially alien to the trading philosophy behind GATT over the last twenty years? How do the new exporters relate to GATT? Are they being singled out for special attention under the new protectionism?

A third set of questions relates to how the AICs have, or have not, been adjusting to developments in the chosen sectors. Are we merely seeing an emerging crisis in certain technologically mature industries, or are we seeing a faltering of the adjustment process across the whole range of industries in the AICs? Are the AICs' 'dynamic' industries sufficiently dynamic to play the role expected of them in the debate about positive adjustment? Does it make economic or political sense to require AICs to get out of industrial sectors where the NICs seem to have some long-term comparative advantage? Assuming that the NICs will extend their penetration of at least a limited range of industries, what particular adjustment problems are caused by these new Third World exporters? Are there specific institutional factors which hinder certain AIC industries or regions from adjusting to the new challenges facing them?

THE SECTORS

The five sectors chosen for closer analysis are textiles and clothing (treated as a single sector), colour televisions, steel, automobiles and petrochemicals.

Inasmuch as there is no other manufacturing industry as important to the Third World, the selection of clothing and textiles was automatic. The trade and adjustment politics of this sector, in addition, are a particularly rich area for analysis. The other sectors were chosen to complement this immediate choice of clothing and textiles. Consumer electronics make up a sector into which leading NICs such as Hong Kong have been rapidly and successfully diversifying. The problem is that this is an extremely amorphous sector, including everything from transistor radios and electronic watches to colour televisions and hi-fi systems. We chose to concentrate on colour televisions as being at the more technically complex end of this sector, thus posing a problem for any NICs wanting to dominate consumer electronics to the extent they do the textiles and clothing sector.

Iron and steel was chosen as a sector which contrasts very markedly with textiles and clothing, being right at the other end of the scale in capital and skill intensity. It further appealed because trade tensions are already marked within the AIC world, and leading NIC producers such as Mexico, Brazil, India, Taiwan and South Korea are easily identifiable. It also serves as a proxy for the development of heavy industries in the NICs.

The petrochemical sector has many similarities to the iron and steel one, with the important difference that its technology is generally more dynamic. This sector had the added attraction of potentially involving some of the leading oil producers, which have the capital and the raw material (gas) to enter the industry, if they should so choose.

Finally, the automobile sector was chosen to represent one of the core AIC industries, the technology of which has matured, in which leading LDCs such as Brazil, Mexico and South Korea are emerging, and where the product is much less of a commodity than, say, petrochemical and steel products, which sell to intermediate customers rather than to end consumers. At the very least, this sector will test the NICs' ability to design a complex, expensive product which, after a long lead-time, must ultimately find acceptance with AIC consumers.

Some of the basic distinctions between these various industries are summarized in Table 1.1, which is the result of remodelling some detailed statistical work done at the World Bank (Balassa, 1980, pp. 14–15).

Table 1.1 *Physical and Human Capital per Worker in Selected US Industries (US$)*

Industry	Physical capital ($)	Human capital ($)
Clothing	2,370	11,000
Textiles	10,000	16,620
Road motor vehicles	12,890	25,400
Chemicals	21,370	25,510
Household appliances (including televisions)	8,290	39,090
Iron and steel	27,710	28,150

Source: Balassa, 1980, table 4.

Physical capital per employee is a relatively straightforward concept and ranged from $2,370 for the US clothing industry in 1978, to $27,710 for the iron and steel industry. The concept of human capital is much more difficult to define and in this case has been calculated from the difference between average and unskilled wages (thus giving some idea of the relative skill intensity of the work-force). In both cases, the clothing industry's performance has been taken as the base. The table confirms the basic picture, with the clothing industry at one end of the spectrum and steel and chemicals at the other.

THE COUNTRIES

The choice of these five industrial sectors was made to bring out the role that certain new exporters – loosely known as newly industrializing countries – have been playing in world trade. As it happens, the NIC concept is used elastically, sometimes encompassing no more than a core of six or eight countries, but sometimes covering nearly twenty. For statistical purposes, this book works with a fairly concentrated core of eight countries: South Korea, Taiwan, Hong Kong and Singapore in Asia (the 'Gang of Four'); Brazil, Mexico and Argentina in Latin America; and India in South Asia. To call such nations (Hong Kong's status is still colonial) 'NICs' is to pass no judgement about how dynamic their economies currently are. Instead, we reflect the fact that these are the eight largest exporters of manufactures in the non-European developing world.

Others are happier with a larger cast of characters. The OECD has included Greece, Portugal, Spain and Yugoslavia from Southern Europe. Britain's Foreign and Commonwealth Office has worked with an even wider list, including Israel and Malta from the Mediterranean area, and Iran, Malaysia, Pakistan, the Philippines and Thailand from Asia. The FCO even suggested that Poland, Romania and Hungary from Eastern Europe deserved analysis within the NIC classification (FCO, 1979). In fact, we have not tied ourselves to any tight categorization when we have come to consider the dynamics of individual sectors or wider political issues. If to refer to countries beyond our core eight has helped to illustrate a point then we have done so without hesitation. So, on occasion, the East European countries get a mention, as do Saudi Arabia and Libya, which are essential to the discussion of the petrochemical case.

TWO WARNINGS

Finally, here are two warnings to the reader. First, this is not a book about Japan, even though this country can be seen as a 'proto-NIC'. Where Japan is relevant, it gets referred to, but we have tried to direct the debate to the next generation of new exporters of manufactures who are somewhat out there beyond Japan. Second, this book is not just about the NICs. Certainly, the industrial sectors were chosen to illuminate the roles that the NICs might, or might not, be coming to play. However, this book is about far more. As it progresses, attention switches more and more to the question of the effectiveness of adjustment processes in the AIC world. Fundamentally, the book must stand or fall on the quality of the case studies and the relevance of the lessons and generalizations drawn from these to a number of current debates.

NOTE

1 This idea of the interplay of the three factor inputs is at the heart of the modified version of the Heckscher–Ohlin factor proportions theory in explaining patterns of trade. Ohlin (1978) has put it thus: '. . . a significant proportion of the variance in the commodity composition of trade in manufactured goods can be explained statistically by variations in three factor inputs, physical capital, human capital and labour. The proportion of variance explained goes as high as 45 per cent.'

2

The Rise of the NICs as Exporters on a Global Scale

Colin I. Bradford, jr

INTRODUCTION

This study focuses on developing-country exports of manufactures and their implications for adjustment in industrial countries. The process of industrialization and growth and the role of import substitution and export-oriented strategies have long been the focus of attention and debate in development economics. The success of several developing countries in implementing export-oriented growth strategies and achieving high rates of growth of manufactured exports in the late 1960s and early 1970s has spawned a considerable literature on these country experiences based on research in the mid-1970s.[1] These studies were primarily concerned with understanding the strategies, policies and processes that led to the dynamic export experience and their relationships to economic growth in the countries themselves.

In the late 1970s, a spate of studies were published which explored the impact of manufactured exports from NICs on the economies of the OECD countries (Edwards, 1979; FCO, 1979; OECD, 1979a). These studies were primarily focused on adjustment in advanced countries to import competition from outside the OECD. Hence, they did not limit themselves to developing countries but included Spain, Portugal and Yugoslavia, in all three of the studies, and one also included Israel, Greece, Turkey, Poland, Romania, Hungary, Iran and Malta, as well as developing-country exporters.

The present study limits itself to examining the current and prospective role of developing-country exports of manufactures in the adjustment process of the United States and Western Europe. A major part of the study consists of the analysis of specific industries. This chapter retains a country frame of reference and is intended to provide an examination of the underlying dynamics determining the role of developing countries in world trade in manufactures in recent years and their implications for the future.

THE ORIGINS OF THE ISSUE

The sequence of perspectives manifested in these two clusters of studies is quite revealing as to the origins of the issue of the role of NICs (among LDCs) in OECD adjustment problems. The first set of studies focused less on the adjustment implications of the export-oriented growth strategies of developing countries because most of the work was completed by the end of 1976 and analysed trends through 1972 or 1973 (Balassa, 1978; Krueger, 1978). Whereas the magnitude of LDC manufactured exports was large relative to LDC trade and GNP by 1973, it was less striking relative to OECD imports, consumption and GNP. What was more important, the period 1960–73 was a period of substantial growth in world trade and of rapid OECD GNP growth as contrasted with the post-1973 period. The fact that European and American adjustment to continued growth in imports of NIC manufactures has been occurring since 1973 in a context of significant disruption due to rising oil prices and the accompanying stagflation is a major reason for the heightened concern about the NICs. As the OECD study stated:

> The shift to outward-looking growth policies and to the fuller exploration of comparative advantage by the NICs had started in the early 1960s. But it only caused major concern in the advanced industrial countries in the wake of the 1974–75 recession; when slow growth, high unemployment and balance of payments difficulties combined to inhibit the process of industrial adjustment and to revive protectionist pressures. (OECD, 1979a, p. 6)

It is the simultaneity of adjustment problems facing the West – inflation, slow growth, unemployment, balance-of-payments deficits, energy adjustment, and industrial adaptation – (GATT, 1980e, pp. 11–21) that creates a context in which dynamic growth in NIC manufactured exports appears to be an additional cause of the European and American economic malaise rather than an attendant development which may indeed relieve these strains.

A second source of the NIC import-adjustment issue for the West, which is revealed by the juxtaposition of these two sets of studies, is the inclusion of non-LDC exporters of manufactures in the later studies on adjustment. It is clear from the data on US and European (EC) imports of manufactures by source that a major reason for the concern over manufactured exports from developing countries in general and the NICs in particular is that they are part of a general expansion of such exports from what one could call 'new' sources. Japan is more an exporter of manufactures to the rest of the OECD than it is an importer of manufactures and, therefore, should be considered a 'new' source. By 1977, Japan, the LDCs, Eastern Europe and Spain, Portugal and Greece together accounted for almost half of US and EC imports of non-chemical manufactures, while US–EC trade accounted for about 20 per cent of each import market – European Community imports being net of intra-EC trade (Bradford, 1981, table 4). It is not the developing-country exporters of manufactures by themselves which are the cause of concern but rather a variety of dynamic exporters that together present the West with an issue of industrial-import adjustment.

This inclusion of the developing-country NICs in the spectrum of more advanced countries capable of dynamic manufactured export growth gives rise to a concern that the current set of NICs are but the leading edge of a trend toward rapid industrialization in the Third World and the eventual emergence of increasing numbers of LDCs with the capacity to both produce and export manufactures, thereby dampening, and even disrupting industrial growth in the West.

> Restructuring (of world industry) is one aspect of the trend towards world interdependence over the last 25 years, a period in which industrial production tripled. Rapid growth has been accompanied by a shift of industrial activity away from old industrial centres to the newly developed countries and to a few developing countries. (UNIDO, 1979a, p. 15)

The success stories among the developing countries, in this view, are not seen as isolated cases but rather as part of a pattern that has larger dimensions in the future than it does presently – larger in volume, growth, product coverage and in the number of LDC exporters. Hence, the issue is raised as to whether indeed the NICs represent the tip of an iceberg, with the rest of the Third World following closely behind as the industrialization process spreads and per capita growth rates increase, or whether the success stories are more unique phenomena with less ominous implications for the West.

> Since countries form a dynamic continuum in the development process . . . [t]he borderline between advanced industrial countries and the NICs on one hand, and between the NICs and other developing countries on the other, is moving all the time and will always be a matter on which views may differ. (OECD, 1979a, p. 6)

We will begin by identifying those developing countries which have been significant exporters of manufactures in world trade. The factors that have been decisive in their export drive will be assessed as a means of evaluating the likelihood of other developing countries following the same path of export-led growth and becoming visible sources of manufactured exports in world trade in the future.

THE RISE OF THE NICs

Which are the NICs?

There is now a good deal of excellent literature that documents the increasing role of developing countries in world trade in manufactures, much of it prepared under the auspices of the World Bank. Treating developing countries as a whole or using regional classifications, without country data, leaves open the possibility that all developing countries are moving along a similar path and participating relatively (or potentially) evenly in the growth in manufactured exports. In fact, the country experiences have been quite different. In his earlier study based on the 1966–73 period, Bela Balassa (1978, pp. 24–5) noted that a dozen countries accounted for 84 per cent of the exports of manufactured goods from developing countries in 1973 and that 'no other developing country accounted for more than three per cent of the total'. (The twelve countries are Argentina, Brazil, Chile, Colombia, Hong Kong, India, Israel, South Korea, Mexico, Singapore, Taiwan and Yugoslavia.)

In the period since 1973, there has been a further narrowing of the range of developing countries that are significant exporters of manufactures on a global scale. By 1976, South Korea, Taiwan, Hong Kong and Singapore accounted for over 90 per cent of the manufactured exports from East Asia; India, 75 per cent of the manufactured exports from South Asia; and Brazil, Mexico and Argentina, 70 per cent of Latin America's industrial exports. Together, these eight countries accounted for over three-quarters of the manufactured exports from the developing world in 1976 (calculated from Keesing, 1979a: manufactures are defined in terms of SITC 5 to 8, minus 68 – non-ferrous metals).

As can be seen in Table 2.1, there is a considerable gap between these eight countries and the 'next tier' of developing countries, with Malaysia, Pakistan, Thailand, the Philippines and Colombia being the next largest exporters of manufactures in 1976. It is clear that without the export capacity of these eight developing countries, LDC manufactured exports would not have surfaced as a global issue.

The latest, yet incomplete, data indicate that in 1979 manufactured exports from South Korea, Taiwan, Hong Kong, Singapore and Brazil alone amounted to $53 billion, up from $18 billion in 1973 (Table 2.2), compared to $70 billion in total manufactured exports from all developing-market economies in 1978 (SITC 5, 6, 7 and 8: UN 1980, Special table B) and to $51 billion in imports of manufactures by industrial countries from non-oil developing countries in 1979 (GATT, 1980e, p. 10).

These data indicate that the East Asian NICs have continued to be the most dynamic exporters of manufactures in the 1973 to 1979 period and that they are the largest in volume, followed by Brazil. Mexico (particularly if the special border trading arrangements between the USA and Mexico are separated out), Argentina and India do not loom as large in global trade in manufactures as the four East Asian countries and Brazil. It is these five countries which are of the greatest interest in understanding the NIC phenomenon. The question is why these particular countries are capable of exporting manufactured goods at such remarkably dynamic growth rates and in such large volume. Is there a set of unique conditions in these countries conducive to high-volume, high-growth exports of manufactures? Or are these developing-country NICs the first wave of new

LDC exporters of manufactures, with other developing countries becoming visible sources of manufactures in world trade as industrialization and growth continues in the Third World in the future?

Two Views

These questions are rooted in two different conceptual views of the role of industrialization and trade in the economic development process. One is that there is a historical process at work, common to all countries in their economic development, which brings about changes in comparative advantage over time, leading to shifts in the composition of output and eventually to changes in the pattern of exports. This view sees the emergence of the NICs as part of a changing world economic structure corresponding to shifts in the international division of labour between countries. These changes occur as a result of a generalized historical movement in which industrialized countries vacate intermediate sectors in industrial production in which advanced developing countries are currently more competitive and advanced developing countries, in turn, vacate more basic industrial sectors in which the next tier of developing countries have a relative advantage. This view, then, sees the process of industrialization as one of historical spread in which the number of NICs will continue to increase.

The other view sees the emergence of the NICs as a process of concentration of industrial capacity in selected countries characterized by special circumstances that make high-volume, dynamic expansion of manufactured exports feasible. This view suggests that the development of substantial industrial capacity of significance in the global structure of production and exports occurs only in unusual circumstances in which a major thrust toward the world market in manufactures is possible. This process is essentially one of concentration in a limited number of countries rather than of spread to a wide variety of countries.[2]

As with all complex problems, neither of these views of the issue has an exclusive hold on the truth. In fact, to a very considerable extent both processes seem to be going on simultaneously. Nevertheless, it is useful to differentiate these two views so that the relative weight of these various forces can be assessed.

Patterns of Comparative Advantage

The degree to which the emergence of manufactured exports can be explained by patterns of economic development is problematic. There is considerable understanding of patterns of industrialization and economic development but the degree of causal relationship between these and the export of manufactures is more elusive. As Hollis Chenery has concluded:

The small, manufacturing oriented countries[3] resemble other small countries in their high dependence on trade but are closer to the large

Table 2.1 *Manufactured Exports from the NICs and the Next Tier of Developing Countries: 1976 (million US$)*

EAST ASIA

NICs		
Taiwan	6,921	
South Korea	6,747	
Hong Kong	6,480[a]	
Singapore	2,920	
	23,068	

Next tier[b]		
Malaysia	799	
Thailand	511	
Philippines	397	
Macao	207	
Indonesia	119	
	2,033	

LATIN AMERICA

NICs		
Brazil	2,332	
Mexico	2,327	
Argentina	976	
	5,635	

Next tier[b]			(1975)
Colombia	384	El Salvador	200[c]
Jamaica	345	Guatemala	155
Uruguay	170	Chile	150[c]
Venezuela	150[c]	Dominican Republic	120
Trinidad and Tobago	122	Costa Rica	119

	1976 increase (20%)[d]	$\frac{(149)}{893}$	2,064
	1,171		

AFRICA

Next tier[b]

Tunisia	203
Morocco	202
Bahrain	200
Senegal	200[c]
Ivory Coast	134
	939

SOUTH ASIA

| NICs | India | 2,803 | 2,803 |

Next tier[b]

Pakistan	677
Bangladesh	220
	897

NIC total 31,506

Next tier[b] *total* 5,933

---

[a] Excludes re-exports.

[b] Countries in the 'next tier' are determined by the amount of manufactured exports in 1976 in value terms.

[c] Estimates based on figures in previous years.

[d] Estimated total increase by these countries in 1976.

Source: Keesing, 1979, annex B.

Table 2.2 *NIC Manufactured Exports, 1973–9 (billion US$)*

Country	1973 $	1979 $	1979÷1973
Taiwan	3·8	14·1	3·7
South Korea	2·7	13·4	5·0
Hong Kong	3·6[a]	13·2	3·7
Singapore	1·6	6·4	4·0
Brazil	1·2	5·6	4·7
Mexico	1·5	3·2[b] (1977)	
Argentina	0·7	1·6 (1978)	
India	1·6	3·4 (1977)	
Global total	17·8		

[a]Excludes re-exports (Hong Kong).
[b]Exports SITC 5 to 8 (minus 68) for 1977 for Mexico are $1·2 billion. These tables exclude imports into free zones in Mexico and exports from bonded factories, mostly to the USA. The value of this export trade was over US$2 billion in 1977 (UN, 1980, country notes for Mexico, p. 24).
Sources
1973: Keesing, 1979a, annex B. Data are based on UN *Yearbook of International Trade Statistics,* SITC 5 to 8 (minus 68) and are consistent with 1979 data.
1979 (except Taiwan): UN, 1980.
Taiwan, 1979: Taiwan is no longer included in UN statistics. See: Taiwan, Council for Economic Planning and Development, 1980, p. 188. Export figures for 'industrial products' are exactly 3·1 per cent greater than Keesing's figures for each year, 1973–7. Therefore, the 1979 export figure is deflated by 0·97 to arrive at a consistent estimate.

countries in the overall composition of their exports. In the majority of cases they are also highly dependent on an inflow of external capital in the early stages of transition. *The result is a unique development pattern whose properties are less easily predictable from general economic reasoning than are those of the other two patterns* (large countries and small primary-product oriented countries). (Chenery, 1979, pp. 121, 130)

In an analysis of the interaction between industrialization and exports, Chenery concludes:

The effects of trade policy on industrial structures . . . are quite striking. Although import substitution is an important feature of early stages of industrialization in all developing countries, it can be accelerated or retarded by trade policy. The later stage of *expansion* of manufactured exports is more susceptible to policy influence. (Chenery, 1980, p. 286)

Nevertheless, there is evidence that the composition of manufactured exports changes as countries progress through different stages of industrialization and growth. Table 2.3 breaks down manufactured exports into three broad categories in roughly descending order of physical and human capital intensity and breaks down the countries into small and large NICs

Table 2.3 *Percentage Composition of Manufactures Exported from Selected NICs and 'Next Tier' LDCs in 1975[a]*

	Capital goods and consumer Engineering goods	Clothing, footwear and other consumer goods	Textiles, inter-mediate goods, miscellaneous
NICs			
Hong Kong	14·1	65·4	20·4
South Korea	12·2	44·7	43·1
Taiwan	19·3	42·7	38·0
Argentina	25·8	7·1	67·1
Brazil	31·5	17·2	51·3
Next tier			
Colombia	7·9	23·5	68·5
Malaysia	15·9	11·9	72·1
Pakistan	2·0	13·6	84·4
Philippines	0·4	39·6	60·0
Thailand	3·8	23·6	72·6

[a]No data for Singapore or Mexico.
Source: Chenery and Keesing, 1979, p. 31.

Table 2.4 *Country Characteristics[a]*

	Investment per capita[b] (US$)	Index of human capital[c]
NICs		
Hong Kong	1,371	60·7
Singapore	1,190	97·6
Taiwan	630	103·5
South Korea	403	66·7
Argentina	2,014	122·0
Mexico	1,067	41·1
Brazil	1,016	29·3
Next tier		
Colombia	752	32·3
Malaysia	495	34·5
Philippines	449	134·2
Pakistan	197	33·1

[a] No data for Thailand.
[b] GDICAP = cumulated gross fixed investment per capita, 1955–71 (US$).
[c] HMIND = Harbison–Meyers index of human resources development.
Source: Balassa, 1977, p. 13a.

and the 'next tier' LDCs that seem the most promising in becoming the new
NICs of the future. These data should be looked at in conjunction with
those in Table 2.4 on capital investment per capita and relative investment
in human capital.

Casual empiricism suggests that the larger NICs (Brazil, Mexico and
Argentina), with relatively high physical capital investment per capita,
tend to have significantly larger exports of capital goods, which are capital-
intensive. Capital-goods exports alone constitute 25·4 per cent of Brazil's
manufactured exports and 18·0 per cent of Argentina's, the highest of any
of the twenty-four countries in the table drawn up by Chenery and
Keesing (1979, p. 31) except for Spain and Yugoslavia (23·5 and 25·4 per
cent respectively). Hong Kong, South Korea and Taiwan, on the other
hand, have relatively higher indexes of investment in human capital, with
the exception of Argentina and the Philippines, and a greater proportion of
their manufactured exports are in clothing, footwear and other consumer
goods, which are more labour-intensive than capital goods and probably
more skill-intensive than textiles, standardized intermediate goods based
on raw materials and miscellaneous manufactures. Also (again according to
Chenery and Keesing, id.) Hong Kong and Taiwan export the highest
percentage of consumer engineering goods (11·3 and 9·8 per cent, respectively) of all the twenty-four countries (the average being 5·8 per cent) and
Korea ranks seventh with 5·2 per cent. This certainly reflects the skill-
intensity of their resource endowment. The 'next tier' countries shown
have the lowest percentage of capital goods and consumer-engineering
exports (except Malaysia) with the bulk of their manufactured exports
being in the third category of manufactured exports requiring the least
investment in physical and human capital. This export pattern for the
'next tier' *vis-à-vis* the other countries selected appears to fit their relative
resource endowment, relying as they do more heavily upon unskilled
labour.

While not conclusive, these data taken together tend to support the view
that the composition of manufactured exports will change in response to
changes in resource endowments as countries accumulate physical and
human capital. This conclusion, in turn, can be extended to support the
notion that the NICs are the 'tip of the iceberg' with other 'next tier' LDCs
following close behind in the capacity to export manufactures. As Bela
Belassa puts it:

[Japan's] comparative advantage has shifted towards highly capital-
intensive exports. In turn, developing countries with a relatively high
human-capital endowment, such as Korea and Taiwan, can take Japan's
place in exporting relatively human capital-intensive products, and
countries with relatively high physical-capital endowment, such as Brazil
and Mexico, can take Japan's place in exporting relatively physical
capital-intensive products. Finally, countries at lower levels of development can supplant the middle-level countries in exporting unskilled
labor-intensive commodities. (Belassa, 1977, pp. 26–7)

All of this evidence and reasoning supports the comparative-advantage view of the evolution of the composition of exports of manufactures as economic development occurs. This thinking tends to be consistent with a 'tip of the iceberg' view of the emergence of the NICs, in that today's advantage for one set of countries is tomorrow's advantage for the next set and new sources are continuously emerging. This evidence is particularly persuasive for our understanding of the evolution of internal productive capacity. The difficulty presents itself in explaining (and projecting) the capacity to export manufactures on a global scale in sufficient volume and at sufficiently rapid rates of growth to become visible in world trade.

The present analysis [of LDC share of world manufactured exports] gives a much less encouraging picture than that provided by the preceding evaluation of performance of selected countries. The contrast reflects the wide-ranging experience of developing countries. Only a few have so far successfully developed several manufacturing export-oriented activities. In terms of the movement of developing countries along a scale of comparative advantage . . . there are, so far, few examples. (UNIDO, 1979a, p. 165)

THE NIC EXPERIENCE

What has been the experience then of the relatively few LDCs that have been successful in exporting manufactures on a significant scale? In the case of Hong Kong and Singapore, the nature of their physical character-istics, location and history seem to have dovetailed to make them centres of manufactured exports. Indeed, these circumstances almost require that Hong Kong and Singapore engage in trade in manufactures as there appears to be little alternative. As Ted Geiger has written:

Hong Kong and Singapore are almost totally lacking in natural resources; their arable land can provide only a small portion of their food supply; nor do they have domestic markets large enough to serve as the initial base for industrialization. Hence, their very existence depends on their ability to import, which in turn rests upon their capacity to earn the necessary foreign exchange by exporting goods and services to competitive regional and world markets. (Geiger and Geiger, 1973, p. 8)

The geographic characteristics were reinforced by the historical development of Hong Kong and Singapore as entrepôts, which in part grew out of their location. The financial, communications and distributional skills associated with entrepôt functions made Hong Kong and Singapore alert to developments in the world economy which facilitated their transition in recent years to manufacturing centres focused on export markets. But, as Balassa has pointed out, these objective conditions should not be over-emphasized; public policy has also played an important role in both countries (Balassa, 1978, p. 26). In 1965 when Malaysia reimposed tariffs and quotas on Singapore's manufactured goods, after eight years as a combined domestic market under the Federation of Malaysia, the Singapore government realized that import-substitution industrialization had come to an end and adopted a conscious policy of export promotion. This was done by specific measures designed to liberalize restrictions and duties on imported inputs for export production and to attract foreign investment and technology. Tax measures were adopted to favour profits and expenses associated with manufactured exports. In addition, an effort was made to restrain rising wage costs and to reduce labour loss due to strikes (Geiger and Geiger, 1973, pp. 156–65; Balassa, 1978, pp. 26–7).

Unlike most developing countries, Hong Kong did not go through an import-substitution phase. It has always been an open economy, even before industrialization. Like Singapore, Hong Kong launched its industrialization and manufactured exports drive in response to adverse circumstances in the early 1950s, in this case the reduction in trade with China resulting from the change in government and the trade restrictions associated with the Korean War. The skilled immigrant work-force, the Shanghai entrepreneurs, and the entrepôt tradition sustained by a free-trade market-oriented regime combined in facilitating export-led industrialization as the central thrust of Hong Kong's successful economic growth over the last three decades. While Hong Kong is renowned for its *laissez-faire* approach to development, this orientation was not preordained; an alternative path toward industrialization could have been adopted. 'The policymakers should thus be given their due for the choice of the policies applied' (Balassa, 1978, p. 26). Also, the government took specific statutory actions that supported the growth of manufacturing industries by establishing the Federation of Hong Kong Industries in 1960, the Hong Kong Trade Development Council in 1966, the Hong Kong Productivity Council in 1967 and the Hong Kong Export Credit Insurance Corporation in 1968 (Lin and Ho, 1981). Manufactured export growth was a deliberate national development strategy in Hong Kong adopted by both the government and the private sector.

Benefiting from a relatively well-educated and skilled work-force, South Korean industrialization first emphasized import substitution in the late 1950s and early 1960s. Small market size and the absence of natural resources made policy-makers aware of the limits of such a strategy. In the two-year period following the election of Chung Hee Park in 1964, major policy reforms were implemented as part of an export-oriented growth strategy. These reforms included a uniform exchange rate, unrestricted access to intermediate and capital goods imports, tax exemptions for exporters, reduced prices on inputs and access to credit for investment. These export incentives were substantial, permanent and uniform across industries. It was not an *ad hoc* system which required daily alteration. Furthermore, it was complemented by a system of export targets by firms which received ministerial and presidential priority. The systematic nature of the reforms meant that they were in effect the organizational basis of the economy rather than an ancillary export-promotion programme. The political commitment to it gave it the element of permanence providing the necessary assurance to exporters to take the risks associated with exporting (Westphal, 1978).

Taiwan appears to be similar to Korea in its development, industrialization and export of manufactures. Japanese occupation of Taiwan from 1895 to 1945 provided a substantial injection of investment and human capital, establishing the basis for modern growth in Taiwan. The movement of numerous talented Chinese from the mainland to Taiwan after the Second World War furthered this development. A successful period of agricultural development and primary-product exports was followed by a subsequent period of industrialization and manufactured exports. Policy reforms in 1960 reducing protectionist tariffs, unifying and adjusting the exchange rate and relaxing exchange controls were of fundamental importance in placing the economy on an outward-looking export-oriented growth path on a competitive basis with the rest of the world. Again, as with Korea, the priority and permanence of these reforms removed elements of uncertainty and engaged other sectors in the endeavour, making it a national enterprise rather than simply another government programme (Fei, Ranis and Kuo, 1979, pp. 21–53; Liang and Liang, 1981).

Brazil's export-oriented industrialization also followed a period of import-substitution industrialization which began in the post-war period and ran through the early 1960s. A military coup in 1964 led to a complete change in economic policy, which first stressed economic stabilization (from 1964 to 1967) and then (from 1968 to 1973) made export-oriented growth, with high priority on manufactured exports, the centre-piece of Brazil's development strategy. This shift in policy met with great success: Brazilian manufactured exports grew at an average of almost 40 per cent per annum in the 1966–73 period, not only leading the export drive but also stimulating Brazilian economic growth, which averaged 10 per cent per annum for the period.

This export-oriented growth phase was in large measure the result of deliberate policy changes in 1968, which built upon and extended the import liberalization measures taken since 1964. The Brazilian government shifted to a crawling-peg exchange rate in August of 1968 and established an elaborate system of export subsidies, tax exemptions and export credits designed to promote exports (Balassa, 1979b; Fishlow, 1975, pp. 35–48). These measures met with great success and the 1968–73 period is now known as the boom period in Brazilian economic development. The boom peaked in 1973 as productive capacity became fully utilized (Bacha, 1977; Malan and Bonelli, 1977). The oil crisis imposed further constraints on Brazil owing to the dependence on foreign sources for 85 per cent of her oil requirements. These effects dampened Brazil's export drive and economic growth. Nevertheless, the boom period showed that Brazil had the capacity for dynamic growth in export of manufactures and brought Brazil into the ranks of the NICs.

From this brief overview of the NICs, it appears that Singapore, Hong Kong, South Korea, Taiwan and Brazil each seemed to have embarked on a highly dynamic export experience in the context of a variety of historical circumstances, economic conditions, market sizes, and physical characteristics which have combined to enable such performance (Bergsman, 1979, p. 74, comes to this identical conclusion when analysing the East Asian NICs). These circumstances, conditions and characteristics do not appear to be the same for each of these countries. In fact, there is considerable variety among them. One common powerful factor, however, appears to be the absence of natural resources. High raw-material import needs seem to drive high export growth, whereas countries with domestic resource supplies are able to sustain the same level of growth in GNP with a lower rate of export growth.[4] The occurrences of some combination of factors conducive to manufactured-export expansion appear to have been more in the nature of necessary than sufficient conditions for dynamic export growth.

The distinguishing feature of the Asian NICs and Brazil is the historic shift in the public policy at a critical point in time to an export-oriented growth strategy which not only gave priority to manufactured exports but made them the central focus of economic policy and development strategy. Several elements were involved in each case. In Korea in 1964–6, in Taiwan in 1958–60, in Singapore in 1965 and in Brazil in 1967–8 there was a policy switch from import substitution to export-oriented industrialization. Whereas Hong Kong has always been outward-oriented, in the early 1950s there was a shift from entrepôt function to industrialization and industrial trade. Secondly, as part of these shifts, liberalized import and exchange-rate regimes were generally adopted, removing quantitative restrictions and surcharges on imports and suspending foreign-exchange controls. Thirdly, the exchange rate was in most cases unified, after a period of multiple exchange rates, the currency devalued, and a realistic exchange-rate policy adopted which attempted to avoid overvaluation, favouring imports. Finally, substantial export subsidies were created in most instances across the board, so as to provide specific incentives for manufactured exports.

The question that arises is how to weigh these various elements to arrive at an explanation of the dynamic manufactured-export performance that has distinguished these few countries. The country experiences surveyed here seem to confirm earlier findings by Anne Kreuger (1978, p. 282) based on the Korean and Brazilian experiences:

> The conclusion is not that export push itself accounts for all the difference in performance . . . it is rather that the logic of an export-promotion strategy seems to condition a number of other policies and to permit a number of other favorable factors to appear in a fairly systematic way.

In other words, export incentives alone do not explain the unusual performance. It is the commitment to the export-oriented strategy by the government which makes it necessary to liberalize imports and exchange controls and adjust the exchange rate, in addition to providing export subsidies. The fact of the public policy commitment to exports drives policies in each of the critical areas: exchange rates, imports and exports. It is interesting that in the cases we have examined of sustained manufactured export expansion – Singapore; Hong Kong, South Korea, Taiwan and Brazil – import liberalization, exchange-rate adjustment and export incentives prevailed *together* over a substantial length of time. What seems to be common, and indeed unique, to the five NICs is a public-policy commitment to manufactured-export-oriented growth which entails a holistic and internally consistent shift in the entire range of relevant foreign economic policies. It is this commitment and the integrated use of various policy instruments to implement it that has enabled these countries to become significant exporters of manufactures on a global scale. These are the features which distinguish this set of countries from others. There are numerous examples of countries maintaining realistic exchange rates without sufficient incentives on either the import or export side to achieve, high export growth (Krueger, 1978, p. 212). There are also examples of countries maintaining liberalized trade and payments regimes without sufficient export incentives to yield significant results (Krueger, 1978, p. 283). But there are very few countries which have been able to implement an export-oriented growth strategy holistically and with consistency among the salient policy instruments.

It should be noted, however, that there is variety in the trade conditions and trade policies of these countries, with Hong Kong engaged in a laissez-faire, free-trade regime, Singapore with an interventionist free-trade orientation and Taiwan, Korea and Brazil having interventionist trade policies which may either fall short of or overshoot the optimality point and therefore could be labelled 'deviationist' (see Krause, 1981). The point here is that whereas export-oriented growth policies on the whole are probably less distorting than import-substitution policies, they are not free of bias and can in fact overdo incentives for exports, creating greater adjustment problems than a less interventionist approach to the international division of labour would warrant. The issue of the extent to which LDC export subsidies go beyond the point of compensating for discrimination against exports and over-subsidize LDC exports is a legitimate and significant international issue.

An important result of this kind of export-oriented policy commitment is the fact that the shift in strategy is seen to be permanent, thereby providing the certainty and stability conducive to eliciting a sizeable response from investors and exporters. 'Brazil's conversion to export status . . . has involved nothing less than a complete realignment of development strategy that has provided the same assurances of policy consistency that the import substitution impetus of the 1950s satisfied' (Fishlow, 1975, p. 89). In the case of Korea, 'the changes in export incentive policies during the first half of the 1960s provided assurance of stable profits on exports and were the concomitant of the government's decision to adopt a strategy of export expansion' (Westphal, 1979, p. 61).

The ability to 'provide assurances' derives in part from the qualitative nature of the change in policy and in part from the capacity to sustain the policy over the long run. Both of these capabilities seem more likely to be characteristic of authoritarian regimes than of democratic governments. Authoritarian regimes have a greater possibility of achieving both the integration of the various elements of policy into a coherent strategy and the implementation of the strategy over the long run. It is significant that of the five NICs focused on here, only Hong Kong escapes these apparent political ramifications. Don Keesing has astutely noted,

> The roster of governments that have succeeded in instituting coherent, pro-trade policies is not exactly a list of repression-free, anti-authoritarian regimes . . . Having labor leaders in jail as well as achieving enough political stability to take a long-run view seem to be very common accompaniments to the creation of pro-trade policies. (Keesing, 1979, p. 152)

FUTURE LDC EXPORTS OF MANUFACTURES

The preceding section analysed the factors underlying the dynamic export expansion of the NICs. The essential elements that seem to yield the necessary and sufficient conditions for a sizeable and successful export drive are: (1) *Commitment by the government* to an export-oriented growth strategy based on manufactured exports; (2) *Holistic* (rather than partial) *implementation* of the strategy, involving consistent exchange-rate, import and export policies; and (3) *Political stability* to ensure the implementation of these policies over a sustained period of time.

These essential public-policy and political elements must converge over a period of time to achieve a historic turning in the direction of the nation. The private-sector industrialists and exporters must respond in a substantial way to the new orientation. These changes must occur in economic conditions and circumstances that are favourable to export-oriented industrial growth, which include requisite labour skills, entre-preneurship, the absence of natural resources as a stimulus, an industrial base, adequate infrastructure, manageable labour costs, access to capital, right market size, etc., even though these favourable conditions in themselves are not the key determinants of dynamic export expansion.

It is clear from this summary that the dovetailing of these economic conditions with the historical evolution of social and political forces leading to a shift in national orientation is not a common occurrence. The capacities of governments to commit themselves to a new economic strategy, achieve consistent implementation and maintain political stability are rare qualities. The uncommon convergence of economic conditions, historical forces and political capacities would seem to account for the quantum leap in manufactured exports from these selected countries and their sustained momentum.

This channelling of human power into an export drive is a deliberate national effort that includes but goes beyond active responses to market signals and forces. To become a major world exporter of manufactures, visible in world trade statistics as a significant supplier, requires an act of national will and the marshalling of energies behind it. These are the unique qualities that have brought the NICs to the fore as significant world economic powers and that have led to the concern about the future growth exports of manufactures from developing countries.

Nevertheless, it would appear that the underlying dynamic that has given rise to the problem is precisely the one which limits it. The NIC phenomenon has not arisen as a consequence of generalized forces of economic growth and industrial spread, but rather is the result of the unusual convergence of a variety of forces and circumstances. The implication would seem to be that, whereas countries will indeed move along a continuum of dynamic comparative advantage, with attendant changes in the composition of output and exports as world trade growth and trade policies permit, these trends in growth will not by themselves yield quantum jumps in manufactured exports from increasing numbers of new LDC suppliers. New LDC sources will surely appear, some achieving new status as exporters on a world scale. But the number will be limited and the occurrences will be unusual. The industrial countries of the West are not facing a generalized phenomenon involving the developing countries as a whole but rather a special phenomenon which only a few countries in any given period in history will be able to undertake and sustain.

Despite the length of time that the current NICs have been able to support an export-oriented growth strategy, it is not clear that the circumstances will remain propitious. Brazil has been pursuing a more balanced development strategy and, since 1979, has been phasing out export incentives and subsidies, leading one observer to suggest that 'an anti-export bias will increase' (Tyler, 1980, p. v). South Korea reportedly faces 'its bleakest prospects in more than a decade' (*New York Times*, 22 September 1980). Since the late 1970s Hong Kong has been going through 'a fretful state of survival adjustment' and an internal debate over the degree to which the government should take an active role in economic diversification (Lin and Ho, 1981, p. 26). Taiwan faces a 'turning-point' in its economic development (Liang and Liang, 1981, p. 34) and Singapore's Prime Minister for twenty-one years, Lee Kwan Yew, has called for a 'second industrial revolution' (*New York Times*, 24 September 1980), as both face rising wage costs and productivity changes. These observations suggest that becoming a NIC is not a once-and-for-all occurrence and that, as new NICs rise to prominence, current NICs may experience periods of slower growth (for more detail, see Bradford forthcoming).

The implications of these various trends for the adjustment problems of the West are that, while manufactured exports from developing countries will surely increase during the 1980s and beyond, the surge of exports from single sources in high volume and at high growth rates is likely to be limited to a group of six to eight developing-country NICs during any given period of time. The forces leading to the rise of the NICs suggest that the West will not face twenty to thirty high-volume/high-growth LDC exporters of manufactures simultaneously in the 1980s. The country composition of the tip of the proverbial iceberg will probably change somewhat in the coming decade but the body of the iceberg will not become more visible.

ACKNOWLEDGEMENTS

I am grateful for the extremely helpful criticisms and comments of three anonymous reviewers for Chatham House of an earlier draft of this chapter. In addition I have benefited greatly from the interest and thoughts of Larry Krause of the Brookings Institution, who has patiently read various versions of my work on the NICs over the last year, and from comments by Peter Kenen, Anne Krueger, Constantine Michalopoulos, and Harald Malmgren, as well as thoughtful discussions with William Branson on this subject, in the context of a study on interdependence sponsored by the US Agency for International Development.

NOTES

1 Two very sizeable research projects gave rise to much of this literature: one, under the direction of Anne O. Krueger and Jagdish N. Bhagwati on Foreign Trade Regimes and Economic Development, was sponsored by the National Bureau of Economic Research and the US Agency for International Development, and the other, sponsored by the World Bank, was directed by Bela Belassa on Development Strategies in Semi-Industrial Countries. See Krueger (1978) and Balassa (1978) for the summary references.
2 Another view would emphasize the role of the international product cycle in the location of production facilities and highlight the role of multinational corporations in the export expansion of the NICs. We have found that 'multinationals do play a role, but it varies heavily by country' and that 'it would be a mistake to put too much emphasis on the multinational phenomenon' (Turner, *et al.*, 1980, pp. 6–9).
3 Egypt, Hong Kong, Israel, Kenya, South Korea, Lebanon, Pakistan, Portugal, Singapore, Taiwan, Tunisia and Yugoslavia.
4 I am indebted to Larry Krause for this thought.

Part One
The Industry Cases

3
Textiles and Clothing
Stephen Woolcock

INTRODUCTION

The textiles and clothing sector exemplifies many of the issues involved in trade between the advanced industrialized countries (AICs) and the NICs. As an industry characterized by a relative ease of entry because of its labour-intensity, especially in the case of clothing, this sector represents an industry of central importance to countries in the early stages of industrialization. At the same time the industry retains significant importance in the AICs, particularly as a provider of regional employment. For this reason trade in textiles and clothing between the NICs and the AICs is highly politicized. Furthermore, trade policy in this sector has far-reaching implications for international trade in general as well as for those affected by structural change in the industry in the AICs. This chapter discusses the importance of the industry, the long-term global trends in the structure of markets and the trade policy responses to the problems brought about by such structural change. Finally, the interrelated issues of trade and adjustment are discussed.

THE IMPORTANCE OF THE INDUSTRY

Industrial lobbies and trade unions in the AICs rightly stress the importance of textiles and clothing for AIC economies. Yet, while important industries for the AICs, they are often the most important industries in the NICs. For example, textiles and clothing account for between 25 and 50 per cent of industrial value added in the leading NIC exporters (World Bank, 1979g) compared to 3 to 12 per cent in the AICs, and they provide up to 50 per cent of industrial employment (around 25 per cent for Greece, Portugal and Turkey) compared to a maximum of 15 per cent in the AICs. Finally, at present, between 30 and 40 per cent of the Asian NIC exports of manufactures are textile and clothing products compared to about 25 per cent for Greece, Portugal and Turkey and an average of 5 per cent for the EC (16·4 per cent for Italy in 1979).

In addition to the industry's importance for the NIC and AIC economies, trade in textiles and clothing will be important for developing countries which are yet to emerge as exporters of manufactured goods. The resolution of trade problems in textiles and clothing may also set a precedent for other sectors in which low-cost sources are considered to cause or threaten market disruption in the AICs. A study of this sector therefore touches on issues as diverse as the sometimes substantial social, economic and political implications of job losses in some AICs and the question of how countries at different levels of development can be accommodated in a multilateral trading system.

NATURE OF THE TEXTILE AND CLOTHING INDUSTRIES

The textile and clothing industries are highly heterogenous and, in the case of clothing, also highly fragmented. As some 50 per cent of textiles are sold in the form of clothing, both industries are also closely linked. Table 3.1 gives an outline of the relative importance of different parts of the industries.

Table 3.1   *Demand for Main Fibre Types by Major Products in Western Europe (percentage)*

Type	Clothing	Household	Carpets	Industrial	Fibre total
Man-made fibres	31	11	10	11	63
Wool	8·5	1	2	0·5	12
Cotton	12	9	–	4	25
Product total	51·5	21	12	15·5	100

Source: Derived from CIRFS figures, 1979.

GLOBAL TRENDS IN THE TEXTILE AND CLOTHING INDUSTRIES

An issue of fundamental importance to both trade and adjustment policy in this sector is whether the industry or parts of it are undergoing sectoral decline in the AICs and if so can, or indeed should, this process be reversed. Product-cycle theory would lead one to expect a progressive shift of such a relatively mature industry to the NICs and then to the less developed countries, but the speed and scale of this shift, especially whether it is inevitable, remains highly contentious. How these global trends are assessed will influence corporate and public policy responses to trade and adjustment problems. For reasons of space we are obliged to confine ourselves to some broad indications of global trends.

Demand for both textiles and clothing is reflected in global fibre consumption. Average annual growth in consumption of all fibres at 4·5 per cent between 1950 and 1977 (Cable, 1979, p. 4) reflects the relative maturity of the industry in the AICs, where growth rates dropped from 5 per cent between 1963 and 1974 to 2 per cent between 1973 and 1979 (GATT, 1980b). The latter figure relates to consumer expenditure on clothing. Expenditure on other products grew even more slowly. Future growth rates will, as in the past, fluctuate but are unlikely to rise above an average of 2 per cent in Western Europe (CIRFS, 1979), a shade higher in North America and a little over 2·5 per cent in Japan, while demand can be expected to grow faster in developing countries under the influence of high population and GNP growth.

Most industrialized countries have had net trade deficits in clothing, especially with developing countries, Italy being one major exception. This has in the past been balanced by a surplus in textiles, except in the USA and the EC from 1976. Table 3.2 shows that the USA stabilized its net trade deficit towards the end of the 1970s while that of the EC has continued to deteriorate since the first overall deficit (in 1975).

Table 3.2 *Net Trade in Textiles and Clothing (million US$)*

	Textiles				Clothing			
	1973	1976	1978	1979	1973	1976	1978	1979
European Communities								
World	1,991	1,295	1,344	545	−757	−2,356	−2,780	−4,197
Developed countries	1,374	917	1,105	951	686	894	1,374	1,578
Developing MFA members	−77	−668	−725	−1,195	−1,143	−2,522	−2,995	−4,030
Eastern Trading Area	290	368	361	387	−227	−314	−441	−576
USA								
World	−77	479	321	1,243	−1,718	−2,801	−4,286	−4,375
Developed countries	−20	549	347	1,031	−448	−368	−540	−267
Developing MFA members	−121	−200	−185	−82	−933	−1,884	−2,847	−3,061
Eastern Trading Area	−5	−34	−60	−21	−8	−41	−112	−202
Japan								
World	1,340	2,650	2,660	2,381	−200	−318	−601	−1,206
Developed countries	233	582	599	353	182	149	101	−135
Developing MFA members	552	849	904	904	−280	−403	−552	−732
Eastern Trading Area	51	181	151	53	−32	−13	−52	−145

Source: GATT, 1980d.

The combined effect of a slowing of growth in demand and increased imports has led to a relative stagnation of production in the AICs, and in particular in the EC in recent years. Production of clothing in AICs has

grown very slowly, at an average rate of 0·5 per cent per annum between
1973 and 1979 and textile output has fallen by an average of 0·5 per cent
per annum over the same period, both experiencing marked year-on-year
fluctuations. In developing countries production of textiles grew by 3·5
per cent on average and clothing 4 per cent between 1973 and 1979. In
Asian NICs clothing production more than doubled over the same period
and textiles grew by about one-quarter (UN, 1979).

Increased domestic and import competition for a stagnating market has
resulted in increases in productivity and a decline in employment
(Table 3.3).

Table 3.3   *Production (P), Employment (E) and Implied Productivity (IP)*
in Some AICs (1973=100)

		Textiles			Clothing		
		1974	1977	1979	1974	1977	1979
EC							
	P	96	94	96	96	98	99
	E	95	83	77	95	86	76
	IP	101	113	125	101	120	130
USA							
	P	93	94	101	97	114	111
	E	93	89	88	93	91	88
	IP	100	106	115	104	125	126
Japan							
	P	88	88	91	89	88	88
	E	92	76	70	101	107	99
	IP	96	116	130	88	82	89

Source: GATT, 1980b.

Various studies (for example, UNIDO, 1978a) of the impact of imports
from developing countries have suggested that productivity has been a
more important cause of the decline in employment than imports. Productivity is undoubtedly the key, but the question of causality between import
competition and falling employment remains uncertain. In very general
terms, the fact that employment in textiles has declined as fast as in
clothing, despite a net trade surplus, suggests that in textiles, at least, productivity advances have been more important than imports. As clothing
accounts for half of textile demand, however, imports of clothing are
probably still an important factor.

The impact on employment varies from country to country. In the EC as a
whole employment fell by 4·5 per cent both in textiles and in clothing each
year between 1973 and 1979, and continued to fall at about this rate in 1980.
In the USA and Japan the respective figures for the fall were about 2·25 and
2·0 per cent in the USA and 6·0 and almost zero per cent in Japan (GATT,
1980b). This means a loss of 1 million jobs between 1970 and 1978 in the EC,

and a fall in textile and clothing's share of total manufacturing employment from 10 per cent in 1973 to 8·5 per cent in 1979.

While precise figures for import penetration are difficult to obtain and open to interpretation, the general picture is one of very rough equivalence between the USA and EC as a whole for imports of clothing by value. If one adds textiles, EC import penetration is far higher, particularly if volume figures are used. Furthermore, the import penetration of some EC member states is far higher than the EC average (about 8 per cent by value for clothing imports in 1978); for example, about 50 per cent in the case of The Netherlands and 20 per cent for the Federal Republic of Germany. On a per-capita import basis the EC also imports more than the USA or Japan from developing countries (GATT, 1980c).

This brief treatment of global trends indicates that structural change is taking place. The AIC industries have been undergoing a process of adjustment for some time, and trade regulation has not slowed the fall in employment. Imports from NICs have been controlled, however, so that the share of developing-country members of the MFA in AIC imports of textiles and clothing has, for example, fallen from 40 per cent in 1976 to 37 per cent in the first half of 1980 (GATT, 1980b). The share of leading NIC exports has in some cases also declined under the MFA. For example, Hong Kong alone accounted for a full 30 per cent of extra EC clothing imports in 1973 but only 20 per cent in 1979 (GATT, 1980c). In the US market the leading NICs appear to have held their position.

THE ORIGINS OF TRADE REGULATION

The origins of trade regulation in textiles and clothing can be traced to voluntary export-restraint agreements reached between the USA and Japan in the mid-1930s. This earlier agreement set a precedent, so that when Japanese exports to the USA grew during the 1950s a further voluntary agreement was reached in 1955. Based on lower wage costs, Japan's share of the world exports of textiles and clothing increased from 8·5 per cent in 1950 to 19 per cent in 1959. As European markets were effectively closed to Japanese exporters their main market became the USA. In 1956, US concern about rising imports of cotton-textile products resulted in the passing of statutory powers to regulate imports unilaterally. In view of its efforts to bring about a general liberalization of trade, however, the US government avoided using such powers, and instead pressed the Japanese to reintroduce voluntary export restraint. For the period 1957 to 1962 the Japanese agreed to restrict exports to the USA, an agreement which not only helped stimulate the spread of export-oriented textile and clothing industries to other countries,[1] but also set the pattern for future bilateral agreements with textile and clothing exporters. In Europe, also, measures were taken to regulate imports of cotton products, for example the UK's bilateral agreements with Hong Kong, India and Pakistan.

By the late 1950s it became clear that, following Japan, other countries

were increasing exports of textiles and clothing. However, the extension of
bilateral agreements to include numerous exporters presented some
political problems. During the late 1950s and early 1960s the US government led the drive for the liberalization of international trade. The GATT,
however, which was of central importance to this effort, was founded on
the principle of non-discrimination, which outlawed bilateral agreements
with specific exporters. The US administration was therefore faced with a
dilemma. In order to facilitate the Kennedy Round of multilateral trade
negotiations which the Kennedy administration believed would consolidate the Atlantic Alliance with the emerging EEC, the administration
required the support of the textile lobby in the 1962 Trade Act.

In order to achieve its objective it was therefore obliged to seek an international agreement which would provide a justification for the bilateral
import regulation agreements the US textile lobby wanted.

The international agreement which emerged was the Short-Term Cotton
Agreement of 1961 followed, in 1962, by the Long-Term Agreement. The
basic conditions of the LTA were that imports should grow at 5 per cent per
annum and that unilaterally imposed quotas should not reduce imports
below existing levels. In exceptional cases, under the bilateral agreements,
zero import growth was possible. The LTA, as the name implies, only
concerned cotton products.

During the 1960s the textile and clothing industries in the industrialized
countries underwent some significant changes. The traditional cotton
industries were in decline, and as man-made fibres (mmf's) grew so did
their importance in exports from developing countries, even though
domestic mmf production in developing countries was limited during the
1960s, growing from only 5·5 per cent of global mmf production in 1961
to 7·9 per cent in 1970.

The effect of import controls on cotton products, combined with
changes in taste and the fact that the leading Asian NICs, Hong Kong,
South Korea and Taiwan, had access to cheap supplies of mmf fabrics,
especially from Japan, resulted in a rapid increase in the export of clothing
of mmfs. Between 1964 and 1972 US imports of cotton clothing increased
by 25 per cent but mmf clothing imports experienced a sixteenfold
increase. In 1971–2 the USA negotiated agreements with Japan (mmf yarns
and fabrics), Hong Kong, Korea and Taiwan (mmf clothing). During this
period in the early 1970s, when an extension of the LTA to include other
fibres was under consideration, the domestic political forces at work in the
USA paralleled those of the early 1960s. President Nixon had made
commitments to the textile and clothing lobbies during his presidential
campaign. The US administration was also in the process of preparing for a
further round of multilateral trade negotiations, the Tokyo Round, and
needed the support of the textile lobby in Congress if the passage of the
1974 Trade Act was to be facilitated. Internationally, there was again the
problem of persuading other developed countries and especially
developing-country exporters of the need for an international agreement
covering clothing, mmf and wool products.

After the USA concluded bilateral agreements with Japan and other leading NIC exporters in the early 1970s, the initial reluctance of the Europeans to a multi-fibre agreement (MFA) changed for fear that bilateral agreements would result in a diversion of exports towards European markets. In order to persuade the NIC exporters to agree on an MFA the USA offered more liberal conditions than the LTA. This was acceptable to the US industry because of the relatively low import penetration of the US market, and a general 6 per cent growth in imports was offered. The fact that import penetration rates in 1973 were not much more than 4 per cent of apparent US consumption (shipments plus imports less exports) shows that, as with the 1961-2 agreements, the 1973 MFA was an anticipatory act of trade protection (Keesing and Wolf, 1980, p. 35).

The 1973 MFA thus extended trade regulation to mmf, clothing and wool products. As was the case with the LTA, it was a means of legitimizing *ad hoc* bilateral agreements, in this case retrospectively. The growth target of 6 per cent was slightly higher than under the LTA, but similar provisions existed which facilitated very low import growth rates on sensitive products under bilateral agreements. Furthermore, if any importing country felt that irreparable damage would be caused to its industry during the negotiation of bilateral agreements, temporary unilateral safeguard action was possible under Article 3. The justification for Article 3 safeguard actions was based on the principle of 'market disruption' originally introduced into GATT by the USA in the negotiations on the LTA.

In order to provide multilateral surveillance of the bilateral agreements and temporary unilateral measures, a Textile Surveillance Body (TSB) was established. The TSB reports to a Textile Committee in GATT, also set up in 1973 to supervise the implementation of the MFA. In practice these institutional provisions developed several limitations which reduced their effectiveness. First, the composition of the TSB evolved in such a fashion that AIC interests were more strongly represented than LDC interests. Secondly, some developing countries used the Textile Committee as a forum for discussing general North-South issues. This is understandable when one considers that, although the 1973 MFA was supposed to be an international agreement, it was in effect a means of justifying AIC import controls against developing countries. While the agreement included reference to equity obligations (in Article 6(1)) and even provided for more favourable treatment for LDCs, the use of bilateral agreements was, as we have seen, a retreat from the principle of non-discrimination embodied in the principle of the Most Favoured Nation. If AICs had wished to control imports equitably, provisions already existed under Article 19 of GATT. There have in fact been only a few cases of Article 19 actions because Article 19 also provides for compensation.

The 1973 MFA also introduced the concept of minimum viable production, included on the insistence of the Scandinavians, who felt that import growth rates of 6 per cent on top of high rates of import penetration would result in the total destruction of their small industries. The 1973 MFA also sought to give preferential treatment to new exporters of textiles and clothing, such as the poorer developing countries. For example, quotas were not based on past export trends alone, as this would indirectly restrict imports from smaller exporters who had not yet developed a large export base.

TRADE POLICY AFTER 1973: A TIGHTENING OF EUROPEAN CONTROLS

Soon after the signing of the 1973 MFA the general economic recession led to a relative decline in consumption of clothing and textiles in all AICs. For example, demand for clothing in the EC fell from an average annual rate of growth of 2·6 per cent during the 1970 to 1974 period to 1·5 per cent between 1974 and 1977. In the USA, production of textiles and clothing also fell in 1974 but recovered after 1975. During the period up to 1977 the position of the US industry was relatively favourable compared to that in the EC. Economic activity picked up quicker in the USA after 1974, and the volume of imports of textiles and clothing into the USA actually declined from 1972 to 1975. Indeed, in 1977 the volume of total imports into the USA was still below that of 1973 (Keesing and Wolf, 1980, p. 54). In Europe there was a growing belief during the 1973–5 period that this was due to the fact that the US administration had been quicker off the mark in concluding bilateral agreements with major NIC suppliers.

The EC did not begin to get its textile and clothing policy organized until 1975 and 1976 (Farrands, 1979, p. 27). There are various reasons for this. First, the EC in general retained a net surplus in textiles and clothing until 1975, when the first deficit was recorded. Second, there were the complications in the EC caused by its heterogeneity. West Germany, supported by the Netherlands, voiced its general antipathy towards any form of trade regulation, and there were in any case the problems of deciding how EC quotas should be shared between the individual member countries. This needed some agreement on the principles of 'burden sharing' (see below) within the EC, but what was more important it required detailed information on extra- and intra-Community trade flows. Until a team of experts was drafted into Brussels the understaffed EC Commission was not willing or able to take on the task.

The EC was finally spurred into action in 1976 as its net trade surplus of US$1·2 billion with MFA member countries in 1974 slipped to a deficit of US$1·06 billion in 1976. In comparison the US deficit over the same period increased by about US$0·5 billion to $2·3 billion, thus strengthening the demonstration effect that the USA had been more effective in controlling MFA imports than the EC. In 1976, France and the UK introduced unilateral measures to control imports. The Dutch and Germans then had the choice of accepting more restrictive MFA controls or precipitating a crisis in the Common Commercial Policy which could have led to restrictions on intra-EC trade. During 1976 and 1977 it was France, the UK and Ireland which pressed for a general tightening of the MFA. Compared to the run-up to the 1973 agreement, the industry lobbies were better organized, at both national and EC levels. Furthermore, the accession of the UK and Ireland strengthened the textile lobby and it was the British Textile Confederation which chaired COMITEXTIL, the EC coordination committee, during the vital period of 1977.

In June 1977 the EC Commission submitted proposals for the EC's negotiating position for the negotiations which were to start in July. These included 'internal globalization', or ceilings on imports of the eight most sensitive products from all sources, which were to serve as a framework for the bilateral agreements with the major exporting countries. The principle of cumulative market disruption was accepted, with the EC agreeing on control of imports from all (low cost) sources, even if the volume involved was very small. To do this the EC devised the 'exit from the basket' mechanism (or basket extraction), which provided for new quotas to be established for any country or product which exceeded a certain percentage – 0·2 for the eight most sensitive products – of extra EC imports into the EC or any member state. A further tightening of EC import controls was to be achieved by increasing the number of product categories from 60 to 123. These categories were divided into six groups depending on sensitivity, i.e. import penetration rates. Once the scope of the EC's overall offer, product by product, had been agreed upon by the Nine, the total import volume was to be divided up between exporters on the basis of 1976 trade patterns (EC Commission, 1978c).

Final agreement on the EC's negotiating position was not given by the Council until September 1977, owing to various member states' efforts to ensure that the EC Commission held a sufficiently tough line. The final Council agreement on the EC Commission's negotiating mandate set the successful conclusion of bilateral agreements as the precondition for accepting an extension of the MFA. The bilateral agreements were therefore rushed through in October and November of 1977 in order to meet the deadline for extension of the MFA. In the process of negotiating these bilaterals, under Article 4 of the 1973 MFA, the EC threatened to redistribute quotas to other exporters if the country concerned did not accept a position acceptable to the EC. This was the case, for example with Hong Kong, which took possibly the toughest stance in the negotiations. South Korea's position was that any agreement on quotas was better than the chaos which would ensue if the MFA were replaced by separate and probably unilateral import controls. Agreement could not, however, be reached with four major exporters of cotton products, Pakistan, India, Egypt and Brazil, who only joined the agreement later after the Commission exceeded its negotiating mandate, to the anger of the UK and France (Farrands, 1979).

During the preparations for the extension of the MFA in 1977, no agreement could be reached in the GATT Textiles Committee on the form the negotiations should take. In order to facilitate the negotiation of bilateral agreements by the EC outside the constraints that the 1973 MFA set on the quotas, a protocol for the renewal of the MFA was drafted by the USA which allowed for 'jointly agreed reasonable departures from particular elements in particular cases'. This 'reasonable departures' clause enabled the EC to conclude the more restrictive bilateral agreements with major suppliers. Because of its effect of weakening the original agreement, the 'reasonable departures' clause remains a bone of contention for developing countries, especially since various countries have used it as a means of tightening import controls. The developing countries maintain that the clause only applies to the EC.

THE MEDITERRANEAN TRADE POLICY

Having gained some satisfaction on the 1977-negotiated MFA, the industry lobbies in Europe turned their attention to other areas of concern. As early as May 1978 the industry and some member states sought to extract commitments from the EC Commission negotiators to a further extension of the MFA in 1982 (UK, House of Lords, 1979, p. 31). Secondly, the 1977 MFA negotiating mandate included provisions that the MFA would not be undermined by imports from Mediterranean countries.

Between 1977 and 1978 the share of Portugal, Spain, Greece and Turkey in the EC's extra-EC imports of textiles increased from 20 per cent to 24 per cent by volume, a growth of 30 per cent, compared to a fall of 2·6 per cent in imports of textiles from developing countries. Clothing imports from these major Mediterranean exporters accounted for 11·4 per cent of extra-EC imports in 1978, up from 10·5 per cent in 1977 and a growth by volume of 13·4 per cent compared to a 3·4 per cent growth rate for the imports from developing countries (Eurostat). But it was not so easy to regulate imports from such Mediterranean countries, owing to the existence of association agreements with the EC which provided for free access of industrial products. Safeguard actions under the association agreements are accompanied by stricter conditions than is the case with the MFA. Indeed, in the case of Greece there was no safeguard clause to fall back on. In 1978 the EC Commission managed to negotiate a series of voluntary restraint agreements, but these were soon exceeded and the industry pressed the Commission to reach more secure agreements. In January 1979 the EC finally reached agreement with Portugal on a three-year voluntary restraint agreement which limited import growth to between 1 and 2 per cent (*Guardian*, 29 January 1979). Agreements were also reached with Greece and Spain and other Mediterranean exporters for 1980 and 1981, but these agreements could only be reached after the Commission had made concessions on quotas which in some cases breached the global ceilings agreed by the Nine. These concessions must be seen in the context of the general need that was felt to support these new democracies, which were in the process of seeking, or indeed negotiating, accession to the EC. From the point of view of the Asian NICs, the enlargement of the EC to include such important textile and clothing producers will inevitably increase competition for markets in the EC and thus the pressure to limit extra-EC imports.

The Mediterranean countries have caused other major difficulties for EC trade policy in textiles. For example, 'burden sharing', in which extra-EC import growth is shared between EC member states, is not possible in the case of imports from the associated Mediterranean countries. This is because the voluntary agreements do not have legal standing as have the MFA bilateral agreements. Under EEC law it is only possible to regulate intra-Community trade for those products which are covered by restrictions under the Common Commercial Policy. For example, if Hong Kong exports clothing to West Germany, which then exports the same products to France or the UK, this intra-EEC trade can be controlled, under Article 115 EEC, if the French or British quotas for the clothing items from Hong Kong have been exceeded.

Outward Processing

A further complication arises from the practice of outward processing of clothing products. In order to secure Mediterranean cooperation in regulating outward processing, the EC Commission was obliged to offer reasonably generous quotas for these products on top of those agreed under the voluntary-restraint agreements for normal imports. The UK refused to accept these additional quotas and continued to count outward processed goods as part of the quota allocated to each Mediterranean country. As German and Dutch producers are very active in outward processing with both the Mediterranean and Eastern Europe, it has been possible for these producers to balance higher domestic costs by relocating the production of some items and thus improving competitiveness. The problem then arises as to how this can be accommodated within the EC burden-sharing principle. In order to solve the problem the EC Commission, pressed by the UK, France and EC trade unions, has made proposals to regulate outward processing. These include, for example, provisions which would limit outward processing for any domestic producer to a certain percentage of his previous year's production (*Agence Europe*, 15 October 1979, 25 February 1981). Similar guidelines have existed in West Germany for some time, but the German measures limit outward processing to 30 per cent of production for any given country. Consequently, if a producer has product sources from three countries, which is not uncommon, he can relocate 90 per cent of his domestic production. The first EC proposals were directed at outward processing with the Mediterranean countries, and future efforts can be expected to be directed towards outward processing with Eastern Europe.

To summarize, there has been a progressive increase in the types of regulation used to control imports of textiles and clothing in the EC. After regulating imports from developing countries under the 1977 MFA, the Europeans, led by the UK and France, then proceeded to press for regulation of Mediterranean imports. As with the USA during the 1960s, trade regulation with one source of supply led to regulation with all sources of supply in order to prevent, or more frequently to anticipate and control, trade diversion. The spread of regulation, however, has not stopped with imports from low-cost sources, but has been extended to include other manifestations of the international division of labour, such as outward processing. There are also implications for trade between developed countries, as evidenced for example by the proposal to include US–EC trade in the MFA bilateral agreements (*Agence Europe*, No. 3101). If the national governments of the EC persist in their objective of maintaining large-scale textile and clothing industries at all costs, regulation can be expected to extend further. If outward processing is controlled with 'the Southern and Eastern European NICs', it can be expected that outward-processing business will shift to other low-cost countries.

DEVELOPMENTS IN THE USA AFTER 1977

On the other side of the Atlantic the demonstration effect of the achievements of the European industry in gaining tighter controls began to operate in 1978. As in 1961 and 1973 the strength of the textile lobby in Congress helped to ensure that the Carter administration also committed itself to treating the textile industry as a special case. This was done by threatening to delay on block the passage of legislation implementing the Tokyo Round agreement on the Multilateral Trade Negotiations (MTNs). After six years of laborious negotiations, the textile lobby was thus threatening to undermine an agreement which was thought to be essential if the general drift towards greater protectionism was to be arrested. The strong bargaining position of the textile lobby in Congress was achieved by linking the Textile Exclusion Bill, which would have excluded textiles and clothing from the MTN tariff reductions, to its support for legislation to extend for a further period the administration's power to waive the imposition of countervailing duties. Both the inclusion of textiles and clothing and the extension of the waiver powers were needed if the USA was to persuade its AIC trading partners to accept the MTN package and thus finally bring the Tokyo Round to a successful conclusion. President Carter did veto the Textile Exclusion Bill, but he was obliged to make certain commitments to the US textile and clothing lobby before they would support an extension of the waiver powers. These commitments ultimately took the form of the Administration Textile Program of 15 February 1979. In this policy document the US government expressed its determination 'to assist the beleaguered textile and apparel industry' and its 'commitment to its health and growth'. The Carter administration also stated its objective of assuring 'that 1979 imports will not exceed 1978 trade levels or 1979 base levels, whichever are lower' and that 'import growth will be evaluated in each of the next three years [1979–82] . . . in the context of the estimated rate of growth in the domestic market, category by category, and adjustments made'. The USA had, therefore, introduced the concept of linking import-growth rates with the growth of domestic demand, an objective picked up by the European industry as its central demand for the next MFA in 1982. US policy followed the European lead by embracing the principle of global import evaluation, 'consisting of a continuous evaluation of imports . . . from all countries', thus opening the way for a form of secondary defence against imports along the lines of the EC's 'basket extraction'.

Textiles and clothing in the USA were excluded from the new GATT code on liberalization of public procurement policies, and the US government committed itself to nullifying MTN tariff reductions if the MFA was not extended in 1982. Furthermore, 'in the event the MFA not being renewed or a suitable arrangement not being put into place, legislative remedies were to be proposed to allow the President authority to unilaterally control imports of textile and apparel products'. As in 1961 and 1977 in the EC, the USA was therefore threatening unilateral action if the leading NIC exporters failed to agree to bilateral agreements. The US government would certainly wish to avoid unilateral import controls, because the necessary legislation would inevitably be seen as a precedent for other industries. With strong steel and automobile lobbies in Congress, there would be pressure to include these other troubled industries in such legislation.

By way of implementing its 1980 programme the USA entered into fresh negotiations with its major exporters in 1979–80 in order to reduce the degree of flexibility in the quotas negotiated only a few years before. The flexibility provisions in the bilateral agreements allowed for quotas to be transferred from one product to another, to 'swing', or to be 'carried over' or 'carried forward' from year to year. While the renegotiations of the flexibility provisions, with Hong Kong then Korea and Taiwan, may have done little to reduce the overall volume of imports, they nevertheless undermined the confidence of the NICs in the sanctity of bilateral agreements.

CORPORATE ADJUSTMENT PROBLEMS

In the clothing industry AIC producers face the problem of high wage costs, especially in Northern Europe, and relatively slow growth in demand compared with other industries. In other sectors the development of large conglomerate corporations has, to a degree, facilitated adjustment from lines of production under pressure to others with better growth prospects. In clothing, however, the industry is still predominantly composed of small-scale companies. Concentration has occurred, and continues at a steady pace, but the clothing industry is still characterized by a large number of small producers, about 10,000 companies in the EC in 1975 and 15,000 in the USA (US Department of Commerce, 1980, p. 368).

Economies of scale in clothing are limited, but some scope exists in handling and to some extent in longer production runs, so that medium sized plants with between 100 and 200 employees do show slightly higher rates of turnover per employee (EC Commission, 1980a). Marketing research and design also offer some scope for economies of scale and

evidence from US apparel companies shows that companies large enough to
strengthen their marketing operations, for example by promoting branded
products, have been more successful than smaller firms for which large-
scale marketing drives are too expensive (de la Torre, *et al.*, 1978). In
Europe, Italy is a case in which wholesale operations, which monitor
fashion and market trends, effectively coordinate the disposition of orders
to a multitude of small, often family-owned, clothing producers. In Japan
also the coordinating function exercised by the major wholesalers has
enabled the industry to defend itself against imports (Nomura Research
Institute, 1979). Where the links between retail and production are
relatively weak, such as in the UK, the domestic industry has been less
successful in competing with imports. The fact that strong retail–
production links help is exemplified by the case of Marks & Spencer in the
UK which places some 90 per cent of its orders in the UK and by the 1979
initiative to improve industry–retail liaison for the whole of the British
industry under the auspices of the NEDO. Effective marketing and promotion of branded products can enable AIC producers to compete with the
NICs as, for example, in the case of US jeans manufacturers. Closer
retailer–producer links, however, are not without international implications. For example, the dominant position of wholesalers in Japan has been
seen as a form of the much criticized 'Japan incorporated' practices.

A further strategy for AIC clothing producers is to exploit their proximity
to AIC fashion markets and concentrate on higher-value-added items. As
this top end of the market accounts for only 10–15 per cent, specialization
on high-fashion items at the expense of standard products would not
sustain AIC clothing industries of any substantial size. Furthermore,
quantitative restrictions on NIC imports have encouraged NIC producers to
move into higher-value-added products in order to maintain export
earnings despite restrictions on import volume. The competition in
higher-value-added products both within the AICs and from the NICs is
therefore intense and profit margins are often low.

Improved production technology is a strategy which is traditionally
employed to counter imports from low-cost sources. This is a strategy that
textile producers have employed. By restructuring of production, in the
form of concentration and capital deepening to improve productivity, the
textile industry has been able to increase economies of scale more than the
clothing industry. As has been shown, however, this has been at the
expense of a more rapid and progressive decline in employment. As such
restructuring takes time the industry has generally sought a temporary
breathing-space from import competition. It is, however, only too
apparent that temporary measures have become permanent. There are
numerous reasons why this is so, but, put simply, it is that the growth in
the market has not been sufficient to support the restructuring programmes. This is illustrated by the mmf industry in Western Europe. As
new capital investment results in improved production speeds, restructuring along these lines also necessitates the closure of older plant if new
investment is not to increase capacity and thus exacerbate the problems

caused by stagnating demand. In Western Europe in particular, there has been a reluctance to close down older textile mills because of employment objectives. Indeed in some cases, such as in mmfs, publicly-backed investment has actually set out with the objective of increasing national capacity, as it did in Italy. There has been also a tendency for governments and producers alike to exaggerate projections of future demand in order to justify, in economic terms, what is in fact a political decision to invest or support investment in order to provide employment or increase national productive capacity. In Western Europe the problem has been exacerbated by the relatively fragmented structure of mmf production, compared with the USA, resulting from residual nationalism, which has inhibited cross-frontier rationalization. As any student of the EC will know, the problems associated with such cross-frontier industrial strategy cannot be overstated. The net effect of competitive investment in order to improve productivity has, therefore, been that profit margins have been reduced because demand cannot sustain the level of production needed to cover the increased fixed costs. Lower profit margins in turn make companies highly vulnerable to fluctuations in demand or increases in imports (Thormählen, 1978).

In the clothing industry the scope for investment in improved production processes is more limited. A study commissioned by the EC Commission concluded that there is some scope for new technology, for example in the use of microprocessors in clothing operations and production control. Robot technology could also be employed in machine loading and stitching operations. There are, however, various problems associated with such a general strategy. First, before investment can take place, confidence in the future viability of the industry would have to be strengthened. This, as the industry has pointed out, means import regulation. If imports are regulated effectively, however, how can one guarantee that the necessary adjustment takes place? This is a problem for AIC governments, especially if they are loath to intervene directly in corporate policy. It also raises the general issue of the links between national industrial policies which influence investment and trade regulation. Secondly, the major importance of the clothing industry for the AICs stems from its role as an employer of predominantly female labour, often in less industrialized regions of the AICs. In order to compete with lower wage economies many AIC producers of clothing have relocated production in semi-rural areas in order to tap a supply of relatively low-paid female labour. This has been the case in the USA, where the industry has moved from New York and Pennsylvania to the Carolinas (US Department of Commerce, 1980, p. 368). It is also the case in Europe; in West Germany for example, there is a relative concentration of the industry in, among other areas, Franken and Niederbayern. In Oberfranken the clothing industry accounts for 8 per cent of industrial employment. As the Conseil Économique et Social (1978) has pointed out, many small towns and even villages in France are dependent on one or two clothing plants for their industrial employment. A policy of increased investment in new technology would, if it is to be successful, lead to a further decline in employment, as it has in the textile industry. There is therefore an unavoidable conflict between the objectives of corporate viability and national employment objectives, which is all too easily solved by import controls. Another possible strategy which exemplifies this conflict is the relocation of some production to low-cost countries (outward processing). The German industry which adopted this general strategy early in the 1970s shed labour faster than the British, which did not. At the same time the German industry has been able to maintain its competitive position *vis-à-vis* the UK industry despite wage costs twice those of the UK during the 1970s.

So far we have discussed the problems of adjustment in the form of restructuring in order to regain or maintain international competitiveness. Rather than attempt to regain a competitive advantage in existing product lines, corporate strategies can aim to diversify into new products. In clothing as we have seen, however, clothing producers are often too small to be able to move out of clothing. In textiles the substitution of mmfs for cotton provided a form of product diversification during the 1960s, but this has now reached a plateau and there are few technological break-throughs in mmfs on the horizon.[2]

Finally, adjustment in the clothing and textile industry poses the problem for AIC governments of deciding between the costs of continuing to support the industry and the costs of allowing the industry to decline. If sustaining the industry at its present size requires investment in capital and human capital in the form of entrepreneurial and technical skills, would it not be better, for the economy as a whole, to release these resources so that they might be employed in sectors with better long-term prospects of retaining international competitiveness?

However, during a period in which industrial employment in general is declining faster than the growth of employment in the service sector, where are the alternative jobs to come from? The problems of adjustment thus often pose difficult and politically unpleasant questions for AIC governments. Given such a situation AIC politicians have tended to avoid having to make unpleasant choices, and to provide assistance for the textile and clothing industries in the form of protection against NIC imports. To date the NICs have not had the power to impose high costs in terms of retaliation. However, as the NICs become more assertive in their retaliation and, what is more important, as trade disputes in textiles begin to spill over into trade between, for example, the USA and Europe, policy-makers may be forced to look again at the relatively neglected issue of adjustment policies.

ADJUSTMENT POLICIES

The principal objective of the MFA was to avoid the disruptive effects of changes in the pattern of trade in textiles. Article 1(4) of the MFA, however, refers to the need for 'industrial adjustment'. The MFA envisaged that the regulation of trade would be 'accompanied by economic and social policies . . . which would encourage businesses which are less competitive internationally to move progressively into more viable lines of production . . . or other sectors of the economy'.

The us Trade Acts of 1962 and 1974 contain provisions which specifically limit the provision of adjustment assistance for workers or producers to imports. Up to the mid-1970s these provisions were seldom used because of the restrictive interpretation of the conditions governing the payment of assistance. The textiles and clothing sector also had little success in its petitions for assistance (de la Torre, 1978, p. 211). In 1977 the us General Accounting Office recommended that assistance be provided to more workers affected by imports. With the more liberal use of the adjustment assistance provisions (Frank, 1977), attention centred on how the financial support was being used. A subsequent study of Pennsylvania apparel workers showed that the scheme was not working well. Payments were often late and inaccurate and it was found that the financial assistance provided to workers was used as a means of extending the period of paid unemployment. Workers rarely sought benefits such as training, job-search allowances or job-relocation allowances (Comptroller-General, 1978). Although financial compensation to workers losing jobs can promote labour mobility and thus reduce resistance to change, the payment of compensation to us apparel workers was delayed and not provided in a lump sum. It has been suggested that if a lump-sum payment had been made at the time of redundancy, the assistance might have encouraged workers affected to take the money and seek other employment (Wolf, 1979, p. 148).

Adjustment assistance for producers was also only provided once it had been proved that the company concerned had been affected by import competition. Studies of various us apparel companies have shown that if adjustment assistance is to be effective it must be not only timely but also based on a sound development plan (de la Torre, 1978, p. 213d). As the provision of assistance to clothing manufacturers, often in the form of finance for consultancy work, took, on average, nearly two years from the time firms petitioned for assistance, the chances of adjustment assistance helping companies bring about a complete reversal in their commercial prospects were limited. The us adjustment assistance programme, therefore, does not seem to have offered an alternative to protection and, as the costs of the scheme grew towards the end of the 1970s, criticism of its effectiveness mounted. Undoubtedly, the scheme can be improved upon, for example, by introducing some form of early warning system so that corporate strategies can bring about the necessary changes before resources and confidence are weakened. But the problems of devising policies with such anticipatory elements are formidable, and import regulation offers an apparently simple alternative. In assessing the pros and cons of adjustment assistance, however, it is necessary to take proper account of the costs. As import regulation does not appear as a visible cost to the exchequer there is inevitably a temptation to use import control as a means of providing assistance. As a 1980 Federal Trade Commission study of US apparel imports has suggested, however, the costs for consumers and thus for the economy in general may, at US$1·4 billion per annum, be considered too high (*Business Week*, 25 August 1980). Following the installation in 1980 of an administration which has made radical cuts in public expenditure on adjustment assistance it remains to be seen whether import controls will be dismantled as part of this economic policy.

In Western Europe, Sweden offers an interesting example of what happens when temporary restrictions on imports from developing countries are not basically protectionist in intent but seek to 'reach a balance between protection and adjustment in an especially difficult case' (ILO, 1976, vol. 11, p. 96). During the 1960s, imports of textiles and clothing grew at 22 per cent. In a relatively small market it was not long before these had a significant impact on the Swedish industry, producing a fall in employment and production. During the 1960s the relatively buoyant economy and generous social-security provisions facilitated adjustment without recourse to excessively protectionist policies. In 1970 an adjustment programme was devised to help the industry cope with the process of adjustment, but no attempt was made to reverse existing trends. By 1974 a reappraisal of the policy found that the industry was declining more rapidly than had been envisaged. As a result, the concept of minimum viable production was applied to the textile industry, and Sweden pressed for the inclusion of this principle in the MFA.

The Swedish case is therefore an example of what happens when import controls are not protectionist in nature but merely serve to regulate the process of adjustment. The resultant decline of the industry then led to a tightening of import controls when the continued viability of the industry was at stake. Sweden's net trading deficit in textiles and clothing in 1974 was more than half that of the massive US market. Therefore, if one accepts Sweden's criteria for minimum viability to be correct and, given the size of the Swedish market compared with that of the USA, one must assume that there is a long way to go before the minimum viability of the US or EC industries is in question.

In the Netherlands also, an open trade policy has been combined with an adjustment policy which has set out to promote adjustment to imports from developing countries (Alford, 1979). In both the Dutch and Swedish industries output and employment have declined faster than in any other OECD countries. In ten years, employment in the Dutch cotton, rayon and linen industry, which was concentrated in areas such as Overijssel (where textiles still accounted for 11 per cent of total industrial employment in 1976), declined by 50 per cent. A reduction of similar size took place in the clothing industry in just five years between 1972 and 1977. In an attempt to cope with the contradictory aims of maintaining employment and promoting trade with developing countries, a policy of 'industrial adjustment with a development dimension' was introduced in 1976. Under the scheme to promote relocation of production in the LDCs, 70 per cent of available funds went to the textile and clothing industries. In addition to the general adjustment policy, tripartite restructuring organizations were established for many subsectors of the industry. In cotton-weaving, for example, it was possible to provide alternative employment or early retirement benefit to all those who lost their jobs during the implementation of a mutually agreed restructuring programme. The cotton-weaving programme also involved a reduction in productive capacity (*Financial Times*, 15 January 1980).

The Dutch adjustment policies were unique in the sense that they not only attempted to promote relocation of production to developing countries, but also aimed at reducing domestic capacity. Other sectoral policies, such as the British Wool Textile Industry Scheme (UK, Department of Industry, 1978), attempted to improve productivity without reducing capacity. Even the early UK Cotton Industry Act, which set out to reduce capacity in cotton-spinning and weaving, effectively increased capacity (Miles, 1968).

In general there is a predominance of general policies of adjustment assistance in Western Europe. These take the form of aid for workers affected by technological change, such as the German Arbeitsförderungsgesetz (Law on Employment Promotion) or regional investment grants. In many cases these programmes help ease the process of adjustment in the textile and clothing industries. In some cases, however, general policies are applied in such a way that they benefit the textile and clothing industry. Under the Temporary Employment Subsidy (TES) in the UK, for example, more than half of the £150 million went to maintain employment in textiles and clothing. As with similar Belgian and Italian schemes which subsidize labour costs, the Commission of the EC attacked the TES as constituting unfair competition, and finally forced the UK to modify the scheme. Provided intra-EEC trade is affected the EC Commission has powers under Community law to prohibit this form of defensive aid. The 1977 agreement between mmf producers is a case in point, in which, although supported by the Industry Directorate in Brussels, the agreement finally had to be modified in December 1979 because it was open to attack in the European Court of Justice.

Such control at EC level over national aid policies can only function if national policies are themselves constrained. EC experience in the textile sector has shown that if national political pressure is too strong, governments will rather risk breaching GATT or EC legal obligations. In this context a major difficulty with the use of import regulation as a means of providing assistance to the national industry is that there is no effective domestic constraint on national policy. The costs of import control are dispersed, and as it is the individual households which account for about 90 per cent of demand, opposition lobbies to import controls are not easy to organize. The view that it is in the general interests not to bind economic resources in less efficient forms of production has not been sufficient to oppose the industrial lobby. Domestic constraints on national policies would be greater if adjustment assistance were accepted as an alternative to protection. The fact that the costs of such policies are a visible burden on national exchequers would help to ensure that assistance is continually evaluated with regard to its effectiveness in promoting adjustment to global market trends. This has been shown to be the case with the US trade adjustment assistance.

CONCLUDING REMARKS

It has been shown that the development of trade regulation in textiles and clothing has been determined by political expediency rather than any clearly defined policy. It is therefore misleading when import controls on NIC imports are justified on the basis of an as yet undefined principle of 'fair trade'. Industrial lobbies have been the determining factor in the development of textiles trade policy. They have been able to exert such pressure because of the continued importance of the industry in the AICs, which has meant that AIC governments have not been able to ignore their calls for assistance.

Once governments assumed responsibility for the industry by selective regulation of imports of some products from some countries, regulations inevitably spread until there was global control of imports from low-cost sources. The LTA and MFA were originally justified on the grounds that selective measures were needed in order to avoid market disruption caused by a surge in imports from a particular source, hence the derogation from the GATT principle of non-selectivity. Selective import regulation, however, stimulated new sources of supply or diversification into other products. These new products were then controlled (under the MFA) as were any new producers. A system of trade regulation has thus developed which has become progressively more global. Initially applied selectively against a few exporters it has grown to include all developing countries, has been extended to EC-associated countries and outward processing, and is now threatening intra-AIC trade in the form of US–EC trade.

In their attempts to deal with the genuine problems caused by the slow growth in demand for textiles and the growth of more competitive NIC industries, neither a majority of AIC governments nor industries have been prepared to accept that even regulated trade in textiles and clothing would eventually result in a decline in the size of the AIC industries. The measures designed to ease the process of change have, therefore, failed to address themselves to the long- and medium-term problems. Failing an acceptance of global market trends, public and corporate policies have been defensive in nature. Corporate policies have often attempted to re-establish lost competitiveness in existing lines of production by defensive investment (Giersch, 1978) in improved productivity and capital deepening. Such productivity advances provide only a brief respite, until NIC or other AIC producers have caught up. This process of restructuring, therefore, exacerbates the problems caused by imports. Although the importance of the industry as an employer has been used to justify trade regulation, productivity advances due to intra-AIC and NIC competition have resulted in a continued decline in employment, especially in Western Europe.

Adjustment policies have found little support amongst AIC industries and governments.[3] Industry resents public intervention, arguing that bureaucrats cannot cope with the intricacies of the industry and take decisions which influence its future shape, and governments concur with this view. Nevertheless, both seem to have little difficulty in agreeing that highly complex trade regulatory measures, which fundamentally influence the shape of the industry, can and should be the responsibility of bureaucrats. Recent trends in the USA and Western Europe suggest that efforts to cut public expenditure will cut even the existing meagre adjustment policies. Regulation of textile and clothing imports can therefore be expected to continue. Import controls against the NICs, however, will not solve the problems of declining employment and stagnating markets, and one can expect increased tension between AICs.

NOTES

1 During the 1957–9 period Japan's share of US imports of textiles and clothing fell from 63 to 26 per cent, while that of Hong Kong increased from 13 to 27 per cent (Keesing and Wolf, 1980, p. 15).
2 One possible exception is the development of water-absorbent fibres. In the USA Du Pont is investing in research into new applications of man-made fibres, in aerospace and automobile construction, for example. Faced with mounting losses, such an R&D effort in Western Europe may be beyond the reach of the industry in its existing form.
3 One example is the uncooperative or indeed hostile industry response to the 1978 EC Commission's proposals for an EC textile and clothing policy (EC Commission, 1978a).

4

Consumer Electronics: The Colour Television Case

Louis Turner

The previous chapter has dealt with textiles and clothing, which have been classic starting-points for countries seeking to industrialize. Though still heavily dependent on these sectors, the NICs have been expanding even faster into a range of other light industries, which include footwear, cutlery, toys and, increasingly, electronics. Table 4.1 gives some idea of the variety of industrial activities that are included in the light electrical or electronic sectors. That Hong Kong is the world's largest exporter of toys may not be entirely due to electronic developments, but the fact that it is by value the third largest exporter of watches predominantly is – since it has established itself strongly at the lower end of the digital-watch market. Looking across the range of activities analysed in the table what is striking is the dominant role of the Japanese and the generally effective performance of Hong Kong, South Korea and Singapore (Taiwan, which is not covered by the United Nations statistics, would show up equally well if it were included). In general, the Asian NICs are more strongly represented in these sectors than their Latin American or South European competitors. India has no significant exports in these sectors.

In this chapter, we concentrate on colour televisions, as a particularly important segment of the whole consumer electronics industry. This is not to ignore the growing fringe of consumer electronics products, which now include calculators, home computers, microwave ovens, citizens' band (CB) radios, home TV cameras, smoke detectors, burglar alarms, electronic watches, electronic games and consumer software (such as audio and video recordings). However, by concentrating on the TV sector, we are dealing with a skilled-labour-intensive industry (Balassa, 1980, p. 21) that the leading NICs are trying to break into, and that illuminates an interesting area in which the AICs are having difficulty in adjusting smoothly to competitive change. Above all, though, colour televisions are interesting because they are a case of an apparently technologically mature product, increasingly fit for manufacture in the NICs, which rejuvenated itself as one part of a research-intensive complex of activities in which the AICs have been able to regain some lost ground.

Table 4.1   The NICs in Electronics and Light Electrical Goods: World Rankers in Exports (1977) (by SITC category)

Country	Telecommunications equipment, including radios (724)		Domestic electrical appliances (725)		Electrical machinery not elsewhere specified (729)		Instruments, apparatus (861)		Watches and clocks (864)		Toys, sporting goods (894)		Calculators (7142)		Computers, statistical machines (7143)		Sound recorders, phonographs (8911)	
	A	B %	A	B %	A	B %	A	B %	A	B %	A	B %	A	B %	A	B %	A	B %
Japan	1	26·7	3	10·5	3	11·8	1	22·4	2	20·7	4	9·2	1	48·8	6	4·2	1	62·9
Hong Kong	10	3·4	9	3·6	13	1·7	12	1·4	3	17·9	1	17·5	4	6·6	21	–	8	–
South Korea	9	3·4	21	0·4	12	1·9	18	0·5	8	2·2	8	5·0	11	–	20	–	5	4·0
Singapore	11	3·2	16	1·0	7	4·0	16	0·7	10	1·4	16	0·9	7	2·8	19	–	12	–
Malaysia	19	0·6	–	–	10	2·6	–	–	19	0·1	–	–	–	–	–	–	–	–
India	–	–	–	–	–	–	–	–	–	–	–	–	–	–	–	–	–	–
Brazil	20	0·5	20	0·5	22	0·4	–	–	–	–	21	0·6	13	–	11	–	20	–
Mexico	14	1·9	–	–	18	0·8	21	0·2	–	–	19	0·8	–	–	–	–	–	–
Argentina	–	–	–	–	–	–	–	–	–	–	–	–	–	–	–	–	–	–
Yugoslavia	–	–	13	1·5	–	–	22	0·2	–	–	–	–	16	–	24	–	–	–
Spain	21	0·5	12	1·6	20	0·7	20	0·3	17	0·2	10	2·0	20	–	13	–	15	–
Israel	–	–	–	–	–	–	–	–	–	–	–	–	–	–	–	–	–	–
Others					Philippines 17 0·9 Thailand 21 0·6				Philippines 11 0·3 Panama 15 0·3		Haiti 20 0·7							
Total exports[1]	24·7		6·8		32·8		17·4		6·2		6·0		1·8		8·7		3·9	

A = Ranking as exporter of given products.   B = Country's percentage of all exports of the product.

[1] Billion US$.

Source: UN, 1979 Yearbook of International Trade Statistics. Copyright, United Nations, 1980. Reproduced by permission.

THE INDUSTRY STRUCTURE

Television production is an important second-rank industry which in employment terms is not in the same class as textiles and clothing and whose companies are outranked by those in the energy, automobile and chemical sectors. One industry source (EECMA, 1978) claims that, in 1977, half a million people worked in the consumer electronics sector of the EC, of whom 150,000 were in colour-television manufacture. Slightly dated statistics (for 1975 and 1976) suggest that between 0·3 and 1 per cent of the industrial labour force of the AICs work in the consumer electronics sector, which falls within the wider electronics category, itself employing between 3·3 and 5 per cent of the total force (see Table 4.2).

Table 4.2   *Turnover and Employment in the Electronics Sector in the Main Producing Countries, 1975–6*

	USA	Japan	Federal Republic of Germany	France	UK
Turnover (all electronics)[1]	39·6	14·2	11·1	7·9	7·07
Employment[2]					
All electronics	1,142·0	600·0	410·0	256·0	489·0
Consumer electronics	129·0	182·0	108·0	23·0	60·0
Proportion of electronics employment to total industrial employment[3]	4·5	3·3	3·6	3·3	5·0
Proportion of consumer electronics employment to total industrial employment[3]	0·51	1·0	0·9	0·3	0·6

[1]Billion US$, 1975.
[2]Thousands, 1976.
[3]Percentage, 1976.
Source: Interfutures, 1979, p. 337.

The other indicator of the ranking of this industry is the size of the leading television producers in 1980, of which only four were in the top fifty largest industrial companies of the world. Two of these, Matsushita (no. 45) and Hitachi (no. 44) are purely consumer electronics companies, for whom television production is particularly important. Philips (no. 23) is somewhat more diversified, but is still primarily engaged in consumer electronics. ITT (no. 21) is one of the more marginal television producers and is not particularly strong elsewhere in the consumer electronics field. The remainder of the leading companies are in the medium rank and are generally highly dependent on consumer electronics and television production (these include Blaupunkt, Grundig, RCA, Sanyo, Sony, Telefunken, Thomson, Thorn, Toshiba, and Zenith).

Television manufacturers around the world are in a state of flux. Market penetration for colour television sets is very high in North America and Japan and is approaching saturation even in the less-developed West European market. As a result, set manufacturers are increasingly dependent on the replacement cycle. In sum, this is a maturing industry, but one which has not yet completely stopped growing. In the circumstances, there is an inevitable shake-out taking place of the smaller companies that could only survive as long as the total market was growing fast.

This trend toward industry concentration is best shown by events in the cathode ray tube (CRT) sector (such tubes generally account for around one-third of the cost of a television set). Already, the technology is highly concentrated, with only two major competing tube technologies left – one from Philips and one from RCA, with some minor competition from Sony. The bulk of the world's industry now bases itself on one or other of these two leading technologies. At the same time, the optimum scale for tube manufacturing has been steadily increasing. The baseload is now up to around 1 million tubes per annum and, given the fact that the world's demand for colour CRTs was 31 million units in 1979, this leaves a limited amount of room for independent tube-makers. There are now only eleven of these left (see Table 4.3) and some of these have still to be shaken out. Given the pressures coming from the steady increase in scale economies, it is inevitable that the relationships between tube-makers and the set manufacturers are increasingly tense. We have now reached the stage where quite large countries may cease to have any tube production at all. Britain, for instance, has but one plant left after Philips rationalized its 1·28-million production capacity.

Table 4.3   *The World's Television Tube-Makers (1981)*

Tube-maker	Technology	Tube-maker	Technology
1. Philips (Netherlands)	20AX	6. Matsushita (Japan)	PIL
2. RCA (USA)	PIL	7. Sony (Japan)	Trinitron
3. Hitachi (Japan)	PIL	8. Mitsubishi (Japan)	PIL
4. Toshiba (Japan)	PIL	9. ITT (USA)	PIL/20AX
5. Zenith (USA)	PIL	10. Videocolor (France)	

New ventures, not ranked

Tatung (Taiwan)	n.a.
Elektronska Industrija (Yugoslavia)	20AX
Glasfabrik von Osvetlovaii Sklo (Czechoslovakia)	n.a.

A further element for instability is the fact that the industry is heavily influenced by developments in micro-electronics. At the level of production technology, it has been possible to automate television assembly lines and thus maintain the competitiveness of highly paid assembly workers. More fundamentally, the growing potential of micro-electronics means that set manufacturers have been developing a number of new functions to be based around the CRT. So, we are entering into the field of videotape-recorders (VTRs), videodiscs, teletext and videotex.[1] All these developments require heavy research and marketing, and the industry is finding itself in a situation where only a handful of companies have the resources to develop these products across the board. The smaller set-makers are thus faced with the problem of getting out of the industry completely, of finding themselves a niche within it (but this is difficult given the extreme fluidity of the industry) or else of taking shelter under the umbrella of one of the research-intensive giants. For the moment, this industry core includes Matsushita, Philips, RCA, and Sony.

JAPAN AND THE NICs

As long as colour television manufacturing was nothing more than a conventionally maturing industry, the NICs could have high hopes of entering it. After all, their emergence into other parts of consumer electronics had come about without posing too much of a strain on the economies of the advanced industrialized countries. Hong Kong, for instance, is strongest in electronic watches, radios and pocket calculators. In two of these sectors, the AICs have given ground quite calmly. The radio companies moved into television manufacturing (RCA originally stood for Radio Corporation of America), and the calculator manufacturers were generally making integrated circuits which they have continued to develop, although firms like Texas Instruments, Hewlett-Packard and Japanese companies like Casio have developed their niches at the upper end of the calculator market. The Swiss have obviously suffered, as mechanical watches have come under simultaneous competition from electronics and cheap NIC assembly capabilities, but, since the Swiss have little international leverage, they have had no choice but to adapt to the new situation.

It looks as though the entry of the NICs into television production is going to be more sensitive. South Korea and Taiwan have already been enmeshed in American Orderly Market Agreements, and the British have tied these two up, along with Singapore, within a network of Voluntary Export Restraints (VERs). Such countries are strongest in black-and-white-TV, a sector of decreasing interest to the AICs. However, some aspects of Korean ambitions in the colour-television field raise issues that, as in other industries, are of wider concern. Thus when Samsung, Gold Star and Kum Ho laid down their colour-television plants, they were hoping between them to export 1·3 million colour-television sets to the USA. In effect, in this single planning decision, they intended to take from 4 to 5 per cent of the world market for colour televisions. This really was an ambitious operation, which might be contrasted with operations in the petrochemical industry, where Saudi Arabia intends to muscle its way to 2 per cent of the world ethylene market by the end of the 1980s. Clearly, Korea's ambitions for the colour-television industry do pose relatively novel problems for free-market economists, and we shall return to these later in this chapter.

Japan

Japan's success in the television field is a classic example of the 'virtuous circle'. In the course of about ten years, its companies have moved from a predominantly black-and-white industry, through small-size colour televisions, to large ones, finally developing video-recorders, in which Philips is the only credible non-Japanese competitor. There are parallels with their successes in the steel industry, in that they benefited from the 'late-comer' phenomenon. A booming home market allowed constant new investments, which could take advantage of optimal-scale economies. These investments built up the industry's export competitiveness, which in turn encouraged further rounds of world-scale investments. Once such a cycle was established, older, more fragmented competitors in the maturer AICs were inevitably left in some disarray. However, consumer electronics has proved a technologically more dynamic sector than the maturer steel industry, and the Japanese have added a research dimension to the virtuous-circle process, in that they have increasingly developed indigenous technology. They have thus done more than simply move down the learning curve until they reached the best of existing AIC technology. By ploughing profits back into R&D, they have become technological leaders in their own right (DWIT, 1978).

The Japanese industrial and political establishment seems to have picked electronics as a growth sector as far back as 1957 (*Far Eastern Economic Review*, 14 December 1979) and there are two aspects of the subsequent success story that catch the eye. First, the industry used offshore assembly as a positive part of its strategy. In the late 1960s and early 1970s, Japanese companies invested in other countries in the region such as South Korea, Taiwan and Singapore (though the Koreans have proved adept at squeezing them out of this sector). There seems to be no convincing historical interpretation of the competitive advantages that the Japanese companies gained from this strategy, but conventional Western opinion is that it allowed them simultaneously not only to slough off ageing, uncompetitive products, but also to provide themselves with a cheaper source of intermediate components. In more recent years, though, the Japanese companies have been facing increasing competition from companies like Samsung (Korea) and Tatung (Taiwan), which they originally helped into the industry. One also suspects that the Japanese interest in Taiwan and Singapore now has a lot to do with the greater flexibility this gives them in taking maximum advantage of gaps in AIC restrictions on television trade. This would seem to be particularly the case with Singapore, where a Japanese investor, Mitsubishi Electric, makes no particular secret that its subsidiary there is to be built into a large export producer, aiming not just at South-East Asia, but also at the USA, Western Europe and the Middle East (*Electronics Weekly*, 7 March 1979).

The second major development is that, around 1973–4, the Japanese companies took advantage of developments in micro-electronics to redesign sets so that production lines could be automated, and thus they avoided being priced out of the market as the value of the yen rose during the 1970s (DWIT, 1978, p. 4). This meant that, by the time the Boston Consulting Group had done a study of the structure of the global television industry for NEDO (Britain's National Economic Development Council), the Japanese had a 25 per cent cost advantage over European producers. One aspect of the policy debate within Western Europe and North America is whether non-Japanese set-makers now have the time to automate in turn and thus reduce some of this competitive distance between themselves and the Japanese.

The result of all these developments is that Japan moved from being a marginal exporter of colour televisions in the very early 1970s to a situation where by 1976 it was exporting nearly five times as many as West Germany, which was the next most important competitor. This did not matter too much to the West Europeans, who were still able to hold the Japanese off by refusing them access to the PAL patents on which the bulk of the West European industry is based. The brunt of the Japanese export expansion was thus borne by the United States. The result of all this is that Japan, with 25 per cent of the world market for colour-television sets, produced 46 per cent of the world's colour TV tubes (see Table 4.4). In particular, this market dominance has fed through into a lead in R&D, with one Japanese company, Matsushita, spending around five times the total UK budget for R&D in consumer electronics (DWIT, 1978, p. 4). It is this expenditure which guarantees Japanese companies a central role in all future developments within the consumer electronics field.

Table 4.4 *Production and Consumption of Colour Televisions and Tubes in 1979 (millions)*

	Tubes			Colour televisions		
Country	Production	Consumption	Balance	Production	Consumption	Balance
Japan	14·5	11·5	+3	11·5	6·8	+4·7
USA	9·4	9·1	+0·3	9·0[a]	10·0	−1·0
Europe	7·8	10·5	−2·7	10·0	10·2	−0·2

[a]Includes over 2 million sets made by US subsidiaries of Japanese firms.
Source: *Europe*, 2 April 1981.

The NICs

What is less clear is how the NICs fit into the slipstream behind the Japanese. Undoubtedly, the East Asians are becoming a significant force across the whole range of electronic and light electrical industries (see Table 4.1). The one quirk in this picture is that Hong Kong, so successful throughout most of this sector, barely registers as a television manufacturer. This is because television assembly is a space-intensive operation, and plentiful land is one factor which Hong Kong does not possess.

Excluding Hong Kong (and Japan), the other three East Asian NICs are strongly entrenched in TV production, with foreign investors having played a key role in developing their activities. Singapore seems to be most clearly a 'front' for the Japanese industry, with Taiwan depending on Philips and RCA as well. The Korean case is the most fascinating, in that it has followed the most aggressive stategy of squeezing out Japanese investors. Thus Sanyo and Matsushita have both divested themselves of their stakes in significant Korean operations. What is more difficult to assess is the level of technological independence which such NICs have achieved. The Koreans claim that their black-and-white television industry is 90 per cent based on indigenous components, and that their colour-television sector is 85 per cent independent (Cable and Clarke, 1981, pp. 37–42). The latest news is that Samsung has developed a videotape-recorder, but there is as yet no evidence as to how much of it is original. It is, though, a sign of the times that the NICs should be entering the market with a product so very much at the research-intensive part of its life (*Newsreview*, 18 October 1980, p. 16).

THE UNITED STATES

From 1948 till 1962, the USA was totally self-sufficient in television manufacture. In 1962 the first Japanese imports developed in the black-and-white sector. The first imported colour television sets were introduced into the US market in 1967 and within three years, imports were making up 17 per cent of the US market for colour sets and about 50 per cent for black-and-white. From 1969 to 1974 the import penetration of the colour sector held steady at somewhere between 15 to 17 per cent of the US market (with Japanese sets making up about 82 per cent of this total). Beginning in late 1975, there was a marked acceleration of this import penetration. By 1976, imports made up 35 per cent of the US market and this rate was maintained through the first half of 1977. In May 1977 an Orderly Marketing Agreement was made between the US and Japan, by which the Japanese were cut back from their 2·5 million sales in 1976 to an annual total of 1·75 million units for the next three years. In December 1978, South Korea and Taiwan were brought into the net through their own OMAS.

The US colour-TV industry was a sitting duck, having insulated itself almost entirely from industry development elsewhere in the world. During the 1960s, US firms undoubtedly had a technological lead but, apart from a very tentative attempt by Zenith to export to Japan in the early 1960s, the industry simply did not bother with foreign markets. In the early 1970s, the total number of sets exported by US companies never rose above 3,000 units per annum. There is some evidence that Zenith was thwarted by Japanese government intervention (DWIT, 1978, pp. 44–68). However, the US industry did not make a serious onslaught on the West European market, seemingly being discouraged by the technical complexities of coming to terms with the PAL and SECAM transmission systems. At the same time, domestic marketing strategies within the United States were aimed at pushing consumers toward the upper (and more profitable) ends of their product lines, while virtually abandoning the lower end of these lines to imports. There was very little consideration given to improving labour productivity to restore competitiveness at the lower end of the product range. Nor did companies give much consideration to radically new products in the consumer electronics field.

The American industry responded to import competition in a number of ways. Most companies were tempted to shift a substantial proportion of their activities offshore. There was nothing particularly new in this, since American electronic companies had been establishing labour-intensive plants overseas at least as early as 1960, and some television manufacturers were shifting part of their operations by the late 1960s. However, the 1974 recession, combined with the increased competition from Japan, further encouraged them to increase their offshore manufacturing capacity. The major study prepared for the US Department of Labour, on which much of this analysis rests (DWIT, 1978, pp. 55–7), has identified a number of the most visible of such moves:

- Admiral came to make both colour and black-and-white sets in Taiwan.
- General Electric moved the manufacture of circuit-boards and other colour components to Singapore.
- Magnavox (a Philips subsidiary) imported from a Taiwanese plant owned by its parent.
- RCA used Taiwan and, in 1975, began moving colour-chassis operations to Mexico.
- GTE Sylvania opened operations in Mexico in 1973 and bought a plant in Taiwan in 1975 for production of both kinds of televisions.
- Zenith built up subsidiary plants in Taiwan and Mexico, and, in late 1977, announced a major shift of jobs to them.

It is estimated that of the 9 million sets sold in the USA in 1977, US added value was probably no more than 30 per cent.

A second approach to Japanese competition was to seek legal redress. The US industry made its first dumping appeals against the Japanese in 1968, and this strategy was developed in the mid-1970s, with the industry lobby called COMPACT (Committee for the Preservation of American Colour Television) leading the attack. But, it was Zenith which led this legal battle, arguing before the US Customs Court that Japan's rebate of commodity taxes was a 'bounty or grant' within the definition of the US tariff laws. This particular dispute rolled on through 1977 and 1978, with the Customs Court upholding Zenith's arguments, thus forcing Japanese exporters to post bonds against any eventual fines which might be imposed. Simultaneously, in spring 1977, the International Trade Commission independently ruled that Japanese television imports were creating serious injury to the American industry, and recommended a substantial increase in tariffs. The combination of these two rulings was enough to force the Japanese to accept the OMA of May 1977. As it happens, Zenith's legal case was eventually thrown out by the Supreme Court in June 1978, which upheld the US Treasury position that export-tax rebates were an accepted international practice. However, by this time the USA had entered on the OMA path. Ironically, Zenith, which was the company which had most strongly resisted the temptation to shift manufacturing operations abroad, celebrated the OMA by announcing its major offshore movement a mere four months later (Meltzer, 1979).[2]

Some companies simply chose to get out of the business. Admiral sold out to Rockwell in 1973. In the next year, Motorola sold out to Matsushita, Magnavox to Philips, and Ford Motor sold its Philco consumer electronics business to GTE-Sylvania, which, in turn, sold its TV business to Philips in 1980. In 1976 Sanyo bought out Warwick, which was primarily a supplier to retailers like Sears. Of these transactions only the GTE-Sylvania deal reflected a serious attempt to get higher-volume production, and thus reduce cost per set. Even those companies which have stayed in the business, such as RCA and General Electric, have shown signs of diversifying away from this sector. General Electric, for instance, moved into minerals by acquiring Utah International, while RCA moved into publishing (Random House), car hire (Hertz) and convenience foods. Since 1966, the number of US-owned colour-television manufacturing companies has declined from sixteen to three (Zenith, RCA and General Electric), and the industry has lost somewhere between 60,000 to 100,000 jobs.

The remaining core American companies have started to come to terms with Japanese technological advances. A great deal is being learned about the need for improved quality control, product design and automated assembly lines. Zenith, for instance, reduced the number of parts in its 25-inch colour televisions by 36 per cent when it went over to its new 'System Three' chassis. Again, with Japanese methods now staring them in the face, the US producers have been radically tightening up their acceptable quality levels ('AQL'). In 1972, RCA would accept up to $1 \cdot 5$ per cent defects in the integrated circuits that it bought in; by 1978, this had been tightened to $0 \cdot 1$ per cent. However, this was still behind the Japanese, who deal not with 'AQL' but in 'PPM' – parts per million. For Matsushita, 10 defects per million is the maximum allowable for transistors that they make (*Business Week*, 9 April 1979, pp. 46b-e-n-e).

There is still the feeling, anyway, that this kind of damage-limitation strategy is not going to be enough for the American industry. It looks as though R&D spending has been low and that most of this has been aimed at essentially cosmetic developments. A particularly interesting example of this reluctance of American companies to capitalize on technological advance was Motorola's delay in using solid-state technology for anything but its top-of-the-line models. It was this unwillingness to capitalize fully on a major technical advance that eventually forced Motorola to sell its television operations to Matsushita (DWIT, 1978, pp. 64–5). Equally, it is significant that the American industry left the Japanese and Philips to develop video-recorders, for this must be the first major consumer product developed over the last twenty years in the development of which US companies have played no part. The remaining hope for the US companies is that RCA's tube technology (Precision In-Line – PIL) may eventually win out over the competing Philips 20AX technology. The one remaining product in which the USA may still have a genuinely innovative role is the videodisc, where RCA has a reasonable chance of finding a mass market.

Ultimately, though, the major structural change in the American market during the 1970s has been the inward investment by Japanese companies. Obviously, they were spurred into this by the knowledge that US resentment against the surging imports from Japan was growing and was leading to a backlash in the form of trade restrictions. So, Sony built a plant at San Diego in 1972; Matsushita and Sanyo bought out existing US-owned TV plants by 1976; and Mitsubishi, Toshiba, Sharp and Hitachi have all launched US factories. Cumulatively, these investments are important in that they have reduced the number of jobs that would have otherwise been lost in the US electronic sector.

Obviously, we should not totally write off the US TV sector to the Japanese. RCA and Zenith are trying to establish themselves in the video-disc sector in competition with Philips and Japan's JVC. On the marketing and software side of the videodiscs, CBS, MCA, General Electric and most interestingly, IBM, are all seeking a part of the action. In fact, it is IBM's interest which reminds us that television manufacturing is just one sector of a much wider telecommunications industry which, thanks to the Federal Communications Commission, is about to be deregulated, thus setting IBM and AT&T to battle it out across the whole telecommunications spectrum. This will provide very much tougher competition for the Japanese as they consider how to build on their undoubted television and video-recorder successes. However, despite this guarded optimism for the future, the overall picture which emerges from the television sector is of US industry having lost a major battle. What lessons can be learned?

First, US sluggishness in this sector seems typical of a continental economy for which trade has been relatively unimportant. The industry has thus lacked the competitive stimulus which should have forced it to look for radical technological innovation, rather than purely cosmetic improvements. Second, with the exception of Zenith, consumer electronics have only been one part of company activities (about one-quarter of RCA's, GTE's and General Electric's total sales; about one-tenth of Rockwell's). In these circumstances, it is not surprising that Zenith fought the hardest, while the others gave the impression of not being 100 per cent committed to the sector. Third, it is sometimes argued that the defence involvement in US electronics has left these companies relatively weak on consumer products – an argument which is also made against the British industry. Finally, throughout the 1970s, the US industry sought to improve its position by controlling imports. It seemed to turn willingly to judicial or quasi-judicial institutions like the International Trade Commission or the Customs Court, without demanding some sort of structural policy on the part of either the federal or state governments. John Zysman (1980) has argued that it is precisely the lack of any such mechanisms for governmental intervention at the structural level that forces US industries to demand some form of orderly marketing arrangement as their main line of protection from competitive pressures abroad.

WESTERN EUROPE

The West European industry had the luxury of growing under the protection of the PAL patents, which were used to limit Japanese penetration to the smaller end of the colour-television market (which, unfortunately for the Europeans, is precisely the end to which demand has been swinging). The main PAL licence is just about to run out and, although associated patents still have a few years to run, the West Europe industry will soon have to come to terms with virtually unfettered Japanese competition.

As with industries looked at in subsequent chapters (petrochemicals and steel), there is a distinct feeling that the West European industry suffers from being notably more fragmented than its Japanese and North American competitors. In tube-making, Philips remains the world's leading company, but the remaining West European contenders are very weak indeed. West Germany's AEG was forced to merge its tube-making division with Videocolor, which was in turn a joint venture between Thomson-Brandt and RCA in Europe. However, the new three-way partnership continued to run in the red (1980). The smallest of them all, Valco of Finland, entered an abortive partnership with Hitachi.

In set-making, the picture is an even clearer one of a relatively vulnerable, over-fragmented industry. Taking just Britain and West Germany in 1980, there were around twenty set-makers in these two countries (of which at least five were Japanese-linked, and two US-linked). Italy had nineteen smallish set-makers, the largest of which was Zanussi (linked with Hitachi), making 150,000 sets per annum. At an educated guess, Western Europe was supporting around thirty-five separate set manufacturers, which was far more than industrial logic would dictate. In the face of growing Japanese competition, there was no absolute guarantee that Western Europe's five major consumer electronic companies (Philips, AEG-Telefunken, Thomson-Brandt, Grundig and Thorn) would all survive the 1980s with their independence intact.

France

The French position is a somewhat peculiar one. To some extent, the French isolated themselves from the mainstream of the TV world by plunging for their SECAM transmission system, which was not widely adopted, and thus did not encourage French manufacturers to think globally. On the other hand, this had the advantage of making the French market relatively unattractive to exporters like the Japanese. In addition, the French – like the Italians and British – used quotas to protect their market further. They have two main tube-production factories; a 450,000-capacity plant of Philips and a 1,050,000-capacity plant owned by Thomson's Videocolor subsidiary. The Japanese (and the British involvement with them) are looked on with considerable suspicion.

The French have had an activist policy within the electronics sector for nearly twenty years (the key event was in 1973 when the USA refused to allow France to import a Control Data computer in case it helped the French nuclear effort (*New Scientist*, 15 November 1979, pp. 515–17)). The stage was reached, under President Giscard d'Estaing, where the whole of the French Establishment from the President downwards was convinced that the French economy had to come to terms with the computing, micro-electronic and telecommunications technologies, which were once known as 'Informatique', but were increasingly called 'Télématique', thus indicating the growing emphasis on the communications aspects.

There have been two main effects of these policies on the television sector. First, there is a determined effort to turn Thomson-Brandt, which is the second largest colour TV producer within the EC (with about 10 per cent of the market), into a fully viable West European force. So, negatively, Britain's Thorn was blocked from buying the French TV rental company, Locatel, in case the perfidious British started undermining Thomson's home market. At the same time, over 1978 and 1979, Thomson made a series of purchases within the West German market, taking over AEG-Telefunken's tube division; a colour-TV maker, Nordmende, which had about 10 per cent of the German set market; and the loss-making French and German television subsidiaries of General Telephone & Electronics (GTE). This all added up to a strategy of expanding Thomson's volume from 1·1 million sets in 1979 (uncomfortably close to the 1 million sets per annum survival point) to some 1·6 million.

If Thomson-Brandt does succeed in surviving as West Europe's number two television producer, it will be a triumph for French industrial policy, which has long identified this company as one of its 'national champions'.

One other area where the French government (like the British) is active is in developing viewdata services. The route it will take is to provide every household with a special telephone receiver-cum-video terminal, which will do automatic dialling and act as an electronic telephone directory. To British eyes, this approach is somewhat odd, but the French are clearly gambling that they can take a lead in electronics for the home through official channels, while in countries like Britain it is assumed that the business market will provide the initial growth. There is, perhaps, a feeling that key decisions are being taken by administrators, rather than by people with a direct sense of the market. However, what cannot be doubted is the overall French commitment to the whole video field.

West Germany

The West Germans have by far the largest tube-producing sector in West

Europe, with Philips producing 1·28 million units per annum, ITT some 1 million and AEG (with Thomson-Brandt) 860,000. Yet the observer is left with doubts about the ultimate potential of consumer electronics in West Germany. The facts are that AEG-Telefunken has had a very rough time in this field; Grundig has partially sold out to Philips; Siemens has stayed relatively aloof from the sector; and the Japanese have not shown much interest in setting up high-labour-cost production facilities there. All these developments go to reinforce the feeling that West Germany's strength in mechanical and electrical engineering may not necessarily spill over as strongly to the consumer electronics field. Obviously, there are a number of reasons why a company like AEG-Telefunken got into financial trouble in the late 1970s, but it is significant that this was a company which had failed to maintain a reputation it had once had as a technical leader in the video field. For instance, it actually pioneered a videodisc system with the Axel Springer group, which flopped because it was ahead of its time and had too many shortcomings.

What is particularly interesting, though, is the acceptance by the West German financial community that such a company could not be allowed to go bankrupt. So the winter of 1979–80 saw a substantial rescue operation which involved the writing down of the company's capital by two-thirds. The brunt of the rescue was borne by the West German banking system, and this only goes to show how even the most *laissez-faire* country is still reluctant to let a company the size of AEG (turnover of abour $4 billion) go to the wall (*Financial Times*, 14 August 1979, 5 December 1979). Otherwise, the West Germans still seem to be running the most open consumer electronics market in Western Europe.

Philips

Philips is an extremely interesting test case as to whether a purely West European industrial policy can emerge in sectors in which one company predominates, and not (as in the case of steel and synthetic fibres) a number of comparably sized companies scattered throughout the EC. There can be no doubt that this company is the only consumer electronics company from Europe or North America which can legitimately be placed in the same technological league as the Japanese companies. The future of its video-recorder strategy is still in doubt, but it has other strings to its bow, like its laser-based videodisc and a miniaturized audio disc. It has established itself as a force in the North American market through its purchase of Magnavox and GTE's consumer electronics interests. It is strong in integrated circuits (a position it has strengthened by its purchase of Signetics, which now makes Philips either the second or third largest semi-conductor manufacturer in the world).

Despite this, Philips is calling on Brussels to protect the European market from Japanese tubes – which would seem to clash with the Franko–Stephenson theory in Chapter 13 that multinational companies are less likely to call for protection than purely national ones. Nevertheless, one can have some sympathy with Philips because, as well as trying to stay technologically competitive with the Japanese, it was faced with the fact that it had tube-production facilities in at least seven West European countries, which inevitably led to over-fragmented, uneconomic production. This spread of production is a reminder that Western Europe is still nowhere near as much a single economic unit as the United States or Japan.

Philips has thus had to reduce its labour force against the knowledge that any decision to rationalize production will inevitably lead to the ruffling of some national susceptibilities. In fact, its plans to reorganize across West Europe actually led to Mr H. Vredeling, the EC vice-president responsible for social affairs and employment, attending a Philips board meeting at which the reorganization plan was discussed. This indicates how sensitive every Philips move is; and one can argue that it is far less free than its North American counterparts to rationalize production according to what it sees as economic priorities. One senses, then, that the call by Philips for trade restrictions at a European level is at least partly based on a perception of the inability of the West European political culture to accept the type of ruthless rationalization of production facilities which is found in the United States.

The British

In its turn, the British industry is going through a fairly eventful period. Set-making has been fragmented, with too many companies assembling 150,000 sets a year or less, which is well below the optimal scale. At the same time, the industry's R&D record has fallen way behind that of the Japanese, and production efficiency has been low. The result has meant that the balance of payments within the consumer electronics sector has been declining badly in recent years, with a deficit of £105 million in 1975 growing to £363 million in 1980. At the tube-making end, the situation is particularly dire, with only one producer (Philips' Mullard) left in contention that has been rationalizing its production, limiting itself to a single plant with an annual capacity of 1·5 million tubes a year. To add to the country's vulnerability is the fact that this plant is concentrating on the 20-inch and 22-inch tubes at a time when the country's consumers seem to be swinging in the direction of smaller sets.

On a more optimistic note, it should be observed that the British market is the second largest in Western Europe, following only West Germany. This presumably reflects the quality of the programmes actually on offer in Britain, along with the fact that well-developed rental chains have played an important part in stimulating demand for sets, even when consumers have not been able to afford to buy them.

The British have been active on a number of different levels. First of all, there has been some reorganization within the British-owned sector, with Decca being bought by Racal. Similarly, Thorn acquired EMI which, though not a set manufacturer, had a strong library of films to strengthen

Thorn in the video sector. On top of these reshufflings within the British-owned electronic sector, there was a significant incursion of the Japanese. Two British set-making companies signed up with Japanese partners: GEC with Hitachi; and, in a short-lived partnership, Rank with Toshiba. In addition, Sony, National Panasonic (Matsushita) and Mitsubishi all set up their own set-making facilities, leaving only Philips, Rediffusion and ITT temporarily outside any corporate reorganizations.

In addition to moves at the corporate level there was rationalization at the plant level as well, with Thorn and Philips making significant plant closures. Simultaneously, Thorn took a leaf out of the Japanese book and has developed its new TX10 model, at a cost of nearly £15 million. Components in each chassis were reduced from 618 to 410, and nearly 75 per cent of these are now assembled by auto-insertion, in which a computer controls their insertion into printed-circuit boards.

There are a few general points to be made about the British experience. First, trade restrictions against the East Asian exporters (Japan, Singapore, Taiwan, Korea and, perhaps, Thailand) were an important part of the industry's strategy at the beginning of the 1980s, and the government came under strong pressure to maintain these until at least the mid-1980s, either bilaterally or else through Brussels.

Second, the industry and Whitehall have worked quite closely with each other in the relevant Sector Working Party (SWP) of NEDO. It was this SWP which hired the Boston Consulting Group to see how British competitiveness compared with that of countries like West Germany, Japan and Korea (the obvious answer was not very well). The SWP used this report to justify a strategy for the industry intended to rationalize the industry around Thorn, Philips and the Japanese; tighten production and quality control; improve R&D; and devise better products. Maintaining import controls was one part of this strategy.

A third notable aspect of British policy has been the positive acceptance of Japanese investment. After some initial hesitation, when Hitachi was discouraged from setting up a 'green-field' plant, it was accepted that the Japanese would be investing in Western Europe anyway, whence they might as well be persuaded to base themselves in the UK – thus maintaining jobs, expanding exports, and demonstrating just what Japanese production techniques could do in the British industrial environment. (Sony has already won awards for its export performance from its British base.) In following this policy, the British are clearly taking a distinct line from the anti-Japanese policies of France and, to some extent, Brussels.

Fourthly, there is the interesting case of the state post and telecommunications facility, British Telecom, which has masterminded Britain's pioneering entry into the videotex/viewdata arena with Prestel. This is an interesting case of state-led entrepreneurship, in that British Telecom has shown a sensitivity to market realities, inasmuch as, for example, the set-makers have been left very free to identify those sectors of the service which seem most promising. In this, there seems to be a qualitative difference between the strategies of the British and French PTTs.

The European Community

The EC is under strong pressure from Philips and Thomson-Brandt to buy the European industry a 'breathing-space' of between five and seven years. The argument is that the industry needs this period of relative protection from Japanese imports if it is to come to terms with a world in which the PAL patents are no longer a barrier. The point of note is that the rest of the West European television industry is not united behind the Philips/Thomson-Brandt initiative. Most other companies feel that existing French, Italian and British restrictions on such imports may be more effective than a common EC approach. In the meantime, though, this leaves France and Italy controlling television imports by direct quotas, and the UK and Benelux doing so by informal agreements. Even if Brussels does decide against protective action in consumer electronics, it will be interesting to see if it feels like challenging these national initiatives, which should really have been phased out a long time ago. If the EC industry directorate does take up this matter seriously, it will be because it is sensitive to Western Europe's weakness in the whole 'Télématiques' sector. However, this is a concern not just with consumer electronics, but with across-the-board European weaknesses in computers, software, electronic components and microchips.

GENERAL OBSERVATIONS

Trade Policy and the 'Virtuous Circle'

Of all the industries we have looked at, the free-trader (whether a Friedmanite or not) has the hardest time with this consumer electronics sector. Clearly, the Japanese were able to build on their general industrial efficiency and booming domestic market to wrest the maximum advantages out of the relevant scale economies. Once they started developing export markets, these economies increased and, within a decade, by ploughing back profits into R&D, they moved from being good-quality imitators to initiators of products throughout the consumer electronics field. How the world economy is supposed to adjust to such a development is known in theory. The new industrial power will have successes across a number of major industrial sectors, eventually reaching a situation in which it will start running chronic balance-of-payments surpluses, with the result that its currency will rise; eventually it will be priced out of the markets in which it had its initial industrial success. (To some extent, this has actually happened with Japan, which was unable to fulfil its 1979 television quotas for the US market – though that will have been affected by the only partially voluntary Japanese direct investment within the US television sector.)

Put abstractly in this way, the argument sounds reassuring. However, the television sector raises some questions. First, the speed of the process is now extremely fast, and there is a real sense that an industry which has fallen marginally behind the best of world practices will not have the time to reorganize before it is subjected to very strong competition from the 'late-comer' economies. Building a new, world-scale plant when one's markets are rapidly expanding and profitable can be done much faster than when such an investment can only take place once two corporations have merged, or two or three small, obsolete plants have been closed down. Almost by definition, it is the older industrial countries which are faced with such reorganization problems, and the argument for temporary trade protection to give the old industry a 'breathing-space' is attractive if the competitiveness of the new supplier rests on scale economies, rather than cheap resource inputs.

A second worry about the abstract argument is that, although a Japan might rapidly price itself out of a given market (thus allowing the traditional producers to re-establish themselves), in fact, the 'virtuous circle' is not just limited to Japan. For instance, the latter's export-oriented model of industrial development is being imitated by some of the NICs, and it could be that we are dealing with a steady supply of new competitors, all in turn taking full advantage of the relevant scale economies. In this case, the fact that an early competitor like Japan will eventually price itself out of a given market will provide no relief if the next generation of new competitors moves in to the very sectors that Japan is vacating. The Koreans and Taiwanese, for instance, seem to have been genuinely competitive in their exports to North America, and are already aware of the need to strengthen their R&D activities to move closer to the technological frontier. Thus we find the Koreans already developing their own video-recorder, and a Hong Kong-linked company, Radofin, to be one of the very first companies to offer cheap viewdata adaptors, which permit a normal television set to be linked to the wider viewdata services.

So, if we have to have any controls against imports from Japan and the NICs, then there would seem to be a far more genuine case for some temporary protection of the consumer electronics sector than for textiles and clothing, which is where the bulk of the controls now occur. There is a qualitative difference between the cases of clothing, where industrial relocation is taking place primarily because of the cheaper wages found overseas, and consumer electronics, where the major issue is not relative wage costs, but the way a managerial lead can be remorselessly developed into a 'virtuous circle', whereby the late-comers can move into a genuine technological world leadership.

Format Choices

One further aspect worth noting is how important the choice of the dominant format for a product has become. There have been incompatible systems before, notably in television transmission, where the PAL, SECAM and American systems were each adopted in different countries. However, the world is now faced with a series of decisions along the lines of those involving the format choice for the long-playing record and audiotape cassette. The world is being offered incompatible systems in the field of video-recorders, videodiscs, audiodiscs and viewdata. There is a lot that the competing companies can do to try to ensure that their particular format becomes the industry standard (as Philips managed to do with audiotape cassettes) by forming strategic alliances with each other. However, this is a high-risk area, in which the NICs are disadvantaged. In some cases, such as consumer electronics, developments in the most advanced market (increasingly the Japanese one) will determine which format wins out: it is significant that Philips is having to present its prototype compact audiodisc to a Japanese standard-setting committee. In other sectors, such as radar equipment for airports, governments (particularly the US one) will make the key decisions. In the viewdata sector, governments will be less important, though state-owned PTTs will still be central.

In this world of high-powered commercial diplomacy, the NICs can do little but wait on the sidelines. They can move into world markets once global formats are settled. However, the fact that they do have to wait like this, while AIC companies and governments battle with each other, indicates that the NICs are still second-ranking commercial powers, unable to dictate the environment within which they will compete.

Regulation as a Disincentive to Innovation

The mention of the PTTs is a reminder that the evolution of consumer electronics will involve steps such as linking domestic television sets to the telephone system, thus taking the industry into a highly regulated sector. For instance, Canada's viewdata effort has been delayed by demarcation disputes over who has rights to what part of the system. In West Germany, a row broke out between newspaper publishers and the television services over who should dominate the new technology. In these circumstances, a nation will get a competitive advantage if its government can navigate the shoals of telecommunication regulations, arbitrating where vested interests clash and knocking heads together where necessary. So far, the British record seems good in this area, but the USA may take the lead through the action of the Federal Communications Commission, which has been deregulating much of the country's telecommunications sector. The effect of this has been to open a way for a single company to supply not just the hardware and software, but also the transmission media, such as fibre-optic cables. So, in consumer electronics, the USA may not be hampered by the over-regulation that has sometimes affected other industries (such as banking). It is therefore necessary for others to maintain a constant, critical eye on their own institutions like PTTs, which may have certain monopoly powers. Their vested interest in maintaining sole rights in key telecommunication sectors may hamper the commercial competitiveness of the rest of the industry.

Government roles

Whether we like it or not, governments are now involved with consumer electronics. The Japanese government, for instance, protected its fledgling industry in the 1960s, when Zenith was trying to establish markets there. The Korean export thrust is masterminded by its government. The French have a clear sense of the importance of electronics and are even protecting their industry from EC members like the British, when these are seen to be acting as a trojan horse for the Japanese. The Americans have protected their industry through orderly marketing arrangements. In the UK, the deals between trade bodies such as BREMA and the Radio Industry Council and their opposite numbers in Japan, Singapore, Taiwan and South Korea have had tacit governmental support.

At the same time, as the boundaries between consumer electronics and other parts of the information and communications industry get blurred, all governments with state-controlled PTTs are inevitably drawn into consumer electronic strategies. It is not inevitable that governments should become involved in the rationalization process triggered when a 'super-competitor' like Japan arrives on the scene. It is doubtful, though, if Thomson-Brandt could have been established as Western Europe's second largest television manufacturer without very active backing from the French government. Similarly, in the UK one can argue that the work done by NEDO has been an important catalyst, if only by bringing home to the British industry exactly how far behind best world practice it really was.

WHITHER THE NICs?

The impression left by studying this sector is that the NICs are stalking a target which is moving ever faster in front of them. In the early 1970s, colour televisions were based on precisely the kind of maturing technology which plays into the hands of the NICs. However, the application of micro-electronics to component assembly suddenly swung the balance of comparative advantage back to those AICs like Japan who saw what was happening. Then, the explosion of new uses for television sets, and the devising of ever new products to be linked to them, meant that the industry became an ever-more technologically dynamic one, as instanced by the emergence of companies like IBM on its fringes. The result was that the basically imitative strategy of the NICs was no longer adequate. They too will have to automate (if only to guarantee quality) and to increase their R&D effort in order to stay in touch with the technological leaders. In many ways, what is happening in consumer electronics is another variant of what has happened in the automobile sector. A maturing technology has suddenly found a new lease of life. This may not pose too many problems for the leading East Asian NICs, who have already learned many lessons from Japan. It will, though, pose problems for the NICs following on behind them. However, the speed with which Korea and Hong Kong have got themselves on to the fringes of the new video recording and viewdata technologies should remind us that the capacity of the NICs to innovate has been increasing as well.

NOTES

1 Some definitions of the terminology are needed here. 'Teletext' is text broadcast over the air to slightly modified television sets. The viewer can, typically, call up 100 to 200 'pages' of text on each channel. These may cover news items, sports results, weather forecasts, etc. 'Videotex' or 'viewdata' describe systems whereby the television set is linked by telephone lines to outside computers. This gives the viewer access to a much greater volume of information and also allows interaction between the viewer and the system; in other words, the viewer is not restricted just to calling up details of available holidays, but will be able to book them directly through instructions keyed into the set.
2 The dumping case was finally settled in an out-of-court agreement in the summer of 1980, but on terms that left the US industry somewhat dissatisfied.

5
Automobiles
Neil McMullen and Laura L. Megna

As the 1980s began, the motor-vehicle industry in the West was under-going significant and far-reaching change. One of the worst slumps in the industry's history was making its impact felt on trade, production, and employment patterns. The malaise did not originate with this slump; rather, it began to develop in the early 1970s when Western motor-vehicle markets reached saturation, the price of oil shot up, and consequent changes in consumer demand, reinforced in the USA by government pollution-control regulations, generated a need for new technology. At the same time as Western motor-vehicle industries grappled with a slump, the NICs were developing potentially dynamic domestic markets and placing increasingly stringent restrictions on the operations of foreign motor-vehicle firms in NIC markets. Changes in trade patterns, compounded by developments in the NICs, have resulted not only in fierce competition between US, European and Japanese firms, but also pressures on their governments for protection from, and assistance in adjusting to, changing patterns of demand, trade, technology, and location of production.

Right up to the mid-1960s, the world automobile industry showed a certain degree of stability and prosperity. Production grew with demand until the industry became a sector of primary importance in several developed economies. As Table 5.1 shows, the average annual rate of growth of car production by these traditional producers (the USA and the EC) exceeded growth in GDP up to 1973; however, changes in demand, technology, and particularly the influx of imported vehicles from Japan reversed this relationship after 1973. Now, reliance on the motor-vehicle industry as a source of dynamic growth has shifted from these countries to the NICs in Latin America, Asia and Eastern Europe. As these NICs embrace the motor-vehicle industry as a means to drive their economies forward, Western producers are concerned about it for wholly opposite reasons: dynamism has given way to slow growth and widespread concern about the impact of the motor-vehicle slump on other industries and on employment in the AICs. While it is generally acknowledged that the NICs are not the cause of the Western motor-vehicle industry's problems, concern nevertheless exists about their likely impact in the next decade.

Table 5.1 *Average Annual Rates of Growth of GDP (Constant) and Motor-Car Production, 1950–79 (percentages)*

Country	1950–60		1960–73		1973–9	
	GDP	*Motor cars*	*GDP*	*Motor cars*	*GDP*	*Motor cars*
West Germany	7·7	23·1	4·5	6·0	2·4^a	3·7
France	4·5	18·5	5·7	8·0	3·0	0·6
Italy	5·3	19·8	5·0	9·4	2·6^b	−3·0
UK	2·4	11·4	2·9	3·1	1·2	−7·5
USA	2·9	0·6	4·0	5·7	2·5^d	−1·0
Japan	7·7^c	62·5	10·3	30·0	4·1^d	5·9
Argentina	3·4	n.a.	4·5	25·8	2·3	0·5
Mexico	6·3	15·5	7·0	15·1	5·0	7·0
Brazil	5·7	v.h.	6·8	21·9	6·9	2·0
Spain	3·5	n.a.	7·0	25·1^d	2·7	7·5^d
South Korea	5·0^c	−	9·0	140·6	9·8	59·7

^{a}Real GNP.
^{b}1973–7.
^{c}1952–60.
^{d}1973–8, from UN, *Yearbook of International Trade Statistics*, various issues.
v.h. = 'very high'. n.a. = not available.
Sources:
GDP: UN, *Yearbook of National Accounts Statistics*, 1978, vol. II, 1969, vol. II; 1973–9 from IMF, *International Financial Statistics Yearbook*, 1980.
MOTOR CARS: Unless otherwise indicated, MVMA of the US, Inc. data as shown in *World Motor Vehicle Data 1980*.

THE STRUCTURE OF THE WORLD MOTOR-VEHICLE INDUSTRY

The world's motor-vehicle industry is characterized by a small number of very large firms. Nine firms – General Motors, Ford, Toyota, Fiat, Nissan, VW–Audi, Peugeot–Citroën, Renault and Chrysler – accounted for 77 per cent of all motor vehicles produced in 1979. Several factors reinforce this structure. Because it takes as many as five years to move a model off the drawing-board and on to the road, the success of a firm depends crucially upon management's ability to predict demand (range of models, component specifications, etc.) and to meet long-term investment costs for redesign and tooling up. The importance of the ability to predict demand and the long lead time needed to create new models cannot be over-emphasized. Generally, large firms can bear the risks easier than smaller firms, forcing smaller firms to regroup for survival by folding subsidiaries (Chrysler), merging (Peugeot–Citroën with Chrysler in Europe), or undertaking joint ventures (Saab and Lancia). In addition to risk, the need to achieve economies of scale also promotes large firms at the expense of smaller companies. It is generally held that a firm must produce 2 million vehicles annually to benefit from scale economies. General Motors (with 8·5 million motor vehicles), Ford (5·2 million), Toyota (3·0 million), the Fiat Group (3·0 million), Nissan (2·7 million), and VW–Audi (2·5 million) produced that minimum before 1979, and the Peugeot–Citroën–Chrysler merger brought that firm into the 2 million production category with 2·4 million motor vehicles in 1979. Once the 'world motor car' takes hold, the only way to compete in the mass market will be with annual production of 2 million vehicles or more.

The convergence of world-demand patterns from highly differentiated car models to small, fuel-efficient cars reinforces the need for scale economies, and hence large firms. Several of the world's larger firms are now designing one basic small-car type, drawing on specialized plants in several countries and selling this 'world car' to an international market. Production facilities, particularly in components such as body pressings, engines and transmissions, in several localities are being integrated into one large overall structure. To compete, several smaller firms, unable to take advantage of production facilities around the globe, are using a variety of approaches, from consolidation to cooperative agreements with rival firms. This need for large-scale production will be an important constraint on the international competitiveness of NIC motor-vehicle industries and their ability to break into the world market independently of Western multinationals.

In addition to a change in the type of car demanded by consumers, particularly in North America, the slowdown in the rate of growth of demand for cars can be expected to continue through the 1980s and 1990s in North America, Europe and Japan. The closer automobile demand gets to saturation, the more sensitive output and employment become to business-cycle fluctuations, since replacement purchases can be postponed during slumps. The motor-vehicle industry in the developed countries experienced two such troughs in 1974 and 1977, and was in the midst of a third as the 1980s began.

Despite some unsatisfied demand for cars in the early 1980s, over the long run it can be expected that saturation will combine with slower economic growth and high energy prices to depress even further the rate of growth of demand for cars in North America and Europe. In fact, OECD predicts that the growth of demand will probably not exceed 2 per cent annually in the 1980s, falling further to almost nil by 1990, after which replacement demand will account for 85 per cent of total demand in North America, Japan and Europe. In contrast, the growth in demand for cars in the markets of countries which have not yet reached saturation, such as the NICs, will be considerably stronger. Table 5.2 projects that US and West European shares of total world demand will fall from a total of almost 90 per cent in 1960 to just over 60 per cent in 1990, while the shares of Japan will increase from 1·5 to 11 per cent, Eastern Europe from 2 to 8 per cent, Latin America from 2·4 to 10 per cent and Asia from 1 to 3 per cent.

In addition to demand and technology changes, the location of motor-vehicle production has shifted over the 1960s and 1970s away from the USA to new producers in Latin America, Asia, the Middle East and Southern and Eastern Europe. The US share of world car production has fallen steadily over the last thirty years, from 76 per cent in 1950 to 28 per cent in 1979, while Japan's share grew from less than 1 per cent to 23 per cent over the same period. While not expanding their output as dramatically as Japan has, several NICs have increased their shares of world car production: Brazil from nil to 3 per cent, Spain from nil to almost 3 per cent, Eastern Europe from 4 to 8 per cent and South Korea from nil to over 1 per cent.

Table 5.2   *Share of World Demand for Cars, 1960–90 (percentage)*

	1960	1970	1980	1985	1990
OECD	*92·5*	*90·9*	*84·7*	*80·8*	*76·1*
North America	56·8	44·5	35·3	33·9	30·8
Western Europe	32·1	34·9	35·3	33·9	32·6
EC	−27·8	−28·9	−27·3	−25·5	−23·3
Other	−4·2	−6·0	−8·0	−8·4	−9·2
Japan	1·4	9·3	11·9	10·8	10·6
Oceania	2·2	2·1	2·2	2·2	2·0
Other regions	*7·5*	*9·1*	*15·3*	*19·2*	*23·9*
Eastern Europe	2·2	3·1	5·8	6·8	8·1
Latin America	2·4	3·3	5·7	7·9	10·2
Asia (excl. Japan)	1·0	1·3	1·9	2·4	3·0
Africa	1·9	1·4	1·9	2·1	2·6
World	*100·0*	*100·0*	*100·0*	*100·0*	*100·0*

Source: Ifo-Institute forecasts, in Interfutures, 1978, p. 55.

The increasing unification of world demand around converging tastes, the changing character of foreign investment, and the emergence of the NICs as new producers are all affecting international trading patterns. Increased Japanese car exports have eroded US European producers' shares of the US market itself and individual European producers' shares of the EC market, intensifying pressures in both continents for protection from Japanese imports. Table 5.3 shows trends in motor-vehicle imports in Europe, North America and Japan.

However, because of the need for large investments in motor-vehicle production and the importance of marketing, economies of scale, and access to new product technology, the Latin American and Asian NICs are not expected to be significant exporters of assembled vehicles to Europe or North America. It is actually parts production, rather than car production or assembly, that will experience a pronounced dispersion to the NICs. A good deal of this kind of dispersion has already taken place, particularly to

Table 5.3 *Share of Imports in New Car Registrations, 1950–79*
(volume-based percentage)

	1960	1970	1975	1979
USA	6·8	24·0	25·1	29·1
From Japan	−ᵃ	2·8	8·6	14·9
Less imports from Canada	6·8	15·7	16·2	22·5
Canada	37·9	63·6	66·3	84·4
Less imports from US	31·7	24·0	0·6	14·0
EC				
France	4·1	23·0	26·9	30·6
Germany	9·8	34·2	39·3	43·4
Italy	4·8	33·7	36·0	47·8
UK	6·3	14·0	37·0	61·2
Japan	2·4	0·8	1·7	2·1

ᵃLess than 0·05 per cent.
Source: Derived from MVMA data.

Spain, Mexico and Brazil. This will continue, but it is not clear that the process will accelerate or spread to new countries in a significant way.

DEVELOPMENTS AND FUTURE ASPIRATIONS IN THE NICs

The sequence of development of the motor-vehicle industry in NIC economies can be characterized by a four-stage model. First, an LDC with no motor-vehicle assembly facilities imports cars. Then as personal incomes, and thus demand, grow with development, LDCs enter the second stage. They invite in a number of multinational motor-vehicle firms to set up small assembly plants, and try to avail themselves of the comparative advantages offered by low labour costs, via wholly owned subsidiaries, licensing arrangements or joint ventures. Using imported parts, components and technology, these firms assemble a variety of models. To encourage domestic manufacture of these imported parts and final products (import substitution), local content requirements are imposed and tariffs raised to protect the industry. A significant number of the world's LDCs have reached this stage.

In the third stage, limited growth, excess capacity and the balance-of-payments costs of import substitution begin to weigh heavily on the more rapidly growing LDCs (the NICs). Policies switch from import substitution to export promotion and protective tariffs are lowered, exchange rates revalued and tax subsidies offered. Attempting to achieve some benefit from scale, NIC governments use a variety of policy tools to reduce the number of firms and models. The motor-vehicle industries in Brazil, Mexico and Argentina reached this stage in the 1970s.

Sometimes NICs use a combination of the import-substitution and export-promotion policies, increasing local-content requirements at the same time as they impose import quotas tied to export performance (Mexico and Brazil are two examples). Either way, these countries are heavily dependent on the willingness of the multinationals to cooperate with overall government policies. There are advantages and disadvantages to the NICs from such a multinational-dependent strategy. On one hand, it facilitates NIC access to developed-country markets, technological know-how, management skills, and the scale necessary to overcome the risks in trying to make accurate long-term investment decisions. On the other, the dependency relationship which develops links the export performance of the NIC motor-vehicle industries to the global marketing and export strategy of the multinationals, and NIC policies and the strategies of the multinationals do not always coincide (Bennett and Sharpe, 1979).

So far, only South Korea is pursuing an alternative third stage: it is attempting to follow Japan's lead and establish a motor-vehicle industry independent of the multinational network. This is a much more costly and risky strategy, and many analysts feel that, given the constraints, Korea's approach is not likely to yield a motor-vehicle industry which will affect world markets in the 1980s in the way that Japan's industry did in the 1970s. However, the Koreans have produced a good automobile and will make an impact if they can market automobiles as well as they manufacture them.

Latin America

Brazil. Operating under the protection of a prohibition on imported automobiles and a 250 per cent tariff on other motor vehicles, Brazil produced over 1 million motor vehicles in 1979, just surpassing Spain in volume as an NIC motor-vehicle manufacturer (see Table 5.4). While multinational firms dominate motor-vehicle production, Brazilian components manufacturers are numerous and of consequence. Although sales of Brazilian-produced finished vehicles concentrate on the home market, with some exports to developing countries, Brazil's output of components is a notable source of supply for OECD motor-vehicle producers. There is clearly a potential for trade and adjustment problems for OECD in the 1980s and 1990s in the components subsector.

The multinational auto firms are the principal channels through which auto component exports from Brazil penetrate the OECD markets. Within this network, Brazil has the potential to develop as a very competitive supplier of components. Already, the value of total auto component exports to the OECD alone exceeds that of motor-vehicle exports by $132 million (1979), and investment is growing. General Motors plans to manufacture engines for its 'world car' in Brazil by 1982, exporting 70–75 per cent to Germany and the UK. Fiat will export small Brazilian-made diesel-engined cars to Italy. Ford announced a 5-year investment programme totalling $500 million to expand its Brazilian operations.

Table 5.4 *Motor-Vehicle Production of Selected NICs, 1960–79 (thousands)*

Country	1960	1970	1975	1979
Brazil	*133·0*	*416·0*	*929·8*	*1,128·0*
Motor cars	37·8	249·9	524·2	498·3
Commercial vehicles	95·2	166·1	405·6	629·6
Mexico	*49·8*	*174·3*	*356·6*	*444·4*
Motor cars	28·1	121·6	237·1	280·0
Commercial vehicles	21·7	52·7	119·5	164·4
Argentina	*90·2*	*219·6*	*251·1*	*266·2*
Motor cars	30·3	163·4	185·7	187·8
Commercial vehicles	59·9	56·2	65·4	78·4
South Korea	*1·8[a]*	*28·8*	*36·3*	*204·4*
Motor cars	1·7	14·5	17·5	113·6
Commercial vehicles	0·1	14·3	18·8	90·8
Spain	*n.a.*	*n.a.*	*814·1*	*1,122·9*
Motor cars	n.a.	n.a.	696·1	965·8
Commercial vehicles	n.a.	n.a.	118·0	157·1
Soviet Union	*523·6*	*922·0*	*1,964·0*	*2,173·0*
Motor cars	138·8	352·0	1,201·0	1,314·0
Commercial vehicles	348·8	570·0	763·0	859·0

[a]1962. n.a. = not available.
Source: MVMA, 1980.

Brazil is encouraging motor-vehicle exports by negotiating incentive programmes (so-called BEFIEX agreements) with virtually all the major multinational motor-vehicle firms. These agreements link their export performance with tax exemptions on their imports. Thanks in part to such agreements, Brazil will make some inroads in OECD finished-vehicle markets in the future as the impact of the internationalization of world auto production and other government industry promotion efforts are realized.

The bulk of Brazilian exports of auto components occurs as intra-multinational trade rather than as autonomous penetration of the US market by Brazilian exports. All of the major auto-component exports to the OECD are traceable to exports by a multinational auto manufacturer: for example, all of the car radios exported from Brazil are exported to Ford in the USA. All but a trickle of Brazil's exports of ignition-starting equipment are US multinational exports to the United States. Of the forty-four firms exporting engines from Brazil, the only ones to penetrate OECD markets are the major multinational auto manufacturers, rather than the smaller Brazilian firms. Moreover, even though most of Brazil's components exports go to the OECD, the penetration is small relative to the size of the

OECD market and, again, intra-firm trade is the prevailing pattern. (In fact, developed countries account for the major proportion of OECD imports: 69 per cent for car radios, 78 per cent for ignition-starting equipment, 95·8 per cent for internal combustion engines, and 99·1 per cent for other auto parts in 1976. Thus, intra-OECD trade is currently the predominant pattern.)

As for Brazilian auto parts firms, production is basically oriented towards supplying the Brazilian market. The smaller and more numerous Brazilian firms focus on the internal market because of their scale and the lack of marketing channels necessary to become a major factor in world markets. It is a rare firm that exports more than 10 per cent of its production. Brazilian auto parts manufacturers do not depend on external markets and are not in business in order to export, as are many components manufacturers in Asia. As Brazil feels the strains of reduced international and domestic economic growth, auto components exports will be important, but they will not be central to Brazil's development or its export strategy in the 1980s. Similarly, they should not be a significant source of market disruption for the auto-component industry of the OECD, whether within the OECD, or in third markets.

Mexico. The Mexican motor-vehicle industry has benefited from a host of government promotion measures since the 1960s designed to increase the productive efficiency of the industry. Using import quotas, tariffs, local content requirements and other import-substitution and export-promotion policy tools, the government reduced the number of motor-vehicle firms from sixteen in 1964 to eight in 1980 and increased the level of finished-vehicle exports from zero in 1960 to 3,000 in 1975 and 18,245 in 1980. The government mandated that local content increase from 22 per cent (1962) to 70 per cent (1980) and 75 per cent in 1981.

The government plans to expand production at an average rate of 14–15 per cent a year in the 1980s, and increase exports by 25 per cent by the end of 1982. In response to requirements that firms must export 10 per cent more in value than they import by 1981, the seven multinational auto firms (four of which – Chrysler, VW, General Motors and Ford – accounted for 80 per cent of Mexico's motor-vehicle production in 1980) will undertake major investments to expand productive capacity from its present 350,000 vehicles to over 1 million in 1990. The government hopes a large part of this production increase will be for export. Chrysler is building a new plant to produce 270,000 five-cylinder vehicles a year, mostly for export, beginning in 1981. General Motors plans to double its current productive capacity in Mexico, a large proportion of which will be exported, while Ford is using a joint-venture operation with a Mexican firm to produce auto parts for 800,000 Ford vehicles to be assembled in Europe and Latin America. A Dina and Renault Mexicana merger into Renault de Mexico expects to invest 1·6 billion pesos over 1978–83, 50 per cent of which will be allocated to the establishment of new plants for local production of parts.

Though substantial, those expansion plans when viewed in a broader perspective are not the threat to world markets they might appear to be. Although the government strongly promotes exports, the bulk of production initially will supply a dynamic domestic market fuelled by cheap gasoline and oil revenues. The industry's total auto output (280,049 in 1979) is only 3·3 per cent of US production: except for American Motors Corporation and Chrysler Corporation's Chrysler model, output of *each* model produced in the USA exceeded Mexico's total car production (and that spread over seventeen models). The achievement of world-scale production levels generally requires large assembly-plant operations totalling 500,000 units with many, if not all, standardized components. In all of Latin America, only VW in Brazil has reached this level of output. Even with production of over 1 million vehicles in 1990, Mexico's motor-vehicle industry will not be sufficiently rationalized to compete effectively on world markets. If growth prospects for the economy as a whole are realized, Mexico could achieve world-scale output in two or three plants in the 1980s; however, it is unlikely that the government will be able to intervene as dramatically as would be required to attain this level of consolidation and rationalization. One way to attempt to achieve scale would be via a Mexican–US automotive pact similar to that which set up a free-trade zone between the United States and Canada in 1965. However, the prospects for such a pact with Mexico are slim. Opposition from US labour (which would be negatively effected by inexpensive Mexican labour) would probably be sufficient to block Senate ratification of a Mexican–US automotive agreement.

In terms of sales, Mexico's domestic market for motor vehicles is still much smaller than Spain's (267,000 cars in 1979 against 584,000 cars sold in Spain). But potential demand is there and, until it is filled, Mexico's significance for OECD adjustment problems will continue to be in exports of components and engines going to the USA with limited, but increasing, exports to Europe.

While finished vehicles accounted for 22 per cent of the value of Mexico's automotive industry exports in 1978, the remaining 78 per cent were parts exports. The subsector is characterized by a good deal of concentration: in 1975, forty (of about 730) auto parts firms had some exports but one firm (TREMEC) accounted for 42 per cent and ten firms for over 80 per cent (Bennett and Sharpe, 1979, p. 193). Increased exports are thus likely to come from these firms (which happen to have strong foreign-equity participation) rather than the 370 or so fully Mexican-owned firms (all parts firms are, by law, majority-owned by Mexicans). In addition to the obvious advantage provided by ready access to the technical sophistication needed for success in international markets, the joint-venture parts manufactures also enjoy long-standing relationships with the international automobile firms, which prefer to buy from these parts manufacturers rather than from independent Mexican firms (Bennett and Sharpe, 1979, p. 199).

Argentina. Of the three Latin American countries with major automobile industries, Argentina has probably had the most difficulty establishing an efficient, competitive industry. Throughout its history, the industry has been characterized by small-scale, high-cost production; because Argentina's exports have not been competitive on the international market (up to 1971, Argentina automobile exports were negligible), sales have had to focus on a domestic market constrained by low income growth. A pro-liferation of firms and models, all depending on this small market, have made for limited standardization and small production runs – in short, difficulty in achieving economies of scale. The consolidation of the industry that has occurred (twenty-one firms in 1960, ten in 1980) has generally been among Argentine firms. Competition from large foreign firms forced Argentine companies to consolidate, drop licensing agree-ments with foreign firms, or go out of business. Whereas in 1960 foreign motor-vehicle firms accounted for about 75 per cent of Argentina's production, by 1979 that share had risen to 84 per cent.

Although its installed capacity is every bit as large as Mexico's, high costs and under-utilization frustrate any attempts by Argentina's motor-vehicle industry to be a serious competitor in international markets outside the multinational framework. With a capacity of about 350,000 vehicles, production reached only 266,200 in 1979, having dipped down to 179,160 motor vehicles in 1978.

There is some disagreement among multinationals about the potential for recovery of the Argentine industry. While General Motors shut down operations at the end of 1978 (citing depressed domestic demand and a weak competitive position), vw took over Argentina's Chrysler Fevre plants with plans to invest $100 million and produce 10,000 vehicles in 1981 and 70,000 annually after that. vw feel that the problems plaguing the small Argentine market (which have forced Fiat to cut its work-force by 21 per cent, Renault by 13 per cent and Citroën by 39 per cent) are temporary distortions due to depressed lower-middle-class incomes and the emergence of a speculative market for large cars as a hedge against inflation. By 1982 vw expect these distortions to be ironed out and the market for small cars to have expanded to 300,000–350,000 units a year. The Argentine government is equally optimistic about the growth of the entire motor-vehicle industry. Assuming an 8 per cent annual increase in motor-vehicle production (based on a rate of growth of population of 1·5 per cent), it projects production of 307,049 vehicles by 1985; 451,155 by 1990; 974,009 by 2000; and 1,431,139 by 2005. The present government's policy of opening the industry to international competition (to bring down prices and increase exports) is designed to ensure that a large proportion of future production is exported. It is questionable whether the means to this end will succeed: dropping restrictions on imports has so far encouraged (foreign) firms to import components and parts needed for assembly, rather than utilize much more expensive Argentine components and parts.

oecd analysts see the demand for cars in Latin Americas as a whole increasing from less than 5 per cent of total world demand at present to over 10 per cent in 1990, despite inflationary pressures and high energy prices. Moreover, it can be expected that this dynamic car demand will be almost exclusively met by producers already established in Latin America. These firms may also supply the demand of Latin America's LDCs for finished and knocked-down cars, parts and components. Whereas Latin American exports of auto parts and components have been and will continue to be important to the traditional car producers, shipments of cars are of minor importance. Given the intense competition on international markets inevitable in the future, this present supply network is very likely to continue.

The Latin American NICs will not be making serious inroads into international finished-vehicle markets at any time in the near future. They will continue to supply their domestic markets first, following this by meeting demand in neighbouring countries and Africa for finished motor vehicles; at the same time, they are increasingly being integrated as component suppliers into international production.

European NICs

Spain. Spain is not usually thought of as a major force in international trade; however, investments in recent years by Ford and General Motors to develop Spain's auto industry are changing that picture. Four factors are encouraging the multinationals to develop Spain's motor-vehicle industry: political stability, favourable long-term growth prospects, Spanish entry into the EC in the early 1980s, and geographical location (good for supplying not only European markets, but those in the Middle East and Latin America as well).

Whereas Spain's output of motor vehicles registered 16,159 units in 1955, by 1979 that figure had climbed to over 1 million vehicles, 38 per cent of which were exported, predominantly to the EEC. The investment now planned by the multinationals could increase output to 1·6 million vehicles by the mid-1980s, with exports of 900,000. Imports are not significant, reflecting Spain's comparative advantage and significant non-tariff barriers to automotive imports.

Historically, Ford has been the primary multinational catalyst of Spain's motor-vehicle industry. Its plants operate on the same scale, and with the same technology, as comparable plants in the USA with the added advantage of lower labour costs. Ford's Spanish operations have long been integrated into an international production structure, so that production of Ford's Fiesta has been able to benefit from concentrated component production at different plants throughout Europe. This strategy gives Ford the kind of competitiveness in Europe it needs to export two-thirds of its total Spanish car production, mostly to southern Europe.

Intensified international competition among the multinational auto firms stimulated General Motors to respond to Ford's future investment plans in Spain with plans of its own. After exporting 189,000 of the 258,000

Fiestas produced in Spain in 1978, plus 95,000 engines for cars produced in other European plants, Ford is talking of spending $450 million to double present capacity, despite labour problems. At the same time, General Motors plans to invest in Spain for the first time, with $1·6 billion (80 per cent of the $2 billion earmarked for Europe) in a 270,000-unit assembly plant (with relatively non-unionized labour) plus a components factory; two-thirds of output is for export. Production is expected to begin around 1982–3 when entry to the EC brings liberalization of existing restrictions on investment. Renault and Peugeot–Citroën–Chrysler (now known as Talbot) each export about one-fourth of their Spanish production, but their investment plans are not yet clear. Toyota is considering a production move into Spain. Trends in the predominantly home-market-oriented Spanish commercial-vehicle sector are less dynamic; only Ibérico-Ebro is a significant exporter.

Spain's largest automotive manufacturer, SEAT, exported about 30 per cent of its 1978 output; however, its inefficient product mix and low productivity forced the firm into the red. Fiat decided not to integrate SEAT into its own production structure, and SEAT has been shopping around for a new investment partner. Despite labour and structural problems, and the uncertain future of SEAT, the internationalization of the Spanish auto business is almost complete, and the foreign firms will clearly dominate Spanish auto production in the 1980s.

Portugal. If Ford does not further expand capacity in Spain, it may build a $650-million export-oriented factory in Portugal (Edwards, 1979, p. 63). Renault has decided to invest $400 million to increase its vehicle-assembly output by stages from 11,000 in 1978 to 50,000 by 1982 and 80,000 by 1987 – one-quarter for export. In a more important operation, Renault's engine production will increase to 222,000 by 1984, two-thirds for export, with 80 per cent local content; and a new component plant is in the offing. Inevitably, Renault's investment plans will affect market prospects for the many small assemblers operating in Spain – Fiat and British Leyland in particular.

EASTERN EUROPE

Because the East Europeans have acquired much of the latest European technology and can set exchange rates and prices at effectively any level they choose, some European producers (for example, BL and Renault) feel that these countries pose a greater competitive threat to Western Europe than the NICs. Like Japan, East European producers first exported to countries which had no major national car manufacturers, as well as to the UK with its weak car industry. Now, they are following Japan with exports to France, Germany, Italy and Canada, where the motor-vehicle industries are relatively strong. Cooperative agreements negotiated between East and West European motor-vehicle firms considerably aid this strategy. Three

East European firms (two with strong links to Fiat) are among the world's twenty-five largest motor-vehicle firms. While their western counterparts suffered the cyclical fluctuations characteristic of their motor-vehicle industries, the output of East European producers has increased steadily since the 1960s. OECD expects the volume of East European car sales to Western Europe to increase to about 300,000 units by 1985, more than double the 1976 volume and about 2 per cent of the total market for passenger cars in Western Europe. In total, it is expected that by 1985 exports of cars will reach 440,000 units; commercial vehicles are reserved for domestic use and therefore will not be exported in any significant volumes.

To make exports more competitive internationally, the East European countries are integrating more than forty plants in Bulgaria, Hungary, East Germany and Poland, as well as fourteen Yugoslav suppliers, around production of parts and components for passenger cars assembled in the USSR and Poland. Technology for this auto is to a considerable extent imported from Western Europe.

While exports will be growing, East European imports of finished cars will not. Instead, imports of engineering services, machine tools and other equipment, as well as parts and components, primarily from Japan, will be used to produce cars for export to Western Europe. Thus growing domestic markets, supplied by local production, and intensified export drives in Europe will stimulate an increase in East European motor-vehicle production from 2·9 million units in 1976 to 6·2 million units in 1985. OECD estimates that this expansion, if successful would correspond to a share of world production rising from 8 per cent to more than 10 per cent.

SOUTH KOREA

South Korea is attempting to develop an internationally competitive motor-vehicle industry independent of the multinational framework. In 1976, the Hyundai Motor Co. began to move from assembly of imported components for Ford vehicles to production of a Korean model, the Pony with about 90 per cent local parts and components. South Korea's primary motor-vehicle markets, the Middle East and Latin America, expanded in 1978 to include Europe; in addition, Hyundai is test-marketing in the United States. Their goal is to achieve an annual volume of exports of 150,000 (half of production) by 1981, and exports of 900,000 on a production base of 2 million vehicles by 1990. However, recent drops in motor-vehicle production (car production fell 50 per cent from 1979–80) cast some doubt upon South Korea's ability to meet these goals.

Because of their cost competitiveness, the primary impact of Korean motor-vehicle exports in the 1980s will be to increase competition in LDC markets, while the difficulty of penetrating complex and relatively saturated markets will constrain success of Korean exports in more developed economies. Unlike Japan, South Korea did not develop the domestic market first, and it may suffer from this approach. In addition, Korean manufacturers lack access to multinational scale and face the challenge of making a number of correct long-term investment decisions. Nevertheless, South Korea has been approached by the multinationals and, given these risks, may hedge its bets with a partial multinational strategy. Until late 1980, General Motors appeared to have the edge in this respect. But negotiations between Hyundai, GM and another Korean firm about a joint venture broke down. It appears that the three firms will now continue as independent manufacturers.

THE MIDDLE EAST

The importance of the motor-vehicle industry in the Middle East may also be expected to grow, pulled primarily by surging regional demand, although problems in achieving significant scale economies will not permit these producers to be major competitors in international markets. In 1977 OECD estimated that production of, as well as demand for, cars in the Middle East could grow by more than 10 per cent annually into 1985. It noted that present and planned projects indicate that by 1985 as much as 36 per cent of the expected demand for cars might be met by local production (compared to none in 1975), another 18 per cent by local assembly. However, these projections assumed political stability in the region; the turmoil in Iran was a serious blow and will probably set back the timetable for regional production by a decade or more.

OUTLOOK

Table 5.5 breaks down the NIC shares of OECD imports of motor cars and parts, revealing that in 1979 almost 100 per cent of total OECD automotive imports from Latin America came from three countries; 58 per cent of OECD assembled auto imports from Eastern Europe came from the Soviet Union and 45 per cent of parts and components imports came from Yugoslavia; almost two-thirds of all assembled car imports from the Far East originated in South Korea. Yet, the sum total of OECD imports of both parts and cars from all five regions amounted to a very small share of such imports. In 1979, 99 per cent of OECD imports of cars and 98 per cent of parts imports came from other OECD countries, leaving about 1 per cent of car imports and 2 per cent of parts imports for Latin America, Eastern Europe, the Middle East, Africa, and the non-OECD Far East *combined*. So the importance of intra-OECD auto trade can be lost if one focuses solely on the three or four NICs that are successfully building up motor-vehicle industries.

Except for South Korea, the NIC motor-vehicle industries are essentially parts of the multinational motor-vehicle industries. Mexico and Brazil are strong exporters to the USA of engines and parts within this network;

Table 5.5 *NIC Shares of OECD Imports of Motor Cars and Parts, 1970 and 1978 (percentages[1])*

Source	1970	1979
Passenger cars		
Latin America	*0·002*	*0·198*
Mexico	−[a]	(80·1)
Brazil	(50·0)	(16·1)
Argentina	(50·0)	(3·0)
Eastern Europe	*0·25*	*1·00*
USSR	(24·7)	(58·4)
Portugal	−[a]	−[a]
Spain	0·20	2·50
Far East	*0·001*	*0·044*
South Korea	(n.a.)	(64·9)
Middle East	0·001	0·011
Parts and accessories		
Latin America	*0·25*	*1·46*
Mexico	(83·9)	(55·1)
Brazil	(12·7)	(38·4)
Argentina	(3·4)	(4·0)
Eastern Europe	*0·37*	*0·67*
Romania	(19·5)	(12·7)
Yugoslavia	(43·7)	(44·9)
Portugal	0·03	0·03
Spain	0·36	1·03
Far East	*0·01*	*0·25*
South Korea	(14·3)	(7·32)
Middle East	0·01	0·07

[1]NIC percentage of total value of OECD imports from the world; figures in parentheses are individual NIC shares of OECD imports from the region.
[a]Less than 0·05 per cent. n.a. = not available.
Source: Derived from OECD, *Foreign Trade Statistics*, series C, 1970, 1979.

indeed, intra-multinational firm trade characterizes the bulk of Mexican–OECD and Brazilian–OECD motor-vehicle trade. Thus the potential of NIC exports of motor vehicles and/or parts to cause adjustment pressures in the OECD is tied to the overall strategies of these firms. To speak of NIC ability to cause such pressures is to recognize NIC ability to 'pressure' a firm to export (that is, to convince the parent firm to buy, through local content and other production requirements). Along with price and quality of production from NIC factories, the willingness of parent firms to buy the products of the subsidiaries will determine the impact of the NICs on international motor-vehicle markets (Bennett and Sharpe, 1979, p. 192).

Shifts in production to the NICs should continue as the multinational car firms increase their subcontracting activity to meet production requirements imposed by the NICs and to take advantage of cheaper, labour-intensive operations. NIC parts plants are often directly competitive with parts plants in the USA and Europe, facilitating the speed with which production can be shifted. Meanwhile, assembly facilities in the traditional producing centres will be increasingly capital- and skilled-labour-intensive. Thus, multinational corporation integration of NIC firms into their global production network will cause adjustment problems in North America and Europe, but they are not likely to be significant or persisting problems. This is because they will be managed within the firm and often subject to negotiation with unions in the auto sector.

Spain will clearly be an important actor in international motor-vehicle markets in the 1980s and 1990s. The multinational producers are investing considerable resources in Spain and, once these plants come on stream and the country joins the EC Spain will be one of Europe's leading exporters of assembled motor vehicles.

Strong demand, government local-content requirements and attempts to capitalize on NIC comparative advantages will lure production shifts to the NICs and LDCs with growing domestic demand for motor vehicles. The OECD predicts that Latin America's share of world car production could come close to 10 per cent by 1990 compared to less than 5 per cent in 1978. South Korea and Eastern Europe could also become modest car-production centres. Eastern Europe plans to increase its share of world motor-vehicle production from 8 per cent (1978) to more than 10 per cent (1985).

On the whole, though, the export-oriented strategy of Japan will continue to affect international motor-vehicle trade more than the NICs. The impact of the NICs on OECD motor-vehicle markets will depend on the degree to which the major multinational producers need to retool and shift more standardized production to their subsidiaries in Latin America or Spain. Such a shift would favour the role of foreign subsidiaries supplying the OECD with imported auto components and consequently, a somewhat larger quasi-NIC penetration of US and European auto components markets. General Motors appears to be reducing that possibility by investing in vertically integrated parts production in Europe, but the skirmish over whether Ford would close its Ohio engine plant, moving engine production to Mexico, instead of retooling the US plant to make smaller engines, illustrates the kind of shift that could take place. In this instance an 'adjustment problem' was avoided when Ford assured its employees that new work would be found for the plant's employees. This arrangement may be a trend setter, as some adjustment problems are handled within the firm. In the auto sector, there is certainly scope for settlements of this type.

As production becomes increasingly standardized and internationalized around the 'world car', domestic NIC part and component producers may be in a better position to expand their production of replacement parts for their domestic market. Conversely, if they are to become suppliers of original equipment to the local or overseas assembly operations, they will have to make the necessary investments so as to reduce prices, maintain high quality and fulfil delivery schedules.

The NICs will be competing with established subsidiaries of multinational part and component producers, but by the late 1980s a few NIC parts producers, most likely Brazilian, may emerge as serious competitors on world markets. Brazilian firms already supply parts and components for local assembly plants, and some of these firms will probably become internationally competitive during the coming decade. While important for the NIC economies, the NIC penetration of OECD parts and vehicles markets will not be large. NIC production of motor vehicles and parts will be quite dynamic in the 1980s, but will primarily be aimed at meeting demand in developing-country markets. During the 1980s, the significant adjustments in investment patterns and trade flows will be intra-OECD adjustments, with OECD–NIC realignments being secondary reflections of the larger process.

The integration of the key NICs into the world auto market should be managed reasonably well. The major adjustment problems in the 1980s are more likely to result from increased Japanese exports, the slow growth of demand in the leading markets, the enormous capital requirements needed for the redesign and production of new products, and the decline in employment due to the increasing automation of the assembly process.

ADJUSTMENT

The problems that have challenged the motor-vehicle industry in the 1970s, which will continue with increasing intensity into the 1980s, are at this moment lending a sense of urgency to developing and implementing adjustment programmes in the traditional producing countries. Governments are reacting to these pressures – of reductions in employment and more intensive competition – with a variety of adjustment strategies. Some are responses common to all the traditional producers; others are strategies unique to the specific pressures confronting individual firms. Five broad approaches to adjustment can be distinguished (Shepherd, 1980, p. 25): protection, promotion of new technology, specialization, internationalization, and diversification. Governments in the traditional producers rarely rely on any single strategy, preferring instead to draw from each with varying degrees of intensity. The approaches are:

Protection. To protect national motor vehicle industries from damaging import competition, governments sometimes resort to trade protection, by measures ranging from voluntary export-restraint agreements to import quotas.

Promotion of new technology. Governments may attempt to promote new motor-vehicle technology, often by encouraging increased automation and product innovation, to improve the domestic industry's international competitiveness.

Specialization. To achieve economies of scale, governments are increasingly providing incentives for firms to specialize in various stages of production, either on their own or in cooperation with other national firms (or even with foreign competitors).

Internationalization. In an adjustment strategy closely related to specialization, governments encourage firms to shift production to new areas of dynamic demand abroad. Direct investment, cross-border mergers and intra-national consolidations permit national firms to benefit from comparative advantages of new localities, longer production runs and economies of scale from a new international market.

Diversification. Rather than attempt to strengthen the nation's car industry with various supports, some governments, notably those of West Germany and Italy, encourage their motor-vehicle firms to diversify into such other sectors as machine tools, aircraft, computers and electronics.

As Table 5.6 shows, adjustment strategies vary with the country, so generalizations are difficult. It is therefore useful to examine individually national approaches to easing change in motor-vehicle industries.

United States

Before 1973, American demand for large luxury cars effectively protected a large part of the US market from serious import competition. Three to four firms were able to build a solid industry upon a large domestic market for a product only they produced in any volume, and to use substantial profits to support production moves abroad to Europe. But soaring fuel prices in 1973, followed by uneven government policies, changed everything. Although the US motor-vehicle industry is, on the whole, still quite strong both at home and abroad, after the rise in energy prices in the 1970s it faced expensive long-term adjustment to produce fuel-efficient cars. Government and industry reacted with a variety of the adjustment strategies. To encourage domestic production, the government, primarily at the state level, offers investment incentives to foreign firms to set up production facilities in the USA – at the same time that US firms are lured out of the USA by foreign investment incentives.[1] Within the industry, Ford is relying on its very successful international small-car production experience to help it meet domestic demand for smaller cars and, similarly to General Motors, is expanding and integrating its international operations. Both Ford and GM are expanding or setting up major production facilities in the NICs, including Spain, and have minority-ownership links with Japanese firms (GM with Isuzu, Ford with Toyo Kogyo).

After years of oil-price controls which perversely encouraged demand for large cars, government energy and environmental legislation combined with the second surge in world oil prices in 1979 to increase demand for small, fuel-efficient cars. This caught US auto producers, particularly Chrysler, without enough cars competitive with Japanese imports.

The most visible US policy intervention in automobile production is the loan-guarantee package that began to support Chrysler in 1980. Guarantees totalling $1·5 billion were provided to enable Chrysler to switch over to producing smaller cars for the 1980s. It is not clear that the Chrysler reclamation programme will establish a trend in US policy towards industries. On the one hand, the success of the programme would make it more likely that the same formula would be tried again, so a lot depends on whether Chrysler succeeds. On the other hand, the prevailing view among most US businessmen is that involvement with the government, apart from sales to it, is a losing proposition. Among the public ar large (and the Republican administration, elected in 1980) the preference is also for less government rather than more. As US industry faces adjustment problems in the future, this feeling may change, but the trend in the early 1980s is to less government involvement, especially when it implies expenditures. A more *dirigiste* and supportive policy towards industry could evolve, but it does not appear that the Chrysler approach will become a model for future US policies.

The first years of the 1980s found US auto firms and the United Auto Workers busily lobbying Congress for a variety of new measures designed to help the industry 'adjust' to increased import competition and the burden of federal energy, safety and environmental regulations. These measures include import surcharges, extension of the mileage deadlines, and increases in the depreciation allowance. The Reagan administration was divided in its approach to this issue; but, anxious to avoid legislated quotas, it asked Japan to restrain car exports to the USA voluntarily. Some restraint by Japanese exporters will probably result, but it will not be a significant factor. The impact on world trade could be more serious if the Europeans move more aggressively to keep Japanese exports out of their markets.

West Germany

The strength of firms in technological innovation, a tradition of high quality, strong domestic demand, high productivity and early exposure to international competition built a strong motor-vehicle industry in Germany. Because some firms, such as VW, were forced to restructure in the early 1970s, they may be able to survive the 1980s without significant government support. An appreciating deutschmark and relatively high labour costs resulted in an early rationalization of the German motor industry through mergers, overseas production, specialization in production of luxury cars and some government R&D support, ownership and credit guarantees. Nevertheless, increasing pressures from competition in export markets and Japanese imports are intensifying the efforts of German producers to manufacture specialized luxury cars domestically and transfer production of fuel-efficient smaller cars abroad. Using com-

Table 5.6 *Summary of Automotive Sector Policies of Major Producing Countries, 1979*

Roles of government	USA	Japan	West Germany VW (40%) BMW (5%)	France Renault (100%)	United Kingdom BL (99%)	Italy Alfa-Romeo (100%); Fiat (indirect share)
Owner	Nil	Nil	VW (40%) BMW (5%)	Renault (100%)	BL (99%)	Alfa-Romeo (100%); Fiat (indirect share)
Underwriter						
General subsidies	Loan and interest-rate subsidies	Nil	Nil	Major funding of Renault	Major funding of BL, Chrysler UK	Major funding of Alfa-Romeo
General credit	Significant loan guarantees for Chrysler	Major credit role by government banks	Negligible	Major funding for Renault and Peugeot–Citroën merger	Major funding of BL, Chrysler UK	Major funding of Alfa-Romeo
Regional programmes	Nil	Negligible	Active in 1960s	Actively promoting investment in distressed regions	Actively promoting investment in distressed regions	Very actively promoting investment in the south
R&D programmes	Major programme under way	Some assistance	Major programme under way	Medium-scale programmes	Small-scale programmes	Negligible
Regulator						
Design/safety	Very extensive NHTSA standards	Extensive regulation	EC directives; extensive safety and noise regulation	EC directives; additional safety regulations	EC directives; additional safety regulations	EC directives; limited additional safety regulations
Emissions	Very extensive EPA regulation since 1970	Very extensive regulations	EC regulations in force since late 1970s	EC regulations in force since late 1970s	EC regulations in force since late 1970s	EC regulations in force since late 1970s
Fuel economy	Mandated standards since 1975	1979 standards: 6½% to 13% by 1985	Voluntary agreement between industry and	Voluntary agreement between industry and	Voluntary agreement between industry and	Voluntary agreement between industry and

			government (1979)	government (1979)	government (1979)	government being finalized
Competition	Extensive antitrust oversight; FTC investigation	Competition law limits some activities	Cartel office regularly challenges price rises but allows extensive cooperation	Cartel law exists; government promotes cooperation	Monopoly commission approved BL merger; Peugeot–Chrysler UK takeover	Cartel law exists; negligible impact on industry
Taxation	Auto sales and excise tax in state hands; lowest tax on gasoline	Weight and road tax; auto commodity tax on car size; acquisition tax; moderate tax on gasoline	Auto-use tax on engine displacement; high tax on gasoline	Road tax; auto tax on engine displacement; very high tax on gasoline	Auto VAT; moderate tax on gasoline	Auto-use tax on engine displacement; auto VAT; very high tax on gasoline
Trade	Low tariff (3%); anti-dumping investigations; possible protection	No tariff; slow to eliminate non-tariff barriers	EC tariff (11%)	EC tariff; negotiated unofficial restrictions with Japan (3% of market)	EC tariff; assisted in negotiating unofficial restrictions with Japan (11% of market)	EC tariff; GATT exception limits Japanese exports to 2,200 cars/year
Intermediary With other car-makers	Nil	Provides administrative guidance for industry	Plays significant consultative role	Provides direction; arranged Peugeot–Citroën merger	Assisted in BL merger (1968)	Negligible
With other governments	Has presented industry views to EC and Japan	Actively involved in trade questions	Occasionally represents industry in foreign markets/countries	Actively promotes industry in foreign markets/countries	Occasionally represents industry in foreign markets/countries	Occasionally represents industry in foreign markets/countries

Source: Fuller and Salter, 1980. Reproduced by permission.

ponents manufactured in Mexico and Brazil, vw is collaborating with other German firms to produce a full range of commercial vehicles, and simultaneously diversifying into other industry-related activities. Daimler-Benz and BMW are concentrating their German production on luxury cars, and Ford and GM (Opel) are following suit. The industry's strategy has been significantly helped by government R&D subsidies to develop new technologies (for example, small diesel engines) for more energy-efficient cars and engines. Such government support will probably play an important role in future adjustment efforts.

The German regional governments have at times supported mergers and takeovers (such as the vw–Audi merger), and sometimes attempted to rescue small firms from bankruptcy (BMW). However, the possibilities for future mergers may increasingly run up against anti-trust policies that have already blocked the merger of two sets of components producers. The government also promotes the location of new production in areas earmarked for regional development.

France

While on the whole the German motor-vehicle industry developed without significant government intervention, the French motor-vehicle industry has typically been sheltered by tariff walls and quotas. The government has promoted industry rationalization in a variety of ways.

To a great extent French policy-makers have been able to 'encourage' the industry in desired directions through Renault, a 100-per cent government-owned motor-vehicle firm and an important employer of French labour. The firm's management, appointed by the state, tends to be sympathetic to government objectives, and because it has not needed to satisfy private stockholders with growing profits, Renault has often been free to pursue those objectives. However, this relationship between the state and management is subtle, and the ability of the government to force Renault in particular directions is not assured and should not be over-emphasized.

The bulk of Renault's exports go to other members of the EC; however, the firm is following the trend towards foreign production, purchasing a share of American Motors in order to produce cars and commercial vehicles in the USA. In addition, the company is integrating its subsidiaries in Spain and Portugal into its domestic operations. Renault has links with Dacia in East Europe, which produces Renault models under licence, and jointly produces engines and components with Talbot and Volvo.

Although the French government has tried in several instances to prevent foreign takeovers of French motor-vehicle and parts companies (GM–Citroën, 1919; Chrysler–Simca, 1963; Lucas–Ducellier, 1977), it has supported intra-national takeovers. Examples include the loan provided by the government to Peugeot to absorb Citroën and the Ferodo–Marchal components merger. Since then, Peugeot–Citroën has acquired Chrysler's European operations, moving the new firm, known as Talbot, ahead of vw as Europe's biggest car producer. Talbot has cooperative agreements with Renault, Volvo and Fiat, as well as a buy-back arrangement with Romania. But the inevitable rationalization of Talbot's three separate model ranges in three major countries (Spain, France and the UK) will result in adjustment pressures on employment in Britain.

The government-encouraged mergers of French components firms with other French firms and sometimes with foreign firms is illustrative of the sorts of efforts the state is making to create internationally competitive components companies. These firms are actively reacting to international pressures by diversifying (for example, into construction-industry products by Ferodo), consolidating around key components and developing an overseas network. In general, healthy demand, high productivity and the rationalization which is occurring both within France and across borders will strengthen the French motor-vehicle industry and enable it to withstand competition from imports, despite French fears. The weak, underdeveloped components sector is being reorganized with government support, so it, too, should be able to withstand competitive pressures.

United Kingdom

The British car industry is suffering from a host of problems: poor management, technological weaknesses, skill shortages, labour relations problems, a fragmented industrial structure, low productivity, overcapacity, high import penetration, declining exports, loss of all overseas production facilities, and increasing foreign control of domestic production. Parts of its assembly production are near collapse, while the more competitive components industry cannot diversify its markets fast enough to ease adjustment.

Government intervention has been largely concerned with rescuing firms in trouble by increasing protection from imports and domestic subsidies. After entry into the EC, tariff protection gave way to a voluntary export restraint agreement with Japan to limit the Japanese car share to 11 per cent of British domestic sales. Large foreign firms strengthened their presence in the UK, so the government used subsidies to promote consolidation of British firms into one firm, British Leyland. When BL later faced bankruptcy, the state took over ownership, propping the firm up indefinitely with considerable (£1 billion to date) government aid. Moreover, when Chrysler UK threatened to shut down in 1975, the government again came to the rescue with loan guarantees and agreed to fund Chrysler's losses (£72·5 million), which it did from 1976 until the firm sold out to Peugeot–Citroën in 1978.

Other government policies hurt the industry more than they supported it. Regional development programmes fragmented the industry and manipulation of the industry as a tool of demand management engendered uncertainty and slow growth.

Any good news for the British motor-vehicle industry will come from its historically strong components sector; Britain has traditionally had a surplus in components and engine trade with every major manufacturing country except Japan. While BL will be suffering, the foreign components firms in the UK will be increasingly integrated into their respective international networks and thus able to draw strength from size and specialization. On the negative side a strong pound could make British components less price competitive and undermine future growth.

CONCLUSIONS

It is clear that slow growth in demand, technological change, changes in the location of production and patterns of trade, and the increasing dynamism of motor-vehicle industries in the NICs and Japan will intensify pressures for adjustment in traditional motor-vehicle-producing nations. So far, firms have been reacting to these pressures in a variety of ways, some defensive, postponing change for as long as possible, and others meeting the pressures and adjusting accordingly. No country adheres exclusively to one strategy, and all except West Germany provide some type of non-tariff protection. Nevertheless, a spectrum of countries does emerge (Shepherd, 1980a, p. 31). At one end, West Germany is meeting the problems of an appreciated deutschmark and costly labour with specialization in luxury cars and internationalization stimulated primarily by market forces and relatively liberal import regimes. Although US firms have traditionally been leaders in internationalization, without impetus from the government, the direct and indirect role of the government in easing adjustment could be on the increase. France and Italy approach the other end of the spectrum. Both countries have histories of active intervention and support in addition to quotas on voluntary export restraints. Finally, the UK is moving towards more protection and government support, hoping to maintain its auto industry, but not quite sure as to how it should be done. While the German strategy is one of anticipatory, active adjustment, Britain's is largely defensive; the countries between these extremes mix defensive with active, depending on the extent of the cost.

In general, European car firms have received much more government support (protection and subsidies) than US motor-vehicle firms, and the number of European motor-vehicle firms would definitely be smaller had this government intervention been absent (Shepherd, 1980a, p. 27). Because all this support creates obligations on firms, particularly in France, to adhere to government economic and social objectives, these firms have not had the freedom to pursue an internationalization strategy to the degree that, for example, US firms have had. For these 'obligated' companies, the overseas investment which has occurred has been primarily of a defensive nature, compared with the offensive integration strategies of Ford and GM.

NOTE

1 For example, in 1978 the province of Ontario and the Canadian central

government paid Ford a total of $68 million to build a plant in Ontario instead of Ohio. Meanwhile, the USA extended tax and other incentives totalling $70 million to Volkswagen to set up in Pennsylvania and $50 million for a plant in Michigan.

6
Iron and Steel

Stephen Woolcock

The problems facing the iron and steel industry in some industrialized countries in the late 1970s and early 1980s are by no means caused by the NICs. If one measures the problems of the North American and European steel industries by a decline in their relative shares of global steel production, then it is Japan that has caused most problems. The growth of the Japanese steel industry, and thus the relative shift in production from North America and Western Europe, was brought about by the growth of steel-intensive industries such as shipbuilding in the 1960s and then automobiles in the 1970s. This chapter will show that shifts in the location of the steel industry are associated with the growth of major steel-intensive industries. As the NICs industrialize, their economies will become more steel-intensive and their share of world steel production will increase. In general terms, therefore, the steel industry reflects the problems associated with the need, within the AICs, to adjust to changes in industrial structure brought about by a maturing of steel-intensive industries. In the longer term the growth of the steel industry within the NICs will depend on the growth of steel-intensive production, as was the case in Japan. In such a longer-term perspective the steel industry therefore offers an insight into industrial development in the NICs, in the sense that it can be seen as a proxy for the fortunes of steel-intensive industrialization.

In the past the steel industry was considered of vital strategic importance. Despite a progressive decline in its direct strategic significance, it has remained a strategic industry in an economic sense because of its importance as a major input into manufacturing industry. In economic terms the industry has also declined, for example from a share of 6 per cent of industrial value added in the EC in 1970 to 4·5 per cent in 1977. These figures refer to metal minerals, which are predominantly iron and steel. In 1977 the industry supplied 4·5 per cent of industrial employment in the EC compared with 5·4 per cent in both 1970 and 1973, and employment fell by 23 per cent in the EC between 1974 and December 1980. The value of US steel shipments was 3·5 per cent of all manufacturing in 1979 (USA, Department of Commerce, 1980), which suggests a share of perhaps 1·5 per cent of industrial value added.

The decline in importance of the industry is reflected in its share of intra-EC trade, down from 11 per cent in the 1960s to 4 per cent. Direct steel exports accounted for 4 per cent of extra-EC exports in 1978 and 1 per cent of imports from third countries (Eurostat, 1979, p. 79). In Japan, steel accounted for 15 per cent of all exports in 1970 and 20 per cent in 1974, but this is expected to drop to 13 per cent in 1980 and 7·5 per cent in 1985 as the Japanese economy 'disengages' from steel (Nomura, 1979).

Trade in steel-intensive products will also influence the development of the steel industry. For example, imports of steel-intensive products will undermine the domestic steel market. In the case of the UK, a NEDO estimate suggested that 1978 imports of automobiles alone effectively reduced the domestic market for the British steel industry by 1 million tons of crude steel. At the end of the 1970s the automobile industry accounted for some 10 per cent of finished steel consumption. Although the NIC presence in the car industry is still relatively small, there are also steel-consuming industries in which the NICs are already active or can be expected to become more active, for example hardware and cutlery (5 per cent of finished-steel consumption), shipbuilding (3·5 per cent of steel consumption in 1972, but only 1–2 per cent in the late 1970s), as well as parts of electrical and mechanical machinery (about 15 per cent) (EC Commission, 1978d, p. 11).

HISTORICAL TRENDS IN STEEL PRODUCTION

The progressive shift in the location of the steel industry is shown, for example, by the decline in the UK share of world steel production from 37 per cent in 1870 to only 2·8 per cent in 1979. Similarly the US share declined from 49 per cent in 1950 to 16·9 per cent in 1979 as output expanded faster in the new steel-producing countries. Above all, it was the output of the Japanese industry which grew – from 2·5 per cent of world production in 1950 to 16·5 per cent in 1975. In the period of rapid expansion in the 1950s and 1960s, Japan's output grew at 30 per cent per annum, compared with 1·5 per cent in the USA, 2·7 per cent in the UK, 6·8 per cent in West Germany and 13·3 per cent in Italy (Cockerill, 1974). Since 1973, however, production output has stagnated in all AIC countries. As growth in output has continued in the developing countries, their share of world steel production has grown from 6 per cent in 1960 and 7 per cent in 1970 to 13 per cent in 1978 (Wienert, 1980; this figure includes the Asian centrally planned economies of North Korea and China).

A history of the steel industry shows that the period of relatively free trade during the 1950s and 1960s was an exception rather than the norm. Even the 1960s were not free from tensions in international trade in steel caused by the need to adjust to the relative shifts in the pattern of steel consumption and production described above. In this context it is important to stress the significance of demand for steel. The USA experienced the boom in steel-intensive industries earlier than the EC or Japan, and by the

1960s the growth in steel consumption in the US was already slowing. From 1967 to 1977 US steel consumption grew only 6 per cent despite a real GNP growth of 30 per cent (USA, Department of Commerce, 1979). Within the European Coal and Steel Community (ECSC), the income elasticity of demand for steel fell below unity in the early 1970s (EC Commission, 1978d). The UK was affected relatively early, while at the other end of the ECSC spectrum demand remained relatively dynamic in Italy. In Japan, on the other hand, the average annual growth in steel demand was 13 per cent between 1964 and 1973, and it was not until 1974 that the growth in demand for steel fell below that of GNP.

Such dynamic growth of demand at home enabled Japan to establish a strong presence in export markets. This is clearly shown by Table 6.1, which shows Japan's share of world export markets growing from 8·5 per cent in 1960 to 32·5 per cent in 1973. Shifts in the pattern of trade shown in the table were not solely brought about by changes in the pattern of demand, but also by the relative competitiveness of the Japanese steel industry. Up to the early 1950s steel industries had developed close to locations of raw materials (either coking coal or iron ore or both), and proximity to bulk raw materials was considered essential for a competitive steel industry. In the early 1950s, therefore, economists of the World Bank advised Japanese planners against ambitious plans to expand capacity. (The World Bank gave similar negative advice to the Koreans when they came in their turn to consider entering this industry.) Seen in the context of 1980, when the Japanese industry was the only one resilient enough to make significant profits despite low capacity utilization rates, this appears especially paradoxical. Such a paradox will not have gone unnoticed by steel planners in the NICs. In a recent statement via the OECD Steel Committee, which will be discussed below, the AIC representatives stated that governments should work together to 'avoid encouraging economically unjustified investments while recognizing legitimate development needs'. One wonders whether the (unspecified) criteria for assessing what are economically unjustified investments are any better in the 1980s than they were in the 1950s.

The strategy of the Japanese steel producers in the 1950s and 60s was to compensate for the high costs of transporting raw materials by increased economies of scale. This involved the construction of large integrated coastal steel plants using the basic oxygen furnace (BOF) conversion process for steel-making. The BOF process reduced the steel conversion cycle from eight hours (as for the then dominant open-hearth process) to forty-five minutes. As this increased output per furnace from 3,300 tons for the older open-hearth (OH) furnaces to 60,000 tons per week (Cockerill, 1974, p. 25), the scale of iron-ore reduction (blast furnaces) and preparation plant also had to be increased. Consequently, the minimum economic scale of integrated plant grew from 4 mmt (million metric tons) in the mid-1960s to 8/10 mmt in the early 1970s. In order to exploit such economies of scale, and to cover the very high fixed costs involved, it was necessary to have a rapidly growing market. As we have seen, this was the

Table 6.1   *Structure and Growth of World Steel Trade (percentages)*[1]

	Country composition			Average annual growth rates	
	1960	1973	1978	1960–73	1973–8
Exports					
Industrialized countries	90·9	86·5	87·2	8·1	5·5
Japan	(8·5)	(32·5)	(31·2)	(20·3)	(4·5)
EC (7)	(57·6)	(34·7)	(34·3)	(4·3)	(5·0)
Developing countries	0·8	4·0	5·6	22·9	13·0
Other Asia	(–)	(1·9)	(3·1)	(–)	(16·9)
Latin America	(0·5)	(1·9)	(2·1)	(19·2)	(7·2)
Centrally planned economies	8·3	9·5	7·2	9·6	(0·5)
World total	100·0	100·0	100·0	8·5	5·3
Imports					
Industrialized countries	48·2	52·3	45·7	9·1	2·8
USA	(10·8)	(18·5)	(19·7)	(13·0)	(7·0)
Developing countries	36·9	33·7	36·8	7·7	7·5
Other Asia	(7·8)	(11·6)	(13·3)	(11·8)	(8·6)
Latin America	(11·9)	(9·2)	(6·0)	(6·2)	(3·0)
Middle East	(6·1)	(7·7)	(11·1)	(10·4)	(13·5)
Centrally planned economies	14·9	14·0	17·5	7·9	10·5
World total	100·0	100·0	100·0	8·5	5·3

[1]Excluding intra-EC and intra-COMECON trade.
Source: Nippon Steel Corporation.

case in Japan but not in the USA. By comparison, the European industry had a moderately rapid growth in markets during the period. Higher growth in output meant that Japanese producers were able to build newer, more productive plant quicker than either the Europeans or Americans, so that labour productivity in Japan averaged 372 tons per man-year in 1973 compared with 199 in the USA, 255 in the Federal Republic of Germany, 244 in Italy, 166 in France and 139 in the UK (Merrill Lynch, 1977).

Such changes in production technology had implications for the location of steel production. For example, if European and American producers were to compete with Japan in both domestic and third markets, it was necessary to build large-scale coastal plants and close obsolete plants located near iron-ore and coal mines. In general the rationalization of production in Europe was moderately successful. In 1960, 30 per cent of EC steel was made by the open-hearth (OH) process and only 10 per cent by oxygen (BOF) processes, but by 1978 OH held only 9 per cent and BOF more than 70 per cent (electric furnaces accounting for the bulk of the remainder). In the USA old plant has been modernized rather than new, 'greenfield' plants constructed. Despite this modernization some 15 per cent of US production in 1978 still employed the OH process, and as late as 1980, 30 per cent of the US Steel Corporation's capacity was in the form of OH furnaces.

Size of plant as a measure of efficiency gives a similar picture. As early as 1961 no less than 75 per cent of Japanese capacity was concentrated in the ten largest plants, compared with only 31 per cent in the US and 39 per cent in the EC. In 1976 these figures had hardly changed, with 69 per cent for Japan, 34 per cent for the USA and 35 per cent for the EC. It is the structure of production rather than the corporate structure that has characterized the differences between the USA and Japan. Between 1961 and 1976 the share of the eight largest firms in each country accounted for between 75 and 83 per cent of total steel capacity. In Europe the company structure was initially more fragmented, the eight largest producers accounting for only 32 per cent of steel capacity in 1961 (Mueller and Kawahito, 1978, p. 7), but substantial inter-company rationalization raised this figure to 63 per cent by 1976. Finally, Japan has also led in the use of the higher productivity, energy-conserving continuous casting of steel. In 1976, 35 per cent of Japanese steel was continuously cast, against 22 per cent in the EC and only 10 per cent in the USA. By 1979 28·8 per cent of EC capacity employed continuous casting and investment plans suggest a rapid expansion to 46 per cent by 1983 (ECSC, 1980).

The blast furnace/basic oxygen furnace (BF/BOF) integrated mode of production, the dominant technology of the 1960s and 1970s, was not without drawbacks. High capital costs of plant, about $1 billion per million tons of steel capacity, made the giant integrated plants vulnerable during periods of weak demand. This problem was exacerbated by the failure, particularly in Europe, to close obsolete plant. Thus serious excess capacity developed which further depressed prices and resulted in large losses by many steel producers.

OECD STEEL POLICIES DURING THE 1970s

Following pressure on the US industry and increased imports from Europe and Japan, three-year voluntary export restraint (VER) agreements were concluded in 1968 and 1971. The VERs were justified on the grounds that imports were creaming off what growth there was in US steel demand, and that 'temporary' relief was needed to help the industry invest and thus improve competitiveness. Europe also agreed VERs with Japanese exporters, and imports from Eastern Europe were controlled by quotas.

The voluntary agreements were allowed to expire in 1974 because steel demand in the USA, as elsewhere in the AICs, was booming. Following the 1973–4 record boom, however, came an unprecedented fall in steel demand in the North American and West European markets, which precipitated a series of anti-crisis and defensive measures during the 1970s. Soon after the beginning of the crisis in late 1974 consultations began within the ECSC on whether to apply the Community's Article 58, which would have given the EC Commission statutory powers to establish a system of production quotas. In line with procedures in the Treaty of Paris, the Commission first sought voluntary actions (EC Commission, 1975a). The French, on the one hand, convinced of the long-term structural nature of the crisis, pressed for the introduction of minimum prices (Article 61 of the ECSC) and the declaration of a manifest crisis (the precondition for application of Article 58). On the other hand, the German producers and the federal government strongly resisted market regulation on the grounds that it would precipitate retaliation against EC exports. German producers also believed that any EC market regulation would effectively support the less efficient, in some cases state-run, producers in other ECSC countries. A slight improvement in the market in 1976 delayed any further voluntary measures. However, in December 1976 voluntary delivery guidelines were drawn up for each producer (the Simonet Plan: see EC Commission, 1976a). These guidelines were not effective for one of the six main steel products (reinforcing bars), and as a result minimum prices were introduced for this product in May 1977, along with guidance prices for the other five prices.

During 1977 the initiation of nineteen anti-dumping actions by US producers reflected the increased tensions in international markets. Pressure for action in the USA increased as plant closures were announced, and the 150-strong steel caucus in Congress threatened to act against imports to hinder the progress of the Tokyo Round unless steel was given special treatment. In response the US government produced a comprehensive programme for the steel industry (Solomon Report, 1978), with the objective of strengthening the competitive position of the US steel industry. The main instrument employed in this policy was that of the trigger-price mechanism (TPM). The trigger-price mechanism sought to strengthen US prices but at the same time to reduce the need for anti-dumping actions by providing for accelerated anti-dumping actions once predetermined import prices, based on Japanese production costs, were undercut. The TPM was seen by the Europeans and Japanese as part of a wider understanding on steel trade. This understanding, which later emerged in more formal terms in the objectives of the OECD Steel Committee (OECD, 1978b), was a political approach to the national and international problems in the industry. The alternative, quasi-judicial approach, resting heavily on anti-dumping investigations, was seen as second best, because such an approach increased uncertainty and thus potentially friction in trading relations.

In Europe also the pressure to take more active anti-crisis measures increased, and, as in the USA, the full Davignon Plan was aimed primarily at strengthening prices (EC Commission, 1977). The ECSC policy entailed mandatory minimum prices for a further two of the total six product groups, and the negotiation of arrangements with major exporters on price and volume. The Japanese contributed to the stabilization of the steel industry by agreeing to continue to pursue its policy of export restraint. In return the Japanese stood to gain from increased prices in export markets resulting from the TPM and ECSC price mechanisms. By 1977 there was at last a recognition of the structural nature of the steel crisis. Thus both US and ECSC programmes included not only anti-crisis measures but also set out the objective of medium- to long-term restructuring of the industry.

As will be shown, this international consensus, elaborated within the OECD steel committee, which aimed to include both short term anti-crisis and long-term restructuring measures, proved fragile. This was in no small part due to the divergent assessments of future regional and global market trends. There was thus a tendency for national producers to exaggerate future demand projections in order to justify maintaining existing capacity. Failing a genuine adjustment which brings supply in line with demand there can be little prospect of reducing frictions in international trade in steel. While these tensions have to date been between the AICs, the relative growth of new steel-producing countries can be expected to lead to growing tensions towards the end of the 1980s or early 1990s unless the AICs can accept and accommodate such shifts in the location of steel production.

GROWTH IN NIC STEEL PRODUCTION

Although consumption in the AICs has stagnated during the 1970s, steel consumption in the developing countries has continued to grow. Even during the period 1960–73, steel consumption in developing countries grew at 8·8 per cent per annum, against 5·5 per cent in the AICs. Between 1973 and 1978 global steel consumption increased by 3 per cent, AIC consumption falling by 14 per cent, thanks to an increase of 53 per cent in developing-country consumption, and future steel consumption in developing countries is generally expected to grow at least twice as fast as in the AICs (Kono, 1980; see also UNIDO, 1976). In 1978, developing countries accounted for 12 per cent of total world steel consumption of 729 mmt, against 51 per cent for Western AICs. If one assumes that global demand will grow at 3 per cent per annum to 900 mmt in 1985, the faster growth in developing-country consumption will increase their share to 15 per cent, against 49 per cent for the AICs (Kono, 1980, p. 22). Further ahead the respective shares could be 20 per cent and 41 per cent in 2000, by which time the relative share of Western Europe and Japan will be following the downward trend already experienced by North America. One estimate (Wienert, 1980) puts the relative shares at 17 per cent in 1990 for the mature North American market, down from 20 per cent in 1980. The EC and Japanese markets, being less mature, will fall from a combined share of 26 per cent in 1980 to 23 per cent in 1990, while the share of developing countries (including Asian centrally planned economies) will grow from 17 per cent to 24 per cent by 1990.

If steel consumption in developing countries is going to continue to grow, an important question is whether this demand will be covered by

Table 6.2 *Crude Steel Production, 1974, 1978–80 (mmt)*

Region/country	1980	1979	1978	1974	1980/79 %	1979/78 %	1980/74 %
Western world							
EEC	127·8	140·2	132·6	155·6	−8·8	+6·0	−17·8
USA	101·7	123·2	124·3	132·2	−17·4	−0·9	−23·1
Japan	111·4	111·7	102·1	117·1	−0·2	+9·3	−4·9
Other industrialized countries	66·6	67·1	62·0	58·6	−0·7	+8·2	+13·6
Total	407·5	442·0	420·6	463·5	−7·8	+5·1	−12·0
Developing countries	57·9	54·0	47·4	30·9	+7·2	+13·9	+87·4
Total, Western world	465·4	496·0	468·0	494·4	−6·1	+6·0	−5·8
Communist countries							
USSR and Eastern Europe	209·5	209·4	211·0	185·1	0·0	−0·4	+13
China and North Korea	42·8	39·3	36·9	29·2	+8·9	+6·5	+46·6
Total, Communist countries	252·3	249·3	247·8	214·3	+1·2	+0·6	+17·7
World total	717·7	747·4	717·1	708·9	−3·9	+4·2	+1·2

Source: International Iron and Steel Institute estimates.

imports or increased domestic production in the NICs (the leading seven developing-country steel producers account for 90 per cent of LDC steel production). LDC net imports of steel increased from 15 mmt in 1967 to 44 mmt in 1974 before falling again to 35 mmt in 1977, owing to slower growth in consumption and increased domestic production. Estimates based on announced expansion plans suggest that the LDC export market for AIC producers would remain relatively constant between 20 and 30 mmt, as Table 6.3 shows (Wienert, 1980, pp. 11, 19; CIA, 1979, p. 7). Table 6.3 also shows that AIC surplus capacity can be expected to decrease by 1985 but that there is unlikely to be a supply shortage in the mid-1980s, as has been suggested (Marcus, 1979).

Table 6.3   *Capacity and Demand Projections by Region (mmt)*

Region	1978	1985	Region	1978	1985
Industrialized countries			*Developing countries*		
Effective capacity	560	562	Effective capacity	68	114
Consumption	376	445	Consumption	91	135

Source: Kono, 1980.

The ability of the NICs to increase steel production and thus take a growing share of their own domestic markets will depend on a range of factors. In the past, high capital costs of steel plant have caused problems for various NIC producers. There are now signs, however, that changes in steel technology may favour the NICs. The BF/BOF process will remain the dominant mode of production for some time, even in developing countries. In 1977, 75 per cent of developing-country capacity was BF/BOF against 7 per cent for the direct reduction electric-arc furnace (DR/EF) route to integrated steel production and 18 per cent for electric furnaces fed largely by scrap. An analysis of NIC capacity plans suggests that the DR/EF mode may account for 20 per cent by 1982, and countries such as Mexico, which not only developed the direct reduction process but also has abundant supplies of natural gas, were switched to this process. UNIDO estimates based on reports by developing countries suggests that of the 173 mmt nominal capacity in 1987, more than 70 per cent will still be BF/BOF despite a 20 per cent annual growth in DR/EF capacity (UNIDO, 1978b, p. 26). Problems arise in estimating capacity because the effective capacity of plant varies. While effective capacity is always lower than nominal capacity, it can vary from 95 per cent of nominal capacity (USA) to 75 per cent (India) or 50 per cent in the Middle East. This UNIDO estimate of 173 mmt nominal capacity in 1987 does not therefore necessarily conflict with the figure given in Table 6.3.

The advantages of the DR/EF process for developing countries, especially those with natural gas such as Venezuela, Mexico, and in the Middle East and South-East Asia, are the lower capital costs. Thus, whereas BF/BOF plants need a capacity of (optimally) 5 mmt per annum at US$1 billion per mmt capacity, but at least 2–3 mmt to become economic, plants as small as

0·6 mmt using the DR/EF route do not suffer excessively from sub-optimal economies of scale. In addition, DR steel-making and finishing plant for 0·5 mmt per annum would cost about US$213 million (1976 prices: UNIDO, 1976, p. 199).

In summary, therefore, the NIC steel producers cannot be expected to become major exporters of steel. They will not become self-sufficient before the end of the 1990s, but the NIC export markets for AIC producers cannot be expected to grow, as NIC production will increase to cover growth in NIC steel consumption. With regard to the AIC producers an increase in exports to the developing world can, in the long term, not be seen as a means of easing the adjustment problems within the AICs. It is in this global context, therefore, that one must view adjustment in the AICs.

AIC STEEL INDUSTRIES – PROBLEMS OF ADJUSTMENT AND POLICY OPTIONS

The problems experienced by major AIC steel-producing countries during the 1970s can be summarized as follows: an exceptionally low level of demand and long-term structural changes in demand which do not allow for optimism in terms of a rapid return to the traditional growth rates of the 1960s. These changes in demand have resulted in persistent excess capacity which has depressed prices on world markets and thus had a dramatic effect on the financial performance of companies that have not been able to adjust rapidly. Poor financial performance has in turn resulted in major retrenchment, with employment falling particularly quickly. The investment needed to restructure and modernize, or to diversify into new products, has also been inhibited. At a national or regional (such as the EC) level, excess capacity or poor financial performance has led to greater public intervention in the industry as governments have provided various forms of assistance. At the international level this public involvement has increased the frictions in trading relations caused by the shifts in traditional trade patterns brought about by the divergent performance of national steel industries.

Estimates of surplus capacity vary according to how capacity is measured. Table 6.4 shows one estimate for capacity utilization, based on effective capacity. Capacity utilization is lower for finished products, for example hot-rolled coils in the EC, with only 47 per cent capacity in use in 1978, a relatively good year. Detailed EC figures also show that West German capacity utilization has been consistently lower than that of other EC countries. Belgian capacity utilization is also below EC averages while France, Italy and especially the UK have operated at higher rates.

Capacity utilization is only partially reflected in financial performance. Generally speaking, US producers returned to profitable operation quicker than most European producers after 1975, although the US Steel Corporation still returned losses in 1979 owing to the costs of closing old plant. The more diversified companies, such as Armco in the US or Mannesmann

Table 6.4   *Capacity Utilization (Effective Capacities) (percentages)*

Country/region	1970	1973	1975	1976	1977	1978	1979	1980
USA	90	101	80	85	82	91	92	78
Japan	94	100	81	84	75	75	81	78
EC	100	97	75	77	71	75	79	72
Other Western Europe	95	101	87	85	79	80	86	84
Oceania	–	98	98	96	97	100	106	103
Total OECD	95	99	79	82	76	80	84	77

Source: Suzuki and Miles, 1980, p. 14.

in Europe, performed relatively well during the 1970s as did the stronger European producers such as Thyssen. The slightly improved market conditions, combined with some radical restructuring, enabled the worst European loss-makers to improve performance in 1978 and 1979. For example, Sacilor and Usinor in France did so; Cockerill of Belgium halved its losses between 1977 and 1979; Estel (Dutch–German), Krupp, Klöckner and Salzgetter were back in the black in 1979; and even Italsider reduced losses. A notable exception to this trend was BSC, which showed little sign of improvement even in 1979, because of the costs of its closure programme. Most notable, however, was the improved financial performance of the integrated Japanese steel producers, despite relatively low capacity utilization. By inventory adjustment, reduced energy consumption, increased automation and assisted by the efforts of US and EC price measures on export prices, the Japanese producers were able to make record profits in 1978 and 1979. In many respects the Japanese producers were, at the end of the 1970s, reaping the benefits of past efforts which had given them by far the strongest steel industry in the world. Therefore, as the 1980s begin with a further fall in the market, the Japanese will be better placed to ride out the recession than most US and European producers. The latter in particular will have received a blow, which may well jeopardize the success of some of the restructuring programmes that were beginning to show some signs of working by late 1979.

In an effort to avert bankruptcies and major dislocations of employment in areas that in many cases were highly dependent on the steel industry, all national governments intervened, but some more than others. The US and German producers were particularly critical of the 'unfairness' of assistance provided to competitors in other countries (for a discussion of what is 'unfair', see Marks, 1978, p. 223). Therefore, in addition to the tensions caused by low-priced steel exports, there were increasing claims (and counter-claims) that exports were being subsidized, and that the various forms of assistance provided by national governments constituted unfair competition. Initiatives were then taken at both EC (by the Germans) and OECD (by the Americans) levels to begin discussions on the international implications of domestic steel policies.

POLICY OPTIONS FOR CORPORATE STRATEGIES AND POLICY-MAKERS

When considering the various responses of the steel producers and governments it will be useful to bear in mind the range of options available. For corporate planners the options can be summarized as follows: press for relief from import competition or seek to reduce domestic price competition by market-sharing agreements or other restrictive practices; restructure in order to re-establish lost competitiveness, by retrenchment and modernization of remaining plant; product diversification into higher-value-added steel products such as special steels or high-strength low-alloy steels, or downstream into engineering; finally, relocate steel production in areas with lower costs or stronger demand. In practice, most steel companies have employed a mixture of restructuring and defensive policies. Those who have diversified have performed relatively well.

The policy options for governments depend on a number of factors, not least of which is whether they exercise direct or only indirect control over investment decisions. There are two general policy options open to governments, to provide help for restructuring or reconversion. Operations to help steel industries to compete or to ease their decline cannot be carried out overnight and some form of anti-crisis assistance to reduce import competition or increase prices is generally necessary. Governments must also decide whether they are going to provide financial assistance to companies and in what form. Direct assistance by grants or loan guarantees is not open to all governments because they lack the instruments for providing such aid. Therefore, countries such as the USA must rely heavily on indirect means such as tax concessions. Finally, one extreme policy option might well be to accept the permanent subsidization of steel production because of its importance for steel-consuming industries. In recent years, however, both the UK and France have rejected such policies and moved towards the OECD norm of market-oriented policies.

Public policy will be influenced by how market trends are assessed. It has been suggested that to speak of the industry as declining has strengthened protectionist sentiment (Florkoski, 1980). This depends very much on whether one considers a stagnating industry to be one in decline. Past experience in Europe suggests that it has been the failure to accept that the industry is undergoing extensive structural change that lies behind defensive policy responses. Certainly, inflated market projections have been used to justify, in economic terms, what have in fact been political decisions to maintain existing (surplus) capacity or indeed expand capacity.

The state of government/industry relations and the structure of the industry will also influence policy decisions. For example, the organic relationship between public policy objectives and the objectives of the steel industry in Japan differs markedly from the often antagonistic government/industry relations in the USA. In Europe public control over the industry is facilitated by control of investment funds. In addition the

Commission of the EC can influence investment decisions, especially when public money is involved.

Policy is also influenced by the impact of adjustment, for example in terms of dislocation of employment. Finally, the degree to which decision-making takes place in corporatist settings, for example in tripartite planning or policy-making bodies, will also influence its outcome.

The Response in the USA

It has been shown that the US steel market was the first to be affected by a slowing of the growth of steel-consuming industries. The response of many US steel producers to this market trend was to adopt a cautious investment strategy. As investment decisions were based on short-term economic criteria, such as return on investment, major rationalization and restructuring of the industry did not take place. New production technologies were exploited when the opportunity arose, but as output was growing very slowly during the 1960s, US steel plant became relatively obsolete (estimates suggest the average age of US plant to be seventeen years compared to eight to twelve years in Japan and the EC; *Europe Bulletin*, No. 2902, p. 7) and internationally uncompetitive.[1]

The lost competitive edge of US producers contributed to the increase in imports, from 4·7 per cent of apparent steel consumption in 1960 to a maximum of 18 per cent in 1978 (AISI, 1980, p. 9). Whenever imports have exceeded 15 per cent of apparent consumption there has been pressure to control import competition (first in 1968 in the form of VER agreements, and again in 1972, when the import growth rates were reduced). Import penetration remained below 15 per cent from 1973 to 1977 when it reached 17 per cent. In 1977 the TPM (trigger-price mechanism) was introduced: this strengthened price discipline but imports still took 18 per cent of the market. The year 1978 saw a fall in imports to 15 per cent of apparent consumption but dissatisfaction with the TPM increased as import penetration again exceeded the 15 per cent mark at the end of 1979. This informal limit to import penetration was finally formalized in the revised TPM of 1980. When the 15 per cent point is passed the Commerce Department or steel producers can start anti-dumping actions without the government suspending the TPM. Under the October 1980 package the US government also proposed a 40 per cent liberalization of tax depreciation and a 10 per cent tax credit for new investment. A further $600 million in public finance was to be made available to promote R&D, and compliance with US Environmental Protection Agency (EPA) regulations was relaxed to allow an extension of three years on compliance deadlines.

Experience therefore suggests that the implicit objective of the US industry, in seeking to ensure 'fair' trade, was to limit imports. When the TPM did not serve this purpose, anti-dumping actions were started. Anti-dumping actions are, of course, a perfectly legitimate means of ensuring that import competition is fair, but the mere suggestion of taking action can and has had the effect of reducing the volume of imports. For example, there was a drop of nearly 50 per cent in US orders for EC steel in the second quarter of 1980 following the US Steel Corporation's anti-dumping petitions.

For many years the US industry has claimed that it has been hindered in its attempts to invest in restructuring of the industry by unfair subsidization of foreign competitors, who subsequently dumped steel on the US market. Furthermore, it is claimed that 'jawboning' (that is, indirect pressure to hold down prices), government price controls (mandatory from 1971 to 1974 and informal thereafter), regulations on pollution control and relatively unfavourable capital depreciation provisions have contributed to the industry's plight (AISI, 1980, p. 1). While all these factors have had a greater or lesser effect, they cannot explain away the problems of the US industry. It is significant that perhaps the major problem, namely slow growth in demand and thus output, is hardly touched upon in the AISI report. The industry's case is that given 'fair' competition and less government interference it will solve its own problems.

It is, of course, too early to attempt any assessment of the chances for success of the 1980 policies, which are to run for five years, but past experience suggests that such anti-crisis measures will be needed for some time to come. In 1968 the US industry was given six years breathing space, but the reduction of import competition was used more as a means of improving profits than for a major effort to restructure the industry. Annual investment fell from $2·3 billion in 1968 to $1·17 billion in 1972 (USA, Federal Trade Commission, 1977, p. 75). Over the 1972–7 period, average US capital expenditure lagged behind that of major competitors, with US$19/ton of crude steel production, compared with $26 in Japan, $24 in FRG, West Germany, $35 in the UK and $28 in France (AISI, 1980, p. 11).

There seems little doubt that the US producers believed, as did many European producers, that the problems of 1975 and 1976 were merely cyclical. By 1977, however, it was clear they were not and there was a general acceptance that major restructuring was needed. Here the government's programme (of 1977) was to provide the means, predominantly indirectly, of increasing investment. Some steel producers have been criticized for investing not in steel but in real estate or chemicals.[2] The lack of direct means of stimulating investment, therefore, presents the US government with something of a dilemma. The industry majors have refused to accept capital grants and attempts to improve government/industry relations have not been very successful. Tripartite machinery was set up in order to improve the flow of information between industry and government, and this has enabled agreements on, for example, the reinstalment of the TPM in 1980 in return for dropping anti-dumping actions. But given the cool, arms-length relationship between the US steel industry and government, it will be some time before any consensus evolves on longer-term policies. As the industry points out, 'temporary, short term measures to cope with serious market disruption need to be part of a long term *trade policy*'. If the 'revitalization programme' (AISI, 1980) will take five to eight years of intensive investment at levels at least three times higher than the general investment trend, and a full twenty-five years before completion, it would seem likely that some form of trade regulation will be needed for some time to come. Without dramatic improvements in the adjustment capacity of the US industry, or acceptance of higher import penetration levels, this regulation can be expected to involve some NICs sooner or later. There has already been a relative shift in the pattern of US imports, so that the EC and Japan now only account for about one-third of total US imports each. Other major exporters are Canada, with 11 per cent in 1978, and South Korea and Spain, with 4 per cent each (Eurostat, 1980). The fact that trigger prices, rather than import quotas or VER agreements, are being used to limit import competition,[3] does, however, suggest that the trade diversion effect of US trade measures will be limited.

The Response of European Producers and Policy-Makers

The moderate growth in output and demand enabled European steel-makers to respond to changes in production technology relatively quickly. In Italy, in particular, fast growth in demand during the 1960s, combined with strategic corporate planning, enabled Italian steel-makers to make rapid advances into the upper rungs of the European steel league. The Italian industry has a dual structure. On the one hand, the public enterprise Italsider, which accounts for most of Italian crude steel production, built large integrated plants, some of which, such as Taranto in the Mezzogiorno, also constituted part of the programme for stimulating industrial development in the underdeveloped south of Italy. On the other hand, there are a large number of independent steel-makers, many using scrap-fed electric furnaces (EFs), in the north of Italy, who resist all forms of regulation whether national or from the ECSC. As scrap-based steel production is particularly competitive during a general recession when scrap is cheap, these northern Italian producers have caused numerous problems for German and French producers, especially in long products such as steel bars, which are easily produced by EF processes. Price competition from the Italians on German and French markets was an important factor behind the introduction of mandatory minimum prices for concrete reinforcing bars in May 1977.

In addition to divergent long-term patterns of demand, the impact of short-term cyclical down-turns in the market has varied from country to country. Short-term market fluctuations during the 1970s have hit traditional steel-making areas highly dependent on marginal plants particularly hard. In areas such as Lorraine, Wales and Wallonia, steel provided up to 25 per cent of total industrial employment in 1976. Dependence on the steel industry will vary according to the reference area, the 25 per cent figure applying to regions such as Gwent or Clwyd (Shotton), where the steel industry provided 28 per cent of total industrial employment in 1976. Very similar conditions existed in other EC countries, for example around Thonville or Rodange in France. Owing to the potential impact of plant rationalization or closures on these areas, restructuring was often delayed, thus exacerbating the problem of surplus capacity. European producers have responded to the problem of surplus capacity by retrenchment and modernization, particularly in the UK and France. Table 6.5 gives a breakdown of EC production and capacity (nominal) by member state. The figures show that there will be no expansion of capacity in the early 1980s, indeed there will be a slight decline. Given the continued weakness of markets, greater effort in retrenchment will be needed before the EC industry can achieve some degree of stability.

Table 6.5   *ECSC Crude Steel Production (mmt)*[1]

Country	Actual production			Production potential			Expected production potential	
	1975	*1978*	*1980*	*1975*	*1978*	*1980*	*1980*	*1983*
West Germany	40·4	41·2	43·9	62·9	68·9	66·9	68·5	67·2
Italy	21·8	24·3	26·5	32·7	35·7	39·4	37·3	39·9
France	21·5	22·8	23·2	33·7	32·4	32·5	30·7	30·0
UK	20·2	20·3	11·3	27·0	27·9	28·0	28·4	25·3
Belgium	11·6	12·6	12·3	19·0	20·0	19·7	19·7	19·1
Netherlands	4·9	5·6	5·3	6·3	8·3	8·5	8·6	8·6
Luxembourg	4·6	4·8	4·6	7·5	7·6	6·4	7·3	6·5
Denmark	0·6	0·9	0·7	0·7	1·2	1·1	1·2	0·9
Ireland	0·1	0·1	0·0	0·1	0·1	0·1	0·2	0·3
Total EC	125·7	132·6	127·8	189·9	202·1	202·5	201·9	197·9

[1]Effective capacity = nominal capacity × 0·88. This gives a figure of 177·9 mmt in 1978.
Source: EC Commission, General Objectives (for steel), Investment Surveys, various years, position as of 1 January 1980.

The social and political impact of closures helps explain the slower output adjustment of French, British and Belgian industries. In West Germany, output adjustment has been quicker than in most other EC countries (Stegemann, 1976), which has enabled German producers to operate relatively profitably when compared with other EC competitors. It is often suggested that this is because only 10 per cent of the German industry is publicly owned. In practice, however, the situation is far more complex. When the impact of rationalization and plant closures on the industry and the communities affected has been relatively great, for example in 1978 in Saarland, where the industry provided 12 per cent of total industrial employment compared with between 3 and 7 per cent in other steel-making areas in Germany, special measures have been taken to help. These in this instance were in the form of loan guarantees to Arbed, which then took on the task of restructuring the Saar industry. Extra regional and social policy assistance was also provided for Saarland. For a critical analysis of the restructuring of the Saar steel industry, see Esser (1979). Compared with other EC countries, the West German steel industry was less concentrated in areas affected by industrial decline. The German producers had also diversified into downstream engineering activities earlier than many EC competitors. For example, Mannesmann went into energy-related steel piping and construction. Thyssen, the largest German producer, has diverse engineering interests which makes it less dependent on bulk steel production than some of the 'one-eyed giants' in other EC countries. Significantly, diversification by the BSC has been restricted by statute as well as lack of finance. Furthermore, the need to meet financial targets has led to the sale of some non-steel operations which makes BSC more, rather than less, vulnerable to the relatively volatile steel market. In comparison, recent increases in public control and ownership in France have led to restructuring that has included diversification. For example, the government encouraged both Usinor and Sacilor, the companies around which the 1978 restructuring programme was developed, to take over the Péchiney-Ugine and Creusot-Loire groups in order to diversify into special steels and plant construction.

Both French and especially West German producers made extensive use of short-time-working compensation schemes, which were introduced in France and Germany before they were in the UK. For example, the number of hours worked was reduced by 2·3 million in the German industry, compared with only 85,000 in the UK in November 1975. Furthermore, the German industry employed some 21,000 foreign workers in 1977, nearly 9 per cent of the total labour force. When one combines these factors with the co-determination (*Mitbestimmung*) laws, which provided German workers with parity on supervisory boards of steel producers in 1952, it is easier to understand why labour has been more flexible in Germany, thus enabling faster output adjustment and reduced losses during periods of weak demand.

The policy response of the various EC steel producers has therefore varied. The restructuring of the German industry was coordinated by the private sector by means of the Walzstahlkontore (rolled-steel offices) and cooperation groupings, and at a relatively early stage (Kohler, 1968). The cooperation group for billets (Stabstahlkontor) in fact dates from 1964. In the UK, 90 per cent of the steel industry was nationalized in order to bring about the necessary restructuring. However, delays caused by political disputes over nationalization and the balance between commercial and social objectives meant that restructuring did not take place during the 1960s and early 1970s when relatively rapid growth would have made it easier. French public control was more flexible and was facilitated by pro-gramming contracts. Public policy promoted restructuring but this was not complete when the recession bit in 1974. Public ownership increased in France in the 1978 restructuring programme, which combined anti-crisis protection, restructuring of steel companies and reconversion for areas, such as Lorraine, affected by closures.

Unlike the French, German and, especially, British producers, the Italians and Belgians did not take decisions to reduce capacity during the 1977–9 period. In Belgium, increased public ownership did not neutralize antagonistic sentiment within the industry, especially among the traditional steel producers. The need to compromise meant that no producers were prepared to reduce capacity, and the strength of the corporatist tripartite policy-making body and parastatal steel financing corporation was not enough to bring about a significant restructuring of the decision-making process and counter the strength of the remaining steel 'barons'. Italian policy-makers justified the maintenance of capacity on the grounds that domestic steel demand and imports were growing, which they were. During the 1970s, therefore, the Italian industry continued to be out of step with trends in the rest of the EC as it had during the 1960s (Stegemann, 1976). This has led to some friction between both private and public sectors in Italy on the one hand, and the EC Commission and northern European steel workers on the other. (For a more detailed account of the national steel policies, see Woolcock, forthcoming.)

The Policy of the European Commission

As has been shown, the EC Commission first introduced voluntary measures in an attempt to stabilize the European steel market. The internal anti-crisis measures consisted of delivery guidelines, first by country and then by company. These were based on quarterly forward programmes which estimated trends in supply and demand. Voluntary guidance prices and finally mandatory minimum prices (for three of the six product groups) were introduced in 1977. These had the effect of increasing European steel prices by about 20 per cent between 1977 and the end of 1979. The external anti-crisis measures consisted of bilateral arrangements on price and import volume with major exporters. These agreements included some NICs, South Korea, Brazil, Spain in 1978 and 1979, but bilateral agreements were not sought with the NICs in 1980.

This short-term anti-crisis policy, however, went hand in hand with a longer-term policy of restructuring. Inevitably the initial objective of the steel producers was to ensure that the defensive, anti-crisis measures worked. Agreement, for example in Eurofer, did not extend to a balanced reduction of surplus capacity. By means of the powers invested in it by the Treaty of Paris, however, the EC Commission attempted to ensure that real adjustment took place, despite the divergent structure and performance of the respective European steel producers.

The instruments for achieving this aim were fourfold. By means of the long-term *indicative guidelines* of the General Objectives, the Commission attempted to develop a consensus on longer-term market trends (EC Commission, 1978d). Based on these projections and on the ability to pass an opinion on investment decisions (Article 54 of the ECSC), the Commission sought to avoid unwarranted capacity expansion. The provision of ECSC *restructuring assistance* under Article 54 of the ECSC or via the European

Investment Bank (EIB), has provided the Commission with a further lever with which it can bring about a modification if not change of investment plans. In particular the Commission's *policy on state aid* enables it to regulate national steel policies. Despite powers to ban all state aid, the Commission has had to adopt a flexible approach because of the political nature of many restructuring efforts. Pressed by the Germans, however, a new code on state aid to the steel industry was initiated in 1979. This provides for more Commission influence in that EC acceptance of national aid for restructuring is subject to the provision of a restructuring programme, but once such a programme is provided, aid has been generally accepted with only a few modifications, and the Germans consider this insufficient.

The European Community also provides *reconversion assistance* in its own right via the ECSC's Article 56. In this context, regional and social policies under the EEC have been coordinated with the ECSC aid for retraining, rehousing and provision of alternative employment in order to achieve maximum impact (EC Commission, 1978e). In a more far-reaching initiative the Commission has proposed a form of work-sharing, involving, *inter alia*, early retirement, restrictions on overtime and a shorter working week. The initial ambitious proposals were scaled down following the opposition of the producers and most governments. The significance of the proposals and the strength of opposition to them was reflected in the failure of the German union, IG Metal, to achieve the progressive introduction of a 35-hour week, despite fighting, on the issue, the first major strike in the German steel industry for fifty years.

The Davignon Plan was therefore an attempt to combine the use of instruments promoting restructuring and reconversion with temporary anti-crisis measures. The defensive anti-crisis measures have not been so restrictive as to protect inefficient producers, who have been forced to retrench. At the same time the EC policy has been strong enough to prevent unilateral, competitive national policies which would without doubt have been more restrictive, and to prevent the development of private cartels. By 1978 a consensus was emerging between the different national steel policies, despite divergent performance and structures. Both French and British governments had accepted the need for more market-oriented policies, while the German government accepted EC regulation of competition during the transitional period. Progress was made between 1977 and 1979, but a good deal more adjustment will be needed. In the early 1980s the European industry cannot expect a rapid improvement in domestic demand to ease the pressures for adjustment. This continued need for adjustment and the vulnerability of the European industry were reflected in the events of 1980 and early 1981. A further fall in demand in 1980 led to the collapse of the ECSC's voluntary scheme and imposition of production quotas under Article 58. In terms of export markets, access to the US market can be expected to remain difficult for some time. The only market likely to grow will be that of the NICs, where the Europeans will have to compete with Japanese and NIC producers.

The Japanese Industry

The competitive position of the Japanese industry in the late 1970s is mainly due to the policies adopted by the industry itself. The most significant assistance provided by MITI during the 1950s was the promotion of heavy, steel-consuming industries. It was the growth of industries such as shipbuilding and automobiles which provided the Japanese steel industry with its dynamic domestic market. After some initial financial aid, the main steel producers soon grew strong enough not to need public help. As in other AICs, competition in the Japanese market is oligopolistic, with the five largest integrated steel producers accounting for 95 per cent of iron and 77 per cent of crude steel production. Competition among smaller non-integrated producers is less regulated, and it was necessary to introduce a crisis-cartel for the electric steel-makers in order to bring about an ordered restructuring of that sector (Nomura Research Institute, 1979, p. 99).

The need for public intervention is also reduced by the fact that Nippon Steel, the leading Japanese producer, assumes important policy-making responsibilities and often acts in the interests of the Japanese steel industry. As in other countries, prices are determined by price leadership, in Japan on the part of Nippon Steel. But Nippon Steel also provides a lead on wage negotiations and other issues.

In the latter part of the 1960s, domestic competition in the form of capacity expansion had an adverse effect on prices and the government intervened by making recommendations on the phasing of investment in blast furnaces. These recommendations were made on the basis of the information collected by the iron and steel subcommittee of MITI's Industrial Structural Council (Magaziner and Hout, 1980). The form of these recommendations does not appear to differ greatly from the EC Commission's opinions on notified investment decisions under Article 54 of the ECSC. Whereas both are non-enforceable, the Japanese recommendations were probably more effective, for the simple reason that in Japan one is working in a single business culture, and one in which industry/government relations are relatively good. While following very similar indicative approaches, the EC Commission has had to contend with a wide range of business cultures, various degrees of national public intervention in the industry, and sometimes divergent national market trends.

The Japanese industry entered the recession very much stronger than its international competitors, but this did not stop it adjusting. Investment in energy conservation and automation enabled the industry to remain profitable despite operating at only 70 per cent of full capacity. Investment decisions taken before 1974 resulted in an increase in crude steel capacity from 120 mmt in 1973 to 147 mmt in 1978, which was criticized in the US as predatory capacity expansion. Improved productivity and increases in export prices helped the Japanese producers boost profits in 1978/9 by up to 100 per cent. Thus the Japanese industry enters the 1980s with depreciated but still competitive steel plant, plus the financial strength to invest in developing new steel products and diversification out of bulk steel into higher-value-added products. This will not mean a rapid shift out of bulk steel. Japanese industrial strategy is said to be based on the income elasticity of demand for a given line of production and the principle of comparative technical progress (Shinohara, 1980). In the case of the steel industry, income elasticity of demand is expected to follow the pattern of the USA and Europe and fall as the Japanese economy disengages from steel. With such long-term perspectives of industrial change one can expect the Japanese industry to respond to such changes in a more timely fashion than has been the case in the USA and Europe. Japanese exports have already shifted from North America and Europe to Asia, which accounted for 44 per cent of total steel exports in 1975 and 64 per cent in 1978. Japanese steel producers are also active in selling steel plant to developing countries. While steel producers in other AIC countries are concerned about the 'boomerang' effect such sales of plant will have on export if not domestic markets, in the case of Japan the exporting of plant forms part of the steel producers' own diversification policy. Owing to the strength of the Japanese industry it is likely to gain a large share of the NIC export market during the 1980s. As this market shrinks from the increased self-sufficiency of the NICs it is likely to be the Japanese who will have sold the NICs much of their steel-making plant.

THE INTERNATIONAL DIMENSION TO STEEL POLICY

Following the intervention by most governments to support national steel industries during the 1970s, pressure increased for some form of international understanding on trade in steel. As early as September 1975 the EC Commission had suggested that informal consultations should take place within the OECD on the particular structural problems of the steel industry (EC Commission, 1975b). Justification for such a sectoral approach was found in the 1974 OECD Trade Pledge, itself an effort to counter protectionist trends in international trade, which referred to such solutions: 'When several countries are confronted with the same structural and sectoral problems, *ad hoc* consultations could help in finding a positive and mutually acceptable solution' (OECD Trade Pledge of 30 May 1974, renewed in May 1975, and subsequently every year). In 1977 the US government appeared to be undecided between the GATT or OECD as a context for discussing the issue of aid to the steel industry (*Agence Europe*, 28 September 1977). During November and December of that year trilateral discussions took place between the USA, EC (the Commission) and Japan, and agreement was reached on the policies which should be adopted in December 1977. This agreement, finally formalized in the objectives of the OECD Steel Committee in October 1978, involved both anti-crisis and restructuring.[4] The 1977 understanding between the USA, EC and Japan was that anti-crisis measures should not disrupt traditional trade patterns, that excessively low export prices should be rigorously controlled, and that national policies in steel should not result in the costs of adjustments to structural change being shifted on to other countries.

It would be wrong to call this general understanding a cartel. The work of the steel committee soon showed that it could not be expected to provide more than a forum within which the OECD countries could discuss their respective steel policies. Europeans, especially the Commission in Brussels, suspected the Americans of wanting to set up a tribunal to pass judgement on aid by European governments to the steel industry. There was, therefore, as in the GATT negotiations on the subsidies and counter-vailing duties code, a distinct difference of interests between the USA and the EC.

When the US Steel Corporation filed anti-dumping actions against the major European steel producers (in April 1980), there was a feeling in Europe that the US was being forced to go back on the 1977 understanding to avoid disruption of traditional trade patterns. The Europeans also felt that the US administration's handling of the issue, in which it insisted that the US industry had either trigger prices or anti-dumping action, but not both, precipitated the US Steel Corporation's action (*Financial Times*, 18 April 1980). One could justifiably wonder why so much effort has gone into avoiding anti-dumping actions. In both 1977 and 1980 preliminary rulings of dumping were made by the US Department of Commerce, but the 1980 action, as did the 1977 action, stopped short of the final ruling on whether the US industry had suffered material injury. Perhaps the most plausible reason for both sides in the dispute wishing to avoid seeing the anti-dumping actions to the bitter end was that there was too much at stake for the decision to be left to the quasi-judicial process in what was the first interpretation of the new US legislation implementing the Tokyo Round anti-dumping code. The US industry, and in particular US Steel Corporation, had for ten years repeatedly stressed that unfair trade and dumping were at the root of the US industry's problems. If the decision had gone against them it might well have precipitated an accelerated move out of steel by the major producers, with all that that would have implied for the US steel policy. On the other hand, the loss of part of the US export market would have a serious effect on the already depressed European market.

Both the Americans and the Europeans were interested in having truly international deliberations on the problems of the steel industry, and in the 1978 decision establishing the steel committee, specific provision was made for non-OECD members. An invitation was extended to four leading NIC producers to participate in the committee's work, South Korea, Mexico, Brazil and India. South Korea's response was favourable and Mexico's position in 1980 was that it might be interested in considering observer status. India came out firmly against the proposal, its policy being summed up by the minister for steel at the UNIDO conference on iron and steel as follows: 'Developing countries should not allow themselves to be influenced by the industrialized countries' concern with excess capacity'

(UNIDO, 1979c). There was some developing-country representation at the OECD steel symposium in February 1980, which was designed to enable participation of all parties in the international debate (OECD, 1980a). Trade unions had pressed for some time for representation in a global debate on the industry. See, for example, the resolution of the International Metalworkers Federation (IMF) of 1977 (*Frankfurter Allgemeine Zeitung*, 15 April 1977). A truly international approach to the problems of the steel industry is, however, still some way off. For example, the desire to bring some order to the provision of export credits for steel plant, which found expression in the objectives of the OECD steel committee, is unlikely to have any significant effect. With slack investment in the AICs, plant-makers are having to look to the developing countries for orders. As the shortage of finance for steel plant is in many cases the most important constraint on developing country steel plans (UNIDO, 1978b, p. 5), this is an issue of central importance to the developing countries.

CONCLUDING REMARKS

The general picture which emerges is that the problems of the AIC steel producers in the 1970s were caused by structural decline in demand. As the income elasticity of demand for steel varied from region to region during the 1960s, this resulted in imbalances in the performance and relative competitiveness of steel-making. The USA was most adversely affected, followed by some EC industries. The Japanese model shows that successful adjustment to the technologies of the 1960s and 1970s required rapid growth in output and long-term corporate strategies. The shift from large-scale plants during the 1980s and slower growth will mean that the pace of change will slow somewhat. There remain, however, significant imbalances in supply and demand which will mean that some forms of trade regulation or anti-crisis measures will continue until genuine adjustment takes place.

The NICs are significant because they constitute the only really dynamic market for the 1980s. In competition for these markets, NIC domestic steel producers can be expected to gain a larger share and the volume of AIC exports to the developing countries will remain roughly constant. Export markets in developing countries cannot therefore be relied upon to offer any relief for AIC producers under pressure to adjust to stagnating domestic markets and higher energy costs. As in the past, a relative shift in the location of steel production will come about because of the faster growth of new producers rather than the absolute decline of more established industries. The shift to the NICs will be slower than was the case with Japan during the 1950s and 1960s, because the trading environment of the 1980s looks likely to be less favourable and because the most dynamic NIC steel producers, for example South Korea, have a relatively small domestic market. In larger NICs or new steel-producing countries such as India or Brazil, instability in the growth of steel-consuming industries or constraints on finance or infrastructure will limit the growth of the steel industry. Nevertheless, NIC growth at twice AIC steel output will make the NICs a significant factor in the world steel market by the end of the 1980s. If AIC producers do not take account of this in their long-term corporate strategies, trade regulatory measures in steel can be expected to extend to include the NICs.

NOTES

1 There is an extensive literature on this issue and reference should be made to it for qualification of such figures. See Mueller and Kawahito, 1978, 1979; and Putman, Hayes and Bartlett, 1978 for a defence of the US steel industry.
2 For example, US Steel Corporation. Armco, which has followed a policy of diversifying out of steel for some time, hopes to reduce the share of its assets in steel from the present 53 to 40 per cent by 1983. See also Chapter 12.
3 Voluntary restraint agreements will not be accepted by the EC or Japan unless they have government assurances that these will be safe from anti-trust litigation in the US courts.
4 The creation of an OECD Steel Committee was the result of pressure from the US steel industry, which wanted more formal commitments on international supervision of subsidies and the inclusion of some developing countries. See letter from 'Steel Senators' to Robert Strauss (*International Herald Tribune*, 5 June 1978).

7
Petrochemicals
Louis Turner

This chapter concentrates on chemicals derived from crude oil and natural gas, which are known as petrochemicals and, by weight, make up around 90 per cent of world production of organic and inorganic chemicals (Shell, 1980, pp. 24–5). In particular, it concentrates on 'base' organic petrochemicals, which are products such as ethylene, propylene, butadiene, benzene, toluene and the xylenes. These are the building blocks from which can be derived a wide variety of end-products ranging from explosives to plastic films.

To understand the politics of this industry, we must take a few basic points into account. First, this is the industry, *par excellence*, the growth of which was stimulated by the plentiful supplies of cheap oil and gas in recent decades. Therefore, the oil-price explosion of the 1970s inevitably meant that the industry would have to restructure itself. Second, the technology underlying this sector is relatively mature. Companies pay as much attention to improving production processes as to discovering major new products. Third, the great era of petrochemical substitution for established products such as tin, glass, paper, steel and aluminium may now be over. Taking American figures as general indicators of what has happened throughout the AIC world, the petrochemical penetration of the US economy (measured in thousands of tons per billion dollars of real GNP) increased by the following percentages during the past decades: 1950–60, 14 per cent per annum; 1960–70, 6·6 per cent per annum; 1970–80, 2·6 per cent per annum; 1980–90, an estimated 1 per cent per annum (Holmer, 1980, p. 18).

ENTER THE NICs

The oil-price explosion of 1973–4 did not just usher in a new age for the oil industry. One by-product of OPEC's success was that the oil producers started thinking seriously about how they could best use their massive oil incomes for the long-term development of their nations. The petrochemical industry was particularly attractive, because much of it could be built on the basis of using natural gas, which was often merely being flared.

The Middle East and North African oil producers are showing signs that they will become a significant, but not overwhelming, force in the world petrochemical industry of the late 1980s. Qatar actually got an ethylene complex on stream in 1980, while both Iraq and Iran had such ventures close to completion when war broke out between them that autumn (and the Iraqi complex had apparently come through unscathed at the time this book went to press). However, the plans of these countries pale into insignificance beside those of Saudi Arabia, where Mobil, Shell and a Dow–Mitsubishi consortium have been persuaded to commit themselves to constructing major ethylene-based complexes, which should come on stream around the 1984–5 period. In addition, two consortia (one American, one Japanese) have agreed to construct methanol plants; Exxon has agreed to invest in a low-density polyethylene plant which is linked with the Shell complex; and (a sign of the times) a Taiwanese company, Taiwan Fertilizer, has signed to build a fertilizer plant. Adding the capacity of these projects up, it appears that Saudi Arabia should have between 2 and 3 per cent of world ethylene capacity by the latter 1980s.

Petrochemical activities have not just been restricted to the oil-producing world. Taiwan, for instance, entered the ethylene industry in the late 1960s and, by 1979, had an overall capacity which was 50 per cent greater than domestic demand. Similarly, South Korea has two ethylene-crackers in production and Singapore will enter this industry via a joint venture with a Sumitomo-led consortium of Japanese companies.

In many ways, these East Asian NICs are as active in the petrochemical field as a number of their more populous rivals in Latin America. Both Brazil and Mexico were established in the petrochemical industry by the early 1960s. Despite this, and despite the fact that it possesses oil and gas resources, the Mexican performance has not been particularly dynamic. By the end of 1979, its relatively fragmented ethylene capacity was below that of Korea and Taiwan (*Chemical Age*, 23 November 1979, pp. 21–2; *Chemical Week*, 23 May 1979, pp. 25–9). Mexico should move ahead now, given the investment boom which followed the major oil and gas discoveries of the 1970s. Brazil will follow in Mexico's wake, even though it starts with a stronger petrochemical industry. For the moment, some of its chemical effort is being diverted into its pioneering, controversial, alcohol-based, oil-substitution policy.

Eastern Europe is one other region whose chemical production has been worrying AIC policy-makers. Its countries have about 24 per cent of world chemical production, but a good part of this is in simpler products such as fertilizers, which can be based on the Soviet Union's plentiful supplies of natural gas. It is more difficult to assess how aggressively the Eastern bloc will move into the ethylene sector. Soviet chemical officials once talked of achieving parity with the US and Western Europe. However, the USSR starts from a low base of 2·5 million tons a year of capacity, with another 2·4 million tons a year under construction, and it is inconceivable that they could try to wipe out this disparity with the West during the course of a decade.

NIC DYNAMICS

It is possible to make some generalizations about the countries which have been entering the petrochemical industry during recent years. First, the role of the state has been relatively important. It goes without saying that the development of the East European industries has been planned from the centre. In South Korea, the government financed or guaranteed the finance of the first two Korean ethylene-crackers. In Taiwan, base petrochemicals will be kept within the state preserve. In Brazil, the state petrochemical company, Petroquisa, has been given an increasingly large role in all recent ventures. In Mexico, it is the state oil company, Pemex, that will be given the lead role in the planned rapid expansion of the Mexican industry. Again, in the Middle East, it is state companies that will be either the sole owners or substantial partners in all the major base-petrochemical ventures planned for the region.

However, the state does not always reserve this industry as a monopoly for itself. The less radical Middle East oil producers, such as Saudi Arabia and Qatar, have entered joint ventures with foreign partners. The South Koreans have had a policy of bringing in private, preferably Korean, investors as fast as possible into projects, even if these were set up by central planners. Most of the non-Communist NICs become more relaxed about foreign ownership the further one moves away from base chemicals. There is even the case of Argentina, which has liberalized those regulations that previously kept base petrochemicals as a state monopoly. Despite this, the NICs generally see base petrochemicals as being much like the steel industry – a strategic sector in which all modernizing states should be represented.

The most convincing picture, then, which emerges from this case is of a relatively technologically mature industry, which can be entered quite easily by governments with the determination and cash either to buy plants on a turnkey basis, or to bribe multinationals to enter into joint ventures. For instance, the surge of plant-construction deals signed by the East Europeans in the early 1970s shows how widely available a lot of petrochemical technology now is. One list of such deals made during the 1972–8 period names over twenty-four Western companies entering some form of buy-back arrangement with Eastern Europe. Only a handful of these companies (Mitsubishi Petrochemical, Uhde/Hoechst, Mitsui, Dow Chemical and Occidental Petroleum) can be properly described as multinationals. The rest were small-to-medium sized plant constructors or traders, who were only too happy to make a profit out of the decline in international tensions (Sobeslavsky and Beazley, 1980, pp. 123–32).

A further factor benefiting the Third World is that the underlying economics of petrochemical production have been steadily improving for the oil-producing countries within it. This is not to claim that OPEC members will not have problems in entering this industry, for construction costs will be higher than in the AICs, the lack of a technological infrastructure will make it more difficult to run plants at close to theoretical capacity, and there will be relatively high transportation costs, since the major markets are normally some distance from the oil producers (Turner and Bedore, 1979, ch. 6). On the other hand, these basic disadvantages can be overcome if capital and gas feedstock are pumped into these projects at sufficiently cheap rates – and these are two factors which most oil producers possess in abundance. In particular, the relative importance of low gas prices markedly increased over the 1970s, as oil-price increases drove the price of naphtha (the basic feedstock in West Europe and Japan) ever upwards.

TRADE POLITICS

The chemical case is distinct from the other four industries on which this book concentrates, in that trade has mostly been within the AIC world, in which the main bone of contention used to be the American Selling Price System, which meant that various chemicals could only be imported into the United States subject to duties ranging up to 40, 50 and occasionally 58 per cent. This anomaly, resulting from US special-interest pleading, was abolished in the GATT MTN Round. The result is that AIC tariffs on petrochemical products are no longer at levels which seriously affect trade flows in any significant way.

The subsequent irritant in transatlantic petrochemical trade relations has been the alleged affects of regulated gas prices on US chemical and fibres exports to Western Europe. These complaints rose during 1979 and 1980, as the Europeans battled with their own rapidly rising feedstock prices and with the post-1977 fall in the effective value of the dollar. The dispute reached a flashpoint in fibres, with the British getting EC consent to impose temporary import restrictions on polyester nylon yarn during 1980, and with the Americans retaliating with the threat to impose countervailing duties on Community exports of woollen clothing and synthetic fibres.

Eastern Europe

Given that this book is primarily concerned with the way non-traditional manufacturing entrants are integrated into the world trading system, we are faced more with anticipating problems than with discussing their actual effects. For instance, if we take the East Europeans, we find there have been a number of anti-dumping actions by the EC and its member countries, but there has been nothing approaching a full-scale crisis between the two parts of Europe, merely forebodings on the part of Western industrial leaders.

The first of their worries has been over the volume of chemical products which could at some stage flood into established Western markets. Certainly, the Soviet Union and other Comecon countries have been putting an increased emphasis on 'chemicalization', and the Soviet Union's plentiful oil and gas reserves mean that feedstocks should be no trouble. Combining their ambitions to the fact that they plan their plants on a turnkey basis, one can understand why the Western industry has been nervous, though the danger of massive inflows of East European products still remains more potential than actual. Two studies from the OECD (1980b) and the EC Commission (Davignon, 1979) have both stressed the relative unimportance of current imports from East Europe. The EC Commission saw some problems with urea, methanol and caprolactam, while the OECD raised questions about ammonia and soda ash. As the OECD study put it, 'The quantities do not generally appear enormous compared to intra-OECD trade and foreseeable demand' (*European Chemical News*, 7 April 1980. p. 14). In any case, the overall chemical trade balance between Western and Eastern Europe has largely been in favour of the West, varying between US$1·6 and US$1·8 billion per year during the 1970s (*European Chemical News*, 17 March 1980, p. 22).

In trade-policy terms, the interesting question is not so much about the speed with which trade between the two parts of Europe will grow, but about how 'fair' this competition will be. Clearly, anti-dumping actions against the Eastern bloc are unsatisfactory, given the extreme difficulty in estimating what domestic prices actually are and what a proper production cost would actually be. For the moment this is not too serious, in that East European officials are allegedly often quite happy to have Westerners tell them that they ought to be charging more for their products. However, should the volume of Eastern chemical exports pick up at the rate some pessimists assume, then the trade-policy problems will be quite severe. GATT has never come to terms with the state-trading phenomenon and, until it does, one suspects that there could be a spread in the use of devices such as trigger pricing.

The Oil Producers

In many ways, the problems which the oil producers may create for the AICs are going to be fairly similar to those created by the East Europeans. In both cases, the question of what counts as 'fair' trading when state corporations compete with privately owned AIC companies will be well to the fore. The big difference will be that the oil producers will generally have a better political relationship with the AICs than will the East Europeans. Also, multinational petrochemical companies will be relatively heavily involved in the increased flows of chemical products from the oil-producing world.

In particular, Saudi ambitions are going to raise the question of the treatment which should be given to 'infant export industries'. Up to now, it has been accepted within GATT that LDCs can protect or otherwise subsidize infant industries. This tolerance, though, was extended as part of a qualified acceptance of import substitution by which the AICs accepted that certain traditional export markets would be denied them in order that fledgeling Third World industries should be given the chance to stand on their own feet. However, tolerating subsidized or protected LDC industries aimed at export markets from the start is another matter. Nevertheless, it is difficult to see how a country like Saudi Arabia, with its overwhelming asset of under-utilized natural gas, can go by any other route. The only way it can seriously enter the industry is by aiming at export markets, and it is inevitable that the first generation of such investments will need assistance in the form of cheap capital and feedstocks.

The feedstock issue is going to be a particularly fascinating one and its fate must be affected by the EC–USA dispute about the latter's pricing of oil and gas feedstocks. The Community had difficulty in arguing within GATT that the cheapness of American petrochemical feedstocks counted as a subsidy under either the old Article 16 on subsidies or the new MTN subsidy code. Presumably, it will be even more difficult to use such provisions against the oil producers as they emerge as petrochemical exporters. However, they will tend to be vulnerable elsewhere. First, in so far as they make cheap loans specifically to the exporting sector, they will fall foul of the drive to eradicate export subsidies. However, Saudi Arabia may be invulnerable here, since it provides cheap capital just as readily to purely domestically oriented projects. A second area in which the oil producers may face problems is over their membership of GATT. US legislation is specific, in that it only requires an injury test in countervailing duty cases once countries have signed the new subsidy code. As long as countries such as Saudi Arabia and Mexico remain outside GATT, they could be very vulnerable to counter-attacks from the US industry. The Saudi position towards GATT has still to be settled, but the positive Mexican rejection of membership suggests that there will be quite serious trade skirmishes between Mexico and the USA as the former's petrochemical exports start building up.

As it happens, the only serious discussions about such matters between leading oil producers and industrial consumers started to take place under the auspices of the Euro-Arab Dialogue. This was conceived in late 1973 and spawned subgroups which brought together delegations from the Arab League and EC to discuss the problems of the petrochemical, fertilizer and refining sectors. These subgroups became important in early 1977, when they started to concentrate on the conflicting forecasts the two sides were making about likely future productive capacities and market demand for the various products. The two sides started to talk about the concept of complementary investment, whereby the Arab side might be encouraged to concentrate on, say, the commodity end of the petrochemical industry, while the Europeans would trade up to concentrate on its more specialist parts. Most of these discussions were shadow-boxing; however, these groups were evolving and, at the time that they were put into limbo (after the Camp David peace accords), they had been granted funds to consider ways in which the Europeans might give practical technical help to Arab aspirations in these sectors (Turner and Bedore, 1979, pp. 110–17; Allen, 1978).

Given that other authors in the trade-policy field have recently been accepting the desirability of institutions charged with analysing the evolution of the global economy (Camps, 1980, p. 44: Gordon, 1979, pp. 165, 172), it is interesting to note that there have been one or two institutional developments along these lines within the petrochemical sector. The most interesting of these is the work by UNIDO, which has had two major 'consultations' on this industry, the first in Mexico City in March 1979 and the second in Istanbul in June 1981. After producing a survey of the world petrochemical industry from 1975 to 2000, UNIDO is concentrating on preparing forecasts for a decade ahead in ten basic petrochemical products. To this end, it has established a permanent working group on world petrochemical supply and demand. UNIDO will act as the secretariat but has invited active representation from economic bodies such as Comecon, the OECD and OPEC; groups of countries such as the Andean Group; industrial associations such as the European chemical federation, CEFIC; particularly important individual countries; and UN organizations such as UNCTAD. All this would suggest that UNIDO's work is the most serious intergovernmental programme straddling both sides of the north–south divide in petrochemicals.

ADJUSTMENT AND PETROCHEMICALS

Even if it is accepted that the NIC incursions into the petrochemical industry will not overwhelm the AICs, there is a sense that the established companies are coming to terms with their NIC challengers in a rather more relaxed way than is true of their opposite numbers in textiles, steel and, even, consumer electronics. The secret would seem to be that a certain amount of the change in the industry's centre of gravity will take place with the active connivance of established multinationals.

In the case of Japan, there seems to have been a decision in the early 1970s between MITI and some of the trading companies that Japan should become involved with the petrochemical ambitions of the oil producers. In part, 'Japan Inc' was acting within the context of its general resource diplomacy. In part, also, there was an awareness that Japan has a greater competitive advantage in process-plant construction than in petrochemical production, a sector where the Japanese industry is relatively fragmented (Nomura Research Institute, 1979, p. 221). Allowing Mitsui to invest in Iran, Mitsubishi in Saudi Arabia, and Sumitomo in Singapore would be advantageous, even if this was at the expense of the petrochemical industry within Japan itself.

The USA looks as though it will be barely touched by NIC competition in this sector. Some American companies are entering joint ventures in Saudi Arabia, motivated by the crude-oil entitlements available to foreign investors and by the knowledge that this is a key economy in which companies should establish themselves. Otherwise, chemical imports into the USA have not been a serious problem in recent years. With the exception of minor irritation such as Occidental's phosphate-for-ammonia swap arrangement with the Soviet Union and, potentially, an increase of imports from Mexico, the US industry looks reasonably impervious to a trading challenge from new producers.

The West European situation is more complex, in that this continent is the natural target for East European, Middle East and North African would-be exporters. In none of these cases are the established West European companies going to be in control of the process. Part of the tensions with East Europe stems precisely from the fact that the latter's industry is being developed in conjunction with plant constructors which have no vested interest in stable markets. The fact that these constructors are forced to take their payment in products means that the proportional importance of trade flowing outside the control of the existing multinationals will grow.

Adjustment, however, is not just a geographical affair of established producers coming to terms with the petrochemical industry of the nearer NICs. Adjustment is also a case of encouraging the further concentration of an industry (if that is the way the industry's logic is going) and the coming to terms with changes in the economic and technological environment. Compared with the other industrial sectors analysed in this book, the petrochemical sector is a model for how an industry can come to terms relatively smoothly with major changes in its overall business environment.

Japan handled the post-1973 slowing of growth in this sector with its usual efficiency. Depending on whose figures you go by, ethylene production was running at 70–75 per cent capacity during 1977 and 1978, compared with the 90 per cent plus seen for the period 1965–73 (Nomura Research Institute, 1979, p. 243; *Japan Economic Journal*, 25 April 1978, p. 9; *Chemical Insight*, No. 143, pp. 2–5). In marked contrast to Western Europe, however, this problem was tackled quite firmly. By early 1978, there were no further ethylene-crackers under construction in Japan. In general, the government is now relatively hostile to new petrochemical construction and expansion within Japan. The feeling is that an industry which is so dependent on hydrocarbons and is potentially a major polluter is not that suited for a small, highly populated country like Japan which lacks its own hydrocarbon resources. At the same time, in certain parts of industries such as fertilizers, the 1978 anti-structural-recession law was apparently used to squeeze out some of the surplus capacity in the industry (Nomura Research Institute, 1979, pp. 239–40).

The West European chemical industry suffered more in the aftermath of the 1973–4 oil price explosion than the US and Japanese, and, at the same time, it showed itself much less capable of pulling itself out of its troubles. In particular, it was unable to control the investment boom which had been triggered off by the dynamic market growth of the late 1960s and early 1970s. The result has been that, even though capacity utilization of petrochemical plant fell drastically from 1975 onwards, new plants were still coming on stream in 1980, with the result that capacity utilization will not regain pre-1973 levels until well into the mid-1980s. This over-capacity has had a drastic impact on the profitability of European chemical companies (see Table 7.1).

Table 7.1 *European Chemical Manufacturers Pre-Tax Return on Sales (percentage)*

	1973	1974	1975	1976	1977	1978	1980
Akzo	7·0	6·2	−2·5	0·7	0·3	1·9	1·2
BASF	7·4	6·8	4·7	6·7	5·2	5·3	4·2
Bayer	8·9	7·2	4·7	6·2	5·1	5·4	n.a.
BP Chemicals[1]			9·0	9·9	3·8	4·2	−6·8
DSM	7·0	14·9	4·0	2·5	1·0	0·3	0·4
Hoechst	8·7	8·7	5·0	6·2	5·1	5·6	5·1
ICI	16·5	17·5	11·3	13·6	10·8	9·8	5·0
Montedison	0·2	1·2	−2·3	−2·0	−8·7	−4·0	n.a.
Rhône-Poulenc	5·9	9·0	−7·7	−0·7	−0·3	−1·7	−5·9
Solvay	8·6	9·2	4·6	9·4	6·4	6·2	−4·0
UCB	5·3	6·5	−0·8	2·2	−2·1	0·1	1·5

[1]Pre-tax and interest.
Sources: Stuart H. Warmsley, 'Profitability for European chemicals', *Chemistry and Industry*, 5 January 1980; *European Chemical News*, 27 July 1981, p. 55 (European Review).

Many of Western Europe's problems stem from the over-fragmentation of the industry. This is statistically difficult to demonstrate but it does appear that the West European industry does have some distinctive problems. The most convincing explanation is that the continent is going through a period of vestigial nationalism. If we look at Table 7.2 we see that alongside ethylene plants built by Shell and BASF, we have plants coming into operation in Portugal, Sicily and Austria. In the Sicilian case, we seem to be back to the Italian invest-first-ask-questions-later phenomenon. Over-enthusiastic nationalism seems also to be the motivation in the Portuguese case.

Table 7.2 *Major New Ethylene Plants, Western Europe*

Company	Location	Start-up
OMV-Danubia	Schwechat, Austria	1980
Montedison/ANIC	Priolo, Sicily	1980
CNP	Sines, Portugal	1980/1
Shell	Berre, southern France	1980/1
BASF	Ludwigshafen, Germany	1981
Esso	Mossmorran, Scotland	1985

Source: Shell.

There has been an element of 'negative adjustment' within the West European industry. The attempted fibres cartel was necessitated by an unwillingness of companies to get out of an industry plagued by over-capacity. There was even a short period around 1978 in which there was an attempt to set up a plastics cartel as well. In general, though, the last two or three years have seen a considerable amount of capacity transfer within the

West European industry. The most well-known example of this was the sale by Union Carbide and Monsanto of certain of their European chemical properties to British Petroleum – a company which also picked up capacity from Rhône-Poulenc when the latter reorganized its chemical activities in the summer of 1980 (the other main gainer was the French oil group Elf-Aquitaine). A further example of capacity-shedding was Montedison's sale of subsidiaries in Spain and the Netherlands (also, more seriously, in the USA). At the time this chapter was being revised, Gulf was also trying to sell its European petrochemical operations.

So, what seems to have happened in West Europe was that there was a period after 1973 in which governments and companies tried to resist the inevitable corporate restructuring. The major problems were downstream of petrochemicals in the fibres sector where the Italians, in particular, got themselves politically locked into a series of disastrous investments. For a period, the French also took a fairly defensive line, though the British, for once, were on the side of letting market forces sort out the industry's problems. But then Britain's virtue was hardly surprising; not only did North Sea developments mean that its feedstock position was strong, but the country possessed companies like ICI, BP and Shell which were relatively well placed to survive any restructuring of the industry.

STRATEGIES FOR THE 1980s

The problems facing the petrochemical industry in the 1980s can probably be narrowed down to three: high feedstock prices, slow economic growth, and the growing importance of non-AIC petrochemical production.

High Energy Prices

To some extent, the petrochemical industry is quite well placed to adjust to an era of high energy prices. For instance, it can make out a good case that the volume of hydrocarbons needed as energy and feedstock to produce a given quantity of plastics is well below that needed to produce similar volumes of steel, copper or aluminium (see Table 7.3). However, the industry still needs to improve its efficiency in using hydrocarbons, and progress is being made. By 1978, the US industry had improved its energy use per pound of product by 18·2 per cent compared to 1972, saving around 360,000 barrels a day of oil. The industry is now working towards a 30 per cent improvement by 1985, aiming to save 770,000 barrels a day of oil relative to 1972 (Holmer, 1980, p. 19). This search for improved petrochemical processes shows up in a number of ways. For instance, Union Carbide and Dow have had considerable success in reducing the capital costs of low-density polyethylene production, by reducing the production pressures by over 100 times. Similarly, ICI has a new low-pressure methanol process, and Shell and Halcon have been improving the processes for propylene oxide and styrene monomer.

Table 7.3 *Energy Intensity of Plastics and Various Metals*

Energy and raw material needed to produce one litre of	*Kg of oil equivalent*	*Energy and raw material needed to produce one litre of*	*Kg of oil equivalent*
Aluminium	15	100 fertilizer sacks from:	
Copper	11	Paper	39
Steel	8	Polyethylene LD[2]	35
		100 m of pressure pipe	
Nylon (acetal resins)	4	(25 mm diameter) from:	
Styrene-copolymers	2	Iron	500
Polystyrene	2	Copper	96
Polyethylene HD[1]	1·75	Polyethylene HD[1]	38
Polyvinylchloride	1·5	100 m of drain-pipe	
Polypropylene	1·5	(100 mm diameter) from:	
Polyethylene LD[2]	1·25	Cast iron	1,970
		Clay	275
		Polyvinylchloride	154
		100 one-litre bottles from:	
		Glass	23
		Polyethylene HD[1]	12
		Polyvinylchloride	8

[1] High-density.

[2] Low-density.

Source: BASF (*The Economist*, 3 November 1979, p. 72).

The next step that companies must take is to move away from bulk towards 'performance' chemicals, and to increase the amount of product differentiation. The point about bulk chemicals, such as ethylene, is that these are the products where marketing skills are least important (though this is not to say that quality does not matter). So, we find the plastics manufacturers tailoring plastics to the special needs of the two large markets for plastics which have been particularly opened up by the oil crisis: automobiles and thermal insulation for buildings. However, even plastics are becoming a relatively saturated segment of the petrochemical industry, so companies are moving into ever more innovative sectors of the industry, such as pharmaceuticals and agrochemistry, both of which are being greatly affected by developments in biochemistry.

Companies may also seek innovation in the feedstocks they use. As oil prices rise in real terms, there will be a growing potential in coal-based chemistry and in the development of biomass as a feedstock, a sector in which the Brazilians are getting themselves established. However, given the gas reserves within OPEC which should be available for use as petrochemical feedstocks, companies may be somewhat reluctant to push ahead with alternative feedstocks that are vulnerable to the vagaries of OPEC's pricing policies.

Research-Intensive Strategies

One implication of all the above is that successful companies are going to have to become much more research-intensive. This is not an area where statistics come easily to hand, but there is some American evidence to show that the chemical industry's research effort is indeed of growing importance. In basic research, the chemical industry accounts for about 40 per cent of all spending by American industry, compared with 30 per cent during the 1960s (Jefferson, 1979, pp. 366–70).

Clearly, governments are starting to realize the way the industry is going. In 1979, the French government announced plans for promoting biotechnology, and the EC Commission has considered proposals for a five-year programme in this same area. As one would expect, the Japanese have identified this as an area deserving a concerted push. According to *Nature*, between 1967 and 1971 30 per cent of the world biotechnological patents originated in the United Kingdom. But of the patents delivered in the two or three years since 1977, 124 came from Japan, thirty-nine from the USA, nine from the Soviet Union, eight from West Germany, seven from France, one from Denmark and one from the United Kingdom (*Financial Times*, 28 January 1980).

In suggesting that the industry has to become more research-intensive, we are implying that there are parts of the industry, such as commodity chemicals and the plastics, which are now relatively mature and for which stepped-up R&D can do little more than make marginal improvements in the properties of the relevant products. Admittedly, there is still a lot which can be done with humdrum products such as methanol or low-density polyethylene, but, despite this, a research-intensive strategy in the maturer sectors of the petrochemical industry will not protect a company for very long as the NICs seek to enter these parts of the industry in their turn. The companies which will survive in these highly competitive areas are those which can consistently stay about four or five years ahead of the others in terms of the quality of the technology they are drawing on and on their marketing skills. This is the type of environment in which only the very best-managed companies will survive and there will be an inevitable shake-out of the world's middle-ranking ones.

CROSS-INDUSTRY COMPARISON

Of our five industrial cases, the petrochemical industry has been the most successful in coming to terms with changing economic circumstances. The most interesting comparison is with the steel industry, which is clearly declining and is based on companies which instinctively look for semi-protectionist measures when they run into trouble. The petrochemical sector may be maturing, but its leading companies have learned the lesson that they must adapt in order to survive. It is almost as if we are dealing with a different generation of companies. Steel companies come from an era in which their industry was central to their nation's military efforts, while the chemical companies have managed to avoid being too closely identified with national security, with the result that they are not only more multinational, but also seem to be much freer to divest themselves of declining sectors, such as fertilizers and man-made fibres. Given the relative dynamism of the chemical sector and the relative stagnation of the steel one, policy-makers might think about how to reinvigorate the latter. Cannot steel companies be persuaded to sell off unwanted capacity to stronger competitors, just as chemical companies like Union Carbide have been doing in Europe and Rhône-Poulenc has been doing in France? Is it too late to turn 'one-eyed giants' like British Steel and US Steel into more flexible and multinational corporations like the leading chemical companies, Hoechst, ICI and Du Pont?

WHAT ROLE FOR GOVERNMENTS?

Although the petrochemical sector is clearly better than most to look after itself, governments still have some part to play. For instance, they clearly have a defensive role in seeing that new entrants into the industry do not severely distort the sector's price mechanism. This is a real issue because of the role the governments in the various NICs are playing in encouraging the development of the petrochemical sector.

The next, relatively negative role left for AIC governments is the encouragement of rationalization in the industry when it appears to be overly fragmented, as seems to be the case both in Japan and within Western Europe. On balance, such rationalization can probably be left to the industry itself, except that the governments should be looking for any barriers to this process. In Japan, the government may need to persuade the main trading companies to reallocate capacity. In Western Europe, the EC Commission should be trying to encourage the transnational rationalization of this industry, where residual nationalism still seems to be a barrier.

A more positive role for governments which seems to be emerging is the identification of the growth areas of the industry (such as biotechnology) and the evolution of policies to encourage companies to move into these areas. The Japanese seem to have moved well ahead in this area, with the French and, perhaps, the West Germans playing a leading role within Western Europe. This is not to argue that significant parts of the US and West European corporate community are not moving into these areas spontaneously, but it is to suggest that the Japanese example shows that a government's strong identification of such areas can apparently galvanize an industrial sector which was not, in the Japanese case, technically very dynamic.

Finally, AIC governments have to come to terms with the fact that parts of the Third World have decided that the petrochemical industry is one on which they will concentrate. For hard political reasons the AICs are not going to encourage such a development, but then they are badly placed to try thwarting it, given the economic power of some of the new entrants (such as Saudi Arabia) and given one implied aim of AIC–LDC trade diplomacy, which is to encourage the Third World to diversify their industrial exports. In these circumstances, the AICs would clearly be well advised to cooperate with bodies developing relatively realistic scenarios of how the industry might develop.

THE NON-INEVITABILITY OF THE NICs

We should perhaps close this chapter with the thought that the petrochemical sector demonstrates that there is nothing inevitable about the emergence of any one NIC. For instance, the industrial ambitions of Iran can clearly be discounted for the medium-term future. Yet, under the Shah, Iranian petrochemical ambitions were often thought to be more realistic than those of the oil-producers on the other side of the Arabian Gulf. However, it is not just Iran which has 'blown up'. Both Poland and South Korea, in their different ways, have learned that when poor countries make massive capital-intensive investments in industries such as petrochemicals, it has to be at the expense of investment in sectors which may be of more immediate relevance to the man in the street. Both these countries will think hard before making any further major investments in this sector. In any case, the oil and gas price rises of the 1970s mean that hydrocarbon-importing NICs, which could count on entering the industry fairly easily in the past, are now having to rethink their strategies. This is the second consideration which Korean planners have had to take into account and, even in Singapore, Prime Minister Lee Kwan Yew has admitted that he is increasingly uncertain as to whether Singapore has a long-term future in the petrochemical sector. On top of this, one can add the arguments of established AIC industrialists, who claim that new producers will have to devote a great deal of time to assuring the reliability and quality of their products. Certainly, some combination of the oil producers, our core NICs and the East Europeans will increasingly penetrate the bulk end of this industry. However, apart from the gas and the surplus capital which a few oil producers possess, new entrants into this industry have few natural advantages. In these circumstances, the established AIC companies should be able to live with the new competition.

Part Two
Trade Policies

8
Western Europe and the NICs
Louis Turner

The experience of the European Community well exemplifies the tensions inherent in the transition from an era of narrowly nationalistic trading policies to one in which free trade is the norm. On the one hand, the Community's creation and periodic enlargement, along with its linkage to the European Free Trade Association, have produced the world's largest free-trading unit, and have thus given a major boost to the process of trade liberalization. On the other hand, trade relations with relatively powerless and peripheral economies remain quite highly politicized. In particular, the NICs generally qualify for discriminatory treatment which simultaneously leaves them less well placed than both their less industrialized competitors (from the Third World) in the EC trading system and their more industrialized competitors in North America and the rest of Western Europe. The treatment of the NICs is a reminder that trade still has to be seen in a context of power politics.

At the same time, though, the evolution of the EC's treatment of the NICs exemplifies a growing wariness within Brussels and European national capitals of the emerging trading environment. It is the feeling that the NICs pose qualitatively new problems which is behind the EC's growing insistence that the NICs should start 'graduating' (that is, accept increased obligations in the economic sphere), and its concern that the AICs should be allowed to redefine the circumstances in which they can resort to selective safeguards against surges of imports. Behind such initiatives is a growing concern about competition from countries with strong state involvement in the trading sector, or which do not give affected AIC industries adequate reciprocal exporting rights to protected NIC markets. Such concerns may often be overstressed but they are none the less genuine.

NICs IN THE EC CONTEXT

The early 1970s marked the highpoint of the EC's relatively uncritical enthusiasm for trade liberalization. In July 1971 it introduced its generalized preferences in favour of LDC exports, some five years before the United States got round to offering a similar scheme under the Generalized

System of Preferences (GSP). In 1973, the six original EC members were joined by Britain, Denmark and Ireland, as part of a package which included the creation of an enlarged free-trade area with EFTA, and an agreement to produce something approaching an amalgamation of the Yaoundé and Commonwealth Preference schemes. This was also the year in which the Tokyo Round of trade negotiations was launched, a decision which was very much seen as a further step in the drive to maintain the momentum of trade liberalization.

However, if the early 1970s were a highpoint for the EC's trade liberalization, the NICs were being treated relatively grudgingly even then. For instance, even though the EC's GSP scheme involved countries such as Brazil, Hong Kong, India, Iran, South Korea, Mexico, Singapore and Yugoslavia, there were strings attached (Murray, 1977). For one thing, the scheme excluded Taiwan. For another, just as the Japanese and Americans were also to do, the EC limited the scope of its scheme by setting ceilings to the quantity of imports of each product which qualified for tariff preferences. Thus, 67 per cent of the relevant products flowing from LDCs other than those named above were given preferential treatment. However, the proportion for the eight leading NICs in the scheme was only 26 per cent, while, in the case of Hong Kong, the exceptions were so severe that only 9 per cent of its potential exports were covered by the scheme (UNCTAD secretariat calculations).

This picture of a relatively circumscribed EC generosity towards the NICs is strengthened by events in textiles and clothing, the sector in which the NICs were particularly well represented. Here, the EC was a willing partner as the USA led the drive to convert the International Cotton Textiles Arrangement into the much more all-embracing Multi-Fibre Arrangement. The picture is further strengthened by what happened during the negotiations leading up to the Lomé Convention of 1975. The original aim was to add the British colonies to the basically francophone Yaoundé Convention in an expanded trade, aid and investment pact. However, as the negotiations proceeded, core NICs were excluded. Asian countries such as India were deliberately left out as being too populous, and the resultant convention covered fifty-eight LDCs outside Asia and Latin America, with a combined population of less than half that of India. So, when the final agreement was signed, the provision of duty-free access for the industrial products of the selected LDCs was relatively costless for the EC, in that few of the Lomé signatories showed any sign of becoming serious industrial forces (ODI, 1980, pp. 1–2).

In fact, the Lomé Convention (whatever its other virtues) was actually a step back for the Asian LDCs such as India and Pakistan, which had hitherto enjoyed Commonwealth preferences in the British market. This was a further sign of EC wariness of those LDCs with the strongest industrial potential, and marked an actual reversal of the relative preferences given to Asian LDCs such as India. On top of this, the EC has gone on to erect a whole 'hierarchy' (Cable and Weston, 1979, pp. 14–15) of agreements with various trading partners, and the core NICs have been placed very much down the list. For instance, the EC has had a very active Mediterranean policy, which has led to forms of trade and cooperation pacts with all countries round the Mediterranean with the exception of Libya and the Albania, and the result has been that the core NICs have ended up very much as second-class citizens in the EC hierarchy of trading partners.

Admittedly, commercial cooperation agreements were signed with the most populous South Asian states (India, Sri Lanka, Pakistan and Bangladesh over 1974–6), but these deals offered little that the GSP did not do. It was not until the late 1970s and early 1980s that the EC turned its attention to the East Asians, signing a non-preferential trade pact with China in 1978, and an economic cooperation agreement with the ASEAN group in 1980.

The result of all this is that the Latin American and East Asian countries have generally been dealt with as run-of-the-mill LDCs, which have qualified for a GSP scheme that is progressively tougher on the more industrialized Third World countries. In fact, this has meant that the market access of the NICs to the EC has been on terms inferior to those covering the goods from almost all other countries, except for a handful of AICs and the Comecon bloc (Cable and Weston, 1979, p. 16) (see also, Golt, 1978; Meyer, 1978; de Miramon and Kleitz, 1978).

THE TURNING OF THE SCREW

Whatever the good intentions of the EC and its member states at the time the Six became the Nine, the Community was blown off course by the events of late 1973 and early 1974. The excessively fast growth of 1973 and the oil-price explosion of 1973–4 combined to produce an actual decline in the Nine's GDP in 1975, and there was no year between 1974 and 1979 when annual growth topped the average seen in the 1960s and early 1970s. In particular, France, the UK and Italy ran very heavy balance-of-payments deficits that were still significant in 1976. Almost inevitably, demands for protectionist measures grew, and leaders in the Community began to contemplate problems which they might have viewed more calmly if economic growth had been faster.

The NICs were most affected by the tightening of the terms of the Multi-Fibre Arrangement, and this time the EC very much led the way in demanding more restrictions on textile and clothing imports. In Chapter 3, Steve Woolcock goes into the politics of this decision, arguing that imports from the NICs were only moderately responsible for the heavy job destruction taking place in the textiles and clothing sector during the 1970s. Despite this, the NICs were widely seen as being a prime cause of the industry's crisis, and the tightening of controls on textile and clothing imports (first through bilateral deals, then through the 'reasonable departures' clause of the revised MFA) particularly hit the core NICs. In some product categories, the quotas given to Hong Kong, South Korea and Taiwan were actually cut back from levels established in previous years. In the most sensitive products, there was a further discrimination in that global ceilings were set for their import but within these ceilings, Hong Kong, Taiwan and South Korea were sometimes allowed no growth at all, while their poorer Third World competitors were given growth rates which would allow them to close their position on these leading NIC exporters (Cable, 1979, pp. 55–77; Shepherd, 1980b, pp. 90–5).

This tightening of controls on the leading NICs has been justified on developmental grounds, in that it supposedly permits the poorest LDCs to industrialize faster. Most development economists would counter by pointing out that this is achieved at the expense of countries which are still relatively underdeveloped by AIC standards, and that, anyway, should any of these poorest LDCs prove genuinely successful, then they will in turn run into the kind of tight trade restrictions now imposed on the leading NICs. Perhaps a more convincing explanation of what has been happening is that this tightening of controls on the NICs is part of the process whereby the EC has become convinced that such countries are too successful to justify preferential treatment any longer. So, just as the MFA was tightened against them, so was the GSP, when it was renewed in 1981.

The Japanese Analogy

The 1970s did not just see a rise in European concern about the NIC performance within textiles and clothing. Increasingly, the NICs were sucked into disputes in which Japan was the main problem for the EC. The Japanese entered the 1970s as a not particularly troublesome trading partner for the EC. Japan was, for instance, pricing itself out of the textile and clothing sector, where it had indeed been a problem in earlier decades. All the same, it was proving successful enough in newer exporting sectors to be attracting some Western criticism and, as a result, there was a small amount of self-restriction by Japanese exporters from mid-1972 (Hanabusa, 1979, pp. 7–11).

The 1973–4 oil crisis changed this situation fundamentally, by hitting Japan disproportionately hard, and thus encouraging its industrialists to step up their export drive in compensation. By late 1975, concern about Japanese competitiveness in automobiles and shipbuilding was becoming marked, and the Japanese agreed to the limitation of their steel exports to the EC. By December 1977, the EC position had so hardened that, after consultations with both the Japanese and US governments, it insisted on introducing import-control measures, linked to a minimum price regime. Japan was only one of the steel exporters hit by these measures, but there were other sectors such as automobiles where individual members of the EC felt sufficiently strongly either to impose restraints on Japanese auto imports unilaterally (Italy, France), or to come to a voluntary agreement with the Japanese automobile industry about the limitation of exports (UK).

As the 1970s progressed, some of the NICs began to be sucked into such trade disputes where the prime trading problem was seen to be Japan's export success. For instance, the European Community insisted on concluding bilateral agreements on iron and steel products with South Korea and Brazil, even though these were minor exporters compared with the others and despite the fact that their ability to export declined in 1978 and 1979 as their indigenous demand took all the steel they could produce. Again, although the EC has concentrated on controlling Japanese competition in televisions, individual member nations such as the UK, France and Italy have sought to control imports from NICs such as South Korea and Taiwan, while (in the British case at least) pressure has been building for VERs with the next generation of television exporters (primarily of black-and-white sets) such as Thailand. The process at work here seems to be that the NICs are seen to be potential 'super-exporters' along the Japanese lines, and that constraints on Japan's export performance will be nullified unless the first tier of NICs is brought under restraint as well. Some of this reflects a genuine awe of the competitiveness of the NICs. Some, though, reflects the suspicion that constrained Japanese companies will use these NICs as export-platforms to nullify VERs which are narrowly aimed at exports from Japan.

The State Traders

Another development of the 1970s was that the EC increasingly became involved with trading partners who played by a different set of rules, in that the state was their leading economic actor. The East Europeans are the prime examples of this new kind of non-traditional exporter.

In the early 1970s the EC was happy, for both political and economic reasons, to encourage trade liberalization between the two sides of Europe. This political impetus was reinforced by the economic self-interest of West European companies in sectors such as automobiles and chemicals, which encouraged compensation trading deals, whereby they built up East European industrial capacity on the understanding that at least part of their payment would be in the form of finished products. In an era of fast growth, these deals would probably not have posed too many problems, but the later years of the decade were anything but fast-growing. The result was that compensation-trading became a major issue, with voluntary restraint agreements being made with Romania (1977), and with the EC Commission deciding it should monitor such deals in the chemical sector (Kostecki, 1978; Marsh, 1980).

For the moment, the issue of what rules should govern trade between such wildly disparate economic systems is relatively ill-defined. However, the 1970s threw up another set of economies, those of the oil-producers, which look as though they will pose many of the same problems as do those of the East Europeans. In both cases, countries will enter technologically mature industries (such as steel, chemicals or automobiles) as much through government decree as through any workings of the market mechanism. Traditional anti-dumping mechanisms may well prove inadequate to counter the effects of irrational over-investment in such sectors. So the West Europeans, whose geographical location makes them particularly vulnerable to such state-led competition, may well find it necessary to invent institutions to play the role that the Euro-Arab dialogue was starting to do – that is, permit some discussion and negotiation about rational levels of investment in certain sectors before these investments are actually made.

THE TURN OF THE DECADE

Despite some increase in the EC's interventionist tendencies, and despite the second oil-price shock of 1979–80, the Community has still maintained some momentum in improving its commercial and political relations with various Third World and middle-ranking powers. For instance, the Lomé Convention was successfully renewed in 1980, with marginally improved conditions. However, its basic irrelevance for the NICs remains, and this irrelevance is strengthened by the fact that the EC has made it clear that it is not prepared to permit unconstrained growth in textile imports from the Lomé grouping, in spite of the Lomé Treaty provisions. Thus the MFA is seen to take precedence over Lomé.

In addition, the EC has continued its process of improving relations with the more independently minded centrally planned economies, with commercial cooperation agreements being signed with China (1978), Romania (1980) and Yugoslavia (1980). In East Asia, the Community filled one glaring gap by signing an economic pact with ASEAN (1980).

Finally, the EC's enlargement process continues roughly on course, involving countries such as Spain, Portugal and Greece, which under some definitions can be counted as marginal NICs. The significance of this is that each further stage of this enlargement process involves national economies which are increasingly competitive with, rather than complementary to, the economies of the core NICs. There is thus a real possibility that enlargement will increase the pressure for heightened barriers against the latter countries. Meanwhile, there has been a more negative side to recent West European trade diplomacy. For instance, Japan has very much remained the leading individual target of EC concern, as the bilateral trade balance has remained stubbornly in Japan's favour and continued to deteriorate in 1981. In the circumstances, both national governments and the EC Commission are deeply dissatisfied with what they see as a lack of adequate Japanese trade concessions to them. It is particularly significant that the relatively free-trading West Germans retreated in 1981 to a more protectionist position over both colour televisions and automobiles, in both cases getting a Japanese promise of restraint. The Japanese thus have a secure position in the demonology of Western Europe's trade politics, and this can only bode ill for those NICs which are trying, in their turn, to establish themselves in world markets.

In practical terms, the EC's renewal of its GSP scheme for the 1981–90 period was a further sign that the Community was toughening its position towards the leading NICs. In 1980, the EC offered concessions on imports from Brazil, Hong Kong and South Korea cumulatively worth $5.2 billion. The restructured scheme meant that the concessions in 1981 only covered trade worth $2.1 billion. (*The Economist*, 4 April 1981). In particular, the scheme has switched from using global ceilings and quotas to individual ceilings for each product and beneficiary country. In effect, this means that the NICs will be unable to take the lion's share of the tariff preferences on offer, as was the case under the old scheme.

At the time this chapter was revised (July 1981), the NICs were also wary of the EC position in the renegotiation of the MFA (see Chapter 3) and of the GATT safeguard provisions. It is this latter issue which is a particularly interesting indicator of the way EC thinking has been evolving on the NIC issue. The EC position in the Tokyo Round negotiations was that there should be a tightening of Article XIX of GATT which permits emergency action to limit imports. The EC, supported by the Scandinavians, has wanted to have this article amended to allow selective action against one or two suppliers, an amendment which would punch another major hole through the GATT principle of non-selectivity. The proposal was bitterly resisted by the LDCs within the Tokyo Round negotiations, but the EC remained firmly committed to it, with the result that consideration of this issue was permitted to continue after the rest of the Tokyo Round package had been agreed. (It would appear that the main pressure for this amendment came from the UK and France, with important support from the industry and foreign-policy directorates of the EC Commission.)

THE FUNDAMENTAL EC CONCERNS

It is possible to identify some common themes in these various actions: the tightening of the GSP scheme; the tough negotiating stances on the MFA and selective safeguards; and the various actions against Japan.

First, there has been a declining faith in the beneficial workings of the multilateral, free-trading model of the world economy. For instance, the growing concern with bilateral trade balances (as between Japan and the EC) fails to account for the relative resource endowments of different regions (whereby energy-poor Japan will inevitably tend to run surpluses in manufactured trade with less energy-import-dependent economies such as those of Western Europe). The trend, also, has been for European policy-makers to be increasingly concerned with the health of individual industrial sectors. This has inevitably played into the hands of lobbyists from troubled industries with particularly large labour forces, of which the textile and clothing industries are the examples *par excellence*.

On top of this is the belief that much of the competition from Japan and the NICs is damagingly unfair. It is widely held that it is governments which are master-minding the success of these economies, and that some combination of the exploitation of cheap-wage labour forces, pervasive subsidies and heavy use of tariff and non-tariff barriers gives these countries an unfair advantage in those industries which they choose to enter. This has given rise to the concept of the 'laser-like' competition from the NICs, which can only be blunted by an increased resort to some kind of safeguard action. The argument continues that the existing GATT safeguard provisions are inadequate, in that all suppliers have to be hit, when the problem will increasingly stem from ill-advised over-investment by a handful of over-exuberant exporting nations. Hence, the EC's concern with getting GATT acceptance of selective safeguards.

The decision to limit the benefits from the GSP scheme available to the NICs reflects a further strand in European thinking: the belief that the leading Third World exporters should start 'graduating', that is, that they should increasingly lose the preferential treatment available to them as LDCs, and should increasingly shoulder the burdens of being just another set of actors in the world's trading arena. The emphasis more and more is on the obligations of the NICs, rather than on their rights.

FINAL OBSERVATIONS

Some of these EC concerns are legitimate. State-led economies do pose new problems, with which trade institutions like GATT have hitherto been only marginally involved. Again, there is an undoubted quickening of the speed with which new challengers to the established competitive status quo emerge within key industries. There is also some justice in the European claim that democratic AICs have to temper straight economic rationality with wider social concerns rather more than is the case for (often authoritarian) NICs. In particular, the West European policy-makers and industrialists are lumbered with a residue of conflicting national loyalties, which are still strong enough significantly to hamper the region's adjustment to industrial challenges from outside it.

At the same time, the EC position has serious weaknesses. Within textiles and clothing, for instance, the EC rhetoric has stressed the need to hold back NIC exporters in the interests of poorer LDCs. EC action through the MFA, though, has primarily benefited other AIC exporters. In particular, the relative inability of the EC to control fast-rising fibres imports from the USA, in the early 1980s, vividly contrasts with its ability to impose most of its wishes on LDC exporters. The impression this leaves is that it is the diplomatic weakness of LDC exporters which singles them out for EC attention, as much as any objective measurement of their actual contribution to the woes of this particular European problem industry. Again, there are inconsistencies in the EC's concern with the need for NICs to 'graduate'. It is perfectly legitimate to argue that the NICs should be accepting greater obligations, but it then becomes much less respectable to continue to single out genuinely open NIC economies, such as those of Singapore and Hong Kong, for relatively hostile treatment. The EC is certainly in this anomalous position of partially graduating some leading NICs from its GSP scheme, while simultaneously (both in Brussels and leading EC national capitals) tightening controls on imports from such countries. In other words, the EC actions suggest that graduation imposes obligations on the NICs, without necessarily increasing obligations on the EC.

It is precisely this EC unwillingness to accept conditions on its resort to selective protection which is the sticking-point for NICs in both the MFA and selective safeguard negotiations (which continued as this book went to press). One would not deny that the EC has some special adjustment problems, nor that its patchwork of ex-colonial and regional obligations make commercial policy particularly sensitive for it. None the less, its ability to restrict access to its markets is a powerful weapon, which should be used sparingly. The EC and its members have an obligation to ask whether this weapon is not being aimed selectively at a group of countries, the NICs, primarily because their diplomatic weakness makes them a convenient scapegoat. Or do the NICs really pose such an insuperable range of new problems that these cannot be settled with the mechanisms which are adequate for trade disputes with other advanced industrialized countries?

9

North America and the NICs

Neil McMullen

INTRODUCTION: US PERSPECTIVES ON INTERNATIONAL TRADE POLICY

During the three and a half decades of the post-war era, trade policy in the USA has been marked by a continuing tension. On the one hand, the goal of freer world-wide economic exchange has dominated policy, while on the other, the need to compromise in specific cases has been ever-present. So as to maintain political support for the goal of freer, expanding international trade, particular industries, regions and interest groups within the USA have had to be appeased with protectionist concessions. The most notable example is the continuing protection the US textile and apparel industry has received over the years. Footwear is another industry that has a history of being protected. In addition, there have been temporary concessions made to other industries, including steel, television manufacture and, most recently, automobiles.

The movement towards freer trade through reduced tariffs was encouraged by several key factors. Protectionism had been given a bad name by its association with the high unemployment levels of the 1930s, and there was widespread willingness to try new approaches to solving economic problems in the aftermath of the Second World War. A freer trade policy was in line with the US belief in the efficacy of markets and the domestic economic policies being adapted. US policy-makers avoided planning and industrial policy-making which would determine the growth and profitability of specific sectors. In addition, as a part of its foreign policy, the USA was committed to the reconstruction of its allies and former adversaries, as well as the development of the poorer countries in Asia, Africa and Latin America. Free trade was part of a programme which would provide increased market opportunities, economic prosperity and ultimately peace and security in the world. The USA tended to discourage preferential marketing arrangements to promote reconstruction and development, relying instead on free trade coupled with capital and technology flows to provide the basis for rapid economic recovery and growth.

While having expanding trade as its dominant international economic goal, the USA faced several constraints on the movement towards lower tariffs. The whole economy benefited as trade expanded but adjustment burdens and new export opportunities were not evenly distributed among industries, labour groups and regions. Structural adjustments tended to be more difficult for workers in mature sectors of the economy, where demand grew more slowly than in the rest of industry. During the 1950s and 1960s the underlying constraint on US trade policy was 'no increase in unemployment'. In any case rapid domestic growth of output, coupled with slow growth in the labour force, led to historically low levels of unemployment in the USA through the 1960s. By the early 1970s the inevitability of adjustment was accepted, at least implicity, and 'adjustment assistance' for trade-related unemployment was legislated (Morici and Megna, 1981, p. 8). Thus, only in the last decade or so has the United States faced a conflict between the international goal of freer world-wide trade and the domestic goal of reducing unemployment.

This tension within US trade policy has mainly revealed itself in the way tariff cuts have taken place. The average tariff on dutiable imports fell from over 50 per cent in the 1930s to 12·8 per cent in 1952. Then the pace slackened as it was feared that further cuts would injure domestic industries. By 1962 the average tariff rate was still 12·3 per cent. The Trade Expansion Act of 1962 permitted the subsequent Kennedy Round of tariff cuts, and this was followed by the Tokyo Round of cuts of the early 1980s. By 1980 tariffs on average were no longer important barriers to trade, having fallen from 8·7 per cent in 1966 to 5·6 per cent in 1976 owing to the Kennedy Round cuts. The Tokyo Round is expected to cut average tariffs to 4 per cent by 1988. However, the US policy of reducing tariffs, while avoiding the danger of injury to domestic industry and maintaining the necessary political support for the broad goal of freer trade, has resulted in a tariff structure that skews protection to labour-intensive, usually unionized, industries. These industries are often those most vulnerable to import competition from the NICs, so that, despite low average US tariffs, the NICs do face modest tariff barriers to entering the American market. The resulting tariff structure is presented in Table 9.1, showing the average tariffs for all imports in seventeen major industries in 1966, 1976 and the 1980s. The industries are ranked according to value added per employee, and it is obvious that tariff protection is concentrated in leather, textile and apparel products, the industries with the lowest value added per employee. (These industries are also protected by quantitative restrictions, which are discussed in the next two sections.)

This pattern of tariff protection prevails generally in all of the AICs and has the effect of discriminating against exporters of textile, apparel and leather products – that is, the NICs. In the USA, the intent of the policy is not to discriminate against any particular group of countries, but to minimize damage to domestic employment so as to maintain a solid political majority in favour of the general movement towards freer trade. It may be that tariffs and quotas in these sectors provide a maximum of employment and political support for a minimum of tariff distortions and trade diversion. However, the bulk of the cost is paid by the NICs and the

Table 9.1   *Average* Ad Valorem *US Tariffs by Major SIC Group: 1966, 1976 and Estimated Post-Tokyo Round*

Major manufacturing sector (SIC)	Value added per employee (000$)	1966 %	1967 %	Estimated post-Tokyo Round %
Chemicals and allied products (28)	60·39	12·2	5·2	3·3
Paper and allied products (26)	33·51	0·5	0·5	0·2
Transportation equipment (37)	33·38	5·0	1·8	1·4
Instruments and related products (38)	31·63	24·3	9·6	4·9
Primary metal products (33)	30·91	4·9	3·8	2·4
Machinery, except electrical (35)	29·27	8·3	4·4	2·9
Stone, clay and glass products (32)	28·00	21·0	10·8	7·7
Fabricated metal products (34)	26·60	12·4	5·7	3·7
Electric and electronic equipment (36)	26·45	11·6	3·7	2·5
Printing and publishing (27)	25·46	4·1	1·5	0·9
Rubber and miscellaneous plastic products (30)	25·42	14·1	9·0	4·9
Miscellaneous manufactured products (39)	21·52	18·8	8·7	4·9
Lumber and wood products (24)	21·40	5·8	3·6	1·7
Furniture and fixtures (25)	17·32	10·9	4·4	2·2
Textile mill products (22)	16·55	16·5	19·4	12·4
Leather products (31)	14·40	14·5	10·2	9·3
Apparel and other textile products (23)	13·27	22·7	24·5	20·0

Source: Morici and Megna, 1981, p. 10.

other developing countries which otherwise would be able to export more of these products to the USA.

Another trend of recent years which has intensified the international competition facing US labour-intensive manufacturing is the expansion of foreign-exchange earnings from agriculture, services and high technology manufactures. Also as an indirect result of the rise in world energy prices, oil-importing nations such as Japan and Brazil have experienced greater incentives to become more specialized and more export-oriented in sectors where they have a comparative advantage. Table 9.2 indicates the net changes in the balance of trade within major sectors for seven countries between 1973 and 1978. All of the countries included in this table faced higher petroleum bills, with the UK and Canada having the smallest increases in proportion to total output: However, the seven countries paid for their higher-cost petroleum in a variety of ways. Japan, and to a lesser extent Germany, moved strongly to increase exports of manufactured goods and, overall, their current accounts both improved for a time. The USA responded in a quite different way, with agriculture, services and the current account (that is, borrowings) paying for higher-cost petroleum. Brazil, dealing with a smaller economy, countered a sharp deterioration felt in both petroleum and services (largely debt-interest costs) with increased exports of agricultural and manufactured goods, along with new borrowings.

Table 9.2 *Net Change in Current Account Balances, 1973–8 (billion US$)*[1]

Item	Japan	South Korea	Brazil	USA	UK	Canada	West Germany
Merchandise trade							
Petroleum	−15·2	−2·2	−3·7	−30·4	−1·9	−2·3	−14·5
Food and agriculture	−5·2	+0·3	+2·3	+5·2	−3·8	−0·1	−4·1
Other raw materials	−2·6	−2·5	−1·6	+1·3	−1·1	+1·8	+7·3
Manufacturing goods	+53·8	+3·0	+1·6	−3·5	+4·9	−4·6	+23·9
Other goods	−11·3	0	+0·1	−8·5	+6·8	+5·8	−3·3
Net trade balance	+19·6	−1·3	−1·2	−35·9	+5·0	+0·6	+9·1
Net services	−3·9	−0·1	−3·5	17·6	+4·9	−5·0	−4·0
Net transfers	−0·4	+0·3	0	+0·2	−3·4	−0·2	−3·1
Net current account	+15·3	−0·9	−4·7	−18·0	+6·5	−4·6	+2·0

[1] Rounded figures.
Sources: EIU, 1974, 1979; Europa, 1975, 1980.

The patterns shown in the table indicate that some of the pressures on US manufacturing emanated indirectly from world-wide restructuring due to higher energy prices. These pressures in turn led to increased demands within the USA for the protection of those industries which Japan, the NICs, and other oil importers were aiming to use for increased exports – notably textiles, apparel, autos, steel and leather products. Therefore, policies and events which act to reduce the demand for OPEC oil will also act to reduce the enormous pressures on oil-importing countries in Europe, Asia and Latin America to increase manufactured exports, and should thus act to reduce protectionist pressure on the western economies.

It must also be recognized that the US goal of freer world-wide trade combined with the strongly legalistic nature of the US international economic policy-making system has meant that the USA is less favourably disposed toward *ad hoc*, selective trade arrangements than, for example, the EC countries. US international economic perspectives have been global and there has been a general reluctance to strike special deals with individual countries, such as Mexico, because of the wider implications for US policy towards other nations. For instance the growth of 'in bond' industries along the US–Mexico border under Tariff Provisions 806.30 and 807.00 has been due to Mexico's proximity to the US market, not the law itself; many other countries take advantage of these provisions, and nearly all countries are eligible. Further, the legalistic nature of US trade policy involves the intensive, periodic involvement of Congress, with unpredictable and sometimes uncontrollable results. This produces legislative guidelines which are then applied fairly mechanically by the bureaucracy. In most other countries the legislating of trade policy is more predictable and the discretion of the bureaucracy in implementing trade policy is much broader (Nelson, 1981, p. 18). These systemic tendencies combined with greater US belief in the efficacy of market solutions have made the USA less inclined towards special formal arrangements, along the lines of the GSP, for example. The US goal is to move towards freer trade on as broad a front as is politically sustainable, with the minimum number of special arrangements requiring new legislative action or raising market distortions.

In the remainder of this chapter these threads will be woven together by reviewing specific actions that demonstrate US trade policy towards the NICs. The historical account will focus on the exceptions to the general movement towards more open markets, namely, the MFA, restraints on footwear imports, orderly marketing agreements (OMAS) and voluntary export restraints (VERs) in televisions, steel and autos, and the steel trigger-price mechanism. To maintain overall perspective, the reader should keep in mind that these are exceptions to a broad general trend towards freer trade and greater market opportunities for the NICs. Finally, the prospects for the 1980s are not bleak. The general thrust of US trade policy is more market-oriented than ever, and even in terms of specifics, the refusal in mid-1981 to raise the steel trigger price and the vagueness of auto export restraints on Japan give rise to optimism about continuing NIC access to the US market. Ultimately, however, US trade policy is hostage to the success of domestic economic policy, the level of US unemployment, and the ability of US policy-makers to maintain support for the relatively open international system which we now enjoy.

TEXTILES AND APPAREL

Throughout the post-war era, textiles and apparel have been the most protected industrial sector in the United States. In fact, protection in this sector was very high in the 1920s and, in the 1930s, the USA negotiated an export-restraint agreement with Japan. In the 1940s and 1950s the USA did not push for more openness in this market and, since neither did the European parties to GATT, nothing happened. There are several reasons why the USA did not push for freer trade in textiles and apparel, even in the 1950s when there was a low level of external threat to the industry (see Keesing and Wolf, 1980). One is the history of high protection, which extended back to the New Deal era. Another reason is the high level of employment in this sector, not just in the USA, but throughout the developed world. As late as 1963, 17 per cent of all employment in the industrial countries was in clothing and textiles (Keesing and Wolf, 1980, p. 14). Many felt that the survival of the industry was not likely without some protection. The US textile industry was centred in two key areas of support for congressional Democrats: the north-east and the south. Combine this with the normal protectionist inclinations of the west and mid-west, and it is not surprising that textiles and clothing came in for special treatment in trade policy.

The US clothing and textile industry is internally very competitive, with many firms, strong unions and an active industry/trade association. During the late 1950s before quotas on Japanese textiles were implemented, US mills faced higher prices for cotton owing to agricultural price supports. Thus it was argued that quotas were needed to offset this cost disadvantage. Japan did not protest, because plans to switch their focus of their production to ships, steel and motor vehicles were already being implemented. At about the same time, voluntary export restraints were negotiated between the UK and Hong Kong, India and Pakistan. The USA tried to put pressure on Hong Kong to restrain exports, but was unsuccessful. Hong Kong thus emerged as the beneficiary of Japan's restraint, more than doubling clothing and textile exports to the USA between 1958 and 1960 (Keesing and Wolf, 1980, p. 15).

In November 1959 the USA raised the issue of market disruption caused by surges in imports from developing countries and, in 1961, having just been elected by the southern and north-eastern states, President Kennedy moved to assist the textile industry by preventing market disruptions. The result was the Long-Term Arrangement regarding international trade in cotton textiles (LTA), which was part of the compromise paving the way for the Trade Expansion Act of 1962 and the ensuing Kennedy Round of tariff cuts. The LTA was preventive and probably more political than economic in its motivation. Market disruption in the LTA implied rapid penetration of markets by particular exporters, substantially lower prices, and potentially serious injury to domestic producers. The result was not unequivocally restrictive, but rather tried to balance the need for expanding markets for exporters against the need for market stability for importers. Because market penetration implied a specific source country, the effect of the LTA was to expand the number of exporters.

The USA moved quickly under the aegis of the LTA. By 1963 restrictions against imports of cotton textile goods from seventeen countries had been set up and by 1971 some thirty-seven countries were limited (Keesing and Wolf, 1980, p. 39). Other developed nations followed suit, effectively limiting cotton-textile exports. However, there was an explosion of imports of garments made of man-made fibres from developing countries to the developed countries between 1962 and 1973. A compound annual growth rate of almost 30 per cent expanded the value of apparel imports from $240 million in 1962 to $3,800 million in 1973. Expansion was centred in three countries, with Hong Kong, South Korea and Taiwan accounting for fully 75 per cent of the 1973 total. However, this surge of non-cotton exports raised developing-country clothing to only 4 per cent of apparent US consumption in 1973 (calculated from Keesing and Wolf, 1980, pp. 34–5).

In 1971 the USA began to react to the surge in imports of garments made from man-made fibres and by 1973, at its insistence, negotiations on a new agreement were under way. These resulted in the Multi-Fibre Arrangement (MFA). By 1980, the United States had made agreements with twenty-two countries explicitly to limit apparel and textile imports and had stand-by agreements with ten others, if problems were to arise. These countries accounted for nearly 80 per cent of all garment and textile imports into the USA (Morici and Megna, 1981, p. 35).

The MFA formally allowed a growth of imports at 'not less than 6 per cent', except in very unusual cases. In fact, during the 1970s, textile imports grew by 2·9 per cent annually, while consumption rose at a 2·4 per cent rate. Apparel imports grew by 8·0 per cent, exceeding the MFA minimum, while US consumption rose 2·6 per cent (*US Industrial Outlook*, various issues). The MFA agreement has not been a particularly large factor in protecting the US synthetic-fibre industry; since 1974 the USA has exported textiles following a dramatic improvement in productivity based on new technologies and on low-cost petroleum and petrochemical feedstocks. It is in apparel that the MFA has an impact on NIC exports to the USA. Estimates of the impact of the MFA indicate that in 1979 apparel imports into the USA were about half what they would have been without the MFA in effect after 1973 (Morici and Megna, 1981, p. 38). The additional $3·5 billion, or 10 per cent of total US apparel sales, would have been almost entirely from the NICs. Thus, although the MFA allows modest growth of NIC access to the US market for apparel, there is a substantial diversion of trade from NIC producers. Otherwise, the MFA has worked roughly as expected in the USA. Imports of clothing have continued to grow, but employment patterns in the apparel industry seemed to have held up quite well in the 1980–1 growth recession. Steel, autos and housing have been hard hit as compared with textiles and apparel.

However much the MFA is a violation of the principles of the international trading system, the events of recent years have demonstrated that it is an enduring fact of life. The Tokyo Round negotiations pointedly avoided modifications to the MFA; and, in the USA, at least, acceptance of the MFA was an implicit quid pro quo for labour support of the tariff reductions and new non-tariff-barrier codes. The MFA is a singular example of the American tendency to make protectionist concessions to a key domestic industry, so as to get legislative support to proceed with broad tariff reductions and codes limited non-tariff barriers. The MFA is also an example of the universal tendency in developed countries to provide greater protection for industries with the lowest value added per worker. The result is a sizeable reduction in possible NIC exports to the USA. On the plus side, the MFA is a strong incentive for the more able NICs to move quickly out of textiles and apparel into higher-value-added sectors which are not as well protected. Further, the MFA is set up so as to give new textile and apparel exporters a foothold in North American and European markets before the MFA restricts them. The result is to spread the knowledge and skills which go with the experience of exporting to developed markets.

QUANTITATIVE IMPORT RESTRICTIONS

Periodically the USA has resorted to temporary restrictions on imports.

These have principally been in the form of OMAs and VERs. Their effect has fallen on a select range of products: footwear, televisions, steel and, most recently, automobiles. These temporary restrictions are clearly motivated by all of the underlying strands of US trade policy. They should be seen as specific and temporary concessions aimed at maintaining political support for a more general movement towards lower tariffs and reduced non-tariff barriers to trade. Problems of high unemployment are involved, recently coupled with high payments for adjustment assistance in the case of automobiles. Footwear is an industry with low value added per worker, but steel, televisions and autos are not. These are, however, unionized sectors and thus have a good deal of political leverage in defending their positions and gaining, at least, temporary concessions. In addition OMAs and VERs can be arranged without going to Congress for new legislation and, because they are temporary, their market distorting effects can be reduced or terminated over time. Given the influences working on US trade policy and the characteristics of OMAs and VERs, it is not surprising that in recent years these types of restrictions have been the principal means used by the USA to limit imports that disrupt domestic markets or threaten harm to domestic producers.

Since 1975 the United States has used OMAs and VERs to protect non-rubber footwear, colour televisions, speciality steel, and automobiles, in addition to textile and apparel producers. These agreements are summarized in Table 9.3, which demonstrates that the countries chiefly effected are Japan, Hong Kong, South Korea and Taiwan. Only in the case of steel are the NICs outside the impact of the restrictions. The basis for this seeming targeting of the leading NICs – along with Japan – is not a conscious policy, but rather stems from the fact that NIC exports tend to threaten US industries which are able to win protectionist concessions from US international economic-policy-makers. Interestingly, the industries usually do not get the anticipated benefits of the OMAs, as alternative unrestricted exporters quickly spring up to supply the relatively permeable US market.

The non-rubber footwear industry (along with textiles and apparel) is typical of the industries that are sensitive in all the developed countries to competition from the NICs. It is a labour-intensive, relatively highly unionized and low-value-added per-worker industry. From 1971 to 1976, US production of footwear fell by over 20 per cent, while the import share of the US market (measured in pairs of shoes) grew from one-third to about a half. Taiwan led the import surge, capturing one-quarter of the US market in 1976, and the industry, faced with continuing plant closures and declining employment, petitioned for a safeguard investigation in September 1976. This was withdrawn after OMAs negotiated with Taiwan and South Korea became effective on 28 June 1977. From a 1976 level of 156 and 44 million pairs, OMAs set the following limits on exports from Taiwan and South Korea to the USA:

	Year	*Million pairs*		*Year*	*Million pairs*
Taiwan	1977–8	122	*South Korea*	1977–8	33·0
	1978–9	125		1978–9	36·5
	1979–80	128		1979–80	37·5
	1980–1	131		1980–1	38·0

The OMAs curtailed import volumes from Taiwan and South Korea by 51 million pairs of shoes, but the domestic industry did not benefit as fully as anticipated. Imports from other producers – notably Italy, Brazil, Hong Kong, the Philippines, Mexico and Singapore – increased by 85 million pairs. South Korean producers shifted the location of production to Hong Kong and Singapore, successfully evading the OMA. Further, Taiwan and South Korea moved up-market and produced higher-priced shoes in the process of filling their quotas. Thus while volume declined 25 per cent, the value of their exports rose 14 per cent. The response demonstrates the creativeness of NIC and other exporters, as well as the genuine openness of the US economy. The effect of the OMA was threefold: it did cushion the domestic industry somewhat; it encouraged the entry of new producers; and, it forced South Korea and Taiwan to improve their product and aim for higher value added per unit exported. (This discussion draws heavily on the work of Morici and Megna, 1981.)

Table 9.3　*US Quantitative Restrictions of Industrial Imports, 1975–81*

				Total US imports	
Product	*Dates*	*Type of restriction*	*Affected countries*	*Year*	*Million $*
Non-rubber	28.VI.1977 to	OMAS	Taiwan	1976	1,092·6
footware	30.VI.1981		South Korea	1977	1,177·4
Colour	1.VII.1977 to	OMAS	Japan	1976	967·5
televisions	30.VI.1980		Taiwan	1977	973·5
	(Japan)		South Korea	1978	1,334·9
	1.II.1979 to			1979	1,182·3
	30.VI.1982				
	(Taiwan and				
	South Korea)				
Speciality	VI.1976 to	OMAS	Japan	1975	194·6
steel	13.II.1980	(Japan)	EC	1976	213·2
		Quotas	Sweden	1977	210·7
		(others)	Canada and	1978	250·8
			others		
Textiles	1973–81	MFA	Hong Kong	1976	5,311·7
and apparel		allows	Japan	1977	5,890·3
		bilateral	South Korea		
		agreements	Taiwan and		
			others		
Automobiles	1981	OMAS	Japan	1977	10,920
				1978	13,645
				1979	13,780

Source: Morici and Megna, 1981, p. 23.

In the case of colour televisions, the outcome was somewhat different. Production shifted away from Japan as a result of an OMA beginning in July 1977. As with shoes, new producing countries entered the market with, exports from Taiwan and South Korea rising sharply, but, more important, a total of four Japanese companies set up production facilities, and three others expanded existing operations, in the USA. Some of this shift was due to the OMA, but some of it would have occurred anyway. The quotas for complete Japanese colour receivers were not filled at any time between 1977 and 1980. The Japanese shifted final assembly to the USA and subcomponent assembly to other countries. The television OMA with Japan is an apparent success in terms of keeping jobs in the USA, but it can be argued that much of the movement of final assembly operations to the USA would have occurred even in the absence of the OMA.

Steel is a sector that has a long history of protection in the USA, as well as in other AICs. Although speciality steel accounts for only about 1 per cent of the value of US steel production, relief was requested and an OMA was negotiated when the sector's utilization rates fell to 48 per cent in 1975. Although principally aimed at Japan, a number of other producers were included, none of them NICs. More recently, when the US steel industry petitioned for relief from dumping by Japanese and other producers, the response was not an OMA, but the steel trigger-price mechanism (TPM). This is a more constructive trade policy concession than OMAs. The TPM is not protectionist, if it is applied correctly, and indications are that this continues to be the intention of the US administration. Initiated in 1977, the TPM is an administrative arrangement based on powers granted in the US Anti-dumping Act. The prices for various products used in the TPM are based on the production costs of the most efficient world producer (judged to be Japan), a profit mark-up of 8 per cent, plus the freight insurance and interest costs required to sell on the three coasts and in the middle-west region of the USA. Prices are reviewed quarterly and these quarterly adjustments have led to recurring conflicts between the administration and some of the firms.

In March 1980 the trigger price was not raised, and US Steel Corporation countered with a number of suits against EC steel firms (which were, strictly speaking, dumping, though not in violation of the TPM rules). Until the 1980 slide in demand, the TPM had helped reduce imports and increase profit margins domestically. The share of the market to imports fell from 20 per cent to 13 per cent between 1977 and 1979, while the domestic return on sales rose from 0·06 per cent to 3·6 per cent (*The Economist*, 29 March 1980, p. 106). However, in early 1980, imports shot up above 18 per cent, as the EC firms, facing slow domestic sales, moved to expand exports to the USA. In the autumn of 1980, a compromise was worked out which raised the TPM by 12 per cent, bound the US administration to scrutinize imports when they get above 15·2 per cent of the market, improved steel-industry depreciation allowances, reduced pollution constraints, and provided benefits for trade-displaced steel workers (*The Economist*, 4 October 1980, pp. 70–1).

Even with this boost, the American steel industry will have a hard time keeping pace with the most efficient international producers, especially the Japanese. Employment in the steel sector fell to 360,000 in August 1980 and has since recovered to only 400,000, as compared with 454,000 in 1979 (*Survey of Current Business*). At best the US industry will have 50 per cent of its capacity based on the efficient continuous-cast process by 1988, while in Japan 90 per cent of capacity will be continuous-cast by 1984, ('Business brief', *The Economist*, 14 October 1980).

From 1975 to 1981, the steel industry has been the most active and aggressive lobbyist in the US trade-policy arena. Therefore, it is worth looking at the steel case closely, even though it does not directly involve the interests of the NICs. It continues to indicate the commitment of US international economic policy-makers to make concessions when necessary to maintain support for the wider goals of freer trade. More important, it indicates a commitment to making concessions which have a minimum distortion on markets. The TPM introduces much less distortion to domestic and world markets than OMAs, and may be the preferred mechanism for avoiding dumping and reducing market disruptions in the 1980s. The August 1981 decision by the US administration to allow only a 1 to 2 per cent price rise (owing to higher interest costs) indicates a continuing determination to avoid protectionist policies.

The 1981 auto agreement points in the same direction. The export restraints agreed to by the Japanese are not likely to offer real or lasting protection to US producers. The limits agreed to for Japanese export volumes are not particularly constraining when one considers the overall weak level of demand in the US auto market, increased competition from new and smaller US-produced autos, and Japan's plan to move up-market and sell fewer, but more expensive, automobiles. As with the quotas discussed above on non-rubber footwear, reduced export volume does not necessarily lead to reduced export earnings.

CURRENT TRADE ISSUES AND THE NICs

With the conclusion of the Tokyo Round negotiations in 1979 and the subsequent widespread acceptance of most of the resulting agreements and codes by the AICs, US trade policy enters a new era. The six post-war series of formal trade negotiations, culminating in the Tokyo Round agreements, have reduced nominal tariffs to a level of insignificance for the bulk of the industrialized nations. Average tariffs are now below 5 per cent for all the major industrialized countries, except Canada. Further tariff reductions are possible and may be highly desirable in specific cases, but tariffs are no longer an important barrier to exports from developing countries.

While tariffs have to a large degree been removed as a major obstacle to international trade, to the benefit of both developed and developing nations, important barriers still remain, and the number of current trade-policy problems continues to be quite ample. These include the traditional non-tariff barriers, such as import licensing, customs valuation, technical standards, public procurement and export subsidies. In addition there are 'industrial policies', performance requirements, selective safeguards, and issues relating to NIC graduation into the ranks of the developed countries. In the remainder of this section the US positions on these issues will be discussed as they effect the NICs.

It is becoming widely recognized that the Tokyo Round may well have ended the era of formal rounds of negotiations over across-the-board tariff reductions. The new era will be more concerned with non-tariff barriers to trade, and will probably be marked by continuing negotiations dealing with specific trade-distorting practices. Recognizing this, the Tokyo Round negotiations established codes of conduct governing a range of non-tariff barriers to trade. Both individually and collectively, these codes are of importance to the NICs.

The effectiveness of the codes will be determined by the degree to which they are supported by the ratification of implementing legislation by signatory countries, and by the elaboration and application of the codes in continuous negotiations to form a body of precedents established on a case-by-case basis. In this process, the dispute settlement procedures for each code will be crucial. From the standpoint of the NICs it is essential that they be well represented on the Committee of Signatories for each code, for only through NIC participation in the process is there any chance that NIC interests will be served over time. As of early 1981 most of the leading NICs had signed one or more of the codes (see Table 9.4); however, very few other LDCs have signed any codes. The vagueness of the language in many areas has moved the rule-making power to the case-by-case decision-making process. If the LDCs are to participate in this process and legally claim other code benefits, they must sign the codes.

The codes establish a pattern of 'differential and more favourable treatment' of the NICs and the other developing countries. At the urging of Brazil, the 'Framework Group' was established to develop a legal basis to give, continuing preferential treatment to developing countries, particularly where trade measures needed for balance-of-payments stabilization and safeguard actions essential for development purposes are at issue. Reciprocity is specifically waived with regard to the developing countries when such concessions are inconsistent with their trade, financial and development needs. Manifestations of differential and favourable treatment of the NICs and other developing countries are readily evident in each of the codes. Perhaps the most important is in the Code on Subsidies and Countervailing Duties, where export subsidies are permitted as policies of developing countries and injury must be shown before countervailing actions can be taken. This is an important advantage for Brazil and other NICs which utilize export incentives as a part of their development strategy, particularly in that the USA is now required to show injury before taking countervailing action. The USA interprets this to apply only to exports from countries which have signed the code; injury need not be found for countervailing duties to be applied against export subsidies by non-signatories of the code. Thus developing countries which do not sign

Table 9.4   *Signatories to the GATT Codes for Major Non-Tariff Barriers (as of 2 March 1981)*[1]

Group/country	Subsidies and countervailing duties	Anti-dumping	Customs valuation	Government procurement	Technical standards	Import licensing
Developed countries						
USA	×	×	×	×	×	×
UK	×[2]	×[2]	×[3]	×[3]	×	×[2]
Canada	×	×	×[4]	×	×	×
EC	×	×	×	×	×	×
Japan	×	×	×	×	×	×
NICs						
South Korea	×		×		×	
Taiwan						
Singapore			×	×		
Hong Kong						
India	×	×	×			×
Mexico						
Brazil	×	×			×	
Argentina			×		×	×

[1] The six Codes covered here are those discussed in the text.
[2] Accepted by the UK with respect to Territories.
[3] Accepted by UK with respect to Hong Kong.
[4] Accepted by Canada with reservations.
Source: From GATT information supplied by the US Trade Representative's office.

the Code on Subsidies and Countervailing Duties will not be able to participate in the dispute resolution process, and may be countervailed against by the USA without injury being shown. Thus, it is the US position that subscription to the codes is intimately bound up with taking full advantage of the 'differential and favourable treatment' offered.

Industrial policies are much farther advanced in Europe than in North America. These policies will probably be among the first attacked as conflicting with the Code on Subsidies and Countervailing Duties. The interests of the NICs and other developing countries should incline them towards a strict interpretation of allowable domestic subsidies in the AICs when disputes concerning industrial policies are referred to the Committee of Signatories. Strict application of the code will be necessary just to maintain the current degree of NIC access to developed-country markets. When industrial policies are allowed to become primarily protectionist, rather than primarily adjustment-oriented, then market access will diminish for all trading nations, and the NICs – with their economic growth so heavily dependent on trade – will suffer disproportionately. Because of the nature of the Code on Subsidies and Countervailing Duties, the participatory role the NICs can give themselves by signing the code, and the clear interest they have in reducing the protectionist aspects of industrial policies in the developed countries, it is the hope of the USA that the NICs will become more of a force for trade liberalization during the next few years.

In addition to the major issues of non-tariff barriers and industrial policies, which will have important effects on the NICs in the 1980s, there is the selective-safeguard problem, which emerged from the Tokyo Round negotiations. The selective-safeguard issue is concerned with Article XIX of GATT, which permits emergency action to offset a sudden surge in imports, of a specific product, which causes or threatens serious injury to a domestic industry. The debate is principally between the EC and the Scandinavian countries, on one side, and the developing countries on the other. The Europeans want a Code of Emergency Action that would permit selective action against one or a few countries when warranted by their market-disrupting export activities. This clearly departs from the traditional most-favoured-nation (MFN) treatment, which has been the cornerstone of the world trade system. The unresolved disagreements concern: the need for prior international approval as the basis for taking selective action (that is, the question of how to determine the source and extent of a market disruption); the permissible duration of the selective action; the level to which imports can be reduced; and the relationship of the expanding network of OMAs, which are *de facto* selective emergency actions, to Article XIX.

Two points have emerged from the debate. First, it is quite obvious that amending the existing safeguard clause could seriously harm the NICs. Hence, it was left to the EC and a group of negotiators from the NICs and other developing countries to see if some compromise could be reached. Second, in seeking to amend the GATT safeguard provisions, the EC was unwilling to concede that the importers taking selective action should be subject to scrutiny which would limit their freedom of action. This was not just a case of arguing that action might have to be taken before there was proper consultation with the affected exporters (the existing Article accepts that extreme speed is sometimes necessary); it was a more fundamental resistance to the idea that the developed countries might be forced to justify protectionist actions within GATT or some other multilateral forum.

In this debate, the Americans have been relatively passive. This is due to several of the underlying factors mentioned above which effect US trade policy. The EC position, if fully accepted, might well lead to a rash of specific protectionist measures which could begin to reverse the general trend of the international trading system towards greater openness. At the same time, repeated disruption of domestic markets could reduce internal US political support for freer trade. Thus, the Americans have chosen to remain out of the debate in the hope that the EC and the developing countries can work out a compromise. If this does not come to pass, then US involvement at a later stage may facilitate a solution. In any event, the more legalistic and less administrative US system of formulating trade policy makes the Americans reluctant to invest more discretionary power in their international economic bureaucracy. Even more to the point, the USA is not anxious to see the international economic bureaucracies of the EC countries endowed with more discretionary power.

The selective-safeguard issue is at the core of the emerging conflict between the NICs and the developed economies – particularly with the EC. Regarding the criteria for both the safeguards and selectivity, the divisions are severe, and it is hard to be optimistic about the outcome. In this environment the USA has chosen to stay out of the ring. The post-Tokyo Round negotiations on this code are moving into their second year with little to show in the way of progress. As long as world trade continues to grow and NIC exports continue to expand, this conflict may not be of vital importance. However, a general recession could lead to a marked increase in protectionism, directed towards the NICs in Asia and Latin America, and especially towards Japan.

While GATT recognizes the need for differential and favourable treatment for the NICs and other developing countries, it also holds that these countries should fully accept the GATT codes and provisions as the development of their economies proceeds. This has come to be known as the 'graduation' issue, and emphasizes the importance of countries subscribing to the obligations as well as the rights of GATT and various other organizations of the international economic community. This position is criticized by UNCTAD, which claims that graduation discriminates among developing countries. Within the American perspective, this fear is unjustified, particularly with regard to GATT, where NICs are asked to participate more fully once their economic progress warrants it, but without their being required to make any commitments as to how or when this shift in status will happen. Indeed, there are numerous gradations of increasing participation in the various codes and committees of GATT, so the graduation process need not be an abrupt one. The first stage might involve a removal of trade barriers, or be the establishment of preferences by the NICs for the LDCs. These could be managed without the developed countries getting involved.

The NICs accepted the graduation principle in the Tokyo Round 'Framework Agreement', which is the legal basis for 'differential and favourable treatment' accorded the developing countries. The NICs found the arguments for this quite convincing, in the light of the realities of the world trading system.

First, economic progress is by definition a movement from developing towards developed status. All countries were at one time undeveloped, by modern standards. In recent years Japan, Israel and Ireland have moved into the developed category, and Spain, Portugal and Greece are close to making the transition. Similarly, there is reason to believe that Singapore and Taiwan will move toward this status in the 1980s, with Korea, Hong Kong, Mexico and Brazil close behind.

Second, the NICs owe it to the LDCs to support the progressive opening of world trade. Experience has shown that small countries are particularly dependent on trade for the expansion of their output and the improvement of living standards. Thus the LDCs will tend to need preferential treatment and market access more than the NICs.

Third, the world trading system may not be able to survive another

Japan: a system of one-directional concessions and unreciprocated market access is politically unsustainable in today's world. Encouragingly, the NICs seem to be more aware of this problem than the Japanese are. When Taiwan was faced with an uncomfortable bilateral trade surplus with the USA, a mission was sent to America with instructions to buy. They did, and a potentially serious problem was avoided. This approach may be overly direct, but it does indicate an understanding of international political and economic realities.

10
The View from the NICs

Louis Turner

The NICs have only gradually emerged as economic forces, but this process has still run ahead of their emergence as diplomatic powers. Not that there is anything surprising about this, for earlier economic 'late-comers', such as West Germany and Japan, have notoriously been economic giants but political pygmies. This diplomatic backwardness of the NICs makes it difficult to distinguish their strategies from those of other relatively prosperous LDCs, but there are now signs that the NICs are emerging with a distinct set of interests, and with an increasingly assertive diplomatic stance – though this increase in self-assertiveness admittedly starts from a low base.

The reverse side of this particular coin is that the AICs are starting to distinguish between the general run of LDCs and the NICs, by making increasingly specific demands of the latter. Inevitably, then, the NICs have had to form defensive coalitions and to distinguish their particular interests from more general Third World ones. The end result, though, is the same. The NICs are slowly becoming more identifiable players in international economic diplomacy. The open question, though, is whether they yet have the political clout to protect their interests against much more powerful actors on the world stage.

LDCs AND THE GATT

It would be unfair to say that the post-1945 trading institutions were created without any consideration of non-AIC interests. After all, the abortive proposals for an international trade organization were made under United Nations auspices, and there was an LDC majority at the key conference in Havana (Camps, 1980, p. 7; Curzon, 1965, pp. 30–1). Even if GATT eventually emerged from less LDC-oriented origins, it still contained Article XVIII, which permitted some protection of infant industries in the interests of economic development (Curzon, 1965, pp. 209–14). However, even if it is true that GATT's founders were not totally oblivious to developmental issues (as then perceived), it is equally true that those LDCs involved with GATT in the mid-1950s were only starting to identify the issues now seen as central to the 'North–South' debate. Over half these LDCs were from Latin America and the Caribbean, and were led by men not yet influenced by the Prebisch thesis of the deteriorating terms of trade. They were more concerned with import substitution than with export-promoting developmental strategies.

It was only as the 1950s progressed that there was growing awareness of the extent to which LDC exports faced major trade barriers. The Haberler Report (Curzon, 1965, p. 226) showed that AIC tariff structures discriminated against processed-product imports from the LDCs, and it also showed the extent to which such products were subject to quantitative import restrictions and other non-tariff barriers. By 1959, the LDCs involved in GATT were sufficiently aware of such analysis that they met as a group for the first time. However, their pressure within GATT was not enough to fend off the rival UNCTAD, which sprang from a 1961 resolution of the United Nations General Assembly (Morton and Tulloch, 1977, p. 63). Initially UNCTAD concentrated on setting aid targets for the AICs and on the creation of the Generalized System of Preferences (GSP), which was designed to help LDC exporters.

The 1950s, then, were years in which the LDCs were not particularly active in trade diplomacy. In retrospect, Raúl Prebisch turned out to be the most important LDC spokesman on trade, but his impact was not really felt till the following decade, and, even then, his ideas only marginally affected the NICs. In the 1950s, though, really only India had a sufficiently distinctive developmental strategy to test the philosophy behind GATT. Even then, the issues turned primarily round commodity, not manufactured, exports (Curzon, 1965, pp. 234 ff).

JAPAN'S PASSIVITY

In retrospect, two facts stand out in the trading environment of the 1950s and 1960s. The first was that the 'proto-NIC' (Japan) failed to resist the other AICs when they discriminated against Japanese manufactured goods. The second, related fact was that those LDCs which chose to develop through the expansion of manufactured exports fought their battles relatively alone, outside the mainstream North–South debate which was developing within UNCTAD.

Japanese passivity is not hard to explain. The country had lost a major war and boasted a culture totally alien to the Euro-Americans then dominating the global economic institutions. Thus, when Japan did contract to the GATT in 1955, fourteen countries, representing some 40 per cent of the trade between GATT parties, invoked Article XXXV, which basically meant that the GATT articles did not apply between them and Japan (Dam, 1970, pp. 348–9). In practice, these invocations were not used to stop Japan enjoying most-favoured-nation treatment, but were used to justify discriminatory restrictions on imports from Japan. It is precisely this quite wide acceptance of the legitimacy of selective protectionism against Japanese goods, which has spilled over into resistance against these from the next generation of NICs.

The 1955–60 period saw another instance of Japanese submissiveness, which strengthened the AICs' tendency to resort to selective protectionism. This was Japan's failure to stop a series of measures in the textile and clothing sectors which were to evolve into the MFA, with all the implications this now has for the international trading system. The initial Japanese capitulation to unilateral pressure from the USA (Keesing and Wolf, 1980, pp. 14–15) meant there was little serious resistance as other AICs joined the USA in identifying further 'disruptive' LDC exporters and an increased range of 'sensitive' products. Clearly, Japanese passivity in the face of such developments is at least partly linked to the submission to authority which produced the disciplined labour force that has been such an important factor behind Japan's economic success. Moreover, Japan was exceptionally dependent on American help in winning acceptance in the international community, so it is hardly surprising that Japanese diplomats were unwilling to resist strong US demands in the trade field.

WEAKNESS OF THE NICs

It was unfortunate that the next generation of NICs was equally incapable of fending for itself in the diplomatic arena. Hong Kong was a British colony, very much threatened by China. South Korea had only just been saved by Western troops from an invasion by its North Korean neighbour. Taiwan needed Western support in its struggle with mainland China. Singapore was a city-state, with uncertain relations with neigbouring Malaysia. Those countries which were large and independent enough to have offered the AICs some serious resistance (India and Brazil spring to mind) were not in the forefront of the textile battles of the early 1960s, and, anyway, their economies were sufficiently broad that textiles and clothing were not the only sectors which concerned them.

All this meant that the NICs were unable to resist the growing selective protectionism aimed at them. They were too few to count in an uncaring world, and there was some disunity within their number. For instance, there were LDCs entering the textile and clothing industry in their turn which were far from unhappy that the leading NICs were running into protectionist problems. Such a lack of cohesion among the LDC exporters in the 1977 renegotiation of the MFA specifically led to the isolation of the Big Three exporters (Hong Kong, Taiwan and South Korea), which resulted in a general agreement that their export growth would be slowed to allow faster growth for the phalanx of Third World exporters behind them.

NICs AND THE NIEO

By the mid-1970s North–South trade politics involved more than just textiles and the GSP. OPEC's success had triggered off demands for a New

International Economic Order, the 'shopping list' for which was presented at the sixth and seventh UN Special Sessions. These Third World demands included some of particular interest to the NICs, such as those for the removal of non-tariff barriers to products of export interest to the LDCs, and for the restructuring of AIC industries which have lost competitiveness with those in the LDCs. However, despite these demands, most of the rest of the NIEO debate centred on issues which were less central to the NICs, such as the problems of commodities, the financing of Third World development, the building of a scientific and technological infrastructure in the LDCs, and the encouragement of agriculture. The impression that NIC interest was in expanding manufactured exports proved of very limited interest to the rest of the LDCs.

The United Nations Industrial Development Organization (UNIDO) proved to be the Third World-oriented organization which paid most concern to NIC interests in manufacturing. At its 1975 Lima conference, it produced a Declaration and Plan of Action calling for the expansion of the Third World's share of world industrial production from its 7 per cent of the mid-1970s to 25 per cent in the year 2000. There should be international industrialization strategies at both global and regional levels, perhaps aided by an International Industrialization Institute. The AICs would be expected to reduce tariffs on the manufactured and semi-manufactured products of the Third World, and to develop policies designed to adjust their economies out of sectors where the Third World had comparative advantages. These specific adjustment measures should be made a condition of the AICs being permitted to resort to protective actions. The latter should be temporary and degressive, with a timetable for their phasing out.

Although UNIDO's concerns can be taken as symptomatic of general changes in Third World thinking about economic matters, it is not a particularly important institution in North–South affairs. It does cover some important sectors, such as steel and petrochemicals, where it may be able to expand its role. However, the key textiles and clothing sector still effectively falls outside its remit, with GATT very much being the body within which most important developments take place.

GATT AND THE NICs

Despite the creation of competing bodies like UNCTAD, GATT has been relatively successful in keeping the NICs within its orbit. Only two of the core NICs are non-members (Taiwan and Mexico), and of the two, only Mexico has deliberately chosen to stay out.

The trouble is that membership is only one step towards having real influence within GATT. What is also needed is a level of diplomatic commitment which many Third World countries have been unable to afford. For instance, a chronicler of the Kennedy Round of tariff reductions in the 1960s remarks on the fact that:

Developing countries mostly had small delegations with little technical support. Some delegates resided in other European capitals . . . The shallow representation of these countries was to some extent due to the shortage of technically competent people, but it also reflected the fact that developing countries had little of trade value to offer as bargaining leverage and tended to be passive recipients of what other participants were willing to give. (Preeg, 1970, pp. 92-3)

This situation improved in the 1970s. For one thing, GATT responded to the growing turmoil in North–South relations by creating the Consultative Group of Eighteen in 1975. This was designed as a high-level group, representing the diversity of GATT membership, but small enough to permit frank discussion of trade issues as they emerged. Originally a provisional body, it proved useful enough to be turned into a permanent forum in 1979. Its membership in 1980 included Argentina, India and the ASEAN grouping (represented by Malaysia). It also included countries such as Egypt, Hungary, Nigeria, Pakistan, Peru, Spain and Zaire – all countries which have been outside the trade-policy Establishment which dominated GATT in the 1950s and 1960s.

In addition to this, the NICs were winning their spurs in the rather more confrontational environment of the Multilateral Trade Negotiations (MTN), which came to a climax in 1980. They put most of their initial weight behind demands for an Enabling Clause, which would regularize the GSP tariff preferences that, up to then, required special (and revocable) GATT dispensation. This led to the challenging of the trade practices of some NICs, in that the AICs made it clear that acceptance of the Enabling Clause would be conditional on the outlawing of some subsidy practices found widely in the Third World. So, one of the turning-points of the MTN came when Brazil agreed to phase out export subsidies, thus permitting the US administration to sell the other parts of the package affecting the Third World to its domestic constituency.

Another turning-point in NIC diplomacy within the MTN came towards the end of these negotiations when the depth of the EC commitment to the selective-safeguards issue became fully apparent. If the LDCs had tamely accepted AIC demands in this area, they would have been giving their blessing to the kind of divide-and-rule protectionism found in the MFA, and in selective actions across industries such as shoes, steel and consumer electronics. In fact, the Third World, led by the NICs, united in opposition in what was the first significant case within GATT of NIC resistance to AIC protectionist tendencies. Moreover, this resistance was maintained even when it appeared that it could be threatening the safe conclusion of the MTNs.

This rejection of the initial AIC proposals for the amendment of the GATT safeguards provisions was reasonably constructive in that the NICs were not rejecting all the other developments within GATT. Admittedly, there was a period in the summer of 1979 when the Third World (through UNCTAD) came close to rejecting the MTNs in their entirety, on the grounds that the final outcome was fatally hostile to Third World interests (Kemper, 1980, pp. 23–5). Feelings were so intense that only Argentina among the LDCs was initially willing to accept the final MTN package. Since then, the situation has become more complex, with various LDCs (particularly the NICs) breaking ranks to accept key parts of these agreements – most significantly, the various codes. To take but the example of the subsidies and countervailing duties code, this had by August 1980 been accepted or signed by Brazil, Chile, India, South Korea, Pakistan and Uruguay, with another eighteen LDCs (including Argentina, Malaysia and Singapore) settling for observer status. A similar pattern has emerged with the other codes, leaving the impression that once the more extreme North–South rhetoric of UNCTAD V had died down, the leading LDCs did their sums and calculated that it would be better to take part in the continued evolution of GATT, rather than to reject it for its failings.

NIC ASSERTIVENESS

The NIC campaign on the selective safeguards issue is a sign that NIC docility can no longer be taken for granted. In fact, there are now cases of individual LDCs going on to the offensive by retaliating against particularly protectionist AICs. One interesting case was that of Indonesia which, in 1980, was offended by British cutbacks in imports of Indonesian blouses, trousers and woven shirts. The Indonesians were able to force a more generous settlement by threatening a moratorium on new orders from British firms, thus putting in jeopardy a £100-million deal for a small fleet of turboprop aircraft, along with a number of other smaller contracts. The value of these threatened deals far outweighed that of the offending clothing – a lesson that will not be lost on other leading LDCs, which will also have some freedom to switch large purchases away from particularly protectionist AICs. A variant of this dispute was when Singapore involved the rest of the ASEAN grouping in a bitter wrangle with Australia, when the latter's low-airfare-to-Europe scheme was drawn up in the knowledge that it would decimate the stop-overs currently being made in Singapore.

However, NIC assertiveness does not just take the form of unsystematic retaliation against offending AICs. In the first place, some NICs believe that existing GATT procedures should be used more assertively against AICs which are tempted to bend the rules. Hong Kong, for instance, has thus challenged aspects of Norway's actions in the textiles and clothing sector.

Secondly, LDC exporters, led by the NICs, are putting an increased effort into coordinating bargaining strategies in advance of key negotiations with the AICs. Their approach to the renegotiation of the MFA is a case in point. In the previous negotiating round, in 1977, the LDCs were ill-prepared and the AICs managed to split the poorer textile exporters from the more dominant NICs. However, the Third World exporters have prepared for the 1981 round much more systematically. There have been meetings through regional bodies such as the UN's Economic and Social Commission for Asia and the Pacific (ESCAP); and there have been wider meetings of negotiators from all the leading Third World exporters in Bogotá (November 1980) and Hong Kong (June 1981). It may well be that the AIC importers will still be able to drive wedges between various groups of Third World exporters, but the latter feel that there is now an atmosphere of solid cooperation unique within their history.

WHITHER THE NICs?

In neither the MFA nor selective-safeguards negotiations can the stance of the NICs be characterized as inflexible. Nearly all of them accept that it is politically inevitable that the AICs will continue to press for some kind of protectionism, especially in the textiles and clothing sector. The NICs are thus negotiating for the most generous treatment they can win, given this admittedly unwelcome background. In both sets of negotiations, the sticking-point for the NICs would seem to be that they wish the AICs to accept a tightening of the specified circumstances in which the AICs can resort to selective actions, or depart from existing agreements. However, the NICs are still bargaining from a relatively weak position.

The NICs can strengthen their position by resorting to the kind of threatened retaliation seen in the Indonesian example (though this is a risky strategy which risks a full-scale trade war that even an oil-rich LDC like Indonesia will not inevitably win). They can strengthen their negotiating teams in key centres such as Geneva, and they can increase their solidarity by the kinds of measures seen in the case of the textile exporters. Somewhere in the background is China, a country which is interested in textiles and has a political importance transcending merely economic considerations. If China throws her lot in with the NICs, as could happen, the balance of power in trade matters will become more finely balanced.

Elsewhere, the NICs have friends in institutions such as the World Bank and GATT, but these may not count for much in power battles within AICs. To increase their lobbying power within the industrialized world, the NICs need to improve their relationships with AIC-based exporters, whose trade is increasingly skewed towards the richer LDCs; and with retailing and other consumer-oriented institutions in the AICs. The anti-Keynesians in charge of many AIC economies may not accept the Brandt Commission's argument that LDC growth can be a healthy spur to the world economy, but the anti-Keynesians are concerned with inflation, and imports from the NICs are an important source of anti-inflationary pressure.

THE PRESSURES ON THE NICs

This chapter has looked at the world trading environment through the eyes of the NICs and may thus have glossed over some unpleasant truths about the NICs' own trading practices. After all, there are observers who believe that such LDCs have been a predominantly baleful influence on the trading system, with their continuing pressure for preferential treatment: first the demand that protection of infant industries should be tolerated; then the pressures for GSP-style tariff preferences; increasingly the assumption that AICs should open their markets to Third World products, whatever the political consequences.

One should not accept such arguments too readily. After all, tariff structures in most AICs have historically discriminated against industrial products from the Third World. Nor is there much evidence that LDCs which have come closest to playing by the GATT rules have been given any particularly favourable treatment. However, whatever the reservations, such hostility to the NICs does point to some important truths. For instance, whether NICs have followed the Japanese, Fabian socialist or Prebisch models of development, they have nearly all adopted some form of import substitution behind the inevitable tariff walls. (Hong Kong and Singapore are the clearest exceptions.) In addition to tariff protection, the NICs will generally have had recourse to at least some measures across the fields of controls on inward investment, export subsidies and trade-distorting financial inducements. Most recently, countries have taken to imposing 'performance requirements' on inwardly investing multinational companies – the biggest controversy centres on the export requirements imposed in countries such as Brazil, Mexico and Spain.

The trouble is that domestic political fortunes come to depend on the maintenance of such trade-distorting practices, and the NICs have just as much of a problem in unscrambling these as, say, the EC is having in breathing some economic rationality into its Common Agricultural Policy. The political difficulties in opening up economies can be understood, but this understanding does not help when the NICs want the AICs to liberalize yet more parts of their economies. This apparent lack of reciprocal concessions by the NICs only plays into the hands of protectionists in the industrialized world.

The Mexican refusal to join GATT is symptomatic of the difficulties some NICs, particularly the Latin Americans, are having in unlocking their economies. This country rejected the GATT option at least in part because it felt it could use its oil wealth to buy itself the benefits that GATT membership would otherwise have provided. If this strategy succeeds, then other oil producers, who already tend to assume that oil will buy them into world chemical markets, may well be tempted to follow the Mexican route. The Mexicans compounded this strategy by tightening their import controls in the summer of 1981.

In retrospect, this Mexican policy will probably prove badly mistaken. For one thing, main-line thinking in development economics (as instanced by thinking within institutions like the World Bank) increasingly stresses the economic benefits of open, rather than closed, economies. Staying out of GATT will reduce the pressures on Mexico to decontrol a somewhat *dirigiste* economy. There is, though, a second, more tactical consideration, which is that US trade law allows countervailing actions, without any proof of material damage, against imports from countries which do not participate in the various GATT codes. As the one NIC which is staying outside GATT, Mexico is leaving itself in a very isolated position. Its future oil revenues had better live up to its expectations . . . .

Meanwhile, the arguments from Mexican policies towards GATT and from Brazil's reluctance to dismantle its array of export incentives can be misleading. Most policy-makers in the four East Asian NICs, and many of those in Indira Gandhi's India, accept that the reduction of domestic barriers on imports not only makes good diplomatic sense, but can be economically beneficial in its own right. The East Asians, for instance, are very much aware of Western hostility to Japan's apparent mercantilism, and South Korea certainly eased imports under the late President Park, specifically to avoid Korea being seen as restrictive as Japan.

What the NICs now need to do is to publicize those cases among their number, such as Hong Kong and Singapore, which are unexceptionable free-trading economies. Those other NICs that are willing to soften their import policies should, at worst, let the world know they are so modifying them, and, at best, should use their compliance to win concessions from the AICs. There is rather more virtue in the NICs' trading behaviour than many outsiders are aware of. However, virtue has to be positively demonstrated before it will be acknowledged or, even, rewarded.

Part Three
The Adjustment Debate

11
The NICs and
World Economic Adjustment
Colin I. Bradford, jr

INTRODUCTION

The capacity of a limited number of developing countries to export manufactured goods to world markets on a global scale is but one dimension, albeit a crucial one, of the increasing role of the NICs in the world economy. As pointed out in Chapter 2, the emergence of this export capacity preceded the oil price rises of late 1973 and 1974. Since then, the promising economic outlook of the NICs, based in part on their export performance, has boosted their creditworthiness so that they have become the leading borrowers within the Third World. This recycling of petro-dollars to the NICs has been a major feature of world financial adjustment since 1973. In particular, this borrowing has increased NIC capacity to import substantially, turning these countries into increasingly important markets for AIC exports, in addition to making them important competitors. As a result, the NICs have played a significant global role in the aftermath of the oil-price rise in both the trade and financial dimensions. This chapter analyses the main elements of the process of world economic adjustment, and seeks to elucidate the global role of the NICs and to place their capacity to export manufactures in the context of their overall role in the world economy.

WORLD BALANCE-OF-PAYMENTS ADJUSTMENT

Complex though the period since 1973 has been in terms of economic adjustment, the world economy adapted to the oil shock through a set of economic processes which can be seen quite clearly in retrospect. The external impact of suddenly rising oil prices caused an increase in the balance-of-payments surplus of the OPEC countries, as export earnings jumped upwards, while OPEC imports of both consumption and investment goods were restrained by limited absorptive capacity. The OPEC current-account surplus shot up from $6·6 billion in 1973 to $68 billion in 1974 and remained at the $30–$40 billion level for the next three years, returning to near balance in 1978. The real price of oil stayed virtually constant following the initial price hike until the period from late 1978 to March 1980, when it rose by 130 per cent (IMF, 1980). The second oil shock led again to large OPEC current-account surpluses in the 1979–81 period.

As can be seen in Table 11.1, the non-oil developing countries have run current-account deficits through the post-1973 period which have been nearly sufficient to offset the OPEC surpluses both annually and cumulatively. A new development in the 1979–81 period has been the occurrence of sizeable current-account deficits in the industrial countries, but even in these years the non-oil LDC deficits have been significantly larger.

By the end of 1978, total outstanding external public debt of developing countries was just over $300 billion. The eight core NICs – South Korea, Taiwan, Hong Kong, Singapore, Brazil, Mexico, Argentina and India – accounted for nearly 40 per cent of the total LDC external debt (Table 11.2). The six potential NICs in the 'next tier' accounted for another 16 per cent, so that together these fourteen countries incurred 56 per cent of the total debt accumulated by the end of 1978 by nearly ninety developing countries. Whereas there was substantial addition to reserves in this period, increased foreign borrowing was a significant stimulus to world trade through the financing of greater imports. Hence, the selected few countries that have achieved a dynamic manufactured export performance have been the principal LDC borrowers in the post-OPEC period, when LDCs have played a major role in global balance-of-payments adjustment.

WORLD ECONOMIC GROWTH

As is well known, the period since 1973 has been one of sluggish economic growth in the AICs. By contrast, the higher-income developing countries in Asia and Latin America have, by and large, experienced rather higher rates of growth (Table 11.3). The industrialized countries experienced increased inflation relative to their historical norms, but inflation rates in developing countries, especially in Latin America and to a lesser extent in Asia, were even higher.

A question arises about the source of this more rapid economic growth in high-income developing countries during the post-1973 period. If faster growth was derived from inflationary consumption growth, the degree to which the foreign borrowing of the LDCs facilitated global financial adjustment in the 1970s may jeopardize balance-of-payments adjustment in the 1980s, as such developing countries face greater debt-service burdens without having added extra productive capacity. However, if consumption growth in the high-debt LDCs has been less than economic growth, and investment growth has been more rapid than economic growth, the outlook is more promising.

Table 11.1 *Summary of Current Account Balances, 1973–81 (billion US$)*

Group	1973	1974	1975	1976	1977	1978	1979	1980	1981	Total 1974–81
OPEC	6·6	67·8	35·0	40·0	31·1	3·3	68·4	112·2	96·0	453·8
Non-oil LDCs	−11·5	−36·8	−46·5	−32·9	−29·6	−37·1	−56·1	−80·4	−96·5	−415·9
LDC/OPEC (%)		(54·3)	(132·9)	(82·3)	(95·2)	—	(82·0)	(71·7)	(100·0)	91·6
Industrial countries (IC)	19·3	−12·4	17·1	−2·1	−5·5	30·1	−10·7	−44·0	−29·5	
IC/OPEC (%)		(18·3)	—	(5·3)	(17·9)	—	(15·6)	(39·2)	(30·7)	

Source: IMF, 1981, table 14, p. 123.

Table 11.2 LDC Debt and Additions to Reserves (billion US$)

Group/country	External public debt,[1] 31.XII.1978 (1)	Additions to gross international reserves 1970–8 (2)	Group/country	External public debt,[1] 31.XII.1978 (1)	Additions to gross international reserves 1970–8 (2)
NICs			*Next tier*		
South Korea	18·2	2·2	Indonesia	18·9	2·5
Taiwan	4·3	1·3	Malaysia	4·4	3·0
Hong Kong	0·9	–	Philippines	7·6	1·8
Singapore	1·4	4·3	Thailand	3·7	1·6
Brazil	33·4	11·0	Pakistan	9·9	6·0
Mexico	31·2	1·5	Colombia	4·3	2·6
Argentina	8·9	5·3	Subtotal	48·8	17·5
India	20·6	7·3			
Subtotal	118·9	32·9			

[1] External public debt is defined as . . . a direct obligation of, or has payment guaranteed by, a public body in the borrowing country' (World Bank, 1980b, p. 128).

Sources
Col. (1): World Bank, 1980b, table 3, pp. 134–5.
Col. (2): World Bank, 1980a, table 15, pp. 138–9.

Table 11.3 *Rates of Growth and Inflation in Industrialized and Developing Countries (percentage changes)*

	1962–72	1967–72	1973	1974	1975	1976	1977	1978	1979	1980	1981
Economic growth											
Seven larger industrialized countries (GNP)[1]	4·8		6·4	0·3	−0·7	5·4	4·3	4·4	3·8	1·2	1·6
Developing countries (GDP)											
Africa		5·0	3·6	6·9	1·9	4·2	1·4	2·2	3·2	4·9	4·2
Asia		4·6	5·4	4·0	6·1	6·4	6·4	8·3	3·3	3·5	5·8
Latin America		7·2	8·3	7·2	2·8	4·6	4·4	4·6	6·5	5·8	5·3
Inflation											
Seven larger industrialized countries (GNP deflator)[1]	4·0		7·0	11·5	10·9	6·9	7·1	7·2	7·9	9·0	8·9
Developing countries (consumer prices) (weighted averages)											
Africa		4·6	9·8	15·3	15·1	15·0	19·2	15·6	19·2	19·4	17·4
Asia		6·7	12·7	17·5	14·7	12·5	16·2	21·1	27·5	40·3	24·5
Latin America		15·4	32·1	37·5	52·0	66·2	51·4	42·4	49·3	60·2	61·4

[1] Canada, France, West Germany, Italy, Japan, UK and USA.
Source: IMF, 1981, tables 1–3, pp. 111–13.

The evidence in Table 11.4 suggests that, in general, the latter pattern of investment growth outpacing economic growth, with consumption growth lagging behind, prevails for both the core NICs and the 'next tier' of potential NICs. The most significant general divergence from this pattern is that in seven of the fourteen countries, the growth of public consumption (that is, government consumption expenditures) has been faster than economic growth, but in six of these seven countries, public consumption (in 1978) was 11 per cent or less of GDP. This suggests that high government expenditures may have been more important in spurring inflation in these countries than in eroding the balance between investment and economic growth. In all cases, except Argentina and Singapore, investment growth has been faster than private consumption growth.

This pattern is further substantiated by figures which show a steady increase in gross investment as a percentage of GNP for East Asia and Latin America in the 1970s (Table 11.5). This evidence indicates that the high rates of economic growth of higher-income LDCs since 1973 have not been consumption driven, but rather that foreign borrowing has helped finance rapid investment growth. An examination of the product composition of world trade confirms this view by revealing high LDC imports of capital goods.

It is interesting to note in Table 11.5 that, during the post-1973 period, when industrialized country savings rates have been substantially lower than previously, domestic savings in East Asia and Latin America have jumped upwards. This is consistent with relatively low consumption growth. Indeed, GATT has found that consumption growth in the combined

Table 11.4 *GDP, Consumption and Investment, Growth in 1970–8
            (average annual growth rates)*

Country	GDP	Public consumption	Private consumption	Gross domestic investment
NICs				
South Korea	9·7	8·7	7·5	13·7
Taiwan	8·0	5·4	6·8	8·2
Hong Kong	8·2[a]	9·2	8·8	10·2
Singapore	8·5	6·4	7·1	5·5
Brazil	9·2	8·6	9·0	10·7
Mexico	5·0	10·6	3·8	7·1
Argentina	2·3	−3·1	2·4	1·2
India	3·7	4·2	3·0	6·1
Next tier				
Indonesia	7·8	10·9	7·6	15·3
Malaysia	7·8	9·6	6·4	10·2
Philippines	6·3	9·4	4·3	11·1
Thailand	7·6	8·3	6·7	7·8
Pakistan	4·4	3·9	3·8	4·8
Colombia	6·0	4·8	5·9	6·3
Average for fifty-two middle-income countries	5·7[b]	7·4[c]	4·9[c]	7·2[c]
Average for thirty-eight low-income countries	3·6[b]	3·7[c]	3·1[c]	3·6[c]

[a] 1970–7. [b] Weighted average. [c] Median value.
Source: World Bank, 1980a, tables 2 and 4, pp. 112–13, 116–17.

non-oil LDCs fell from an average of 5 per cent in 1963–73 period to 3·5 per cent in the 1973–78 period, permitting the average annual growth in fixed investment to remain at 6·5 per cent (GATT, 1980e, p. 31). As the figures in Table 11.5 indicate, all the investment growth in LDCs was not financed by domestic savings. The gap between savings and investment as percentages of GNP indicates the degree to which foreign savings supplemented domestic savings throughout the period shown. Hence, the high foreign borrowing of the higher-income LDCs in the post-1973 years appears clearly to have primarily supported high investment growth rather than consumption growth.

THE COMPOSITION OF WORLD TRADE

Beyond the patterns of growth and balance-of-payments financing already discussed, the structure of world trade provides further insight into the process of world economic adjustment and the role of developing countries

Table 11.5 *Shares of Investment and Savings in GNP (percentage of GNP)*

Group	1961–5	1966–75	1976	1977	1978	1979[1]
Industrialized countries						
Gross investment	20·5	21·2	21·8	22·0	22·4	–
Gross national saving	26·6	29·3	21·6	21·8	22·3	–
Developing countries						
East Asia[2]						
Gross investment	15·9	22·2	25·4	25·2	26·8	29·5
Gross national saving	12·1	17·9	24·1	24·6	24·3	26·7
Latin America[2]						
Gross investment	20·4	22·0	24·4	24·8	25·3	–
Gross national saving	19·8	20·2	21·7	22·8	21·8	–

[1] Preliminary.
[2] Korea, Taiwan, Hong Kong and Singapore represented 58 per cent of the GNP of East
Asia, and Brazil, Mexico and Argentina 66 per cent of the GNP of Latin America, in 1977.
Source: World Bank, 1979g, pp. 10, 14, 18, and 1980b, table 1, pp. 130–1.

within it. For industrialized countries, the large trade surpluses in
manufactures have kept pace with and largely offset the deficits in fuels
(Table 11.6). The developing countries (both oil and non-oil exporting)
ran sizeable trade deficits in manufactures. These LDC imports of
manufactures from industrial countries not only provided a balance-of-
payments offset to oil, but also provided a cushion of added economic
growth to AICs in a period of stagnation. The OECD notes that the export
surplus in the manufactures trade of industrialized countries with non-
OECD third countries rose from $53 billion in 1973 to $116 billion in 1975
(see Table 11.6) and concluded that 'third countries in general, among
them the NICs, thus provided considerable support to OECD manufactured
exports in the recession' (OECD, 1979a, p. 29). LDC demand for investment
goods also stimulated the more competitive industries in the OECD, thereby
facilitating the internal process of structural change, absorbing resources
from slower-growing sectors.

These compositional dimensions and shifts are shown in Table 11.7.
Industrialized countries have experienced sizeable and growing trade
surpluses with non-oil developing countries in engineering products and
chemicals, in which they have a competitive edge, and trade deficits with
non-oil developing countries in consumer goods, principally textiles and
clothing. Machinery and transport equipment rose significantly as a
percentage of exports between 1960 and 1977 for each of the seven larger
industrial countries except for the UK (World Bank, 1980a, p. 127).

This structure of trade in manufactures is consistent with the patterns of
payments and growth discussed earlier, in that non-oil LDC external
borrowing appears to have financed imports of capital goods to support
investment growth by providing the margin of foreign savings needed to

Table 11.6 *Trade Balances by Major Areas and Product Categories (billion $ f.o.b.)*

Category	1973	1974	1975	1976	1977	1978	1979
Industrialized countries							
Fuel	−36	−110	−102	−123	−133	−130	−184
Other primary products	−27	−33	−25	−33	−38	−33	−41
Manufactures	53	90	116	115	130	154	170
Non-oil developing countries							
Fuel	−4	−11	−10	−12	−15	−13	−21
Other primary products	18	25	21	28	35	32	39
Manufactures	−27	−43	−47	−40	−46	−56	−71
Oil-exporting developing countries							
Fuel	37	117	107	128	139	133	190
Other primary products	0	−3	−5	−4	−6	−7	−7
Manufactures	−15	−26	−44	−52	−64	−75	−73

Source: GATT, 1980e, p. 8.

Table 11.7 *AIC Trade in Manufactures with the Non-Oil Developing Countries (billion $ f.o.b.)*

	Exports			Imports			Balance		
Category	1973	1978	1979	1973	1978	1979	1973	1978	1979
All manufactures	40·2	96·0	120·3	15·1	40·7	51·0	25·1	55·3	69·3
of which:									
Iron and Steel	3·6	7·1	9·2	0·5	1·1	1·6	3·1	6·0	7·6
Chemicals	6·6	15·1	20·3	0·8	2·5	2·9	5·8	13·0	17·4
Other semi-manufactures[1]	2·7	6·8	8·0	2·5	5·5	6·5	0·2	1·3	1·5
Engineering products	23·1	58·3	72·6	3·6	11·9	16·2	19·5	46·4	56·4
Textiles and clothing	2·9	4·7	5·6	5·3	12·7	15·2	−2·4	−8·0	−9·6
Other finished consumer goods[2]	1·4	3·7	4·7	2·4	7·2	8·6	−1·0	−3·5	−3·9

[1] Excluding textiles.
[2] Excluding passenger cars and other engineering consumer goods.
Source: GATT, 1980e, p. 10.

fill the gap between domestic savings and total investment. As GATT has recently reported:

> Preliminary estimates suggest that (i) between 1973 and 1978 investment in machinery and transport equipment increased in developing countries at least as fast as investment in buildings and infrastructure, and (ii) for

machinery and transport equipment the volume of imports increased more rapidly than domestic production of these goods. (GATT, 1980e, p. 32)

SOURCES OF GLOBAL SAVINGS

The OPEC current-account surplus has become in effect a significant part of what William Branson (forthcoming) has called the 'world savings pool', which has been recycled to the non-oil LDCs to finance investment growth through imported capital goods from the AICs. The availability of global savings in substantial magnitudes has depended upon continued AIC oil-import demand at levels sufficient to sustain OPEC oil exports at a high enough level to generate a surplus over OPEC import levels. The seven large OECD economies have accounted for nearly three-quarters of OPEC oil exports in the 1977–80 period (Table 11.8). It seems that the inelasticity of demand for oil has generated forced savings from the OECD economies, which have accrued to OPEC and been recycled to the LDCs.

Table 11.8   *Oil Imports by Major Industrial Countries as a Percentage of OPEC Oil Exports*

Category	1977	1978	1979	1980
(1) OECD (seven major economies[1]) net oil imports (million barrels/day)	21·4	20·5	20·9	19·3
(2) OPEC net oil exports (million barrels/day)	29·3	28·0	28·4	25·9
(3) OECD/OPEC (%)	73·0	73·2	73·6	74·5

[1] France, West Germany, Italy, Japan, Netherlands, UK and USA.
Sources:
(1) OECD, 1979f, table 53, p. 124.
(2) IMF, 1980, table 33, p. 112.

It is interesting to note in Table 11.5 that the industrialized countries generated a surplus of savings over investment in the period from 1961 to 1975, and that in the years shown since then savings have roughly equalled investment. This would seem to suggest that the contribution of the industrial economies to world savings in the post-oil-shock period has not been through a direct surplus of savings, but rather through reductions in non-oil consumption, which have been siphoned by oil-price increases.

Data for the USA seem to confirm this view. In the four years immediately preceding the oil-price rise (from 1970 through 1973), gasoline, lubricating oil, fuel oil and coal were a relatively stable percentage of total consumption, averaging 4·23 per cent for the period. This percentage increased to 5 per cent in 1974 and reached 6·5 per cent in 1979. If we assume that the entire increase in the share of US consumption expenditures on fuel was due to the oil-price rise, we can calculate the gap between actual non-fuel consumption in the post-oil-shock period and the hypothetical non-oil consumption that would have resulted if fuel had maintained a constant share of total private consumption. This is done in Table 11.9. This rough estimate of the loss in non-fuel consumption expenditure totals $57 billion for the 1974–9 years. This is the same order of magnitude as the incremental US expenditure on oil imports for the period, which came to $52 billion. While the year-to-year numbers do not correspond exactly, there is some parallel between the calculated consumption loss per annum and the incremental US expenditure on oil imports each year. These are crude calculations, but they are consistent with the intuitive judgement that the OPEC surplus consists of forced AIC savings, derived from forgone non-fuel consumption, which in turn has dampened demand in the advanced economies.

Table 11.9 *Estimated Consumption Loss for the USA, 1974–9 (billion US$)*

Year	Non-fuel consumption expenditure		Difference	Incremental oil imports
	Hypothetical	*Actual*		
1974	850·5	843·8	6·7	18·30
1975	935·0	927·8	7·2	0·40
1976	1,038·4	1,030·5	7·9	7·55
1977	1,154·5	1,146·7	7·8	10·41
1978	1,291·6	1,284·3	7·3	−2.27
1979	1,446·9	1,426·5	20·4	17·69
			57·3	52·08

Source: Council of Economic Advisers, 1981, table B13, p. 248.

WORLD ECONOMIC ADJUSTMENT

The main elements of the global system of economic adjustment since 1973 can be summarized as follows:

– Inelastic AIC import demand for oil in the 1970s (even in the face of rapidly rising oil prices), and limited OPEC absorptive capacity, yielded an OPEC current-account surplus.
– The OPEC surplus in effect consisted of forced AIC savings, derived from compressed non-oil-consumption demand, which in turn caused slower economic growth in industrial economies.
– The OPEC surplus was recycled to developing countries, which together ran nearly equivalent current-account deficits, thus yielding increased imports and higher economic growth.
– The recycled global savings were concentrated in the form of external debt in the NICs and, to a lesser extent, in the 'next tier' of NICs, which achieved fast rates of growth through high investment and high export growth.

- LDC imports of AIC capital goods supported LDC investment growth and somewhat cushioned the sluggish growth of the AIC economies.
- The AIC export surpluses of manufactured goods to oil and non-oil LDCs largely offset the AIC oil deficits.
- The dynamic growth of LDC exports of manufactures increased LDC capacity to import and to service external debt.
- Internal structural change has advanced to the degree that increased trade in manufactures facilitates the growth of more competitive industries.

These patterns of external payments, economic growth, world trade and global savings fit together to delineate the process of world economic adjustment in the aftermath of the oil-price rises. The role of the core and next tier of NICs in this global adjustment process has been central. When focus is solely directed at the manufactured export capacity of the NICs, without regard for their broader role in the world economy, a distorted view is gained. The foregoing analysis elucidates the fact that the role of the NICs in the world economy is at least as significant in the realms of balance of payments, external debt and imports of manufactures as it is in respect of manufactured exports. These other aspects of NICs' role in the world economy facilitate global trade and payments adjustment and work to offset the internal costs to competing economies of their dynamic export expansion. Indeed, it is precisely the volume and the growth of their exports which facilitates world economic adjustment through offsetting imports of manufactures and current-account deficits. Hence, the difficulties caused by NIC exports of manufactures at the micro level should be seen against the background of the macro-economic dimension of their broader role in the world economy.

ACKNOWLEDGEMENTS

This paper has benefited from research financed by the US Agency for International Development for a book on interdependence in the 1980s and by discussions with William Branson, Peter Kenen, Anne Krueger, Harald Malmgren and Constantine Michalopoulos in the context of that study. I am grateful to Vanessa Sherman for statistical assistance.

12

The Concept of Adjustment

Stephen Woolcock

This chapter sets out to identify the major issues in the adjustment debate. From the previous chapters it will be clear that there are factors other than imports from the NICs which influence the adjustment of industries in the AICs. In the steel, petrochemical and automobile sectors, these will remain more important than import competition from the NICs during the 1980s. Nevertheless the general response of the AIC industries and governments to the need for adjustment will influence international trade and thus indirectly the NICs. This chapter seeks to clarify the issues involved in the adjustment debate and to sketch out the general policy options open to AIC decision-makers.

WHAT IS ADJUSTMENT?

In general terms adjustment can be defined as the allocation of resources between and within industries in response to changes in the pattern of demand, trade or technological development. More comprehensively, adjustment has been defined as

> a gradual response of resource allocation to changes in taste and the pattern of demand (e.g. from goods towards services), to changing technology, to changing relative costs and prices (e.g. energy prices or changing relative costs reflecting differential productivity growth) to changes in comparative advantages between countries, and to changes in the composition of the labour force. (OECD, 1979c, p. 81)

Such a very broad definition of adjustment has both advantages and disadvantages. For one thing, it is broad enough to accommodate all those factors of change at work and thus the increased number of instruments available to policy-makers to influence this change in the OECD economies of the 1980s. In the interpenetrated world economy of the 1980s (Interfutures, 1979) not only tariffs but also a range of instruments from incentives for new technology industries to selective quantitative restrictions on imports are the concern of trading partners.

Such a broad definition of adjustment also allows for diverse interpretations of what adjustment really is and what should be done to promote rather than inhibit the process.

IS THERE INCREASED PRESSURE TO ADJUST?

Different perceptions of economic and industrial change, and the role of national and international public bodies in influencing this change, can influence the adjustment debate at the very outset. At the risk of oversimplification one can characterize perceptions as falling into two general categories: the optimistic view and the pessimistic view on industrial structural change. How such long-term structural as opposed to short-term cyclical (Gordon, 1979, p. 7) trends are assessed will inevitably influence policy responses. Optimists will stress that 'adjustment' is and always has been an integral part of economic life, and wonder why there is any reason to assume that it will not continue to be. They would suggest that the process at work is far too complex to describe, and view such efforts to describe it with scepticism and suspicion. Suspicion because efforts to explain change are seen as the first step towards progressive public intervention in the process, or at least to give support to those who favour increased intervention (Golt, 1980). This view has been succinctly expressed by the West German government:

> The need for adjustment [*Anpassung*] which exists in the German economy in general, varies from sector to sector. However, there are also differences within individual sectors. Some companies need to adjust a great deal, while others only to a limited extent. These intra-industry differences show that neither monocausal explanatory approaches (i.e. comparative advantage) nor simple industry (or sectoral) case studies can explain developments, and far less serve as criteria for decisions concerning the adjustment process. (FRG, Bundesregierung, 1978)

This concern at descriptions of the adjustment process which draw attention to supposed rigidities in the market allocation mechanism exists at both the national and international level. At the international level, for example, AIC governments are suspicious of studies on structural change conducted by bodies such as UNIDO (UNIDO, 1979a). It is felt they provide ammunition for the G77 in their attempts to get AIC governments to take active measures to promote industrial adjustment in order to facilitate enhanced market access for G77 industrial exports (UNCTAD, 1970, p. 5; UNIDO, 1979b). At a national level, sectoral studies are also thought to increase the likelihood of collective misinvestment.

So much for optimists; pessimists will argue, meanwhile, that the pressure for change is greater today than during earlier periods and is likely to increase during the 1980s. It is possible to isolate perhaps four factors which suggest that the need to adjust will increase in the 1980s.

These are: energy costs and supply; a general slowing of economic growth in the OECD countries (compared with the 1960s and early 1970s); increased competition from the developing countries, especially the NICs; and technological changes (EC Commission, 1979a; Gordon, 1979; Maldague, 1979; Page, 1980). The energy constraint is of major importance and has stimulated all AICs to pursue specific policies at the national and international level. In the context of this study we are, however, primarily concerned with how changes in energy prices affect the relative positions of industries within the AICs and between AICs and the NICs. Increased energy costs inevitably lead to increased pressure to adjust in energy-intensive industries such as iron and steel and (petro)chemicals, which, for example, together accounted for more than 20 per cent of US industrial energy consumption in 1976 (Page, 1980, p. 6).

Slower growth not only inhibits innovative investment and investment in new capacity, but also exacerbates the problems of industries in which existing major product lines are approaching demand saturation. The industry cases have shown this to be the case for bulk steel, some textile products, bulk petrochemicals and to a lesser degree automobiles. Slower industrial growth also means that alternative industrial employment prospects will deteriorate. If the late 1970s trends continue, the service sector will not be able to absorb all the labour shed by manufacturing (EC Commission, 1979a). Assuming that relatively full employment is not further downgraded as a macro-economic policy objective, the pressure to preserve industrial employment in order to achieve national employment objectives can therefore be expected to increase.

As suggested in the preceding chapters, the growth of demand for various manufactured products will probably be greater in the NICs. If NICs capitalize on this as well as their labour-cost advantages, NIC competition can be expected to increase in some of the more mature product-cycle products. In various lines of production in the AICs, therefore, there will be increased competition for a slow-growing market. In such cases, as has been shown in the case of textiles, AIC producers will be forced to improve productivity at the expense of industrial employment (Berthelot and Tardy, 1978; EC Commission, 1979b; Interfutures, 1979).

In the field of technology also, the technologies on which the rapid industrial growth of the 1960s was based are approaching maturity. New technological innovations can be expected to take their place, but the shift in emphasis from electrical and mechanical engineering to electronics will bring about further fundamental changes.

While there are many who share the view that the need to adjust will grow, there is inevitably a divergence of views on what should be done. Some, for example, argue that adjustment problems are inevitable with slow growth and that governments should concentrate on facilitating an increase in investment, usually by macro policy, and above all desist from inhibition of the adjustment process in the form of selective subsidies and trade regulation (Blackhurst *et al.*, 1978). The middle ground in the adjustment debate, as expounded for example by the OECD Secretariat

(OECD, 1979c), is that government policies inevitably impinge on adjustment and that they should seek to minimize selective intervention and above all ensure that all forms of intervention promote rather than inhibit adjustment. Finally, proponents of what has been termed anticipatory adjustment support rather more active policies. A policy of identifying the need for future industrial adjustment, through sectoral studies, and providing adjustment assistance would, it is argued, help both corporate and public-sector planners to adjust before the company (or industry) is so weakened that defensive anti-crisis measures or 'temporary' trade protection is needed to prevent large-scale redundancies and bankruptcies (de la Torre, 1978; Plässert, 1974).

Even if we assume that the problems of adjustment will not get worse in the 1980s – and there is enough evidence to suggest they will – there remains the problem of phasing out existing anti-crisis measures and trade regulations. This alone will be no easy task. It is therefore necessary to go beyond the often sterile debate on interventionism to consider how existing forms of intervention, both general and selective, can be used to promote rather than inhibit adjustment. In doing so, it is convenient to distinguish between various dimensions of the adjustment debate.

CORPORATE-LEVEL ADJUSTMENT

In the mixed economies of the OECD countries the major responsibility for adjustment falls on individual companies and their work-forces. At the corporate level, firms will be concerned with how they can maintain profit margins, perhaps in the face of increased imports or stagnating demand for their existing product lines. The corporate response to such a situation might be, for example, to improve productivity by automation or the introduction of new production processes. Alternatively, firms may drop low-income elastic products from their product mix at an early stage and develop new lines of production with better demand prospects. AIC producers can also find cheaper locations for production of relatively mature product-cycle goods, perhaps even in the NICs. Invariably such corporate responses entail disruption of employment or net job losses, so that there is often a conflict between corporate viability and national employment objectives. This conflict is particularly marked when relocation of production is relatively easily facilitated by multinational companies, or when a plant affected by adjustment is located in an area of high unemployment.

NATIONAL-LEVEL ADJUSTMENT

National governments are concerned with how the national economy responds to changes in demand, trade or technology, and how the objectives of growth, price stability, employment and balance of payments can be achieved. The means to achieve these include, of course, macro-economic policies such as general demand management, fiscal or monetary policies, exchange rates and so on. Such policies set the general framework and thus influence the pressure to adjust on national economies. Macro policies can also discriminate between different industrial activities even if this is not their explicit objective. For example, higher exchange rates will tend to favour sectors more dependent on imported raw materials and intermediate products, but will intensify pressure on industries in which price-sensitive products predominate. Rising exchange rates were, for example, an important factor in the more rapid relocation of Dutch and German clothing production to low-cost sources during the 1970s.[1]

It is at the national level that the issue of casuality between non-inflationary growth and adjustment applies. It has been suggested that the relative decline in the ability of AIC economies to adjust to changes in industrial structure has meant that resources are being tied in relatively less productive industries. As the AIC economies resist change in an increasing number of industries – clothing, shipbuilding, steel, auto-mobiles and so on – the general level of productivity growth declines and macro-economic objectives of growth and price stability are endangered. There is thus 'a vicious circle whereby slow growth generates behaviour and policies which impair productivity and accentuate inflation; this prompts governments to adopt more cautious demand management policies and hence leads, directly and indirectly, to even slower growth' (OECD, 1979c, p. 85). In other words, the question is whether to promote growth to facilitate adjustment or adjustment to facilitate non-inflationary growth. 'Picking the winners' is a related issue. For example, given the constraints on general demand expansion, should governments promote new industries, such as bio-technology or telematics, as a means of increasing industrial output and growth?

GENERAL ADJUSTMENT POLICIES

The debate on national adjustment policies centres on the degree of selectivity, and inevitably involves the interaction between corporate and national objectives.[2] It is often argued that general adjustment assistance is preferable to selective measures because it reduces the degree of political discretion. General assistance, it is argued, reduces the likelihood of governments becoming hostage to industrial lobbies or basing assistance on political expediency, such as when a particular industry is important in a politically sensitive constituency, by making assistance conditional on predetermined economic criteria. General adjustment policy can take various forms such as public support for depressed regions (regional policy), or increased expenditure on eduction or vocational training to help professional labour mobility. It may also take the form of general support for R&D in the form of, for example, tax incentives for R&D investment or labour costs. Alternatively, it can provide adjustment assistance for those affected by adjustment, along the lines of the US adjustment assistance programme. Under such a scheme assistance would be available, automatically, once given conditions were satisfied. There is no space to discuss the intricacies of such compensation schemes (see Wolf, 1979). Broadly speaking, general adjustment schemes are considered preferable from an economic point of view, but they have various drawbacks. First, they are likely to be very expensive. The US scheme provided adjustment assistance for those affected by changes in certain trade patterns only and has still been a candidate for public-expenditure cuts. Second, as with macro-economic policy, general assistance often has a selective impact. For example, when a certain industry is located in a depressed region, the distinction between sectoral and regional aid becomes blurred. The temporary employment subsidy (TES) is an example of an employment subsidy which, though purported to be general, in fact favoured the clothing industry. Finally, a further example is the supposedly general R&D incentives in the otherwise 'liberal' (that is, non-selective) West Germany, which in fact benefited the few large companies that had sufficiently large R&D operations to use the public funds provided (Bombach & Gahlen, 1977). As general aid can discriminate it has been the subject of discussion at an international level, as we shall see below, because it may be considered as a form of 'unfair' trade by trading partners. Basically speaking, however, general adjustment assistance causes fewer problems internationally because of its non-selective intent. The main international problems arise from explicitly selective actions designed to slow the speed of adjustment.

SELECTIVE ADJUSTMENT POLICIES

Perhaps the major criticism of general adjustment policies as practised during the 1960s, in the form of regional, manpower or science and technology strategies, is that they have failed to prevent the spread of selective assistance. General policies recognize that there are imperfections in the market, but as a means of allocating resources they operate over the medium to long term. The recent increase in selective anti-crisis measures or trade regulation has been in response to the immediate problems of specific 'crisis' industries. For workers and managers of such an industry medium-to-long-term solutions are not seen as a real alternative, especially when industrial employment is on the decline. Selective adjustment policy could therefore be defined as the management of the transition from short-term defensive measures back to a situation in which market forces and/or general policies can regulate the speed of adjustment. Selective measures, whilst usually of a highly political nature, can nevertheless be justified in economic terms. For example, if a rapid and massive fall in demand threatens to lead to wide-scale bankruptcies in an industry, as in the case of steel, it may be cheaper for the national economy to provide 'temporary' aid rather than face the consequences, in terms of the impact on employment and the balance of payments, of importing most of the steel that will be required.

A major problem with selective adjustment-assistance measures is that, in an increasingly 'industry-oriented' (see below) international trading system, trading partners will see them as 'unfair' trading practices designed to shift the costs of adjustment on to others. In this context it is possible to distinguish between different forms of selective assistance according to the degree to which they cause friction in trading relations.

Reconversion assistance seeks to minimize the impact of industrial change or decline, by funding retraining schemes, income support, alternative employment or aid for areas affected on a selective basis. Examples of such aid can be found in ECSC reconversion programmes (see Chapter 6). This form of selective aid provides not production or investment subsidies to maintain or re-establish lost competitiveness, but compensation for those immediately affected. As such, it has less impact on the international distribution of cost and therefore less direct impact on trade.[3]

When selective assistance is provided to help an industry back to viability or competitiveness, *restructuring*, production costs and thus imports and exports are inevitably influenced. Such restructuring aid can take a number of forms, from public payment of accumulated losses to preferential depreciation allowances. As the objective here is often the maintenance of existing, or at least a substantially sized domestic productive capacity, there is a danger that adjustment costs will be pushed on to other countries. In order to avoid this, sectoral advisory bodies such as the OECD steel and shipbuilding committees have been established.

Finally, of course, there is *selective trade regulation*, including 'voluntary' restraint agreements, which is perhaps the most immediate form of relief for an industry. The increase in selective import regulation has rightly caused concern in the international community, because it has often taken place outside the auspices of GATT, which could provide some form of multilateral monitoring. In the case of both restructuring aid and trade regulation a major issue is how one can ensure that such assistance is genuinely temporary. Experience has shown that once committed to providing relief or assistance in such forms governments have found it very difficult to extract themselves. In practice, national approaches to selective adjustment problems have sometimes combined reconversion, restructuring and trade regulation (as in steel), whereas trade regulation has been the main form of relief from adjustment pressures provided in other sectors (such as textiles).

THE INTERNATIONAL DIMENSION TO THE ADJUSTMENT DEBATE

The increased concern with national measures which slow industrial adjustment at the expense of foreigners has contributed to the emergence of the, as yet undefined, concept of 'fair trade'. The competing industry in other countries will argue that to support free trade under such conditions would grant free access to a subsidized competitor. Consequently, industrial lobbies have moved from support of 'free' trade to 'fair' trade, and interest has centred on all manner of policies adopted by other countries which 'unfairly' benefit competing industries. When an industry believes a foreign competitor is being unfairly supported it will press for equivalent subsidies, import regulation or some other form of compensation.

This move towards 'fair' trade is industry-oriented as opposed to general welfare-oriented. For example, under the tradition of general welfare-oriented free trade, subsidies provided to, or dumping practices exercised by, a foreign producer benefited the domestic consumer via lower prices. The shift from 'free' to 'fair' trade, however, has meant that such practices are seen primarily in terms of their impact on domestic industries – hence the industry as opposed to welfare orientation of 'fair' trade. The danger with 'fair' trade is that, failing any clearly defined criteria for what is 'fair' and what is 'unfair', it may be used to justify neo-protectionist policies. The debate on what constitutes fair trade is linked to adjustment debate because many of the measures defined as 'unfair' fall under the rubric of adjustment policies as broadly defined.

There have, of course, been various attempts to define 'fair trade' and thus prevent the escalation effect of subsidies leading to countervailing measures leading to further subsidies. In the Tokyo Round of MTNs, such issues were included in the form of GATT codes on subsidies, public procurement policies and selective safeguards. On the latter no agreement could be reached. Under existing GATT rules, nearly all industrialized countries were committed to the 1960 Declaration giving effect to the provision of Article XVI:4 of GATT, which prohibited export subsidies. There is no prohibition on the use of domestic or production subsidies, only a requirement under Article XVI to notify any subsidy 'which operates directly or indirectly to increase exports of any product, or to reduce imports of any products'. Major differences appeared in the course of the Tokyo Round negotiations on a code for subsidies and counter-vailing duties. Some countries, mainly in Europe, wished to retain a large degree of freedom in the provision of domestic subsidies for social and domestic political reasons, while others, notably the USA, wished to have tighter monitoring of subsidies. An attempt failed to reclassify subsidies according to: prohibited subsidies (that is, those designed to increase the competitiveness of national producers, thereby distorting international trade); conditional subsidies (practices directed towards domestic, economic, political or social objectives, but which may distort inter-national trade); and permitted subsidies (practices with little or no impact on international trade) (GATT, 1979, p. 53). This classification corresponds approximately with that of selective restructuring aid (prohibited), selective reconversion aid (conditional) and general aid which does not distort trade (permitted). As no agreement could be reached on this reclassification, the final GATT code on subsidies and countervailing duties does not cover a wide range of subsidies used in adjustment policies. It remains to be seen whether the evolution of a GATT case-law will bring more subsidies under GATT surveillance in the future. Experience to date, however, especially in the EC which has far more extensive powers to control subsidies, suggests that governments will continue to provide selective assistance to avert large-scale bankruptcies or when social problems are acute (EC Commission, 1978b). It has been shown that either national governments are not prepared to commit themselves to rigorous international constraints, or that even when treaties provide for a total ban on subsidies (as in Article 4 of the ECSC Treaty), these are not enforceable, for social and political reasons.

The degree to which international constraints in the form of rules or norms will be accepted and operable is therefore limited. For these reasons an OECD initiative to promote positive adjustment sought to encourage national governments to modify national policies. The case for modification was put mainly in terms of the negative effects defensive policies can have on national macro-economic objectives. But it was also argued that selective action on the part of one country would lead to similar action by others in order to compensate, thus effecting a general misallocation of resources. This has happened, for example, in the shipbuilding industry, for which even the West Germans have been obliged to provide production subsidies. In order to encourage the use of intervention to promote adjustment rather than inhibit it, the OECD Secretariat introduced the concept of positive adjustment.[4] The OECD programme on positive adjustment set up various working parties and drew on the expertise of existing OECD committees – for example, trade, industry (OECD, 1979e), manpower and social policy (OECD, 1979d) – in an effort to identify the various ways by which policy instruments influence adjustment. By drawing the attention of all governments to the practices employed it was hoped that governments would move towards best practices in various fields. A High-Level Advisory Group on positive adjustment was also created. This had the task of monitoring the various sectoral bodies, such as working party 6 on shipbuilding and the steel committee, which were set up to help prevent adjustment costs being shifted from one country to another (OECD, 1979d). The task of the High-Level Group was to ensure that the sectoral consultations did not stop adjustment and thus jeopardize macro-economic objectives. The two-year work programme on positive adjustment was initiated after the OECD member countries had agreed on general orientations for industrial, employment, manpower and regional policies in 1978 (OECD, 1978a). These general orientations are similar to guidelines developed within the EC (EC Commission, 1978b; Woolcock, 1981), in that they seek to ensure that assistance is temporary, degressive and transparent.

The OECD exercise is not legally binding and it is difficult to judge its effect on national governments. Certainly, knowledge of what other countries are doing helps to reduce the suspicion which often lies behind claims of 'unfair' trade practices. By forcing governments to justify their policies it has also contributed to the national debates on the best form of adjustment assistance. None the less, no government has found any difficulty in classifying its policies as being positive, and few have felt constrained from providing 'temporary' selective assistance.

While international constraints on national policy are essential, they will not work without adequate national constraints on defensive or negative adjustment. As indicated above, national approaches to selective adjustment assistance are likely to involve a mix of reconversion, restructuring and trade protection. There are unlikely to be any simple solutions to the problems of promoting positive as opposed to negative adjustment. As the earlier chapters indicate, trade regulation is likely to continue to be used. However, when considering the question of adjustment assistance as an alternative to trade regulation, it is important to remember that policies which have visible costs and affect the distribution of costs nationally will be more constrained than policies which do not. Thus adjustment assistance to workers, communities or industries incurs a visible cost on the national exchequer. It also has the built-in constraint of opposition from interest groups at the national level who contribute in the form of taxes to the assistance, but do not benefit from it. The effectiveness of this constraint on national defensive policies has been clearly shown in the case of the steel industry in Europe and the trade adjustment assistance in the USA.

During a period in which many AIC governments are attempting to reduce public expenditure, the prospects of increased adjustment assistance are not good. Trade regulation therefore offers a cheap alternative, and it has the added advantage of avoiding politically sensitive distributional issues at the expense of foreigners. Of course, trade regulation shifts the costs of adjustments from the industry to the consumers, but compared with industry, AIC consumers are still under-represented in the debate. This is one reason for the shift from free to 'fair' trade. For national policy-makers trade regulation also has the added advantage of avoiding some of the difficult economic and ideological problems involved in devising effective adjustment policies. For some unexplained reason, trade regulation is considered less of a sin against the open market order than selective intervention in investment decisions or public subsidies. Finally, the political and financial costs of trade regulation are even less of a constraint when NIC imports are regulated.

NOTES

1 For a comparative study of the effect of appreciating exchange rates on industrial adjustment pressures, see, for example, the Maldague Report (1979).
2 See Diebold (1980) and Pinder *et al.* (1979) for a discussion of the interaction between industrial, national and international levels.
3 Such reconversion assistance, as it is termed in EC jargon, has not caused major problems internationally, and is generally supported, for example by the OECD Steel Committee.

4 The nearest the OECD has come to defining positive adjustment formally is to say that what matters is 'whether over the long run the policies concerned facilitate movement of labour and capital from the production of goods and services in declining demand to those where demand is increasing, from less to more efficient forms of location and production, and from production in which other countries are gaining a comparative advantage to new competitive lines of production' (OECD, 1979c, p. 9).

13
The Micro Picture: Corporate and Sectoral Developments

Lawrence G. Franko and
Sherry Stephenson

The thesis of this chapter is that, because of the great differences between the industry and company structures found among different sectors of NIC interest, the adjust-versus-protect choice facing the industrialized countries (and companies) has been, and will continue to be, highly differentiated by industry. Moreover, this holds under a very wide range of high- or low-growth macro-economic assumptions.

The view here is that the adjustment process as played out in the real world is not primarily a macro-economic, market process, but rather a series of micro-economic 'games'. The players in those games have certain characteristics, predispositions and stakes. An understanding of these 'structural' factors could well lead to better forecasts and policies than those based on merely knowing whether the games will be played in more or less agreeable business climates.

PARAMETERS OF PROTECTIONISM

If past is prologue, it can be argued that the ease of adjustment in AICs to the thrusts of the NICs varies largely as a function of five principal characteristics of an industry's structure in the AICs. The 'fit' of that industry structure with the structure of the sector in the NICs also appears to matter.

The relevant industry characteristics appear to be:

(1) 'Multinationality' of the principal company actors;
(2) The degree – or lack of – product diversity of the leading firms in the industry;
(3) The presence or absence of state ownership in the industry;
(4) The importance of the threatened product or industry in total employment in manufacturing; and
(5) The degree to which some companies are very much more – or less – competitive in a given industry, compared with those in other AICs.

The causal relationships underlying these hypotheses are the following:

- A significant multinational spread of production, especially if it extends into the NICs themselves, gives a firm degree of freedom in managing the adjustment process simply not available to a national firm. Multi-nationality of firm structure and a powerful oligopolistic position in an industry tend to go together; market power can allow corporate production location decisions to 'damp' what could otherwise be abrupt and socially disruptive workings of the market. At the limit, the internal decisions of multinational enterprises (MNEs) can act, as Helleiner has asserted, as 'extra-governmental' non-tariff barriers. But one need not ascribe quite such machiavellian behaviour to MNEs to observe that their planning horizons will tend to be geographically broader, and their comparative cost information very much better, than the information available to national firms. This fact alone would enable an MNE, on average, to forecast, plan and thence to 'manage' the adjustment process better than can a national firm. By extension, industries characterized by many MNEs ought to pose fewer adjustment headaches for public policy-makers than those consisting of national firms.
- Product diversity, too, allows firms degrees of freedom to adjust to new competitive thrusts unavailable to few-product firms. Like any other skill, shifting resources from old products to new, from inefficient to efficient modes of production, or indeed from production of goods to the provision of services, appears to be learnt by doing. Although the evidence has not been as systematically assembled as one would like, business history teaches that firms that have already diversified many times are likely to be far more successful at future resource-shifting moves than will firms trying such moves for the first time; especially when the first-timers have sunk vast organizational, human and capital investment into one specialized activity. By extension, industries charac-terized by diversified firms will tend to pose fewer adjustment problems for public authorities than will industries made up largely of mono-product specialists.
- State ownership tends to imply state, indeed public and political, commitment to the national survival of a particular activity. In theory, state ownership need not necessarily imply that a firm or sector will be cushioned or protected against failure in the face of foreign competition. Still, since more or less spurious national-security grounds are often invoked for the taking over by the state of a particular industry in the first place, it is all too easy for honour, patriotism and the like to get in the way of adjustment.
- The more people employed in a threatened sector, the more likely that adjustment will both prove difficult and be resisted with the aid of public policy instruments. The point has often been made that the benefits of free trade are diffuse and benefit many people a very little bit, while the benefits of protection are much more concentrated and obvious, and therefore lend themselves to the formation of political

coalitions aimed at obtaining those benefits. But in the modern AIC democracies this may not be the whole story when trying to predict resistance to adjustment. Modern democracies are sensitive to numbers – especially to numbers of people concentrated in specific regions – and it is numbers of people in particular electoral districts that make or break political careers. The NIC threat may be very nearly total, as it has been in certain sporting goods. However, if there are few people employed in any given AIC in making such products, and they are scattered around electoral districts in such a way as to allow elected representatives to think of other things, adjustment may proceed with minimal overt tension between nations. But when the jobs at stake number in the tens of thousands politics may retard or block the relevant economic processes.

– The more a 'North–North' competitive disequilibrium exists among companies in a particular industrial sector, the more competition from the South may be made a surrogate target for political action. Countries in the North have, through the EC and successive GATT negotiating rounds, disarmed themselves of many trade barriers which could be used to salvage an industry ravaged by competition from other AICs. When the US, French and British steel industries fell seriously behind Japanese, German and Italian rivals, the tension in the 'centre' was necessarily released at the 'periphery'. In contrast, when the company players of most AICs are in more or less similar states of health, exports from NICs may more easily be absorbed into the system.

COMPARATIVE CORPORATE STRATEGIES

Overlapping these general processes which affect sectoral adjustment is an additional micro-factor – the fact that companies of the different continents seem to have developed distinctive strategies towards the export thrust of the NICs.

European Companies

On the whole, the European companies have chosen to stay at home or to seek a 'Limited-multinationality Northern-market solution' to the reality of changing comparative costs. This has taken the form of some mix of moves towards 'rationalization' (by seeking scale economies through plant closures or concentration, or through substituting capital for labour), or moves towards higher-value-added product lines, R&D, innovation and diversification.

By and large, European companies like Philips and Thyssen which attempted to adapt by choosing a strategic mix skewed towards diversification and a search for higher-value-added new products ended the 1970s as viable, if not spectacular, competitors against the Japanese and the NICs (which were often one and the same). Those companies like ICI which pursued a northern-hemisphere strategy and stressed rationalization and cost-cutting more than R&D and diversification tended to find that these measures could never be pushed far enough or work fast enough to avoid losses of market share to the large-scale, low-cost, globally minded Japanese, whose productive operations typically extended into the NICs, and who were meanwhile themselves upgrading their own product lines and innovative capability. European would-be 'cost-cutters' often sought refuge in protection, but even when this protection 'worked', open AIC markets, plus rising currencies, still left many would-be cost-cutters highly vulnerable to intra-EC or to Japanese competition, as well as to the occasionally viable and internationally minded American.

Japanese Companies

While the Europeans have attempted with greater or lesser success to *adapt* to the process of change, Japanese companies have generally *promoted* it. They have done this by often being the first to promote efficiency through scale, improved work methods or advanced process technology. They have also promoted change by continuing investment and R&D during downturns in demand (for example, as in steel and colour television) as opposed to curtailing such activities during recessions in the US or British manner. Perhaps most distinctively of all, they have carried out a programme of active, export-oriented foreign investment in those sectors (synthetic fibres and TVs) where the competitive edge has passed to lower-cost, NIC suppliers.

US Companies

US companies have often been caught in an uncomfortable middle position, being outdistanced both in process and product innovation, as well as doing little, compared with the Japanese, to seek export-production bases in the low-cost, fast-growth NICs.

Some notable exceptions aside, US companies have often ended up neither really adapting to, nor promoting change but instead trying to avoid it, through an overemphasis on the domestic market, a reliance on the (temporary?) advantages of large-scale operations and a reluctance either to export or to move to lower-cost sites. The only alternative to the loss of domestic market share has thus become recourse to lobbying for the closure or protection of the US market from imports. The 'value-added hunt' engaged in by the Japanese and some of the Europeans has been pursued by a surprising number of US companies belatedly or inadequately.

THE SECTORS UNDER STUDY

This chapter tests the significance of such 'micro' factors against developments in three sectors: steel, synthetic fibres and consumer electronics. The other sectors covered in this book are dealt with in somewhat less depth.

Table 13.1 synthesizes the first four of the salient characteristics of the principal sectors with which we are concerned. Stark differences emerge among sectors along the dimensions of the multinationality of the major company actors, their degree of product diversification, the extent to which they are owned by governments, and the degree to which they employ politically significant numbers of people.

STEEL

Steel represents one extreme case. It is the sector with an extremely low presence of multinationals. It not only appears to have an even lower incidence of multinationals than such 'national' industries as textiles and apparel (see Table 13.2), but it is also particularly low in the use of 'export-platform' subsidiaries in the Third World (see Table 13.3). Companies in the steel industry tend also to be just that: companies producing steel and little else. Exceptions to this rule exist, notably among the less troubled German steel firms, but they appear to be rare. Steel is also perhaps *the* sector of industry which has come to be most dominated by state-owned companies in the AICs – at least those in Western Europe.

Steel also employs large numbers of people. Employment data do not appear to exist broken down to the level of discrete products, but the data that do exist suggest that, with the possible exception of automobile assembly, no single industry employs more people in most AICs than does commodity steel production. As Table 13.4 shows, employment in steel certainly looms very much larger in total AIC manufacturing employment than does, say, employment in synthetic fibres, the only other of the sectors under consideration for which detailed employment information appears to be available in Europe.

Table 13.1   *AIC Industry Structures in Synthetic Fibres, Garments, Consumer Electronics, Automobiles, Steel and Base Petro-chemicals*

Industry	Multi-nationality of major companies	Product diversification of major companies	Presence of state ownership	Importance in total employment in manufacturing
Synthetic fibres	High	Medium-High	Medium-Low	Low
Garments	Low	Low	Low	High
Consumer electronics	High	High	Negligible	Medium
Automobiles	Medium	Low	Medium	High
Steel	Low	Low	High	High
Base petrochemicals	High	High	Medium	Low

Table 13.2 *Multinationality of Industry Structure, Major Industries*

Industry	Percentage of US industry sales by US MNEs, 1964 (1)	Number of MNEs in sector, 1972 (2)
Chemicals		
Industrial	80 ⎱	
Other (including pharmaceuticals)	90 ⎰	57
Petroleum refining	77	17
Electrical machinery	76	34
Non-electrical machinery	67	25
Transport equipment		
Autos and parts	90 ⎱	
Other	20 ⎰	25
Non-ferrous metals	62	10
Textiles and apparel	29	4
Steel	7	7

Sources:
Col. (1): Vaupel, 1971.
Col. (2): CEI-Harvard project, 1972, in: Franko, 1976, p. 15

For these reasons alone it should perhaps be no surprise that steel has been a case apart in terms of protectionist measures actually taken up to the present time. Apart from the well-known case of the clothing industry, the 'New Protectionism' as we have known it so far has been strikingly concentrated in steel (see Table 13.5). The protectionist moves in steel turn out, first and foremost, to have been thus far primarily directed or 'targeted' by AICs at other AICs (especially the Japanese) – or at the socialist East (see Table 13.6). Protecting the AIC industry from NIC competition appears to have been little more than an afterthought, although it was – and is – a spectre much conjured up in rhetoric about the industry's problems.

Company Response to Changing Comparative Advantage

It is arguable that most of the debate over the AIC steel problem has been largely a euphemism for what are some quite specific French, Belgian, British and US problems (with some, but only some, segments of the Italian industry also facing acute adjustment malaise). The variance in comparative performance in terms of losses per unit produced, company profitability (Table 13.7) and change in output since 1974 is extraordinarily wide compared with what is known about company performance in the other industries considered in this volume. A 'North–North' problem clearly exists: is it that the losers in the world steel game do not want to admit that they are losing to other developed countries, and thus choose to blame the NICs?

Table 13.3   *'Export Subsidiaries' of 186 Largest US-Based Multinational Companies (as of 1 January 1976) and Number of Active Manufacturing subsidiaries with Exports Greater than 10 Per Cent of Sales in 1975*

Country or Region	Industrial chemicals	Other chemicals	Iron and steel	Radios, televisions and appliances
Canada	5	2	1	2
Latin America	7	9	0	7
Of which:				
Mexico	3	3	0	4
Brazil	1	1	0	1
Europe	23	43	6	12
Of which:				
Portugal, Greece and Turkey	0	0	0	0
Spain	1	0	0	1
North Africa and Middle East	0	0	0	0
East and West Africa	0	0	0	0
South Asia	0	0	0	1
Of which:				
India	0	0	0	0
East Asia	5	5	0	7
Of which:				
Hong Kong	0	1	0	3
Japan	3	4	0	1
Singapore	0	0	0	1
South Korea	0	0	0	0
Taiwan	1	0	0	2
Southern dominions	2	3	0	2
Total export subsidiaries	42	62	7	31
Total manufacturing subsidiaries	208	309	57	115

[1] Chemicals other than industrial chemicals, plastics, agricultural chemicals, cosmetics, and pharmaceuticals, but including synthetic fibres.
Source: Curhan, Davidson and Suri, 1977, pp. 400–3. Reprinted with permission from *Tracing the Multinationals: A Sourcebook on U.S. Based Enterprises*, copyright 1977, Ballinger Publishing Company.

Meanwhile, there can be no doubt that the winners in the world's steel industry in most recent decades have been the Japanese. These companies have increased their investments and operating efficiency (including energy-saving). Their emphasis has been on exports of steel, steel mills and technology (including sales to US Steel for plant modernization in 1980). They have promoted the development of the steel industry in NICs and

Table 13.4 *Employment in Steel and Synthetic Fibres as a Percentage of Total Employment in Manufacturing, 1977 (1976 when 1977 not available)*

Country	Steel	Synthetic fibres
Belgium	4·9	0·3
France	2·7 (1976)	0·5 (1976)
United Kingdom	2·4 (1976)	0·6 (1976)
West Germany	2·4	0·4
Netherlands	2·3	n.a.
Italy	1·8	0·6

Source: ILO, *Yearbook of Labour Statistics*, 1978.

Table 13.5 *EC: Actions to Restrict Imports under Safeguard, Surveillance, and Anti-Dumping Provisions, 1971–8[a]*

Industry sector	1971	1972	1973	1974	1975	1976	1977	1978[a]
Textiles and clothing	–	1	3	2	17	5	22	29[b]
Chemicals and fertilizers	5	3	–	–	2	2	4	1
Steel and other metals	–	3	–	–	–	1	6	45[c]
Machinery and appliances	–	–	–	–	–	4	2	2
Food	–	–	–	2	2	–	2	3
Electronics	–	1	2	–	–	–	1	–
Footwear	–	1	–	–	1	–	–	3
Rubber products, including tyres	–	–	–	–	–	–	2	–
Wood	–	–	1	–	–	1	–	1
Pulp and paper	–	–	–	–	–	–	–	7[d]
Other	–	–	–	–	1	–	2	3[e]
Total	5	9	6	4	23	13	41	94

[a] To the end of August 1978 (inclusive) only. Our criteria for counting 'actions' may or may not be the same as that used in the original IMF compilation. Therefore, comparisons should be treated as indicative only.

[b] Includes one unilateral Italian action (surveillance of wool-product imports).

[c] Includes one unilateral UK action (iron and steel from Romania).

[d] Includes one unilateral French action ('visa' surveillance).

[e] Includes two unilateral British actions (cutlery surveillance; OMA with Japan in motor vehicles).

Sources: *Official Journal* of the European Communities, various issues, and data provided by the GATT secretariat; 1978 data from GATT, *Survey of Developments in Commercial Policy*, No. 2, January–April 1978, and No. 3, May–August 1978; 1971–7 data from IMF, *The Rise in Protectionism*, 1978.

other LDCs via an extensive programme of technological assistance. They have also used 'offshore' low-energy sites for direct-reduction pelletizing of ore to feed Japanese furnaces. In contrast, West European and US companies have shown little of the Japanese dynamism. The more successful private European companies have made some moves towards

Table 13.6   *Exporting-Country 'Targets' of EC Actions to Restrict Imports during 1978[1] (where identifiable)*

Industry sector	Japan	Other developed countries	Socialist countries	'Mediterranean transition countries'	Developing countries
Textiles and clothing	–	2	4	6	19
Chemicals and fertilizers	–	2	–	–	–
Steel	9	34	31	8	4
Machinery	2	–	–	–	–
Footwear	–	–	4	1	6
Wood products	–	–	–	–	1
Pulp and paper	–	9	1	1	–
Total[2]	11	47	40	16	30

[1] Up to and including 31 August only.
[2] Totals may not equal numbers of 'actions' taken (see Table 13.5), because one 'action' may have been taken simultaneously against several countries.

Table 13.7   *Company Performance (1980): Selected OECD-Based Producers of Steel (billion $)*

Company	Country[1]	Sales (1)	Net income (2)	Equity capital (3)	ROI (%)[2] (4)
Thyssen[3]	D	15·2	0·061	1·74	3·5
Nippon Steel	J	13·1	0·5	2·1	24·0
US Steel	US	12·5	0·5	5·3	9·5
Krupp[3]	D	7·7	0·03	0·8	3·75
Mannesmann[3]	D	7·2	0·09	1·2	7·5
Estel	N	7·0	−0·25	0·9	−28·0
British Steel	UK	6·8	−3·89	1·7	−228·0
Bethlehem	US	6·7	0·12	2·6	4·6
ARMCO[3]	US	5·7	0·26	2·1	12·9
Kobe	J	4·5	0·11	0·58	18·9
Italsider	I	4·3	−0·87	1·5	−58·0
Sacilor	F	4·0	−0·47	0·6	−78·3
Cockerill	B	3·5	−0·27	0·79	−34·2

[1] B Belgium, D West Germany, F France, I Italy, J Japan, N Netherlands, UK United Kingdom, US United States.
[2] Col. (2) ÷ col. (3) × 100.
[3] Highly diversified company.
Source: Fortune.

diversification, emphasizing the development of high-value-added product lines. However, the bulk of European companies have unsuccessfully tried to copy the Japanese strategy of large-scale commodity steel production. In the case of the USA, the companies there seem to have tried to avoid any major changes, and have moved to close the domestic market off from imports.

The Japanese companies have been able to pursue their strategy in part because rapid productivity and sales growth have combined to generate sufficient profits for investment in new plant at home. Secure in their technological superiority and ever more modern, efficient plants, the Japanese could promote the entry of LDCs into the industry. Whether the resulting LDC output went for local sales or for export, it was virtually certain to take market share away from non-Japanese producers. In contrast, investment and productivity growth lagged in Western Europe and the USA. With the exception of some individual companies, the response to NIC entry has been much more defensive as well.

European Responses

Companies such as BSC and US Steel which tried to follow the Japanese example of large-scale commodity steel production, but did so defensively and in the face of shrinking market demand, have tended to fail. The British example is a case in point.

BSC

The British Steel Corporation (BSC) is an example of a company in which bad strategic decisions since nationalization, as well as a statutory restriction against diversification, have led to over-capacity in low-value product lines, outdated plants and enormous losses (totalling £2 billion over the six years up to 1980). In stark contrast, the 10 per cent of the British steel industry left in private hands has become stronger since 1967. By pursuing a policy of continuous investment (now running at £100 million a year), it has doubled its crude steel-making capacity and now competes more than successfully with BSC on all overlapping product areas.

This difference in record is partly explained by the strategy each sector followed during the early 1970s. While BSC set out on a course of bulk steel-making after the Japanese fashion, with the target of expanding to between 30 mmt and 40 mmt annually by 1980, the private sector (which involves over one hundred small companies with a combined capacity of 5 mmt of crude steel per annum) embarked upon rationalization and a 'value-added search'. Several small family firms joined together and pushed production towards the speciality areas of steelmaking. The private producers also benefited from the mini-mill concept and by the making of steel in electric arc furnaces – a capital-intensive but (thanks to a large use of scrap) a materials- and relatively energy-efficient technique. By remaining flexible, these firms generally remained profitable as well.

Other private West European steel producers have chosen to go by a different route, that of diversification. Companies which began as steel producers, such as Thyssen (West Germany) and Schneider (France), have moved consciously in recent years to broaden their product lines. For both these companies, basic steel products accounted for less than 30 per cent of total sales in 1979. Thyssen has moved into the trading and engineering services area, along with capital goods manufacture, while Schneider has chosen the areas of construction and civil engineering. For both, steel took only a small part of the new investments made during 1979. The European companies have also moved to the high-value-added end of the product line within the area of steel itself: for Thyssen speciality steel (9 per cent of total sales in 1979) was one of its most profitable product lines.

US Responses

Neither the strategy of the Japanese nor that of the successful West European producers has been followed by the majority of US companies, which have remained in a sluggish middle ground, bothered by low profits and ageing equipment and witnessing an ever larger chunk of the domestic market being taken by imports. While the Japanese (along with some of the new NIC producers) tried to remain at the most efficient end of the production ladder, and the Europeans sought higher-value-added solutions or diversified, the Americans by-and-large ignored changing world competition and markets, stood still and then turned to protectionism.

Since at least 1968, the international relations of the US steel industry have been dominated by a search for protection. A 'voluntary' export restraint was agreed with the Japanese in 1968 and extended in 1971 to the end of 1973. After a brief outburst of free trade during the 1973–4 economic boom, import quotas were introduced in 1976. When the anticipated cyclical recovery failed to materialize in 1977–8, pressure by US steel producers led to the introduction of the Trigger Price Mechanism for monitoring the price of imports. This was then superseded by the series of anti-dumping charges against West European producers, which were subsequently withdrawn when trigger prices were reintroduced at a level 12 per cent higher than before.

By the mid-1970s, the pressure to protect the domestic market was being supplemented by efforts to inhibit the sale of steel plant and technology by US firms abroad, especially sales to NICs. These efforts successfully limited US Export–Import Bank lending for foreign steel-mill projects, as well as official investment insurance against political risks which otherwise might have been available for such plant exports.

The Armco Strategy

One of the exceptions to this rather bleak picture is the case of Armco. Although Armco is only number six in raw steel output, accounting for around 6 per cent of the US steel industry's production, its example of diversification serves as a yardstick for assessing the strategies of the larger producers. It has long ceased to look for growth in basic steel production. Less than half of its $466 million operating income in 1979 was earned from steel, and of the $300 million it planned to spend on capital assets in 1980, only one-fourth was to go into basic steel. This contrasts starkly with the US Steel Corporation, largest steel producer in the USA, which derived nearly three-fourths (72 per cent) of its operating income in 1979 from basic steel products.

Armco's biggest growth area at present is the oil services sector where it owns a subsidiary called National Supply, making drilling equipment. It also has oil and gas exploration interests, along with activities in five other product areas, each of which is managed separately: special steels, mineral resources (coal, ore and limestone), metal fabrication, financial services and industrial products.

Armco is also unique among US steel-makers in the volume of its international operations, with interests in more than thirty countries. Understandably, given its diversified multinational posture, it is less strident about import restrictions than are the other less-diversified, primarily domestic producers. The diversification part of Armco's strategy is being adopted somewhat more by necessity than by choice by US Steel Corporation, which is now expanding as fast as possible into the chemicals business.

A further unique element in the Armco story is its long-standing technical-assistance and licensing link-up with Nippon Steel, a link which dates back to post-war Japanese reconstruction. Whereas Armco technology once helped Nippon Steel rebuild, Nippon Steel technology now helps Armco remain competitive. (In late 1980 a limited cross-equity link between the two firms was announced.) In the light of this relationship, it hardly seems coincidental that Armco should have shown a broader geographical and product awareness than that of its domestic brethren.

The Japanese Posture

As in other industries, Japanese firms are vigorously promoting the entry of the NICs. In steel, however – perhaps because of the heavy state investment in most LDCs – the emphasis has been more on licensing, equipment sales and management contracts than on equity ownership.

Starting with the export of equipment, engineering services and technological assistance to Brazil in the 1950s, the Japanese industry has become the purveyor of steel know-how to the Third World.

Nippon Steel

Nippon Steel became involved with Brazil through the activities of its predecessor, Yawata Iron & Steel Company, which made the first serious technological exports of the Japanese steel industry in 1956. Yawata helped construct the Usiminas steel-mill which, after some twenty years of operation, has now grown into an integrated steel plant, having three blast furnaces and boasting an annual crude-steel output of some 1·2 million tons.

The success of the Usiminas steel-mill encouraged other developing countries to ask for aid, which resulted in the construction of steelworks in Malaysia, South Korea and Italy. By the autumn of 1980, Nippon Steel was engaged in building a steel-mill in Shanghai. In fact, the company's range of technological assistance in 1979 involved 134 cases spread around seventy-one different companies in twenty-six countries. By this time, its cumulative effort in technological assistance involved projects in thirty-five countries.

Nippon Steel's technological link with Armco is the most graphic example of its growing sophistication. However, Nippon Steel is now emphasizing the importance of engineering as a business for the 1980s. Originally, the engineering division sprang from the need to make full use of the surplus technological staffs, resulting from the merger of Yawata and the old Fuji Iron & Steel Company. However, the top management of Nippon Steel now see this engineering division as much more than a way of mopping up surplus labour. At present, as many as 4,000 workers are involved in this division under the direct leadership of three vice-presidents (*Oriental Economist*, September 1980).

There is little doubt that this policy of NIC-promotion is coupled with longer-term plans, not only those of Japanese companies but also of the Japanese economy. Since the début of post-war Japanese economic planning, the steel industry has been the sector, and Nippon Steel the company, closest to the industrial structure committee of the Ministry of International Trade and Industry (MITI). Its wage bargains are to this day considered the model for the economy. The international strategy of the industry was described to one of the authors of this paper in 1970 by a Japanese steel executive who was a participant in a management development programme in Geneva. In a class presentation he outlined his firm's twenty-year plan for 'riding the international product life cycle', that is, for a planned disengagement by Japan from the steel industry as products and technologies matured and standardized to the point where less-developed, lower-wage countries with access to the capital or resources needed for entry could become competitive. (For an elaboration of the argument that low-wage countries can have a comparative advantage in capital-intensive, but low-skill, standardized products, see Franko, 1979, pp. 25–8.) It is of perhaps more than historical interest to note that the reaction of several of the Western executives present was one of some hilarity at the idea that a firm would bother considering something so 'unrealistic' as a twenty-year plan.

SYNTHETIC FIBRES

Of all the sectors under study, synthetic fibres bears perhaps the closest comparison with steel. The industry has already had to cope with extra-AIC competition (albeit primarily from the Socialist countries). The maintenance of employment has proved impossible, at least in Europe. The principal AIC-based companies are less diversified than are the base-petrochemical producers. Also, Italian and French companies in particular have had a notably harder time keeping up with the rest of their AIC competition (see Table 13.8). Moreover, like steel (and unlike basic petro-chemicals), serious LDC expansion of production capacity is not hovering on the horizon, but is already here.

None the less, if there are some similarities in kind between the cases of steel and synthetic fibres, there are market differences in degree. The likes of Du Pont and Hoechst are hardly 'one-eyed giants', the expressive term used by Scott to describe the product-committed US steel firms. Rhône-Poulenc may be having difficulty in synthetic fibres, but as a firm it is hardly bereft of growth sectors (for example, pharmaceuticals) in its portfolio. Most of the firms are multinationals, although with mixed involvement in the NICs: ICI, for example, is basically AIC-centred. Rhône-Poulenc's clear centre of gravity is in France, but it is also the single largest chemical-producing firm in Brazil. ('Multinationals' have been active in the synthetic-fibre industries of South Korea, Taiwan, Indonesia and Thailand, but this has often been on a minority participation basis, and the MNCs in question – in Taiwan, Indonesia and Thailand – have been based in Japan) (CEPII, 1978, p. 75). Perhaps the most marked contrast with steel is that shown in Table 13.4. Employment in synthetic fibres is very small in comparison with that in steel as a percentage of total employment in manufacturing, reaching a high of only six-tenths of 1 per cent in the UK and Italy. However, owing in large part to their substantial interests in textiles as well as fibres, several European companies have put their weight behind protectionist moves.

Table 13.8 *Company Performance (1980): OECD-Based Producers of Synthetic Fibres (billion $)*

Company	Country[1]	Sales (1)	Net income (2)	Equity capital (3)	ROI[2] (%) (4)
Hoechst	D	16·5	0·25	2·7	9·3
Du Pont	US	13·7	0·72	5·7	12·6
ICI	UK	13·3	−0·046	6·5	−0·7
Montedison	I	9·1	−0·52	1·5	−34·7
Rhône-Poulenc	F	7·2	−0·46	1·3	−35·4
Monsanto	US	6·6	0·15	2·8	5·3
Akzo	N	6·3	−0·035	1·1	−3·2

[1] D West Germany, F France, I Italy, N Netherlands, UK United Kingdom, US United States.
[2] Col. (2) ÷ col. (3) × 100.
Source: Fortune.

Companies in Western Europe have a different perspective on the problem of the textile 'chain' than do their US counterparts. Trade regulation in fibres was introduced in Europe because the smaller markets and more numerous and fragmented plants could not match the competition from the NICs through productivity improvements and rationalization. US trade protection is designed primarily for the clothing sector; the US fibre industry is doing well and has recently emerged as a serious threat to European markets. The US industry has larger-scale plants but, previously, demand growth and its corollary, high prices, allowed smaller European plants to be viable ('infra-marginal', in economists' jargon). With a constrained demand and slumping prices, this is no longer the case. In addition, because of the depressed value of the dollar during 1979 and 1980, the US had low labour costs – especially compared with strong-currency competitors. Moreover, it benefited from access to low-cost supplies of natural gas and oil feedstock for its fibre production.

Company Strategies

Behind tariff and MFA protection, companies have responded to increases in imports of synthetic fibres, and of textiles and clothing using these materials, in different ways. Responses have varied according to: (1) the degree of protection the company felt that its products enjoyed; (2) the degree of its diversification in areas other than fibres (or other parts of the textile 'chain'); and (3) the primarily 'national' or 'multinational' nature of its operations and outlook. The responses of Rhône-Poulenc (France) and ICI (UK) to the growing competition in fibres are illustrative.

Rhône-Poulenc
Rhône-Poulenc, the sixth largest chemical company in Europe (after ICI, Montedison and the three German giants Hoechst, Bayer and BASF) was relatively undiversified before the 1970s. The group, which supplies 8 per cent of the world's production of synthetic fibres, is a 'multinational' company but with very strong national roots. Seventy per cent of its production was produced at home in 1977, and this could be subdivided into 30 per cent exported and 40 per cent consumed in France. In 1966 nearly two-thirds of its sales came from fibres and textiles (including some clothing) alone, while by 1977 this figure had fallen to 28 per cent. However, even this much reduced figure far exceeded the importance of fibres in the total product portfolios of most of its major European competitors (approximately 9 per cent for ICI, 8 per cent for Hoechst and Montedison, 4 per cent for Bayer and BASF). Only four Western companies – Du Pont (US), Akzo (Netherlands), Courtaulds (UK) and Snia Viscosa (Italy) – and a few smaller Japanese competitors had a greater concentration on fibres. The result of such a heavy dependence on one troubled product sector meant that Rhône-Poulenc has had a poor financial performance relative to most of its competitors during the difficult years since 1974. For example, losses from textile and fibre operations totalled 707 million French francs in 1977. ICI lost £16 million sterling in fibres in that year. However, while the overall picture for Rhône-Poulenc was in the red for 1977 because of textiles and fibres, the overall operations of ICI were in the black.

Rhône-Poulenc benefited from a stronger MFA through purchases of its chemical fibres by the protected European textile and clothing industry. It was clearly one of the firms pressing its government for a protectionist response. However, it also began to 'adapt' internally through a major reorganization effort – *le Plan Textile* – announced in December 1977. The reorganization effort concentrated on trimming the range of its synthetic-fibre products: eliminating and reconverting some, maintaining others as low-scale operations (fibranne, rayon, chlorofibre and acrylic) and promoting others. Polyester and nylon were singled out as fibres for future expansion and growth, and three plants in France were rationalized and modernized for the production of these fibres.

Rhône-Poulenc's primary response was diversification, accompanied by one of the highest R&D expenditure-to-sales ratios in the industry, with a concomitant effort at rationalization of its fibre production in the home market. Venturing abroad occurred but was not stressed. In mid-1980, in a restructuring move partly sponsored by the French government, Rhône-Poulenc sold off its (also unprofitable) basic petrochemicals businesses to (partly state-owned) Elf-Aquitaine; it retains its fibres business, however.

Before leaving the Rhône-Poulenc story, the puzzle of the company's important US and Brazilian operations (the latter reportedly constitutes Brazil's largest chemical company) deserves a mention. Despite some exports, neither of these undertakings appears to have been really used in an integrated strategy. Was it because of the company's extreme national base or that the structure of management relations was of the loose, 'mother–daughter' variety (Franko, 1976, ch. 8). Or was there some other reason?

ICI

The British multinational, ICI (Imperial Chemical Industries Ltd), is a more diversified company than Rhône-Poulenc, but it also has very strong national roots. In 1978, 49 per cent of its production, 60 per cent of its fixed assets and most of its R&D were located in the UK. As in the case of Rhône-Poulenc, 40 per cent of group sales went to its home market, in this instance the UK. Export sales, however, accounted for only 9 per cent of total group sales, and foreign production for some 51 per cent. Thus, if foreign production is the criterion of multinationality, ICI is a good deal more multinational than Rhône-Poulenc. With a handful of exceptions in protected LDC markets, however, ICI's 'production multinationality' is concentrated in northern Europe and North America. Indeed, an unofficial but common view in the industry had it that this was the result of an explicit managerial decision taken at the end of the 1960s to avoid the political risks of LDC operations.

ICI is a highly diversified company. Large portions of its sales are constituted by general chemicals (20 per cent) and agricultural products (20 per cent). Petrochemicals (18 per cent) and plastics (14 per cent) are also important product lines. Fibres are far down the list, accounting for only 9 per cent of sales. Consistent with this fact, ICI's concern over the depressed market situation in fibres in Europe since 1974 has been less than that of Rhône-Poulenc. However, perhaps because of vertical integration within the company as well as its northern hemisphere orientation, it combined with its British competitor Courtaulds (a company much more dependent both on fibres and textiles) and the clothing industry to throw its full weight behind the pro-MFA lobby.

Although in 1979 it was profitable overall, ICI has shown consistent losses in its fibre operations since 1973 (£16 million in 1977 and £13 million in 1978). It instituted a rationalization programme in 1975 to raise productivity, with the goal of producing 30 per cent more with 30 per cent fewer people. It moved to restructure domestic fibre production facilities at home and abroad. In 1977 it closed the Offenbach factory in West Germany and sold off or closed a number of other small plants in Holland and Germany in order to centre all of its Continental fibre production in one plant near Heidelberg.

ICI followed the trimming of part of its fibre operations with selective investment in modern technology in factories in the UK. It perceives the future and long-term viability of its fibre operations as 'closely linked with those of its downstream customers in the (European) textile industry' (*Annual Report*, 1978). It feels that the problem of over-capacity in the industry at present (nearly 30 per cent in Europe) is one which should be solved by unified action coordinated and endorsed by the EC Commission's Directorate for Industry. ICI does have a minority position in the number two US producer of fibres, Fiber Industries Inc. (Celanese is the majority partner), but it produces no fibres in NICs with the minor exception of a small plant in India.

As of late 1980, ICI's 'protect and rationalize' strategy was not producing the hoped-for results. Its fibres division in particular, and quite possibly the company as a whole, appears critically trapped between the more productive R&D of its Continental European rivals, the scale economies and feedstock prices of the Americans, and the low-cost, NIC-based Japanese.

Asahi Chemical

The response of one of the main Japanese chemical companies, Asahi Chemical Industry Company, stands in sharp contrast to the reaction of the European companies to the increase in fibre imports from low-cost and more productive suppliers. Asahi and its consolidated subsidiaries manufacture a diversified line of products including synthetic fibres and textiles (44 per cent of total sales), chemicals, plastics, synthetic rubber, food products, pharmaceuticals, construction materials and housing units. As in its European counterparts, Asahi's fibre and textile division experienced declining sales in the 1970s. Asahi responded by (1) adapting through organizational changes at home (for example, by the formation of a new sales company for synthetic fibres in June 1978), (2) streamlining production (the company's acetate operations were suspended in September 1978), (3) shifting towards higher-value-added products (fashion apparel), and, especially, (4) shifting its fibre operations to low-cost producers, either NICs or other developing countries. The network of its foreign operations is far-reaching and, by contrast with Rhône-Poulenc or ICI, is concentrated almost entirely in low-cost countries. It has fourteen plants abroad (of which eleven are in LDCs), has been regularly investing abroad, is the largest shareholder in companies producing synthetic fibres in Indonesia, Guatemala and South Korea, and is a minority shareholder in companies in India, Sri Lanka, Nigeria, Hong Kong and Mauritius. Entering into the European market, it chose Ireland as a site for acrylic fibre manufacture and spinning. Its foreign expansion has been particularly marked since 1974, since when it has added the operations in Indonesia, South Korea and Taiwan. Asahi's response to the export challenge has thus been to promote change by increasingly important foreign operations in NICs and other developing countries.

A preliminary survey of the strategies of other Japanese fibres companies, such as Toray industries, suggests that, with slight variations along the lines of somewhat more R&D or diversification, the 'NIC export-platform' route has been chosen generally by the main Japanese firms in the industry.

CONSUMER ELECTRONICS

Of all the industries here considered, consumer electronics presents the most nearly polar contrast with steel in terms of industry structure. The companies are multinational (although those which refused to multination-alize, like Zenith in the USA, experienced difficulties in the face of foreign, mainly Japanese, competition). Moreover, unlike the synthetic fibres case, where the 'multinationality' of some leading firms does not extend into the NICs, here MNCs have actively used NICs as export bases (see Table 13.3). Furthermore, it appears that by far the largest proportion (75 per cent in 1977) of US imports of electrical goods – including consumer electrical apparatus – from LDCs occurred as 'related-party' transactions from subsidiary to parent. In contrast, US imports in other sectors of NIC thrust, such as clothing (12 per cent), textiles (8 per cent) and footwear (4 per cent) were much less 'manageable' by MNCs (Helleiner, 1979). The principal firms in this industry are also highly diversified, with the partial exception of 'leaders of the rearguard action', like Zenith. Indeed, it is hard to find firms in *any* sector more diversified than consumer electronics producers Philips, Matsushita and the unrelated UK and US General Electrics.

Except in the UK and Belgium, employment in the electrical industry as a whole has remained steady or increased. It is far from easy to isolate employment figures for this subsector, but it is clear that consumer electronics account for only a small fraction of total employment within the electrical machinery and electronics sector of Western Europe and North America (see Table 4.2 in Chapter 4).

'North–North' competitive battles are hardly unknown in this sector. Indeed, the picture is similar to that found in steel; there have been severe problems with Japan, the great gainer in intra-AIC competition over the past decade. The 1977 OMA imposed by the US on colour-television imports was quite specifically aimed at Japan. Yet nowhere has the survival of all the relevant companies in whole nations been threatened as was the case in steel. European and Japanese managers in Philips and Hitachi may wonder why the Americans have so nearly disappeared from consumer electronic sectors such as radios, televisions and watches. But however much US companies may have been forced to cut back production in those lines, only the exceptional company has disappeared or been irretrievably damaged. Instead, they went on to other products and other production sites. Financial performance of the AIC-based firms has varied, but nowhere to the extent of steel, or even synthetic fibres (see Table 13.9). For a change, too, some of the greatest variation was within countries (General Electric versus Zenith) rather than between companies in different countries. It is not surprising therefore that in the USA, the trade-policy debate in consumer electronics took place as much between US companies as between them and their foreign rivals. The case of steel shows that a different kind of conflict occurs when countries are, or seem likely to be, knocked off a particular industrial playing field.

Japanese Dominance and NIC development

The success story of the 1970s in colour-television sets has definitely been a Japanese one. Their producers achieved their market success through a combination of lower labour costs, higher technical qualities and larger-scale operations. They have moved through extensive research outlays to the forefront of technological advance and product development in the consumer electronics field. Their advantages in television-set and tube manufacture include:

(1) Labour costs one-half or one-third as high as those in West Germany or the UK.
(2) Designs requiring up to 30 per cent fewer components than West European or US sets, because of a greater use of integrated circuits.
(3) Automation in the assembly of sets (of between 65 and 80 per cent of total components used as against between 0 and 15 per cent in West German and UK plants), meaning that a Japanese company can produce a colour television set with an average of 1·9 work-hours, against 3·9 in West Germany and 6·1 in the UK.
(4) Large scale of plant operations (output per plant of around 500,000 sets a year) with double the capacity of European plants.
(5) Superior-quality components, helped by the fact that the Japanese television suppliers produce a relatively high proportion of their own components. This vertical integration has given rise to a technological cross-fertilization which is difficult or impossible for less integrated Western firms to achieve.

Table 13.9   *Company Performance (1980): OECD-Based Producers of
Consumer Electronics[1] (billion $)*

Company	Country[2]	Sales (1)	Net income (2)	Equity capital (3)	ROI[3] (%) (4)
GE	US	24·6	1·5	8·2	19
Philips	N	18·4	0·17	6·0	2·8
Hitachi	J	12·9	0·50	3·4	14·7
Matsushita	J	12·7	0·54	5·1	10·6
Thomson-Brandt	F	8·6	0·07	0·7	10
RCA	US	8·0	0·31	1·9	17
AEG	D	6·8	−0·16	0·4	−40
GEC	UK	6·6	0·54	2·9	18·6
Sanyo	J	4·0	0·13	1·0	13
Thorn EMI	UK	3·5	0·20	1·2	16·7
Zenith	US	1·2	0·03	0·3	9

[1] The major OECD-based companies producing consumer electronics tend to be highly diversified; consumer electronics in some cases (e.g. Siemens, US General Electric) is only a small part of company activity.
[2] D West Germany, F France, J Japan, N Netherlands, UK United Kingdom, US United States.
[3] Col. (2) ÷ col. (3) × 100.
Source: Fortune.

In an economic climate of generalized recession in Europe and the USA, the Japanese can be considered to have a product/market-segmentation advantage as well. A large proportion of Japanese sets are small, with tubes of less than 20 inches (51 cm). This is due partly to the nature of Japanese home demand and partly to restrictions built into the PAL licensing system. Western producers have specialized in big sets, and are thus best positioned for a return to 1960s-style economic growth, which may never come.

Most of the Japanese success story in colour televisions during the 1970s has been due to process, component, and – with the advent of video-recorders – product innovation within Japan. But, as with black-and-white televisions and tubes back in the 1960s, most Japanese companies have not hesitated to move offshore once automation reached its limits at home, or international trade politics so demanded.

Part of the response of Japanese companies to US trade barriers was to seek locations in NICs such as Taiwan and Singapore which were still unencumbered by restraint agreements and which had efficient, low-cost and easy-to-train pools of local labour. Mitsubishi Electric made it clear that one of its aims in investing in Singapore was to use this subsidiary in an export drive aimed at the US and West European markets. Matsushita and its affiliate JVC have a whole or partial ownership stake in colour-television component factories in South Korea, Malaysia and Mexico, which appear tied-in with US final assembly. In fact, Japanese companies have been using offshore assembly in lower-cost NICs as part of their production strategy since the late 1960s.

However, although it is the Japanese which have recently become the most vigorous promotors of NIC involvement in colour televisions and components, the first 'NIC-promoters' in the colour-television sector were, in fact, US firms responding to the initial Japanese challenge of the early 1970s. At that time, the Japanese use of NIC export-platforms was essentially limited to black-and-white televisions. But perhaps because US offshore production was only defensively motivated, it lost its thrust, and protectionism – or disappearance – became the prevailing US response to the Japanese advance.

US and European Responses to the Japanese/NIC Thrust

The response of television-producing companies in the USA and Europe to the export thrust of the Japanese and the NICs during the 1970s was varied and depended upon several factors, among which were:

(1) The speed at which the problem was presented to the company. For instance, the drive of the Japanese and others was aimed first towards the US market. This was less protected, and producers had left the bottom range of the television market open through having concentrated on the large-screen, higher-priced range of products.
(2) The company's perception of market signals of changing competitive conditions.
(3) The degree of diversification of the company, and the importance of television operations to its total sales.
(4) The company's willingness to risk spreading its assets by investing abroad, rather than concentrating upon modernization and rationalization in the home market.

US Companies: Zenith

Zenith, the US company which, along with RCA, has had the largest share of the US colour-television market (22 and 20 per cent of the market, respectively, in 1977), was less diversified than other US consumer electronic companies and was thus most vulnerable to the surge in television imports. Zenith was also not vertically integrated into components, a fact perhaps not unrelated to its slowness in adopting solid-state technology. It failed to respond correctly to changing market signals, and to assess the growing competition. Along with the other US television producers, it had not bothered about exporting and considered the US market basically as a closed entity. It also pushed ahead with overly ambitious production and marketing plans inappropriate for the economic conditions at hand.

Most US television producers responded to the competitive challenge either by selling their assets to Japanese or European multinationals (the case of Motorola, Magnavox, Philco, Warwick and GTE-Sylvania) or by shifting a substantial portion of their activities offshore (see Chapter 4 for further details).

Zenith, in contrast, attempted an essentially 'US-only' strategy, and was reluctant to shift its operations offshore in any major way. This attitude prevailed, although it already had small subsidiary operations going in Taiwan and Mexico. Rather than expand these operations, Zenith chose initially to lobby for protection of the domestic market, while it was also arguing a case on appeal from a customs court against Japanese television producers for allegedly conspiring to restrain trade. Independently of the Zenith case, the International Trade Commission was also investigating alleged Japanese dumping in the television sector. The combination of such domestic pressure resulted in the May 1977 OMA with Japan.

Besides seeking protection, Zenith invested in R&D (albeit at levels which appear to have been below those of Japanese competition) and attempted to develop a 'quality image' in the market-place. When this strategy gave insufficient results, it reacted belatedly but quickly to trim its domestic operations. After having first pushed for further automation in the USA and spending research money without being able to cut production costs, it was forced to follow the example of RCA: rationalize at home, shift assembly abroad and aim for lower-cost assemblage parts. Zenith closed its colour-television tube factory in Pennsylvania in 1977, laying off one-quarter of its work-force. These colour-television operations were moved to its plants in Taiwan and Mexico. Zenith thus belatedly joined the ranks of the other US television producers in moving investment and assembly abroad and promoting competitive change. It chose not to diversify and in fact sold its small hearing-aid business.

Europe

In Europe, colour-television producers were also forced to think about rationalization, in spite of protective barriers, but thanks in large part to the patent protection from PAL, and the PAL/SECAM split, they faced the Japanese/NIC thrust later than did their US competitors. Only recently has there been a trend towards increased concentration as a solution for the very fragmented and generally small-scale operations in Europe. While Europe leads the world in actual production of colour-television sets, its tube industry is smaller than that of both the USA and Japan. This appears to be an especially vulnerable area, which seems to require a build-up of both larger and more integrated producers.

Philips. Philips of Holland and France's Thomson-Brandt have chosen a relatively positive range of strategic responses. In addition to seeking scale economies, in part via horizontal integration through acquisitions of other television producers, they have actively, albeit primarily defensively, moved to counter Japanese and potential NIC competition through new product development in 'home communications', merging television use with video-recording and playback, and, especially in the French case, with teletext and viewdata systems.

Philips, the Dutch multinational, is the world's largest single producer of colour televisions, and probably has the soundest position in the European market, even though its specialization in large sets and lagging position in video-recorders (VTRs) has rendered it vulnerable to Japanese and NIC competition in the small-set and VTR sectors. It is relatively dependent on consumer electronics compared with General Electric (US), Hitachi and Toshiba, but it is still a diversified company and, unlike the smaller European firms, is a producer of components. A quarter of its deliveries in 1978 were in home electronic products for sound and vision. (Besides television sets, this included videocassette-recorders, cameras, video record-players, audio equipment, clock and car radios, hi-fi equipment, hearing aids, etc.) Although only 8·6 per cent of Philips assets are in the relatively small Dutch market, most of its investment abroad is in the AICs, with only 3·5 per cent of its assets located in developing countries in 1978.

Philips controls about 30 per cent of the European market for colour televisions (one-third of its sales are in West Germany alone) and furnishes about 40 per cent of Europe's colour-television tubes. The prospect of increased Japanese penetration of the European market as the PAL licences expire and Japan is able to sell screens larger than 20-inch, pushed Philips further to integrate its operations horizontally by taking a 25 per cent share in Grundig (the eighth largest world producer of colour-television sets and Philips's main customer for tubes) in 1979. Between them the two companies now have 40 per cent of the West German television market. Philips and Grundig will also collaborate on the development of a second generation of videocassette-recorders and a new videodisc system (Video 2000) to be marketed in conjunction with Siemens. Along with the Grundig and GTE-Sylvania tie-ups, Philips has moved towards adapting its European operations through production standardization and model rationalization. Despite important television production operations in Singapore and Taiwan, Philips appears to be giving comparatively limited emphasis to LDC/NIC 'export platform' investments in its overall strategy.

On the negative side, Philips has heavily encouraged the EC to pressure the Japanese to accept a voluntary export restraint (VER) agreement in the colour-television sector. This is not the action of a company confident of its future, despite the fact that Philips has generally been more positive in its response to Japanese competition than its US rivals.

Thomson-Brandt. The French have isolated themselves somewhat from the rest of the European market through their adoption of the SECAM transmission system. However, the French government has been actively promoting one of its national champions, Thomson-Brandt, to prominence in the West European consumer electronic market. Thomson now controls 10 per cent of the European market for colour television sets and, through its specialized subsidiary Eurocolor (owned jointly with RCA and Telefunken), furnishes 25 per cent of colour tubes.

As is pointed out in Chapter 4, Thomson-Brandt has made a series of acquisitions aimed at taking it out of the narrow confines of the isolated French market and into the wider West European one. Its acquisitions of (and from) Nordmende, AEG-Telefunken and GTE-Sylvania are signs of its horizontal expansion within the colour-television sector, but these purchases will allow the company to integrate its operations vertically and to rationalize them through a greater specialization in set designs and models.

Thomson's chief involvement in the NICs is through an operation in Singapore, producing 100,000 colour televisions for the south-east Asian market. This is a bit reminiscent of Philips, whose operations in the Asian NICs are not a central part of its strategy. Rather, also like Philips, Thomson-Brandt is primarily concentrating on strengthening its home base in Western Europe, through a rationalization and modernization of its operations, and a rather greater concentration on product and process innovation. The development of operations in the NICs is very much an afterthought.

Conclusion

While US television producers have been absorbed or forced to contract through misreading or ignoring the world market situation, and have belatedly reacted with some offshore operations, and while the Continental European producers have sought to develop a 'Northern market' solution by rationalization and product upgrading at an EC level, the Japanese producers have adopted a global outlook in the consumer electronics market, for both production and sales. (The UK is in the process of being drawn into the Japanese orbit, by imports, import-linked licensing accords and production joint ventures.)

Accordingly, Japanese companies first invested in NICs, both to sidestep trade-restraint agreements and to take advantage of lower-cost production sites for assembly of components and manufacture. As other AIC markets were penetrated, the Japanese added US and UK production sites to get within the rising trade barriers round such economies. Hitachi has twenty-two overseas manufacturing plants, of which fifteen are in LDCs, while Matsushita has thirty-nine plants abroad, of which thirty-three are in LDCs. In 1979 alone Hitachi established joint venture companies in the Philippines, Singapore, Mexico, Thailand and Taiwan.

Matsushita's goal of expanding overseas production is to 'combat [the] unfavourable effects of currency fluctuations and import restrictions in major markets' (*Annual Report*, 1979). Hitachi's production philosophy is stated more forcefully as the development of a 'system of decentralized production through the establishment of production bases throughout the world, especially in televisions . . .':

Our business must be carried forward from a worldwide view and not from the viewpoint of a single country . . . true internationalization is something to be realized in the future. (*Annual Report*, 1979)

Thus the Japanese companies have both remained at the competitive head of the general television and consumer electronics sector and have acted to promote the development of this industry in the NICs.

Perhaps the major risk facing the Japanese companies that are following this global strategy is the possibility of their being gradually forced to lose a share of the market to lower-cost NIC competition, which they are now helping to promote. Adaptation to such change, be it through increased process automation, large-scale component integration or new product R&D would not seem to be easier for the more flexible Japanese than it has been for the more inward-looking, defensive US and European companies.

PETROCHEMICALS

The petrochemical industry has proved even more resistant to protectionism than consumer electronics. In this, it is at the opposite extreme to steel and textiles (even though there are companies which straddle both the petrochemical and synthetic-fibre sectors).

In base petrochemicals, the post-oil-crisis fears of imminent 'disruptive' competition by Third World producers, especially those based in OPEC, have receded a good deal since the Iranian revolution disrupted that country's industrialization drive. But there are other, more fundamentally persuasive, reasons for thinking that the oft-forecast adjustment 'problem' in this industry may, like the earth's horizon, recede continually the closer we get to it – even if a serious OPEC presence in the industry is established one day. On both sides of the North–South divide, the structure of this sector is substantially different from that found in the other sectors under study.

Here, multinationals are the rule in the AICs, whereas in steel they are hardly even exceptions (see Table 13.2). Despite the fact that petrochemical multinational involvement in LDC–NIC export subsidiaries is low (perhaps because there just are not yet that many LDC export subsidiaries – see Table 13.3), the firms active in *developed* countries do have world-wide cost and market-scanning capabilities, as well as some remnants of oligopolistic control over markets through the advantages of scale, logistics and delivery capabilities.

Above all, these chemical MNCs are highly diversified. It is not even possible to put together a table of comparative company performance in 'basic petrochemicals' analogous to the comparison of steel producers in Table 13.7 – because it is virtually impossible to identify such a thing as a 'basic petrochemicals company' any more. Many are more commonly known as oil companies; these, in turn, may mine coal or uranium, own department stores, or be world leaders in laser and word-processing computer technology. Others are purer 'chemical' companies, active in the literally thousands of product groups which comprise that industry. State champions are few in number and importance, and that state ownership that exists is largely a derivative of state shareholdings in the oil-company

Table 13.10   *Employment in the Chemical Industry, 1973–7 (000s)*

Country	1973	1974	1975	1976	1977	Percentage change 1973–7
Belgium	74·6	76·9	77·2	76·2	76·3	+2
France	342·4	352·6	350·7	353·1	n.a.	+3 (1973–6)
West Germany	n.a.	617·1	610·7	587·4	579·9	−6 (1974–7)
Italy	282·0	293·9	293·6	302·2	n.a.	+7 (1973–6)
Netherlands	90·1	93·0	95·9	92·3	89·5	−1
UK	n.a.	479·8	482·4	465·4	470·9	−2 (1974–7)

Source: Eurostat.

parents of the affiliates producing petrochemicals. Moreover, these oil companies with state shareholdings, such as ENI, CFP, BP, Elf-Aquitaine and Veba, are – unlike the national steel companies – also multinationals.

Perhaps again because of the fact that the companies in the industry are so highly diversified, statistics on employment in the basic petrochemicals sector *per se* seem unavailable. One can only surmise that, because the sector involves one of the most highly capital-intensive production processes, and because 'chemicals' covers so many thousands of products, the numbers of people employed are tiny relative to all manufacturing. Still, the data on employment in the whole chemical sector in various European countries presented in Table 13.10 allow some inferences to be made about this industry's adjustment potential. It is perhaps most noteworthy that, even in the face of the most severe slump in the West since the great Depression, total employment in chemicals either remained roughly constant, or even increased between 1973 and 1977 – West Germany being the only (modest) exception to this general rule. Also, most of the few declines in total chemicals employment which did occur seemed to be particularly concentrated in synthetic fibres.

CONCLUSION

Broadly speaking, this survey of industry and company responses to the NIC challenge confirms the hypotheses with which we started. In particular, the multinationality, diversity and intra-AIC competitive position of the leading *firms* active in each sector matters if we are to understand the accommodating or protectionist responses of the developed *countries* to developments in the NICs. However, there are nuances.

First, multinationality matters, but only if it extends in an important way to the NICs themselves. Despite their multinational spread within the northern hemisphere, ICI, Rhône-Poulenc and Philips eventually found themselves lobbying for protection. Perhaps this was because their strategies had treated LDC production sites as desirable only as a response to local market protection, not as bases for world-wide exports in the Japanese manner.

Secondly, although state ownership, especially in steel, has not notably facilitated adjustment, it cannot be said that it bears major blame for anti-NIC protectionist pressures. That must be assigned to management myopia on a much broader scale.

Thirdly, although these particular case studies have tended to cast the Japanese firms as the dynamic, NIC-promoting, adjustment-prone firms – and Western companies as resistant to change – such generalizations are too simple. The West does have its Armcos and Thyssens, its General Electrics, Du Ponts and Hoechsts, which are adjusting and not looking to reactive, public policy for protection.

The real public and private policy challenge is thus one of preventing firms from falling into product and geographical management myopia. How to do that is, however, the subject of a different study.

14
Adjustment in Western Europe
Stephen Woolcock

In Chapter 12 the issues involved in adjustment policy were discussed on three levels, the corporate or industry level, the national level and the international level. In this chapter we look at adjustment policies in a predominantly national context, taking France, the Federal Republic of Germany and the UK as examples of West European approaches to adjustment. Where relevant, reference is also made to the role of the EC.

HISTORICAL TRENDS IN APPROACHES TO ECONOMIC POLICY OF WEST EUROPEAN GOVERNMENTS

In this volume we are concerned with the 1980s. The present and future policy responses in Western Europe are, however, influenced by historical factors. In the nineteenth century the economic policies of both France and Germany were more state-oriented than were those of the *laissez-faire* British. The strong empire-oriented trade policies of the British cushioned the effects of the world recession in the 1930s, but influenced the development of attitudes and policies in the post-war period (Walker, 1980). British banking was developed to finance trade with colonial and Commonwealth markets and did not develop the close links with industry which characterize the German banking system.

The development of economic theory and political forces in the UK resulted in the creation of a post-war economic policy based on the mixed economy and Keynesian demand management. Indeed, during the 1950s the UK was the only real Keynesian economy in Western Europe (Postan, 1977). While other West European countries employed demand management and global steering of their economies, the commitment to Keynesian ideas was greater and longer-lasting in Britain. (For a comparison of British 'Keynesianism' with German 'Schumpeterian' policies see Giersch, 1978, and Wolter, 1976.)

In the Federal Republic of Germany the past importance of the role of the state in the tradition. of the *Nationalökonomie* was broken by the general discrediting of the state and the need for politicians in the West to distance themselves from the central planning of what was then the Soviet Zone (now the German Democratic Republic). The domestic political and international climate therefore effectively precluded the choice of the 'middle way' of the mixed economy. Economic freedom in the form of the social market economy was intrinsically linked to political freedom, and the formal commitment to the social market economy by the Social Democrats (the SPD) (Godesberg Programme, 1959) consolidated the existing non-interventionist ground rules of West German economic policy. The SPD line – 'competition as far as possible, planning as far as it is necessary' – meant that there was little pressure from the SPD for greater intervention as long as the German economic miracle lasted.

France began the post-war period with a comprehensive effort to bring what was still a relatively inward-looking fatalistic economy into the twentieth century (Monnet, 1978, pp. 232–63). The initial modernization committees built on a tradition of state involvement in the economy, and set a precedent for a more active role on the part of government in industry than in any other West European country in the post-war period. While the tripartite modernization committees were not to last, the corporate approach to indicative planning fostered close 'technocratic' (Shonfield, 1965) government–industry relations and a relatively harmonious relationship between civil servants and industrialists which continues to influence French adjustment policy (Stoffaes, 1980, p. 7). As comprehensive, indicative planning became less effective with the increased openness of the French economy, it was replaced by contractual links (for example, programming contracts or growth contracts) between government and industry. In this way it has been possible for government to influence investment and industrial structure in a more flexible fashion than by the full nationalization of sectors of industry as in the UK. The ability to control the private sector without full public ownership was also facilitated by public control of a significant share of the banking sector. It is estimated, for example, that publicly controlled banks (such as the Banque Nationale de Paris, Crédit Lyonnais and Societé Générale), hold 40 per cent of French bank deposits or 80 per cent if one includes savings banks.

The differences between the French *économie concertée* and the German social market economy meant that no agreement could be reached on the common approach to industrial development in the EC (Woolcock, 1980; for a specific discussion of the role of the EC in industrial adjustment, see Woolcock, 1981). During the early stages of the EC this was of no great importance. Relatively strong economic growth meant that adjustment to new trading patterns within the customs union was relatively painless. The need for an EC approach to what is now termed adjustment policy emerged as national governments began to adopt separate policies. Notwithstanding the differences in national approaches, all governments had, by the end of the 1960s, adopted some form of regional policy. This was particularly true in the case of Italy, but West Germany had also begun to develop structural policy instruments (FRG, Bundesregierung, 1966). The role of the EC soon emerged as one of seeking to ensure that national regional aid programmes did not distort intra-Community trade. The late 1960s also saw the emergence of more active industrial policies, such as those promoting advanced-technology industries, in order to redress the technological gap with the USA. France promoted national champions under its policy of *l'impératif industriel.* The British Industrial Reorganization Corporation (IRC) encouraged corporate restructuring in important industries and in West Germany this period saw the beginnings of public support for R&D in electronics, aerospace and nuclear energy. During the 1960s all countries developed increasingly sophisticated social and man-power policies, with the Scandinavian countries in the lead (Franko, 1980).

At the beginning of the 1970s, however, adjustment policy consisted of predominantly general, non-selective means of influencing factor allocation. It was not until the post 1973/4 period that more selective forms of adjustment policy were introduced. There had been problem industries during the 1960s, with textiles and coal-mining both in relative decline. But it was not until the 1970s that a majority of governments actively intervened to slow the process of adjustment in such industries as ship-building, textiles and steel.

POLICIES IN THE 1970s: A PERIOD OF REASSESSMENT

Even before the energy-price shock in 1973 some West European economies were beginning to consider how to respond to change in industrial structures. France was promoting her national champions in an effort to move French industry into industries such as aerospace and electronics. In the early 1970s Britain was still struggling with generally poor industrial performance, so the response was not one based on selective promotion of growth sectors. General investment incentives were used when it became clear that the enterprise package of the Conservative government was not having the desired effect. Indeed the 1972 Industry Act was used more as a general defensive response to the problems of British industry than a means of promoting selected growth sectors. Both Labour and Conservative governments accepted that 'selective aid would be justified in the case of an inescapable contraction of an industry . . . where to precipitate dissolution [of the industry] may occasion problems of unemployment and hardship which no government could reasonably tolerate' (UK, House of Commons, 1971–2).

In West Germany there was some consideration of structural trends as reflected in the production for the first time of a structural report on the economy (FRG, Bundesregierung, 1969) in 1969. As early as 1966 it was recognized that 'in future there [would] be greater need for structural adaptation due to technological change, new materials, European inte-gration, changes in the international division of labour and a slowing of demand for basic consumer goods as income levels rise' (FRG, Bundesregierung, 1966). An attempt was also made to devise criteria for industrial structural policy. Any subsidy or assistance should not maintain existing structures but promote adjustment (*Anpassung*) or technological innovation and productivity (FRG, Bundesregierung, 1966). Therefore, while West Germany was and remains relatively non-interventionist, it was forward-looking in the sense that it attempted to specify criteria for intervention in advance rather than respond to particular problems as they arose in an *ad hoc* fashion. Adjustment became an issue because it was recognized that it had been held back by a relatively undervalued Deutsch mark and the importation of semi-skilled labour (*Gastarbeiter*). By 1970 West German labour costs were second only to those of Sweden, in Europe, and the number of *Gastarbeiter* had risen from 1·1 per cent of total employment in 1960 to 6·8 per cent in 1970 (13 per cent of manufacturing employment) (Wolter, 1979, p. 4).

With high trade dependency it was therefore recognized that adjustment would have to take place if manufacturing was to remain competitive. This adjustment was to be brought about by industry itself under the pressure of a rising Deutschmark and external competition. But this did not stop the government taking steps to promote new technologies and R&D, and in 1972 the Federal Ministry of Research and Technology was formed for this purpose.

Following the oil-price shock of 1973 all West European countries introduced anti-cyclical measures to minimize the impact of the recession. The anti-cyclical or trade regulating measures were in many cases defensive in that they slowed adjustment. How defensive each country was depended on the interaction of a range of factors including the structural problems of the economy and the political climate (Franzmeyer, 1979).

The energy-cost constraint on the balance of payments led many countries to reassess the value of general demand expansion. This was particularly true in France with a deficit of 6 billion francs in 1976 which forced her to introduce deflationary policies. But France's supply-side response in the form of the Barre Plan did not stop at fiscal and monetary policy. There was also a commitment to bring about far-reaching structural change by active intervention if necessary. The view gained ground that French industry must respond to changes in the international division of labour and technological developments if it was to become more competitive and thus pay for France's increased oil bill (Stoffaes, 1980, p. 10). The Barre Plan involved a liberalization of the economy, with the removal of price controls, but, what was more important, it recognized that French industry and French industrial policy would have to become more outward-looking.

French public and semi-public bodies are more prepared than most to describe and seek to influence structural changes in trade and production, and comparative studies (Maldague, 1979), mostly of French origin, have shown that France's industrial structure is still relatively dependent on price-sensitive lines of production in which the NICs have been becoming

increasingly competitive (Stoffaes, 1978) (the comparative work shows the
UK and Italy to be even more dependent). Furthermore it was thought that
French industry had not moved into growth sectors – sectors, that is, for
which global demand was growing relatively fast – as well as the Japanese,
Dutch or West German industries. Once again the UK came bottom of the
AIC league table in this regard (Baron, 1978). During the 1970s, therefore,
French policy has increasingly accepted the view that the pressure of
structural changes would increase, and that French industry would have to
adjust if the vicious circle of low-growth/refusal to adjust/structural
rigidity/weak growth was to be avoided. The French could therefore be
classified as 'growth pessimists' (Pinder *et al.*, 1979, p. 3), who consider
that it is government's responsibility to ensure that such measures as are
necessary are taken on the supply side. The country also remains relatively
interventionist, but showed signs of becoming more outward-looking and
positive in her adjustment policies towards the end of the 1970s.

It has been shown that West Germany attempted to codify public
structural-policy intervention at an early stage. In the UK such a
codification was not possible, perhaps because of a general suspicion of
codification, but a fundamental lack of consensus on the role of government seems a more likely reason. It has been argued that clear policy
guidelines laid down in advance would help avoid defensive *ad hoc* intervention (Wolf, 1979). Part of the reason for Britain's more defensive
approach to adjustment problems could therefore be this lack of generally
accepted policy guidelines. Probably more significant, however, is the fact
that Britain's problems have been greater. For this reason greater emphasis
was placed on the general improvement of UK industry, as in the Labour
government's Industrial Strategy, which established no less than forty
sectoral working parties (SWPs) under the auspices of the National
Economic Development Office (NEDO). With a relatively vulnerable
industrial base UK policy in the 1970s was more defensive, with the
emphasis on maintaining existing industries when these were under
pressure rather than more forward-looking adjustment policies (Silberston,
1980).

In what could be considered as an initiative to consider the role of
industrial strategy in a new international division of labour, an
interministerial committee was set up. Indeed, in a speech at the time
Foreign Secretary David Owen suggested that the industrial strategy
should be formulated to help adjustment to industrial growth in the
developing countries (*Financial Times*, 30 November 1977). The Foreign
Office, as in some other countries more outward-looking, of course, than
the Department of Industry, produced a study (FCO, 1979) of the impact of
the NICs on British industry. But discussion of links between trade and
industrial policies has either not taken place or has not permeated beyond
Whitehall.

The question of growth and adjustment was, however, an issue in the
UK. In 1977 it was recognized that macro policies would not be enough (for
example, Eric Varley, Minister of Industry, *Financial Times*, 15 January

1977). But progress towards more selective policies was blocked by the inability to employ planning agreements, and the effect of the National Enterprise Board (NEB) was circumscribed. Furthermore, the NEDO, a stabilizing influence on the otherwise volatile British industrial policy, argued, in 1977, that devaluation and import controls (policies supported by the TUC and Labour left) would not be effective without an effort to improve the supply side of the economy. It was also recognized that the UK was becoming increasingly dependent on lines of production which faced either growing NIC competition or a stagnating world demand (UK, NEDO, 1977). NEDO economists also stressed the need to promote R&D and innovation, and were prepared to consider the case for letting go some activities characterized by price sensitivity and standard technology (*Financial Times*, 17 September 1979).

Such an appraisal echoes the West German consensus view that German industry must become more human-capital (that is, skill) intensive (Wolter, 1976). Both the Federal Republic of Germany and France are, as we shall see, more actively promoting innovation and technology. In the case of the more forward-looking West Germany such a policy has been followed throughout the 1970s, in terms of both technical and vocational training and public R&D support via the Federal Ministry for Research and Technology. In 1979 in the UK a Conservative government was brought to power committed to reducing the public sector. By reducing support for industry, allowing sterling to rise and demand to fall, it has exposed British industry to the full force of adjustment pressures. Given the structural weaknesses of British industry, this shows more faith in the market as a mechanism for adjustment than any other country in Western Europe.

Because of divergent views on the scale of the adjustment problem and the appropriate policy response, no overall policy on EC adjustment has evolved. In December 1977 the European Council recognized the need to restructure those industries undergoing structural crises, and in 1978 the Commission of the EC produced a document entitled *Towards a Community Growth Policy* (EC Commission, 1978f). But the lack of a consensus on the question of growth and adjustment precluded any proposals for more active Community policies. Common EC policies have therefore tended to be defensive actions in declining sectors.

All countries have assumed responsibilities for ensuring a relatively equitable distribution of economic activity throughout the country, via regional policy, and responsibilities for manpower and social policies. This has effectively ensured that regional and professional labour mobility is an issue in the adjustment debate.

REGIONAL POLICIES

There is little evidence from France, the UK and West Germany that regional policy has been consciously used to subsidize particular industries, most aid being automatically provided when a company invests in specified regions. For example, of a total of £1·66 billion spent in the UK on regional grants between 1972/3 and 1977/8, only £0·2 billion was selective aid. Selectivity is introduced, for example, in the form of selective aid under Section 7 of the British Industry Act of 1972, whereby regional aid is augmented in order to enable the region to compete with other locations in attracting multinational investment. Any comparison of incentives would have to be done on a case-by-case basis, but generally competition for investment between regions in Europe helps to ensure that the level of subsidy is roughly equivalent, if different in form (by grant or tax concession, for instance). Within the EC all subsidies are already monitored and controlled, under Article 92 (EEC), when they distort intra-Community trade. While regional policy is considered a desirable objective under the Treaty of Rome, there have been cases where the Commission has intervened in order to remove discriminatory aspects of regional aid programmes.

EMPLOYMENT

Employment subsidies have been used for regional policy, for example, the Regional Employment Premium in Britain. This was phased out after British accession to the EC, and replaced by the Temporary Employment Subsidy (TES). The TES certainly helped the British textile and clothing industry to retain labour during 1976–7, when jobs in the rest of Europe, especially in the countries with strong currencies, were being lost very much more rapidly. The case of the TES shows how the EC Commission, under pressure from competing clothing industries in the rest of Europe, has controlled some defensive aid programmes. The TES was finally replaced by a short-time-working compensation scheme (for textiles and clothing and then for all industry). This practice of compensating workers for lost income had been introduced in West Germany in 1969 and adopted by France in 1975, and is considered less of a distortion to trade because payment is made to workers and not to employers. Apart from controlling trade-distorting employment subsidies, the EC Commission has promoted such worker-income compensation schemes by using them in the coal and steel industries. Under Article 56 of the ECSC Community funds are used for the reconversion of labour in these industries. When Community funds have been used to provide adjustment assistance in the form of regional or social funds under the EEC, the aid has also been in the form of reconversion or non-selective regional aid. For example, the bulk of EEC regional aid grants are provided for infrastructure or in the UK in the form of 'advanced factory' construction.

It has been argued that lump-sum redundancy payments would facilitate labour mobility more than compensation spread over an extended period (Wolf, 1979). Comparing the redundancy schemes in Western Europe it is difficult to find any evidence to support this claim. Britain has a lump-sum redundancy-payments scheme, introduced by statute in 1965. The French and German schemes, however, provide for a set percentage of past earnings to be paid over an extended period: between 65 and 80 per cent in France and 68 per cent in Germany (for the first year, followed by 58 per cent thereafter). Our industry cases suggest that labour mobility has been higher in West Germany than elsewhere. Studies by the OECD (OECD, 1979d) also suggest that social policy has at the most a marginal effect on labour mobility. At this level of abstraction, therefore, one must conclude that it is the general uncertainty about future employment prospects (worse in the UK than in West Germany) which reduces labour mobility and thus the speed of adjustment, rather than statutory social-security provisions.

There are specific cases where job-security legislation may have hindered adjustment. For example, the statutory requirement for authorization of large-scale redundancies (*licenciement collectif*) by employment authorities in France. During the period prior to the 1978 elections, such instruments helped slow labour shedding.

All West European economies face major problems of rising unemployment. Estimates put UK unemployment as rising from 1·5 million over 1978–80 to 2·7 million over 1980–5 and 3·7 million over 1985–90, French at 2·5 million in 1985 and 2·2 million in West Germany by 1985. All these estimates depend on certain policy assumptions. Generally they reflect figures expected if present policies are pursued (see *Cambridge Economic Policy Review*, April 1979, No. 5, p. 34; *Frankfurter Allgemeine Zeitung*, 14 August 1980; Stoffaes, 1980). Since 1977 the service sector has failed to absorb enough jobs to keep pace with jobs shed in manufacturing (Maldague, 1979, ch. 10). Faced with increased unemployment all trade-union movements have pressed for a shorter working week. In West Germany a major strike was fought on the issue in the steel industry. Although national agreements have been reached in specific sectors, the efforts of the EC Commission to introduce temporary reductions in working time in the steel industry failed. Efforts to introduce measures at a national level for all manufacturing have also failed. For example, a government-supported compromise proposal in France, based on annual hours worked rather than weekly hours, finally collapsed in July 1980. Discussions in the EC have made little progress because of opposition by the employers' association UNICE (*Europe Bulletin*, No. 2908). There are clearly immense difficulties in introducing general measures in even a flexible fashion in all the EC countries. But action in specific industries, such as the steel industry, has been opposed because it is seen as setting a precedent for a general reduction in working hours. Any reduction in working hours would certainly make it harder for the West European AICs to compete internationally in labour-intensive or price-sensitive products. Given increased tension in the labour market in all countries, however, the pressure to introduce more labour-market supply policies (such as retraining and shorter working hours) will increase. High and rising unemployment can be expected to slow adjustment.

INVESTMENT

Our industry case studies have shown that defensive investment based on short-term market conditions, and often in existing lines of production, is not an appropriate corporate response to adjustment pressures. During a period of slow growth, however, with uncertainties about exchange rates and inflation, the capacity and will of the private sector to invest in innovative processes or products is severely constrained. In all mixed economies governments are concerned about the level of investment, and measures which are designed to raise the level of investment can scarcely be considered as adjustment policy. Here we are concerned with how the existing forms of public intervention have influenced the direction of investment.

Even in West Germany there is the usual divergence between supporters of more active policies aimed at influencing the direction of investment and supporters of less-interventionist policies. Building on our case studies it is interesting to note that it was the problems of surplus capacity in the man-made fibre sector in 1972 which led the German chemical union, IG Chemie (supported by the DGB, the West German TUC, which is to the left of the SPD) to press for sectoral committees to monitor investment decisions (Mitteilungen, WSI, 1976). The objective of such committees was to prevent the kind of investment which has resulted in excess capacity in man-made fibres in Europe throughout the 1970s. The proposals also recognized the need for international action, and considered the EC Commission's monitoring of investment in the steel industry as a model. Under Article 54 of the ECSC the Commission can only give a 'reasoned opinion' on investment decisions and has no veto powers unless public aid is provided. No such monitoring of investment has been introduced in West Germany, but the discussion of *Investitionslenkung* (steering of investment) continues. For example, the 1977 SPD congress called for structural advisory panels to augment the SVR, the advisory panel on macro-economic policy, and *Investitionsmeldestellen* (registration and publication of large investments) (*Handelsblatt*, 1 December 1977). Through its opposition to more selective investment incentives and its control of the Ministry of Economics, which is the sponsoring ministry for industries such as textiles, steel, shipbuilding and chemicals, the liberal Freie Demokratische Partei (FDP) has prevented the SPD/FDP coalition from adopting a more active industrial policy. For example, the SPD sought to provide more generous capital depreciation for selected industries in 1977 (*Financial Times*, 7 September 1977) and again in 1980 (*Frankfurter Allgemeine Zeitung*, 16 September 1980). On both occasions it was blocked by the FDP. The consolidation of the FDP position following the 1980 general elections suggests that its free-market philosophy will continue to play a key role in West German policy.

One area in which West German policy has taken a more active approach is in the promotion of technological innovation. This is done by indirect investment incentives, for both R&D capital expenditure and R&D

manpower. The support for employment in R&D reflects the West German objective of promoting human-capital-intensive industries as a means of adjusting to changes in the international division of labour and the decline of employment in industry. The increasingly active Federal Ministry for Research and Technology (the BMFT) which is controlled by the SPD, has also provided R&D finance for the energy, aerospace and electronics/telematic sectors. The more active approach of the SPD has, therefore, been channelled into selected industries with high innovative potential (Hauff and Scharpf, 1975).

Sixty per cent of total West German R&D expenditure is financed by the private sector, but in 1978 the BMFT provided DM1·76 billion for energy and raw materials, DM554 million for aerospace, DM310 million for data processing and DM149 million for telematics (*Financial Times*, 19 February 1980). Much of this aid has gone to a few large companies – Siemens for example received DM2·3 billion in 1977–8 – although efforts are being made to reduce this concentration of aid. A new departure in the policy of the BMFT in response to the need to restructure more mature industries has led to support for the modernization of the steel industry and consideration of similar actions in shipbuilding (*Frankfurter Allgemeine Zeitung*, 8 September 1980).

UK aid to science and technology, £254 million in 1978–9 (*Financial Times*, 28 March 1980), was less than West German aid to energy and raw materials R&D alone. Certainly aid to the nationalized industries (£199 million in 1978–9) and the aerospace, steel and shipbuilding industries (£172 million in 1978–9) is partly used to promote R&D, but there can be little doubt that British R&D aid is less than German. The UK R&D effort has been selective, but it has been selective in the promotion of defence and defence-related R&D activities. For example, defence took 46 per cent of UK public R&D expenditure in 1975 (Pavitt, 1980, p. 45), and this share appears to be increasing (52 per cent in 1978 and 55 per cent in 1979) (*Europe Bulletin*, 9 October 1980, No. 2995, p. 16). Only France comes anywhere near spending as much on defence-related R&D, with 35 per cent of public R&D expenditure in 1979. West Germany, Italy, the Netherlands and Belgium all spend more on the general promotion of technology (between 35 and 45 per cent of the R&D budget against 20 per cent in Britain).

In France a recent interministerial study (*Le Monde*, 29 May 1980) has recommended a reallocation of public aid to industry, estimated at 12 billion francs in 1980. These proposals suggest that, within this overall budget, expenditure on R&D should be increased by 30 per cent to some 7 billion francs per annum, and indirect assistance in the form of a 1 per cent reduction in VAT for R&D work is being considered.

Recent policy suggests that the state will 'not hesitate to play the role of innovator' (André Giraud, Minister of Industry, *Le Monde*, 22 September 1978) in new technology-intensive industries. Public policy orientations in France are important because government can influence the direction of investment via its control over substantial bank deposits, and its flexible contractual links with public and private industry. In comparison, the state in West Germany has no control over the industrial investment provided by the private banking sector. However, the large universal banks do fulfil a vital role in industry, which in other countries might fall to public bodies. For example, private bank consortia twice bailed out the troubled AEG within the space of five years. In the UK, where the commercial banks are less committed to the long-term needs of industry, it has been the government or NEB that have helped, for example, Ferranti.

While both the UK and France are relatively interventionist in providing capital investment, the British approach has been more rigid than that of the French or, for that matter, the Italians. In the UK the emphasis has been on nationalization (or opposition to public ownership), whereas French policy has been more concerned with influencing without necessarily taking a rigid line on public ownership. Various attempts have been made to devise a more flexible approach to public control over investment, through, for example, the IRC and the (NEB), both public bodies with powers to invest in public equity holdings, and the Labour government's attempt to introduce planning contracts. But public enterprise in this form has failed in the UK: the IRC was abolished by a Conservative government wishing to reduce the role of the public sector and the future of the NEB as a significant factor in British industry is in doubt. Planning agreements have also failed in the UK. The failure of such agreements probably rests on the lack of close personal links between government and industry, which have enabled such contractual relations to work in France.

This brief survey shows important differences in the role of government in influencing industrial investment. In general it confirms the view that the French approach is relatively interventionist, but this intervention is becoming more positive and forward-looking under the influence of the 'new realism' in industrial policy. West Germany, as France, has remained consistent in its policy. Although relatively non-interventionist, it has consistently pursued the active promotion of R&D and new innovative industries (Fleischmann, 1976). British policy has been volatile because of the lack of a general consensus on the role of public finance for industry. It has also been influenced by the need to defend existing industries. The Conservative government elected in 1979 is again attempting to reduce defensive intervention, but this has not been accompanied by more forward-looking support for innovation in new industries where the UK lags behind both West Germany and France. In sum, therefore, it is necessary to qualify the conventional wisdom that has tended to see intervention and 'positive' policies as opposites. In this context 'positive' is used in the sense of the OECD definition of positive adjustment (see Chapter 12). On this general point see also Pinder *et al.* (1979).

PUBLIC POLICY TOWARDS SPECIFIC INDUSTRIES

A study of Western Europe and our three countries in particular shows that there are three rough categories of selective intervention. There is intervention on a more or less permanent basis in industries that are undergoing progressive decline or experiencing problems in adjusting to long-term structural changes. As the industry case studies show, this has been the case in textiles and clothing over the past twenty years, and in steel and shipbuilding (the past seven to twelve years). A further characteristic of these industries is that the majority of, if not all, AIC governments pursue some form of selective policy. The second category of intervention involves the provision of temporary assistance to an industry suffering from a short-term drop in demand, an import surge or that has temporarily fallen below the current technological level. Here one is concerned with the automobile industry and the consumer electronics industry. It is characteristic of this type of intervention that, because the difficulties of the industry are short-lived, only one or two countries are intervening in a given industry at any one time, and not most countries all the time as with permanent intervention. There is of course a danger that temporary assistance to intermediate industries can become more global and permanent in nature. At the time of writing the automobile industry was in danger for going this way.

Finally, there is intervention in industries which are considered to offer favourable growth prospects. To students of the adjustment debate this involves the issue of 'picking the winners'. Contrary to the case of permanent intervention in 'declining' industries, the West European governments have shown little interest in cooperating in order to prevent competitive provision of assistance. This is due to the belief that the industries involved, such as telematics, face a growing world demand, and every country wishes to gain as large a share of this market for its own industry as possible. In the case of industries facing stagnating world demand, such as shipbuilding, there is greater awareness that assistance provided by one country shifts the costs of adjustment on to other countries. We shall return to this question of different forms of intervention after considering the experience of selective policies in Western Europe.

THE FEDERAL REPUBLIC OF GERMANY

As we have seen, West Germany has distinguished between structural maintenance, adjustment and the promotion of productivity and technological advance. In practice it has been difficult to apply this classification. For example the aid provided to the shipbuilding industry was classified as adjustment assistance. All West German aid to industry is classified in the 'Subventionsberichte' (subsidy reports) (see FRG, Bundestag, 'Subventionsberichte', 1977). In practice aid has been provided to maintain employment and production. That such aid was classified as adjustment assistance reflects the dilemma facing market-oriented economists. As structural maintenance or semi-permanent intervention in an industry is considered incompatible with an effective market order, such aid is simply classified as adjustment assistance and justified, retrospectively, on the grounds that it is only a temporary derogation from the market order.

In the case of textiles and clothing the Federal Ministry of Economics has on numerous occasions strenuously resisted requests for help. As a large exporter of textile and clothing products, the Federal Republic wished to avoid the escalation of trade regulation in this sector. Textiles and clothing, however, is a sector in which many countries have provided selective assistance in the form of import controls. Under pressure from the French and British, West Germany was therefore obliged to go along with the 1973 and 1977 MFAs rather than see unilateral measures, on the part of her trading partners, undermine her largest export market, the EC.

In our intermediate group of industries, automobiles and consumer electronics, the federal and *Länder* governments have only provided temporary assistance, if at all. In line with the social market economy, assistance has been provided when the impact of the adjustment process has resulted in social hardship. For example in 1975, when Volkswagen was undergoing a process of adjustment, a one-off social action programme was mounted to retrain workers. This took large numbers of redundant workers off the labour market for a time and helped ease the adjustment process. The impact of increased petrol prices had at that time also affected other EC car producers, but initial soundings within the EC Commission for a coordinated policy were soon scotched. The industry (rightly) assessed that the problems were only of a short-term nature and no attempt to coordinate lobbying of national governments or the EC was made. The drop in demand and growth of Japanese imports in 1980 has affected all EC producers. The automobile industry is, however, more dynamic and international (cf. the adjustability factors described in Chapter 12). With little prospect of significant direct competition from NIC national industries developing in the 1980s, Japanese exports are likely to remain the main object of efforts to regulate trade. As with all temporary measures, there is a danger that defensive measures in the USA or Europe could escalate into a widespread problem of regulation of automobile trade and production.

The case of the West German steel industry clearly illustrates the problem of a predominantly privately owned industry competing in a world market which is more or less permanently regulated. German assistance to the steel industry has been limited to a few specific actions, such as the loan guarantee of DM900 million for Arbed, which took on the job of restructuring the troubled steel industry in the Saar. Federal and *Land* assistance was also provided to mitigate the social impact of the rationalization programme. West German steel policy has not totally excluded ECSC anti-crisis measures, but both industry and government have sought to prevent regulation of the steel market becoming permanent. In line with EC steel-restructuring policy, West Germany has also provided investment aid for modernization. There has been no selective aid provided to the consumer elect ⁀ ˑcs industry in the Federal Republic, but pressure for import controls has grown in this sector as in automobiles (*Financial Times*, 28 August 1980). However, as noted above, the banks have assumed certain responsibilities for restructuring companies such as AEG. Since the banks operate according to medium- to long-term commercial criteria, however, one can be assured that the assistance for AEG will be temporary.

Compared with France West Germany has not actively promoted mergers as a means of restructuring an industry. One exception, however, has been in the aerospace industry where the federal government, when granting aid to the industry, has repeatedly stressed that it expected the two major airframe companies, VFW and MBB, to merge (*Bulletin des Presseamts*, 1977; also *Financial Times*, November 1980). The federal and *Länder* governments (Bremen and Bavaria) have provided assistance to the aerospace industry over an extended period of time; and have done so despite commercial setbacks such as that over the VFW 614. The support for the aerospace industry has therefore had the objective of ensuring that West Germany has a domestic industry, even though cooperation with other countries, such as in the case of the Airbus, is also encouraged. Similar objectives have been pursued in the computer industry, where West German aid has been estimated to be four times that provided to the British industry (*Financial Times*, 2 September 1980). As in all countries West Germany has also provided considerable aid to the energy sector on a long-term basis.

FRANCE

The French approach to selective intervention distinguishes between three types of industry. First, there are the industries in which the NICs are becoming increasingly competitive, such as: textiles and clothing; raw-material or energy-intensive industries (such as base petrochemicals and steel); and industries characterized by mature product-cycle goods. In these industries 'adaptation' should take the form of innovation, product diversification or automation in order to compensate for the ineluctable decline of certain markets. Second, there are the classic AIC industries such as automobiles and electronics. Here adjustment must enable the industries to consolidate their share of domestic markets. In order to do so, companies must invest in foreign technology and production locations. Finally, there are the new industries such as telematics, aerospace and nuclear energy in which the state must play an innovative role in developing a French industry (*Le Monde*, 22 September 1978; Franko, 1980).

The French government has been careful not to classify certain industries as condemned, but since 1978 it has taken a somewhat less defensive line on industries such as textiles and clothing, steel and shipbuilding. In the past France has provided substantial aid to the shipbuilding industry and has been one of the leading countries in pressing for regulation of trade in textiles and clothing. The shift in French policy is based on a greater acceptance that some industries are less suited to the 'characteristics of the French economy' (André Giraud, *Le Monde*, 22 September 1978), and the need for French industries to become more outward-looking if they are to compete internationally and pay for the increased oil bill. A strong franc, which also helps the oil balance of payments, inevitably increases pressure on price sensitive industries.

In textiles this new policy direction has been reflected in Rhône-Poulenc's sale of much of its man-made fibre capacity, and the fact that the government allowed Boussac to collapse. French industrial policy in textiles has long been to promote concentration in the industry (Mytelka, 1980). This has helped bring about a change in policy, because the large companies are far more receptive to the more positive adjustment government sought to promote towards the end of the 1970s. There remains, however, a sizeable number of more protection-oriented smaller clothing and textile producers, and French policy, as elsewhere, has been sensitive to the social significance of such companies. In shipbuilding the Terrin shipyards were restructured via the bankruptcy mechanism (Stoffaes, 1980, p. 21), but a major restructuring of shipbuilding has been delayed. In line with its policy to restructure energy-intensive sectors, Rhône-Poulenc sold off its heavy chemicals to ELF-Aquitaine and low-density polyethylene to CDF-Chimie in order to free resources for investment in higher-value-added lines such as fine chemicals (*Financial Times*, 5 August 1980).

Plans for restructuring the steel industry existed as early as 1976, but were not fully implemented until after the 1978 elections. By means of financial restructuring, the state taking 15 per cent equity but exercising control over some two-thirds, the steel industry was restructured around two companies. The full steel plan involved diversification into special steels and engineering, retrenchment involving closures of obsolete plant and substantial reconversion (retraining, and alternative employment for workers) (Stout, 1980, App. D6). By means of contractual agreements and financial aid the government also induced both Renault and Peugeot-Citroën to invest in areas affected by steel closures. Of the total package of £2·15 billion, ECSC funds will provide £93 million. In steel as in textiles the 'new realism' has been tempered by French support for EEC or ECSC measures to regulate the speed of adjustment. In the discussions on the ECSC declaration of manifest crisis it was France which pressed hardest for its introduction in 1976. Unlike the West Germans the French diagnosed the existence of long-term structural problems at an early stage. It remains to be seen how far France is prepared to allow such industries to run down, but the new approach to policy at any rate reflects greater acceptance that a certain degree of decline is inevitable.

In the intermediate industries, cars and electronics, policy is directed at strengthening what is, in the case of cars, an already relatively strong position. In line with the trend towards global production patterns in the form of the world car, the publicly owned Renault has invested in production plant in Portugal and concluded various joint ventures. The electronics sector is more dynamic than most and this is reflected in corporate restructuring. In order to promote a domestic component industry the French government has provided loans to French companies seeking joint ventures with US companies. French aid to these intermediate industries has been of a predominantly temporary nature, with emphasis on public support for mergers and similar operations. But France has always had a restrictive approach to Japanese car imports. The fact that policy in these industries is outward-looking suggests a more positive form of intervention than is available in the more introvert, defensive policies for the nationally based steel, shipbuilding and textile industries. At the time of writing (autumn 1981), it was still too early to see how this approach to industrial adjustment would be changed by the Mitterrand administration.

THE UNITED KINGDOM

In textiles and clothing the UK, like other countries, has slowed the process of adjustment in the industry for social and political reasons. The industry has undergone a long period of adjustment, as is shown by the effort to adjust the industry in the 1950s with the Cotton Industry Act. As competitive NIC exporters appeared the UK, along with many other countries, pressed for regulatory measures to ensure 'fair trade'. During the 1970s price-sensitive industries such as textiles and clothing were given indirect protection from AIC competitors by the relative devaluation of the pound. Furthermore, the Temporary Employment Subsidy (TES), while designed as a general, anti-cyclical employment subsidy, effectively slowed adjustment in the industry. By 1979 a strong and rising pound and no TES meant that the industry was exposed to the full force of external competition.

Assistance for the steel and shipbuilding industries in the UK was provided at an early stage, largely as compensation for the relatively slow growth in steel consumption following British industry's generally poor performance. This meant that steel-making in the UK was caught in the downward spiral of slow output growth/lower profit margins/low investment and loss of markets sooner than in many other AIC steel industries. The British approach was to nationalize in order to restructure. However, political controversy over extension of public ownership and lack of resolve in pushing through painful rationalization meant that the British Steel Corporation's recovery strategy took shape just as steel was moving into a global recession. Rather than adjust during the relatively favourable climate of the 1960s, the steel industry made the attempt during the 1970s. Consequently, when modern plant was finally installed, there was no market to enable profitable production. BSC was further inhibited by the narrow concept of public ownership in the UK in that its 1967 statute severely limits its ability to diversify. As shown in Chapters 6 and 12, diversified companies such as Thyssen or Armco have been able to adjust more easily. Whereas the simple costs of maintaining the steel industry forced more rapid adjustment from 1978, control of nationalized industries by cash limits has resulted in further sale of diversified profit centres.

British policy in the intermediate (product cycle) industries has had some success. For example ICL, formed by one-off aid in the form of an IRC-inspired merger, had an early success in the European computer industry, when French and West German attempts to launch an industry were suffering setbacks. BL (previously British Leyland) was also created by the IRC and has received substantial public investment finance. Although it will be a close thing, BL may survive. It has perhaps the disadvantage of being more nationally based than many of its more multinational competitors, but has entered into a joint venture with the Japanese company Honda. The British television industry has evolved in a similar fashion and under strong external competition it has incorporated Japanese technology. The role of government has been marginal here, but the NEDO consumer electronics sectoral working party was able to stress to government that Japanese joint ventures should only go through subject to certain safeguards for the domestic component industry.

Another example of UK policy in what the French call classic AIC industries is provided by the electrical power-plant industry. In 1976 it became clear that a lack of domestic orders would mean the loss of part of the power-plant industry and some of the 30,000 jobs involved. A Central Policy Review staff study concluded that if nothing was done this 'core' industry would collapse, and recommended bringing forward orders by the nationalized Central Electricity Generating Board (CEGB), combined with a restructuring of the industry to reduce capacity. After a long debate the orders for power-station plant were finally brought forward and the CEGB compensated. The necessary reorganization of the industry, however, did not take place. This is symptomatic of British selective industrial aid. Support is given before restructuring programmes are devised and as major problems occur. This is a more 'hands-off' approach than that of the French, who use investment aid as a lever to bring about restructuring programmes which are devised with active public involvement. The lack of national guidelines on a long-term strategy has therefore contributed to Britain's relatively *ad hoc* approach and lack of forward-looking policies.

CONCLUSIONS

There are no specific trade-related adjustment policies in Western Europe. With extensive structural-policy instruments of a both selective and non-selective nature, there is little need to introduce any new policy instruments. What is needed is better use of existing intervention, and, if policies are to become more positive, a change in attitude by various interests. The study of selective intervention shows that it is possible to distinguish between permanent or semi-permanent regulation of industries undergoing long-term structural change, temporary help for industries which have not yet gone ex-growth, and long-term help for new industries.

In those industries in which selective trade regulation and subsidies are widespread, international sectoral bodies such as the TSB and the Steel Committee are likely to develop as a means of preventing adjustment costs being pushed on to trading partners. Such bodies, however, can only control the spread of negative policies; positive actions to adjust (for example by reducing surplus capacity) must come at the industry or national level. Whether adjustment assistance is provided must be decided at the national level, because it is only at this level (at present) that decisions can be made on the balance between economic efficiency and social costs of adjustment. Such a policy can, however, only succeed once the ineluctable decline of certain lines of production is accepted and trade is regulated in such a manner that external competition continues to provide the ultimate sanction against industries which refuse to use the 'breathing-space'. Adjustment assistance for both labour and capital would have to be voluntary and take the form of reconversion assistance.

For intermediate industries there is a stronger case for providing restructuring aid, as the chances of it being genuinely temporary are better in more dynamic industries. This is not to say that there should not be a strengthening of the multilateral surveillance procedures for safeguard actions, but the fact that these intermediate industries are not regulated by a majority of countries makes surveillance easier. In general, the assistance provided to this range of intermediate industries should be governed by the criteria evolved in the EEC and called for by the OECD, that is, limited in time, degressive and transparent. Finally, launching aid for growth sectors must be seen as preferable to support for declining sectors.

In practice there will inevitably be cases where no clear consensus will exist on whether adjustment problems are of a short-term or long-term nature. Here the provision of studies on global structural change and market trends will help to ensure that temporary assistance is not used to maintain industries undergoing long-term change. There may be cases where an industry in a particular country is suffering long-term structural problems while the same industry in other countries is still relatively buoyant. In these cases there may be some advantage in the international or European community providing adjustment assistance, in order to impede the dynamic spread of trade regulation, since trade regulation or aid by the country concerned provokes compensatory measures by others.

15
Adjustment in the USA
Neil McMullen

CONCEPTUALIZING ECONOMIC ADJUSTMENT

Adjustment is the continuing and dynamic response of resource allocation to changes in fundamental economic determinants, including demand patterns, technology, labour-force composition, public policy, the availability of resources and raw materials and productive patterns in the rest of the world. Changes in fundamental economic determinants, such as the change in energy prices that occurred in the 1970s, have an impact on all levels of economic activity: on individuals, firms, industries, regions, nations and the world. Adjustment is occurring all the time, often to positive developments. New technologies, more skilled labour and more plentiful resources during the 1950s and 1960s led to massive economic adjustments. These were generally of the positive kind: real incomes rose, working hours fell, employment in the service sector soared, railroads declined and highway transport rose, energy usage shifted away from coal to cheap petroleum, population shifted to the suburbs, and so on. The USA and the world as a whole adjusted well to these favourable developments in fundamental economic determinants, especially the decline in the real price of energy. In the 1970s many of the underlying trends went into reverse and the challenge now is to adjust to negative developments in a number of fundamental economic determinants.

In the USA the issues of economic adjustment are being addressed on five levels: the macro level; the level of general competitiveness and productivity; the industry level; the level of the firm; and the individual level. These shade into each other, but provide a useful scheme for analysing the likely trends in adjustment policy in the USA during the 1980s. At the macro level, interest in policies is shifting away from interest-rate-oriented monetary and fiscal policies aimed at managing demand. More emphasis is being placed on managing demand via quantitative monetary aggregates and on boosting output via supply-side policies. Supply-side policies also have an impact on the level of general competitiveness and productivity. Policies aimed at enhancing productivity and competitiveness across the economy include reduced taxation of factors of production, measures to stimulate investment in plant and equipment, incentives for increased R&D

and reduced regulatory burdens. These incentives are available for all and could be utilized by the service sector in addition to industry. These economy-wide supply-side policies are being implemented by the Reagan administration, but also with the support of many Democrats in Congress. Policies at the industry level are like general supply-side and productivity-enhancing policies, but are targeted at particular industries. Reducing regulatory costs or requirements on automobiles is clearly aimed at helping that industry. The steel industry is the proposed object of a package of policies, including loan guarantees and relaxation of regulation, aimed at reviving steel production. Industry-level adjustment policies of necessity shade into firm-level adjustment; in particular, loan guarantees are focused on individual firms, sometimes to the detriment of competing firms which have maintained their creditworthiness in private capital markets.

Historically, US programmes intended to facilitate adjustment to changes in international trade patterns have focused on affected firms and individuals. These programmes were initiated in 1962 by the Trade Expansion Act, which authorized US participation in the Kennedy Round trade negotiations. It manifested the political need of pro-trade groups to respond to the concerns of businessmen and trade unionists that reduced tariffs would result in the loss of sales and jobs. The current US programme of adjustment assistance to trade-affected firms and employees grew out of the earlier programme, but assistance was expanded and made more accessible by amendments which were part of the 1974 Trade Expansion Act authorizing the Tokyo Round negotiations. It is widely recognized that these programmes were not particularly successful in the 1960s and 1970s, and the 1980–2 recession is the first real test of the new programme established in 1974. Indications are that it has made adjustment assistance benefits much more accessible to unemployed workers in industries directly affected by imports, for example, automobile assembly. The unemployed in indirectly effected industries such as auto parts and components have not received similar benefits. Perhaps more important is that it is unclear whether any adjustment has been encouraged by the new programme.

Adjustment policies aim to minimize and share equitably the costs of change. Some aspects of adjustment policy focus directly on increasing the efficiency of resource allocation and thereby reducing the costs of economic change. Incentives to invest in plant and equipment and innovation are efficiency-oriented. Payments to workers or firms made redundant by economic change are examples of redistributional adjustment policies. Most adjustment policies combine efficiency and redistributional aspects. Manpower policies aiming to retrain unemployed workers improve efficiency while helping those most directly hit by change. Regional policies also combine efficiency and redistributional goals. Adjustment assistance is a subset of adjustment policies implying conscious inter-vention by the government to help the domestic economy respond positively to the impact of increasing competition. This positive response combines domestic efficiency and distributional goals with international efficiency and distributional goals. Positive adjustment maintains, or enhances, the openness of the international trading system, while advancing domestic efficiency and distributional goals. Positive adjustment policies are structured so as to increase the political acceptability of greater import penetration in the affected sectors. Interaction between economic policies and political forces is irresistible, and to understand current and prospective US adjustment policies one must keep in mind the political forces at work. Therefore, the Chrysler loan guarantees and the programme to revitalize the US steel industry must be viewed in a political as well as an economic context. This will be analysed in more detail below when US industry-level adjustment policies are discussed.

In analysing a nation's adjustment policies five 'essential distinctions', noted by Wolf (1979, pp. 103–6), should be kept in mind. These distinctions help explain the types of adjustment policies which countries tend to establish. The first distinction, suggested by Giersch, is that between 'Schumpeterian', market-oriented, economies and 'Keynesian', interventionist-oriented, economies. Wolf notes that there is not currently a strong correlation between the 'Schumpeterian' economies and openness in world trade, on the one hand, and the 'Keynesian' economies and protectionism, on the other. Giersch (1978, p. 6) argues that over time the NICs will become 'natural partners of advanced Schumpeterian countries'. Thus in analysing likely trends in US adjustment policy we should keep in mind the long-standing US predilection for market solutions. The second distinction is made between whether intervention, when it does occur, is forward-looking or defensive. Forward-looking policies would intervene in the adjustment process so as to accommodate the emergence of new exporters of older, more standardized, less skill- and technology-intensive products. This implies intervening so as to focus domestic production on newer, more unique, more skill- and technology-intensive products. Japan is perhaps the paradigm for forward-looking intervention and many Asian NICs are consciously adapting similar policies. Recently, the tone of US intervention in automobiles and steel has been more defensive than forward-looking; however, the case can be argued both ways. Auto production is in a transitional period and may well emerge in the late 1980s as a high-technology sector in which the USA is very competitive. The third distinction is the extent of the welfare state. In the USA the welfare state is not as extensive or comprehensive as in the European nations, so that adjustment-assistance legislation has as a result focused on providing additional income security for workers and firms adversely affected by imports. The fourth distinction concerns the relative importance of trade in the national economy. Where trade is large relative to the entire economy, it is unrealistic to treat trade-induced adjustment differently from other types of change. Special treatment for trade-induced change is more feasible in the USA, because trade is a smaller part of total economic activity than in any other AIC. The fifth distinction noted by Wolf is 'the extent of political bias against change brought about by trade . . . ' (Wolf, 1979, p. 106). The key factors here seem to be fairness and influence. If the trade-induced change results from foreign actions that are widely felt to be unfair, for example, subsidies, predatory dumping, cartelization, or exploitation of labour, and the USA has the power to influence the situation, then political forces are likely to build up in opposition to a particular trade-induced change. The strength of these forces depends very much on the strength of the case in terms of generally accepted business criteria and the numbers of adversely affected workers.

Based then on Wolf's five distinctions, adjustment policy in the USA has been fairly strongly market-oriented, but shows signs of becoming somewhat more defensively interventionist in the early 1980s. Because trade is not large relative to the total economy and because the welfare system is not comprehensive, trade-induced adjustment is treated rather differently than general economic adjustment. Finally, a political bias against change induced by imports, particularly Japanese imports, may be developing. Rightly or wrongly, Japan is beginning to be perceived as being unfairly competitive in a number of sectors. The NICs are not perceived as negatively as Japan, but may be less able to defend their interests if they are perceived as resorting to unfair practices in the 1980s. To maintain access to the US market, it is imperative that the NICs make it clear that they are abiding by the applicable GATT articles and codes. Further, their observance of the principles of fair trade must be made known. In this way, a political bias against imports from NIC producers is less likely to develop in the USA.

PRODUCTIVITY AND MACRO-ECONOMIC ADJUSTMENT

Our assessment of economic adjustment policies in the USA begins at the macro-economic and general-productivity level. Although economy-wide adjustment is not generally emphasized when considering trade-induced changes, there are two good reasons for including it. First, as the 1980s begin, this is the major area of economic-policy activity and debate in the USA, for concern with high unemployment, low and even declining rates of growth of output per man-hour, low savings rates and a comparatively poor investment performance have focused the attention of the media, the political parties and the public on issues at the macro-economic and general-productivity levels. Second, a country's performance at the macro-economic and general-productivity levels is extremely important in determining its willingness to adjust at the industry, firm and individual levels. When unemployment is low, output per worker is increasing and the economy is growing it is much easier to adapt and implement positive adjustment policies at the industry, firm and individual levels. Thus successful adjustment at the macro-economic and general-productivity levels is essential if the response to trade-induced changes is to be positive at the other levels.

During 1980 the discussion of the USA's economic malaise emphasized supply-side economics and the reindustrialization of the US economy. There was at least verbal agreement among all three of the 1980 presidential candidates that demand policy should be based on quantitative monetary management, which the Federal Reserve Board has been trying to implement, and reduced public-sector deficits. There was also agreement that demand management was not enough to affect macro-economic adjustment. The three candidates all put forward economic programmes which featured tax cuts aimed at encouraging investment and R&D by firms and savings by individuals. These programmes varied in terms of the size, timing and incidence of the tax cuts, but they all accepted the premise that tax cuts are needed to stimulate capital formation and macro-economic growth via the supply side. As presented in the media, these policies were termed the 'reindustrialization of America' (*Business Week*, 30 June 1980, pp. 55–138). While the complete reindustrialization of the USA is unlikely, and probably undesirable, a reassessment of US economic problems and policies is a positive development. Demand-management policies which worked in the 1960s have diminishing usefulness when expectations of high and continuing inflation dominate economic decision-making at all levels. In the NIC perspective, the direction of the reassessment is quite positive; the NICs are not seen as a part of the problem. Thus far Americans have tended to blame principally themselves and their economic-policy-makers for their economic ills. The causes of the decline are generally diagnosed as counter-productive government policies, especially in the energy and regulatory fields, high inflation coupled with high taxes which reduces the incentives to save and to make profits, outdated and inefficient plant and equipment, managers who are interested in short-term corporate performance and unwilling to take entrepreneurial risk, a collective bargaining system which is often slow in responding to change, unrealistic expectations, particularly on the part of young workers and, finally, a deteriorating competitive position abroad. The latter problem is attributed to government policies (corrupt practices, trade embargoes, human rights, anti-trust loans, health, safety and environmental regulations, and inadequate low-cost export financing), the attitude that exports are unimportant, and a lack of response to other nations, particularly France and Japan, that are effectively closing off parts of their economies to foreign investments and imports. If these are the perceived problems facing the USA, it is hard to see how resorting to pro-tectionism, particularly towards the NIC, will help. The NICs present problems in a few industrial sectors, which will be discussed below, but they are not a real factor in the main area of US concern: the performance of the economy at the macro-economic and general-productivity levels. Thus, the principle adjustment concerns of the United States do not indicate a strongly protectionist bent, particularly regarding the NICs. Japan is viewed as the problem trading partner in a number of sectors and is liable to be the primary object of US protectionist impulses that arise in the early 1980s.

Although the supply-side and productivity-enhancing policies now being considered will almost certainly help the US adjust at the macro-economic level, it is not clear that they will result in reindustrialization. Although reindustrialization is the stated objective, it raises as many questions as it answers. What is reindustrialization and what does it entail? Is reindustrialization possible at a reasonable cost? Will reindustrialization help to resolve the economic adjustment problems facing the USA in the 1980s?

Reindustrialization means different things to different people and therefore will entail quite different strategies, perhaps even conflicting strategies. To businessmen, reindustrialization means higher after-tax returns on investment, lower cost structures, increased competitiveness internationally and government policies which give a high priority to industrial growth and de-emphasize conflicting policies, particularly regulation. To organized labour, reindustrialization means increased jobs in the traditional, unionized industrial sectors, improved working conditions and standards of living for workers, particularly in industries with lower wages, and limiting foreign access to US markets for traditional industrial products. To those in the north-eastern and mid-western states, it means the revival of local industries, an expanding tax base and an end to the decline of the cities in these regions. To the federal government, it is a way out of the high-employment, high-inflation conundrum at the macro-economic level. To the public, it probably means more of what they want at reasonable prices, more employment opportunities, and a return to traditional production and economic patterns. In the best of circumstances, most of these expectations are likely to be frustrated, and if US reindustrialization becomes thoroughly defensive, it will result in widespread disappointment – as it has in the UK. More fundamentally, it is unrealistic to expect any set of government policies to increase the share by industries of employment, particularly employment by the larger industrial firms. Over time and in every industrial nation, the share of employment in the industrial sector has tended to decline. Even in dynamic and competitive industrial economies like West Germany and Japan the proportion of workers in industry has been falling. In West Germany it fell from a peak of 49·3 per cent in 1971 to 45·3 per cent in 1977 (OECD, 1979a, p. 20). The proportion of the Japanese work-force in industry grew rapidly to a peak of 37·2 per cent in 1973, since when it has declined to about 35 per cent. The comparable decline in the USA is from 33·8 per cent in 1967 to about 29 per cent in 1979.

The sharpest falls have tended to occur in the older heavily industrialized European economies. This group includes some poor performers such as the UK and perhaps Sweden, as well as good performers such as Switzerland and Austria. This tendency for employment to shift to the service sectors is universal among all but the newest industrial countries; it is already under way in many of the NICs. Analysis of US employment patterns shows that in recent years employment by large industrial firms has declined absolutely, even as the total labour-force has grown at historically high rates. Between 1970 and 1978 US employment rose from 78·6 million to 94·4 million, or 20 per cent; of this 15·8 million increase, only 1 million went to manufacturing, raising manufacturing employment by only 5 per cent (USA, Bureau of Labor, 1980). However, analysis at the firm level indicates that employment declined in medium and large companies, while there was a remarkable growth of employment in small firms of twenty people or less. All the evidence, therefore, indicates that industry is not likely to be a dynamic employer in the years ahead, and that reindustrialization cannot be counted on to generate very much employment.

In addition, a programme which focuses solely on industry is likely to miss growth potential in the service sector and would maximize the likelihood of adjustment policies becoming defensive. That is, subsidies would be directed to the shoring up of declining firms, implicitly reallocating resources away from more dynamic, growing firms. One can argue that both welfare (employment-creation) and efficiency (growth-stimulation) criteria call for a broad-gauge, supply-side approach to adjustment strategy at the macro-economic and productivity levels, rather than concentration on industry and manufacturing.

During the 1970s the environment for adjustment in the USA deteriorated, but there is reason to believe that this will improve in the 1980s. In the 1970s there were three factors at work causing a deterioration in the macro-economic employment/inflation trade-off which could moderate or reverse in the 1980s. First, during the 1970s the effective price of international oil rose by some twenty-five times in nominal terms. High energy prices will continue to be a serious problem for oil-importing nations throughout the 1980s, but the rate of increase of oil prices will surely moderate and this will work to moderate inflation in turn. Second, in the 1970s the US civilian labour force grew from $82 \cdot 7$ million to $104 \cdot 5$ million, an increase of $26 \cdot 4$ per cent (*Survey of Current Business*, August 1980, pp. 5–11). It estimated that during the 1980s the civilian labour force will increase to $111 \cdot 5$ million (NPA, 1979, p. 6), showing a ten-year increase of $6 \cdot 7$ per cent. The growth of the labour force will thus slow dramatically and this should lead to older, more experienced and more productive workers with less unemployment and a tighter labour market. Finally, third, the hostility between business and government that marked much of the 1970s should diminish in the years ahead. Indeed, some of the tax proposals put forward by the Democrats in 1980 would have cut business taxes more than those of the Republicans, accompanying a widespread recognition that regulation is becoming counter-productive and often contradictory. The political rhetoric of the 1980 campaign may not flower into policies for the 1980s, but there does seem to be a recognition that improved incentives to save and invest are needed. Along with more stability in energy prices and slower growth in the labour force, better relations between business and government should improve the adjustment process at the macro-economic and general-productivity levels. There is the distinct possibility however (discussed in more detail in the next section) that applied reindustrialization will become thoroughly politicized and be used to impede adjustment. Nevertheless, low growth of the US labour force and less instability in energy prices will improve US productivity and macro-economic performance, thereby increasing the chances that the USA will adopt positive adjustment and trade policies during the coming decade. The real key to a successful adjustment policy in the USA is in getting productivity and macro-economic policy right, particularly in raising savings and investment and restoring historic trends in productivity and growth.

ADJUSTMENT AT THE INDUSTRY LEVEL

Philosophically, the USA has tended to favour a relatively non-interventionist policy towards its industry. Symptomatic of this is the low level of subsidies flowing to US industry. A recent study of the net-tax (taxes less subsidies) position of industry in OECD countries found the rate of subsidization in the USA to be significantly lower than any other country (Mutti, 1980). Current operating subsidies and direct aids to private capital formation totalled $0 \cdot 3$ per cent of GDP in the USA; for competing countries the figures ranged from $2 \cdot 6$ per cent in Italy to $1 \cdot 3$ per cent for Japan. If government expenditures on R&D are counted as subsidies then the US level rises to $1 \cdot 6$ per cent of GDP, compared with a high of $3 \cdot 7$ for France and only $1 \cdot 9$ per cent for Japan. Also, with a larger private sector in the US economy the effect of these subsidies is more diluted. If subsidies to public and private enterprises are combined, the US proportion is $6 \cdot 3$ per cent, compared with a high of $17 \cdot 5$ per cent in Italy and a low of $7 \cdot 1$ per cent in West Germany (Mutti, 1980, p. 10). In practice, US policies towards industry have been interventionist, but usually on the negative side. One current study describes the USA as having an 'anti-industrial policy' (Morici, 1981). Looking across the range of US programmes as they affect the economy the impression is that they provide a whole series of intended and unintended incentives for resources to flow into the agricultural, construction and service sectors. Agriculture is stimulated by public R&D oriented towards the needs of the farmer and the food stamp programme, which stimulates demand. Construction is boosted by the desirability of having tax deductions for interest payments and property taxes paid by home-owners. Home-ownership has been the only investment which protects the middle class from inflation; not surprisingly, savings are diverted from industry to residential construction. Finally, the service sector enjoys a spectrum of intended and unintended attractions for capital and labour. Medical service demand is stimulated through direct public aids and through tax exemptions and tax deductions for medical insurance and large medical payments. The growth of the service sector is encouraged in an indirect and unintended way as taxes and regulatory constraints rise. Young entrepreneurs and professionals are encouraged to seek opportunities in small firms, usually in the service sector, in a number of ways. Small service businesses are not as visible to regulators, involve may tax advantages, as personal and business expenses lose much of their distinction, and provide opportunities for barter and other tax-avoidance practices which just do not exist for workers or managers in the industrial sector. The result has been a marked shift of activity and resources away from established industrial firms to newer and smaller service enterprises. The overall result is to establish a bias against industrial expansion in the USA. The bias probably exists in most other mature industrial economies, but elsewhere the problem seems to have been recognized and positive policies seem to have been crafted to offset much of the bias. In the USA, however, there is a lack of awareness that existing policies are not even neutral, but anti-industry (Morici, 1981).

During the 1980s the USA will probably move haltingly to both correct its current bias against industry and to shore up particular industries which are felt to be candidates for successful structural adjustment. The deregulation of airlines, trucking, rail and communications begun by President Carter is a good sign, but within specific industrial sectors US policy is becoming more interventionist and this may lead to an increase in protectionism during the 1980s. Let us review briefly the emerging trends in five key sectors: automobiles, steel, textiles, consumer electronics and footwear.

As a result of the massive rise in international oil prices in the 1970s, the world automobile industry, and most dramatically the US automobile industry, is being thoroughly restructured. The premium is on smaller, lighter, more energy-efficient vehicles, and the US industry started out in the worst position to meet the new demand patterns of the 1980s. The Japanese industry was well situated because it was already producing smaller autos. The European industry was better off than the US industry with experience in producing large numbers of relatively energy-efficient cars in the 1960s. Nevertheless, in every European auto-producing country some form of government intervention to assist in retooling, carrying inventories or structural adjustment was necessary in the 1970–6 period. In retrospect it is surprising that it took the US government so long to get involved, given the scale of adjustment now required. In fact a careful review of the record indicates that government policies were working against the adjustment to small cars, principally by controlling the price of domestically produced petroleum and thereby subsidizing the consumption of gasoline – another example of an unintended anti-industrial policy. The result was a surge in demand for large US cars in the 1975–9 period. For after the gas lines of 1974 had subsided the price mechanism told the consumer that the crisis was over, real energy prices fell, US firms found themselves with ballooning inventories of small cars and double shifts were required at the Cadillac and Lincoln plants. By 1978 even Japanese cars were selling slowly and inventories were piling up at the ports. The US firms had been planning on a 3 per cent annual increase in the compact car's share of the total US market from 1973 on; however, demand patterns, shaped largely by government-controlled prices on gasoline, worked against this strategy and the small-car share of the market declined between

1974 and 1978. When the second energy-price shock came in 1979 the adjustment process was compressed into two years, and the five years of failure to adjust came back to haunt the US auto industry, particularly Chrysler and Ford. Ford had a strong enough position internationally to get through 1980 without requiring any direct or indirect government assistance. However, Ford, together with the United Auto Workers, appealed for import restraints to limit the number of imported cars, particularly Japanese cars, admitted to the US market in the early 1980s. This appeal was turned down by the International Trade Commission, but the matter did not end there. In 1981 the Reagan administration pressured the Japanese into accepting VERS, the effectiveness of which remains to be seen.

For Chrysler time and resources, particularly cash, were just not available, and to maintain the firm's viability the government stepped in to provide $1·5 billion in loan guarantees. The circumstances of the action were unusual and deserve closer scrutiny, but the Chrysler guarantee does not establish a clear precedent for future interventions. Chrysler was hurt by a lack of attractive big cars in the 1975–8 period. The firm had been out of phase with US demand patterns in the 1960s, with too many small and medium-sized cars, and in the early 1970s with too many big cars. In 1978, as new management took over, the first goal was to develop the larger cars needed to restore the firm's profitability. This, of course, changed dramatically in 1979 and the need to retool and speed up the introduction of a line of smaller cars became essential to Chrysler's existence. By 1980 sales and assets on hand were insufficient, lenders were sceptical about the firm's future, and government loan guarantees became the key to Chrysler's survival. After some hesitation and bargaining these were forthcoming. There were four arguments in favour of the Chrysler loan guarantees: (1) that it was a structural adjustment problem – that Chrysler, once through the initial period, would be able to survive; (2) that it had worked in the Lockheed case; (3) that there was no immediate cost to the US Treasury, whereas Chrysler's liquidation would have required the government to assume the unfunded liabilities of Chrysler's pension fund; and (4) that in an election year it would be unwise to let Chrysler and its suppliers increase the already large unemployment levels in the key 'swing' states of Ohio, Michigan, Illinois and Pennsylvania.

In the adjustment perspective the first two arguments present no problem; if Chrysler survives and is competitive then legitimate adjustment has occurred. As soon as a firm fails and government funds are called, Congress and taxpayers will be increasingly reluctant to guarantee future loans. The last argument is a quadrennial problem that cannot be avoided, but it should be noted that Chrysler is the sixth largest industrial employer in the USA and thus merits more attention than would a smaller firm. The third argument is the most troubling and might incline public policy to defend declining industries, rather than work for a genuine restructuring of the economy. US law concerning private pension plans provides a federal government guarantee to employees of liquidated firms. Thus, federal policy-makers face a cost, which in Chrysler's case was considerable, for inaction. It remains to be seen whether ultimate federal responsibility for private pension liabilities leads to a defensive adjustment policy, but this is a factor that will have to be watched closely in the future. In sum, the Chrysler support programme does not establish a precedent for a more interventionist, more defensive US industrial adjustment programme, for there are several aspects of the Chrysler situation which are not likely to be repeated in other industries for a number of years and the Chrysler loans are unlikely to establish a pattern. If the access to credit of American Motors or Ford were threatened in 1981 or 1982, a similar programme would probably be arranged, but these are the only extensions that seem to follow from the Chrysler case.

The recent assistance programme established to help adjustment in the US steel industry is much more likely to be a trend-setter and poses more of a threat to positive adjustment. Chapter 6 above contains a useful description of the background and events leading up to the current dilemma facing the US steel industry. The restructuring programme announced by President Carter in September 1980, and continued in much the same form by the Reagan team, has six major provisions (*The Economist*, 4 October 1980, p. 70). Trigger prices are reintroduced at a rate 12 per cent higher than those that prevailed when the old TPM was ended earlier in the year. Import surges in excess of 10 per cent for any specific product will be examined for dumping or subsidy violations. Depreciation allowances are to be improved and grants for tax-credit purposes are to be made, Congress willing, which should improve cash flow and the incentive to invest in new plants. Pollution-control laws are to be eased for the steel industry. R&D funds are to be supplemented by the federal government. Finally, the package included a variety of assistance programmes for individuals and communities hit by steel-plant closures. The programme is geared to provide a five-year period during which restructuring is to move ahead and, in particular, investment in modern plant is to accelerate sharply. In the best of circumstances the situation is not bright; by the late 1980s only 50 per cent of US output will be truly competitive, whereas 90 per cent of Japan's production will be highly competitive continuously cast steel by the middle of the decade (*The Economist*, id.). Realistically the current programme is only the beginning of the process of adjustment in the steel industry. The shake-out of employment is well under way with employment in steel-mills having declined by almost 40 per cent, from 490,000 in mid-1979 to 310,000 in mid-1980. Some of this decline is cyclical, as capacity utilization was only 70 per cent, but the bulk of this decline in employment is structural. The longer-term restructuring issues are now in the areas of management, investment and finance.

The problems currently facing the US steel industry are a more acute microcosm of the problems facing US industry as a whole. Outside the USA, governments as a part of their overall industrial strategy set targets for certain industries, and steel has been a target industry in Japan since 1951. Japanese steel producers rely on an enormous leverage of debt in relationship to equity to finance growth and modernization. Including borrowings for working capital, the debt–equity ratio of the Japanese steel industry is about 5 to 1, so that nearly 85 per cent of finance is raised through loans, generally from Japanese banks under the careful supervision of the Central Bank. The ratio for the US industry, however, is 1 to 3 (Putnam, Hayes and Bartlett, 1977, p. 14), so that roughly three times as much investment is generated from the US steel industry's retained earning and stock issues as from the capital markets. This extraordinary difference in the financial base of the industries in Japan and the USA has two effects. First, the Japanese steel industry has greater access to financial resources because it is not as limited by its ability to generate retained earning or sell new issues of stock as is the US industry. Japanese banks, with the support of the Central Bank, are willing to take more risk and lend greater amounts relative to the industry's equity than US banks or bondholders. As a result, the Japanese have greater financial resources and can grow faster. Secondly, the interest on the Japanese steel industry's very large debt is fixed, whereas dividend payment on equity vary as profits vary. Japanese steel firms are thus impelled to market very aggressively because they must maintain high production rates to generate the revenues necessary to repay their loans and break even. The estimated break-even point for a typical Japanese steel firm is at an 80 per cent operating rate, whereas the same firm with a US financial structure would have a break-even point at an operating rate of about 72 per cent (Putnam *et al.*, 1977, p. 17). Thus ultimately the willingness of the Japanese Central Bank to accept the steel industry as a target for financial support has resulted in a much larger Japanese steel industry than would have otherwise existed. Moreover, to meet its fixed financial payments the industry must export and market its products aggressively throughout the world.

Realistically, under these conditions, the USA faces three unattractive alternatives: permanent protection for the US steel industry, with the sizeable implied costs involved; acceptance of the long-term decline of the US steel industry with all that that implies for US security and access to steel in tight or restricted markets; or a long-term programme of government subsidy, support and at least partial control, with the enormous potential for waste, inefficiency and mismanagement implied by public subsidies and/or control. Given the contrived, but real, advantages of the Japanese steel industry, and the support being directed to European firms, it is unlikely that the US steel industry can effectively compete in the 1980s without comparable advantages and support. The current programme mixes protectionism (trigger prices and the surge provisions) with support, but will not close the gap. Fundamental problems remain. On the labour side, wages have risen faster than output per man-hour and steel-workers are among the very few groups in the society that had real hourly earnings increases of 2·5 per cent per annum through the 1970s. (According to Department of Labor data, hourly earnings in the steel industry rose from $3·62 in 1967 to $11·60 in 1979. This is an annual average increase of 9·3 per cent as compared with a 6·8 per cent rise in the consumer price index over the same period.)

Wage costs are one of the factors undermining the cost competitiveness of the industry, but the problems on the management side loom even larger. Management conceded the wage increases noted above and has not been particularly innovative or aggressive in modernizing productive capacity or in presenting the case for steel to the nation. Most important, they have been unwilling to take risks and are defensive in their strategy. As the boom in US oil exploration picked up, the demand for tubular steel exceeded domestic supply in mid-1980. Imports were filling the gap, but world-wide demand was also very high. A new $500-million tube-mill was needed in the USA, but no one seemed to be willing to make the commitment and take the risk that the mill could be built in three years while world-wide demand held up (*Wall Street Journal*, 20 October 1980). Steel-industry analysts felt that such an investment was as close to a sure bet as any investment could be. Finally, in 1981, US Steel managed to put together an innovative programme for financing a new mill, with completion expected in the mid-1980s. This programme is, however, an exception in an industry with a record of a quarter of a century of standing pat that has put the US steel industry in its present situation. The government deserves an ample portion of the blame for failing to recognize what was happening abroad and for failing to adapt regulatory and tax policies to a more competitive international environment. To a lesser degree, these same problems prevail in a number of traditional industries in the USA, and policies adapted to the restructuring of the steel industry could become a model for a broader strategy of US industrial restructuring. Such a strategy will probably include aspects of protectionism, decline, and subsidy, and given US ambivalence about all of these one cannot be optimistic about the likely results.

In textiles, consumer electronics and footwear a gradual reduction in employment has proceeded throughout the 1970s without the sharp shake-out in 1979 and 1980 that occurred in the automobile and steel industries. Employment in manufacturing in the USA peaked in 1969 at $20 \cdot 17$ million, peaked again in 1973 at $20 \cdot 15$ million and reached its maximum level of $21 \cdot 06$ million in 1979 (*Employment and Earnings* (USA), various issues). During this period the proportion of persons employed in manufacturing fell from $28 \cdot 7$ per cent in 1969 to $23 \cdot 4$ per cent in 1979. In 1980, preliminary figures indicate further declines to $20 \cdot 2$ million employed and $22 \cdot 4$ per cent in the proportion employed.

Against this backdrop of relative stability in total manufacturing employment between 1973 and 1980, employment in the industries reviewed in this study declined rather sharply: employment fell 16 per cent in textiles, 30 per cent in radio and television equipment and 20 per cent in footwear. The bulk of the decline occurred in the 1973–9 period. This is in sharp contrast to the auto and steel industries which were up slightly between 1973 and 1979, but fell 25 per cent in the auto sector and 15 per cent in steel between 1979 and 1980. Interestingly, employment in the apparel industry has held up rather well, declining by only 1 per cent between 1973 and 1979 and $2 \cdot 5$ per cent between 1979 and 1980 (calculated from various issues of *Employment and Earnings*). Output data indicate somewhat different patterns for these industries. Output declined for footwear, radio and television equipment and for steel between 1973 and 1979. For textiles, apparel and motor vehicles, output rose 17·3 per cent, 17·0 per cent and 12·6 per cent respectively. During the 1979–80 downturn, output in both autos and steel fell by about 28 per cent. Output in textiles fell 9·3 per cent and all the other sectors had smaller drops (calculated from various issues of *Survey of Current Business*). Thus, the problems facing textiles, apparel, radio and television equipment, and footwear are quite different from those facing steel and autos. Steel and autos have encountered a severe cyclical shake-out, which could be a one-time movement to lower levels of employment in the 1980s. The industries which have had longer-term declines in employment seemed to be less affected by the 1979–80 cyclical downturn. The hope is that this indicates stability and strength, the implication being that a good deal of restructuring has taken place and that these sectors are on their way to being competitive in the 1980s.

The employment and output trends in the apparel and textile sectors deserve somewhat closer examination to discern the impact of the Multi-Fibre Arrangement (MFA). Output in both sectors grew at about 17 per cent between 1973 and 1979; this is less than the 22 per cent growth rate of all manufacturing, but greater than any of the other industries reviewed in this study over the same period. In the case of textiles the growth is accompanied by a shift in trade patterns, as the USA became a net exporter of textiles in 1978 and 1979, and improved productivity with output up 17·3 per cent and employment down 16·2 per cent. In textiles the root cause of unemployment is technology rather than imports, and restructuring would seem to be in progress; moreover, the net export balance indicates that the MFA is probably not having a large effect on the US textile industry. Clearly, cheap petrochemical feedstocks are a big factor here, but these should be rising in price within the next two or three years, and only by then will the shape of the remaining adjustment problem be recognizable. In the apparel industry, employment from 1973 to 1980 held up better than any of the industries reviewed. This would indicate that the MFA has been successful in increasing output and maintaining employment in the US apparel industry during the 1970s, albeit at some cost to consumers. This will probably not change very much during the 1980s, as effective maintenance of the MFA was established as a condition for US ratification of the Tokyo Round trade agreements. Employment in the apparel sector will continue to decline slowly, but the likely erosion of the real wage of clothing and apparel workers could emerge as a greater problem than unemployment in the 1980s. Whether this would lead to a decline in the supply of labour for apparel work or efforts to strengthen the MFA is not clear.

In conclusion, at the industry level a good deal of restructuring and adjustment occurred in the 1970s in a number of traditional industries. In 1979–80 the need to adjust was suddenly and sharply felt in the steel and automotive sectors and the response in those two sectors will probably determine the direction of US industrial strategies in the 1980s. In the automotive sector, with one very strong firm and good management now in place at all of the large firms, there is reason to be optimistic about the outcome. In steel, the firms are weaker and management has been inclined to look to Washington for solutions and is unwilling to take even what seem attractive risks. On balance, US preferences to keep the economy free, while cutting taxes and providing incentives across the board to industry, will probably prevail, and the anti-industrial attitudes characteristic of the 1960s and 1970s will almost surely end in the 1980s. It is to be hoped that this adversary relationship between US industry and government will be replaced by one of cooperation and openness, rather than connivance and exclusion. The key to this will be success in getting macro-economic policy right and restoring aggregate growth.

ADJUSTMENT AT THE INDIVIDUAL AND FIRM LEVEL

Because of fundamental differences in experiences, the attitudes and expectations of US individuals and firms differ considerably from those of their European counterparts. US firms, with relatively low payroll taxes and the ability to lay workers off (as noted above, for example, in the automobile and steel industries), are more willing to hire during the upswing, and conversely the more junior workers are often laid off during recessions. Western European firms, with high payroll taxes and the inability to terminate redundant workers easily, have during the 1970s utilized more labour-saving equipment and held down employment. In turn, those employed have very high expectations of remaining employed. The differences extend to the firm as well. US firms do not expect to receive outright subsidies to cover operating losses. More likely than not, the unprofitable firm will either fold or be absorbed by a more profitable firm that will reorganize and use the losses for tax relief against its own profit. Thus a US firm with losses has a very small expectation of surviving for any length of time. These two facts of economic life in the USA must be seen as fundamental to the natural adjustment process at the individual and firm levels.

The US adjustment-assistance programme, recognizes these facts, but does not fully obviate them. This programme, must be seen as a product of the normal tension between economic and political realities. Economic realities call for restructuring by the removal of workers and firms to more productive lines of operation, as soon as possible; while political realities call for the equitable distribution of the costs and benefits of restructuring, that is, for reduced costs to the individuals and firms affected. The dilemma is that the programme perforce reduces the incentive to adjust, and in assisting those affected may slow or even arrest the adjustment process.

The current US adjustment-assistance programme is part of the Trade Act of 1974, the enabling legislation for the Tokyo Round negotiations. It supplements existing unemployment and aid to business programmes with special provisions which aid workers, firms and communities judged to have been injured by increasing imports. The criteria for individual assistance are that a significant number of workers are, or will become, unemployed in a given firm, that firm production and/or sales have decreased absolutely and that imports 'contributed importantly' to the separation of workers and the decline in sales or production. Imports must be an important, but not necessarily the most important, cause of the decline in sales or production. Certified workers receive allowances equal to 70 per cent of their average weekly wage or the average national manufacturing wage, whichever is less. These payments last for fifty-two weeks and may be extended twenty-six weeks if the unemployed individual is in an approved retraining programme. Funds are available for travel to retraining activities and to cover some job search costs. Prior to the 1979–80 recession, utilization of the programme by unemployed workers was running at about 100,000 per year, with total annual payments of about $250 million (data drawn directly from the Department of Labor). In 1980, estimates anticipated 180,000 beneficiaries and a funding level of $381 million. In fact, 550,000 were involved, at a total cost of $2·8 billion in 1980. In 1981 the total cost will have fallen to $2 billion, with 327,000 beneficiaries, if 1979–80 levels of unemployment persist among manufacturing workers. Individual payments in 1980 were running at $300 per week for unemployed auto and steel workers, or an annual rate of $15,600, which is tax-free. Therefore, loss of employment implies little or no loss in disposable income for import-affected workers. It should be noted that only directly affected workers are included. Auto workers are judged to be seriously affected by imports, but unemployed workers from parts and components firms are not covered. This seems inconsistent, and efforts are being made to include workers from firms indirectly affected.

From a fiscal point of view, the popularity of the programme, in 1980 and 1981 was something of a surprise and an embarrassment to the administration, and in that light efforts are being made to reduce eligibility and/or benefit levels. Beyond this, the current programme, is clearly reducing costs to the impacted worker, but is probably not assisting or facilitating adjustment. The benefits are unconditional and rather high so there is not much incentive to act for at least a year, and then if the affected worker finds a retraining programme, six months remain before alternative employment becomes urgent. On the surface there would seem to be a need to restructure the existing programme, so as to accelerate adjustment while maintaining the assistance aspect. This will not be easy to do and presents one of the major challenges of the 1980s to US international trade policy-makers. Adjustment-assistance benefits might be conditioned on immediate participation in a retraining programme and demonstration of basic proficiency in the new occupation after six months of training. In addition, benefit levels might decline gradually after nine months without employment. Such changes would increase the skill inventory of the labour force and reduce the likelihood that workers will wait a year and a half to be recalled by their original firm. However, before reform can be meaningful, more research into the re-employment patterns of workers in the 1980 recession will be necessary.

The 1974 Trade Act has provisions for adjustment assistance to firms which can meet the same criteria mentioned above, that is, of significant numbers of workers separated, declining sales, and imports 'contributing importantly'. The Department of Commerce certifies the firms and this qualifies them to apply for benefits during the next two years. In order to receive benefits a firm must submit data on its past operation and proposed adjustment plan. Individual firms may receive up to $1 million in direct loans or $3 million in loan guarantees for as long as twenty-five years. In addition, technical assistance in the form of consultants or grants for consultants is provided by the Department of Commerce, up to 75 per cent of the total cost. Under this programme, the most important efforts were directed towards the restructuring and revitalization of firms in the shoe industry. A programme, of special assistance directed to the industry began in 1977. With loans and loan guarantees originally estimated at $40 million, for 150 trade-affected firms, the programme was fully operational in 1979, expanding its budget to $60 million. Only fifty-two firms have received financial assistance, but fully 153 have utilized the technical assistance available. As an aid to stabilizing the industry the programme has been successful: employment in the rubber and leather footwear industry was 222,000 in 1973 and fell to 167,000 by 1979. Since that time it has risen slightly, to about 172,000 for 1980, despite the general economic decline. Production shows similar trends, with a decline of 18·5 per cent from 1973 to 1979 followed by stability in 1980. Thus, in terms of maintaining domestic output and employment in footwear, the 1977 shoe-firm assistance programme has been a success. Detailed analysis of the shoe-industry assistance programme, should be undertaken in a year or two in order that the correct conclusions can be drawn and future US adjustment policies formulated so as to make use of the lessons learned. Only time will tell if a smaller, restructured US footwear industry can be competitive, but it is heartening to see an area in which a US industrial programme has made progress without excessive reliance on protectionist trade measures.

US ADJUSTMENT POLICIES: CONCLUSIONS

US adjustment policies in the 1980s will be an eclectic collection of protectionism, new production technologies, increasing specialization, integration into world-wide production systems and diversification into new activities. The movement towards new forms of protectionism in the short run is clear, with steel the leading example. The duration and extent of this movement towards protectionism will be heavily dependent on the recovery of the US economy from the 1980–82 recession and the performance of the economy throughout the 1980s. The tightening of the US labour market should help to reduce pressures for protectionism in the last half of the decade, but progress must be made with both the unemployment and the inflation problems if protectionism in the USA is not to become a serious matter in the next few years. The use of new, labour-saving production technologies will be central to industrial restructuring. This in turn will put pressure on the economy to continue to generate jobs at historically high rates for the next few years. In many industries restructuring will imply more specialization of production processes with increased subcontracting, more integration of US production into world-wide markets and, for some firms, diversification into new fields which offer advantages of faster and more stable growth. In most cases, firm adjustment and restructuring will facilitate economy-wide adjustment, with the proviso that employment in manufacturing will almost assuredly decrease in the 1980s, and successful restructuring must be predicated on significant employment generation in other sectors.

Part Four
Conclusions

16
An Overview
Louis Turner

The lessons from this book are that the NICs have indeed become a significant part of the world economy, but that theirs is not an irresistible success, with which the AICs cannot come to terms. For one thing, the competition between NICs and AICs is not a zero-sum game – both can benefit from the interplay of their economies. For another thing, there is a fragility about the success of certain NICs which suggests that some of the 'economic miracles' of the last two decades may look less impressive in the years to come.

A number of points can be made to support these non-alarmist conclusions. For instance, Colin Bradford argues in Chapter 2 that the leading eight NICs – Hong Kong, South Korea, Singapore, Taiwan, India, Argentina, Brazil and Mexico – are unlikely to be followed in the 1980s by an equally dynamic 'second tier' of NICs. This is not to claim that countries as diverse as Chile, Colombia, Egypt, Jamaica, Malaysia, Pakistan, Peru, Philippines, Thailand, Turkey or some OPEC members will not expand their manufactured exports. Rather, the process which led to the dynamic expansion of NIC exports of maufactures involves such a high degree of national commitment and policy coherence that it is unlikely to become a generalized phenomenon. Furthermore, most of these countries seem to lack the preconditions behind so much of the dynamism of the NICs (especially of the East Asian 'gang of four'). In some cases, their literacy rates are low. Others have relatively buoyant agricultural or mineral sectors, which will thus reduce their urge to maximize manufactured exports. Some of them are highly unstable. All in all, highly dynamic, large-volume LDC exporters of manufactures are likely to be few in number in the next decade.

At the same time, there is nothing inevitable about the continued success of these classic high-achievers. For one thing, the slow, steady decline of India's relative importance as an exporter of manufactures at least partly reflects an ingrained ambivalence among Indian policy-makers about the virtues of export-led development. For another thing, the social unrest which led to the 1979 assassination of South Korea's President Park was not totally unrelated to social strains connected with the extreme emphasis he put on the country's drive for exports.

Finally, the continuation of Hong Kong as a dynamic export platform overwhelmingly depends on its delicate relationship with China. Of course, it is perfectly possible that the latter will learn from Hong Kong and emerge, in its turn, as a formidable exporting power. For the moment, though, it is equally plausible to argue that the drive for modernization being engineered by China's post-Mao leadership will falter, and that the resultant unpredictable political and social strains will once again call Hong Kong's anomalous, outward-looking status into question.

SPONTANEOUS AIC ADJUSTMENT

If this book questions the universal ability of the NICs to maintain their export orientation, it also suggests that their successes are still quite narrowly based, and that their entry into an ever-widening range of industries is getting progressively harder. For instance, even within textiles and clothing, it is clear that alert managements, combining capital-deepening with fashion flair and good marketing, have been able to preserve substantial pockets of the AIC industry. In consumer electronics, the picture which emerges is of AIC managements capitalizing on micro-electronic developments to automate their production lines and to evolve a range of new products, thus making it far from inevitable that the heart of the industry will migrate to cheap-labour NICs. As the latter were coming to terms (just) with basic colour-television technology, the AICs have been moving into video-recorders, videodiscs and the whole videotex arena, in which information technology is merging with consumer electronics.

In the automotive sector, we also see a quickening of the industry's technological pace, with an increased concentration of corporate ownership. Both developments will make it difficult for basically imitative NICs to duplicate Japan's success in this industry. South Korea's ability to produce a single model is a far cry from producing companies with the strength of a Toyota or Nissan. We still have to see if Brazil can capitalize on its innovative alcohol-based automotive technology. The picture is of NICs feeding into the logistical networks of established multinational companies, rather than sustaining a frontal challenge to these companies, as the Japanese proved capable of doing in an earlier era. The conclusions from the steel and petrochemical sectors are only a little more hopeful for the NICs. Even here, it only looks as though one, extremely debatable, 'NIC' (Saudi Arabia) is likely to emerge as a massive net exporter in either industry during the 1980s.

So what are the general lessons this book points to, given the five sectors on which it has concentrated? Perhaps the most important one is that the clothing–textile chain looks unique, in the way it favours LDC entrants. Clothing is small-scale, technologically mature, non-oligopolistic, generally price-sensitive, and has a natural indigenous demand even in the poorest LDCs. The linked textile operations are again technologically mature, relatively unskilled, and of only moderate scale. All this makes LDC entry into world markets relatively easy. The other sectors, however, call on a rather more complex set of comparative advantages than the mere possession of a cheap but disciplined labour force. Entry into petrochemicals requires capital, feedstocks and a relatively skilled labour force – and although the leading oil producers have the first two, they generally do not have the third. The steel situation is somewhat similar, with an energy-intensity which makes it an increasingly risky prospect for energy-poor NICs.

The remaining two sectors (automobile and consumer electronics) call on comparative advantages which the NICs are only just starting to struggle to possess. These sectors are research-intensive (electronics particularly so), increasingly large-scale, and demand very high levels of management skills, particularly in the management of extremely complex systems and technologies in the context of rapidly evolving market requirements.

In all four of these non-textile/clothing sectors, it has been possible to point to AIC companies that are following the textbook recipes for improving their competitive position: raising their productive efficiency (made easier by micro-electronic developments); moving into higher-value-added parts of their industries; stepping up research into new products and lines of business; selectively divesting themselves of less-promising activities; diversifying into related, but faster-growing areas; and integrating the emerging strengths of the NICs into their overall strategies. In other words, even if times proved hard in the 1970s, the classic adjustment processes nevertheless continued unabated.

Just to strengthen these non-alarmist conclusions, it is worth pointing out that the AIC trade surplus with the NICs in one sector (chemicals) alone more than outweighs the combined AIC deficit with the LDCs in clothing, textiles and finished consumer goods (excluding automobiles and other engineered consumer products) (GATT, 1980a, p. 12). Again, one can argue that there is no sign that the NICs are reaching saturation in their demand for products such as petrochemicals, special steels, machinery, computers, other electrical goods, aircraft, ships, scientific instruments, insurance, tourism, advanced education or consultancy. Obviously, some NICs are starting to produce one or two of these products, but for every South Korea which may become a net exporter of ships, the AICs should have no difficulty in finding new areas (bio-technology, satellite communications, ocean mining) in which to keep a technological lead.

TRADE PROBLEMS

Despite all such reassuring analyses, most AICs still remain wary of the NICs, and this book should have convinced most readers that there has been an increase in protectionist measures aimed against these newcomers. Why is there this gulf between analysis and action? Undoubtedly, part of the problem is a question of timing. The NICs were unfortunate in coming to the fore during the 1970s, a decade of slow growth partly caused by the oil revolution of the early 1970s and probably reinforced by the anti-Keynesian reaction to the inflationary pressures that had been building up even before the oil-price shock. As growth slowed, fewer new jobs were created and it grew progressively more difficult to resist the lobbyists from those industries that were in secular decline. This was also the first decade in which currencies floated, thus giving an extra sense of uncertainty to AIC planners. In addition, the NICs had the misfortune to be emerging in the wake of Japan, a new-coming exporter attracting more than its share of Euro-American ire. The core NICs are considerably more than mere proxies for Japanese exporters, but it was inevitable that the NICs should be sucked into trade disputes which primarily involved Japan.

However, even if the timing explains some of this drift towards selective protectionism, the latter is not just an unthinking, malevolent reaction by Western democracies increasingly unable to compete with new economic competition from abroad. There are some specific aspects of NIC trading practices which raise understandable resistance in AIC circles, even among quite dedicated supporters of free trade.

In the first place, there is the 'laser-like' impact that a handful of investment decisions in an NIC can have on its AIC competitors. One thinks of the three Korean companies which laid down export-oriented colour-television plants virtually simultaneously; or of the way Spanish performance requirements forced Ford into becoming the country's largest single exporter with its first investment in Spain. When trade-affecting investment decisions of this size are taken with the explicit or implicit backing of the NIC governments, from behind tight trade barriers, and within an opaque business environment not permitting the identification of relevant subsidies, it is inevitable that companies and employees at the AIC end of the affected sectors will feel aggrieved, believing they are faced with something more than the normal workings of the laws of comparative advantage.

There is also the issue of the relatively important role of state and para-statal corporations in a number of NICs. These will often be ranged against purely private AIC corporations – a situation clearly found in East–West trade and in parts of the steel industry – and will become a factor as the oil producers move into petrochemicals. How does one reconcile the trading practices of two such different sets of actors?

Then there is the question of fair-labour practices in those NICs which primarily compete on the cheapness and discipline of their labour forces. If welfare spending is low by AIC standards, and trade-unionists are harassed or trade-union activities are actually illegal, can one say that competition from such countries is 'fair'?

In industries where comparative advantages are linked to the optimal scale of operations, there is the problem of fast-growing, middle-income countries which may be able to enter a virtuous circle, in which expanding domestic markets and increased penetration of export ones permit steady investment in the latest world-scale plants. These will tend to out-perform the older, smaller-scale plants in maturing AIC markets, and it may be politically impossible to rationalize these latter plants fast enough for them to stay competitive against best practices within the NICs. At what point does AIC resistance to the natural advantages of scale economies enjoyed by fast-growing NICs become illegitimate?

A further problem is that thrown up by the entry of the oil producers into the petrochemical industry. In so far as they will have to subsidize the first generation of their new plants in this industry, to what extent are subsidies to and protection of infant export industries covered by existing GATT rules allowing them to protect infant, import-substituting ones?

That these are all genuine problems which will tax international trade institutions should not blind readers to the fact that NICs do have genuine comparative advantages. For instance, although employees in the AICs may view NIC employment practices as unfair, it is hard to justify claims that they should so improve these practices that they price jobs out of world markets. All the same, it would be useful if some reasonably objective body such as the International Labour Organization could draw up some indicative list of kinds of wage-levels, welfare benefits and employment practices typically found at different levels of development. Such a list might remain too ill-defined to justify the insertion of 'social clauses' into trade pacts (as the EC has been tempted to do), but it would help single out countries whose export performance relies on an exceptionally harsh exploitation of its citizens.

Again, no one should blind themselves to the fact that LDCs can also have genuine competitive advantages stemming from raw materials, improving skill-intensity, more effective entrepreneurship and the dynamic effects of relatively fast-growing economies. The simple picture of NIC successes resting on cheap labour and massive state subsidies should be discarded once and for all.

THE AIC PROBLEM

Trade politics has always been an arena in which the motes in one's opponents' eyes have always seemed mountainous, while one's own vision has been crystal clear. So, many Europeans and Americans blame their inability to sell to Japan on iniquitous Japanese protectionism, while ignoring cultural factors and sheer Western exporting inefficiency, which are also part of the story. In the wider case of AIC–NIC trade relations this book has gone out of its way to suggest that neither side is perfect, and that some AIC trading practices need very critical scrutiny indeed. Perhaps the most worrying aspect of recent AIC behaviour has been the rather casual way in which the basic GATT principle of non-discrimination has been broken, not just to liberalize trade within regional preferential trading blocs, but to restrict trade with various trading partners. Within GATT, there were the various textile initiatives, culminating in the MFA. Increasingly, since then, the AICs have resorted to various extra-GATT mechanisms such as VERs or OMAs. These have sprung up despite the fact that GATT's Article XIX sets down the conditions in which safeguard action can be taken. It is unsurprising that some AICs, the Europeans in particular, have put the amendment of this Article very high up on their list of priorities. However, what is important is that any such amendment should be carried out carefully.

On the one hand, readers can use this book's analysis to justify the case for occasional safeguard actions. AIC industries and companies do fall behind competitively for relatively peripheral reasons, so some protection to allow their rejuvenation or restructuring can make some sense. There may also be problems with trade surges stemming from state-led investment decisions which cannot be handled comfortably by conventional anti-dumping actions. More debatably, the social cost of the unbuffered exposure of a secularly declining industry to the full blast of foreign competition may be more than a country's political structure can stand.

On the other hand, this book also supports the argument that selective protectionism is often applied arbitrarily, with rather more rigour applied to the diplomatically weak than their trade offences may actually justify. The textile and clothing sector abounds in arbitrary decisions, such as the way in which the NIC exporters are used as expendable bargaining chips in the US formation of interest-group majorities in wider trade politics; such as the different way in which the EC treats its textile trade disputes with the USA and the LDCs; and the way in which the growth rates of the leading Third World exporters are held back, allegedly to favour the development of the poorer exporters. Selective actions in other sectors are still rare enough that generalizations are not easy to make, but one is struck by the exceptionally wide variations in the national quota treatments forced on Japan in the automotive and electronic sectors, and the way the NICs like Taiwan and South Korea come in for even more restrictive treatment when they move into new export markets (for televisions, for instance).

Given that small nations do need some protection from the selfish interests of the richer, larger ones, it would seem desirable that the reform of the GATT safeguards procedures should be part of a wider package. To start with, this should define some conditions which should be met before GATT endorses a country's resort to selective safeguards. There ought, for instance, to be a definition of the kind of market disruption which can be used to justify such actions, and the constraints might reasonably include the need to get prior international approval before action can be taken, or else require prompt vetting if circumstances required action before approval could be granted. There ought also to be time limits set on such actions; an understanding of the precise extent to which imports can be cut back in given situations; much tighter restrictions on the recourse to non-GATT actions such as VERs and OMAs; and the creation of a body within GATT to monitor the observance by countries of these conditions. One part of the package should be to register all existing VERs and OMAs, with the aim of modifying as many as possible such that their forms would satisfy the new requirements.

It would be unfortunate if any initiative on safeguards left the MFA untouched, even though there is a distinct possibility (not certainty) that it will have been renewed before this book reaches the hands of its readers. Be that as it may, the MFA should be a test-case for any new safeguards regime. There are several reasons for selecting it. For instance, it covers the most important industry in which the AICs have widely lost their competitive edge over the LDCs; protection of the industry has lasted for over twenty years in various forms; and the sustainable competitive rump of the AIC industry has still not been touched. It is the worst possible advertisement for supposedly temporary AIC selective protectionism. If the new selective safeguards arrangement proves slack enough to permit the extension of creeping, MFA-style trade controls in other industries, then the arrangement will still be too loose and should probably be delivered still-born. A period of further ambiguity as to what is permissible or not would probably be preferable to a new understanding on safeguards which does not put adequate obligations on the participants.

POSITIVE ADJUSTMENT

Resort to semi-permanent managed trade in sectors such as textiles and clothing is an admission that AICs are reluctant to let their economies adjust out of labour-intensive activities, even though these may have become widely uncompetitive in world markets. This reminds us that trade and adjustment are two sides of the same coin. Countries refusing to let their economies adjust are forced into protectionist actions. Facilitating economic adjustment permits a more relaxed attitude towards trade politics.

Non-interventionist readers can take some comfort from this book. As has been noted earlier in this chapter, many companies are still adjusting to changing circumstances without needing government help. Less conclusively, one can argue that those countries like West Germany and Japan which have been most relaxed about the decline of labour-intensive industries, such as clothing, have been among the most dynamic economies in any global comparison. However, the simple non-interventionist position is unsatisfactory. For one thing, Japan's strong showing in the world economy has been heavily influenced (if not precisely planned) by Japanese governmental bodies like MITI. For another, neither Japan nor West Germany is willing to let every industry go to the wall – both, for instance, protect inefficient agricultural sectors. Even the heavily market-oriented Reagan administration in the USA, is unwilling to expose its textile industry to unfettered foreign competition.

The other trouble with the non-interventionist analysis is that we do not, in practice, start with a blank slate. On the contrary, the overall effectiveness of AIC adjustment processes is affected by a myriad of pre-existing governmental actions (or non-actions) at a variety of different societal levels. Thus, everything from fiscal and educational policies at one end of the spectrum to retraining and redundancy-payment policies at the other may be relevant. Effective adjustment involves individuals, corporations, trade unions, local communities, entire industrial sectors and national cultures. Any policy which seeks to improve the adjustment process merely by trying to minimize the role of governments runs the real risk of foundering on institutional or cultural reefs. In these circumstances, a simple reliance on the pure workings of market forces ignores the fact that electorates may rebel (as the French did against the relatively technocratic President Giscard d'Estaing) or communities can explode into violence (as happened in the UK in the summer of 1981). Those who believe that governments have some role in facilitating the adjustment process would argue, rather, that policies aimed at easing the burdens on those most affected by economic change may permit faster overall economic growth.

This book's analysis of five industrial sectors certainly does not justify the authors' coming to definitive conclusions about what such optimal adjustment policies should be. However, the evidence from these sectors permits some observations, starting from the macro and moving to the micro environment.

The case-study approach is not designed to contribute significant inputs to fundamental controversies, such as that between the monetarists and Keynesians in the field of economic management – although the way an innovation such as the UK teletext service was clearly held back by inadequate consumer demand over 1980–1 suggests that monetarist squeezes might well cripple the innovative industries needed when the underlying health of a country's overall economy comes to be restored. At a less theoretical level, the cases have not revealed a single convincing instance (apart from Japan's initial protection of its infant industries) in which defensive economic policies, involving the protection or other cosseting of troubled companies or whole industrial sectors, have led to such a complete transformation of them that they are clearly going to be able to stand unaided on their own feet for the foreseeable future. The most one can say is that from companies such as RCA, BL, AEG-Telefunken, US Steel or Chrysler a handful will take the chance to re-establish themselves as industry leaders – but most of them will stagger on as companies more and more of the second rank, which will prove less and less relevant to dynamic growth in the 1990s and beyond.

What the role of government should be in picking the 'sunrise industries' is still an open question. The success of Japanese governments (and of some of the NICs) in guiding the development of their economies has very much rested on tracking the success of already established AICs, such as the USA. What has yet to be proved is that governments can usefully identify the growth industries of the 1990s and thus selectively guide their economies towards them.

At the very least, our cases suggest that governments – by omission or commission – are inevitably going to be involved in the evolution of their underlying economies. For one thing, it is quite clear from our cases that the industrial structure of AICs will be increasingly knowledge-intensive, hence the always important link between educational systems and industrial needs will grow stronger. The effectiveness of such a link is something which governments can influence for good or ill. Furthermore, the evidence from consumer electronics is that some industries are evolving towards highly regulated sectors, such as telecommunications. Inevitably, then, the evolution of these industries will be dependent on the way governments handle the regulation/deregulation issue. Sketchy evidence from the electronics sector is that those countries such as the USA and the UK that have been relaxing state telecommunication monopolies have been gaining an advantage over countries that have not done so.

Moving to a more specific issue, our cases suggest that more effort goes into handling the results of over-capacity than in preventing the over-investment in the first place. However, the cases point to the positive role that might be played by institutions like the OECD's sectoral bodies concerning steel and shipbuilding; UNIDO; and the (now defunct) Euro-Arab Dialogue. These have all analysed the economic environment which should underlie investment decisions in certain industries. There are obvious anti-trust implications in recommending that the work of such bodies should be strengthened. However, given that we seem to be moving into an era in which state-led over-investment and AIC reluctance to get out of uncompetitive sectors are basic problems, bodies which permit governments to develop their thinking about the true investment prospects of key sectors will probably do more good than harm.

Continuing at the sectoral level, a couple of basic points can be made. First, governmental intervention in specific AIC industrial sectors will tend to affect NIC prospects. This is because sectoral interventions tend to encourage the lobbyist, and the stronger the political, rather than economic, motivations behind AIC initiatives, the more likely is it that the specific interests of the diplomatically weak NICs will be hit. Therefore, as far as the NICs are concerned, they should be pressing AIC governments to go for general rather than sectoral adjustment measures.

Secondly, the closer one looks at our chosen sectors, the more one is struck by the relative inability of West Europeans to permit any sector to reduce its capacity in line with inadequate demand – and this is a generalization which holds true whether one considers the state-dominated steel industry, the fundamentally privately owned chemical sector, or the more mixed automotive one. In all these sectors, both industrial and governmental decision-makers in Western Europe seem slower in taking corrective action than their opposite numbers in the USA and Japan. So, despite the fact that Western Europe is the world's largest free-trading area, investment decisions are still heavily affected by political consider-ations in the different states. This residual nationalism is one of the biggest problems still facing the market-oriented decision-makers in Western Europe. The fact that Italy and President Mitterrand's France will remain relatively *dirigiste*, and that the UK's Conservative government could well be replaced by an inward-looking, protectionist Labour administration does not suggest that the forces for positive adjustment policies in Western Europe are going to find life any easier.

One American view is that there are lessons to be learned from a comparison of the West European and US examples. Despite the fact that the USA has been faced with a tremendous growth in the overall labour force, its economy has proved sufficiently flexible to generate enough jobs to mop up most of this increase. This contrasts with the less successful record of the West Europeans in job generation, which, in this view, may be attributed to tight European employment laws that, in contrast to the US case, make it relatively expensive and difficult to lay employees off or to sack them. This makes employers in West Europe cautious about taking on new employees in the first place. These transatlantic differences explain why there has been proportionally greater job creation in the USA – and success in creating new jobs helps the whole industrial adjustment process.

This study has concentrated primarily on adjustment at the level of companies, industrial sectors and wider national economies. At this level of analysis, the cases suggest the the AICs can cope with the emerging NICs without too much trouble. Moreover, analytical confidence at the macro level does not necessarily justify confidence at the level of individual employees. The NICs may not be a particularly important force in destroying AIC jobs, but the emergence of these countries has coincided with the initial impact of micro-electronics on assembly technologies (which will mostly affect unskilled labour) and of the oil-price revolution, which has changed the underlying economies of whole industrial sectors (thus affecting skilled and unskilled labour alike). This triple impact of the NICs, micro-electronics and high oil prices may well have speeded the continuing process of job destruction in the AICs, and has certainly made job creation more of an uncertain process than it has been in the past.

Our case studies were not designed to examine the ease with which displaced workers find jobs elsewhere in national economies. However, what one can say with some confidence is that the rise of NICs means that there will be a decreasing role in the AIC economies for tradable goods which depend on a high proportion of unskilled labour – and women (and ethnic minorities) will be particularly exposed to the effects of competition from the NICs (Cable and Rebelo, 1980, p. 25). Quite clearly, the unskilled in the industrialized world will have to upgrade their skills, or else move into non-trading sectors – a move which depends on there being enough new, relatively unskilled jobs in existence (and there are those such as Emma Rothschild (1981) who argue that the transition from manufacturing to service jobs is a much more problematical process than many macro economists are willing to admit).

The fact that this book has concentrated on relatively mature industries means that it has been disproportionately concerned with job destruction, rather than job creation. Even so, from our cases one can see where new jobs will be emerging that will not call for advanced educational or technical accomplishments. For instance, the chemical sector is pushing into bio-technology, which will prove increasingly important for both the agricultural and health sectors – both areas in which the competition from cheap Third World products is relatively unimportant. In consumer electronics, the cost of the hardware is steadily declining in relation to the value of the informational and educational services being transmitted through it. The growth of television studios, publishing-houses, computer-software companies, radio stations, record companies and programme originators for videocassettes and discs will all go to compensate for any decline in the number of jobs involved in making products like radios and televisions. In the case of automobiles, we are dealing with one part of a wider transportation sector which, once the new price of energy has been absorbed, should continue to expand. Even allowing for some substitution of telecommunications for business travel, personal mobility and the tourist industry will continue to increase faster than real incomes, creating a mixture of high- and low-skilled jobs.

The new jobs, then, are potentially there, ranging across the spectrum of skills, from hotel-workers to computer programmers. So why are the NICs viewed with so much suspicion? The evidence from the book suggests that their problem is not that they are posing fundamentally new problems to the world economy, but that they have emerged at the wrong time. At a time of slow growth and high unemployment, there is obvious scepticism about the workings of the economic adjustment process. Inevitably, there will be suspicion of identifiable new actors on the world scene. Given the kind of fast growth seen in the 1950s and 1960s, the NICs would probably have excited not much more than some intellectual curiosity. However, the slow growth of the 1970s has invited the search for scapegoats. The NICs – diplomatically weak and demonstrably alien – have filled this role only too well.

Bibliography

AISI (American Iron and Steel Institute), 1980, *Steel at the Crossroads: The American Steel Industry in the 1980s*, Washington DC, AISI.

Alford, M. D., 1979, 'The Netherlands adjustment policy with a development co-operation dimension', *Intereconomics*, March/April.

Allen, David, 1978, 'The Euro-Arab Dialogue', *Journal of Common Market Studies*, vol. 16, no. 4, pp. 323–42.

Bacha, Edmar, 1977, 'Issues and evidence on recent Brazilian economic growth', *World Development*, vol. 5, no. 1/2.

Balassa, Bela, 1977, *A 'Stages' Approach to Comparative Advantage*, Washington DC, World Bank (Staff Working Paper no. 256).

Balassa, Bela, 1978, 'Export incentives and export performance in developing countries: a comparative analysis', *Weltwirtschaftliches Archiv*, vol. 114, pp. 24ff.

Balassa, Bela, 1979a, 'A "stages" approach to comparative advantage', in: Irma Adelman (ed.), *Economic Growth and Resources*, vol. 4, *National and International Issues*, London, Macmillan, pp. 121–56.

Balassa, Bela, 1979b, 'Incentive policies in Brazil', *World Development*, vol. 7, pp. 1024–8.

Balassa, Bela, 1980, *Structural Change in Trade in Manufactured Goods between Industrial and Developing Countries*, Washington DC, World Bank (Staff Working Paper no. 396).

Baranson, Jack, 1967, *Manufacturing Problems in India: The Cummins Diesel Experience*, Syracuse, NY, Syracuse University Press.

Baranson, Jack, 1969, *Automotive Industries in Developing Countries*, Baltimore, Md, Johns Hopkins.

Baron, Yves, 1978, 'Croissance interne et compétitivité internationale', *Économie et statistique*, no. 105, November.

Bennett, Douglas, and Sharpe, Kenneth E., 1979, 'Transnational corporations and the political economy of export promotion', *International Organization*, vol. 33, spring, pp. 177–201.

Bergsman, Joel, 1979, *Growth and Equity in Semi-Industrialized Countries*, Washington DC, World Bank (Staff Working Paper no. 351).

Berthelot, Yves, and Tardy, Gérard, 1978, *Le Défi économique du Tiers-Monde*, Paris, La Documentation Française.

Blackhurst, Richard, Marian, Nicolas, and Tumlir, Jan, 1978, *Adjustment, Trade and Growth in Developed and Developing Countries*, Geneva, GATT (GATT Studies no. 6).

Bombach, G., and Gahlen, B. (eds.), 1976, *Probleme des Strukturwandels und der Strukturpolitik*, Tübingen, Mohr.

Bradford, Colin I., 1979, *Brazil as a 'New Influential'*, New Haven, Conn., Yale University (mimeo.).

Bradford, Colin I., 1981, 'Advanced developing country manufactured export growth and OECD adjustment', in: Krause and Hong (eds.), q.v.

Bradford, Colin I. (forthcoming), 'Interdependence and trade in manufactures', in: *Interdependence in the 1980s*, sponsored by the US Agency for International Development.

Brandt Report, 1980, *North–South: A Programme for Survival*, London, Pan.

Branson, William H. (forthcoming), 'The macroeconomics of interdependence between the US and the developing countries', in: *Interdependence in the 1980s*, sponsored by the US Agency for International Development.

Cable, Vincent, 1979, *World Textile Trade and Production*, London, Economist Intelligence Unit (Special Report no. 63).

Cable, Vincent, and Clarke, Jeremy, 1981, *British Electronics and Competition with Newly Industrializing Countries*, London, Overseas Development Institute.

Cable, Vincent, and Rebelo, Ivonic, 1980, *Britain's Pattern of Specialization in Manufactured Goods with Developing Countries and Trade Protection*, Washington DC, World Bank (Staff Working Paper no. 425).

Cable, Vincent, and Weston, Ann, 1979, *South Asia's Exports to the EEC – Obstacles and Opportunities*, London, Overseas Development Institute.

Camps, Miriam, 1980, *The Case for a New Global Trade Organization*, New York, NY, Council on Foreign Relations.

CEPII (Centre d'Études Prospectives et d'Informations Internationales), 1978 *Les Économies industrialisées face à la concurrence du Tiers-Monde: le cas de la filière textile*, Paris, CEPII.

CEPII, 1979, 'La concurrence industrielle à l'échelle mondiale: mutations et perspectives', *Économie prospective internationale*, 2nd qr.

Chenery, Hollis B., 1979, *Structural Change and Development*, Oxford, Oxford University Press.

Chenery, Hollis B., and Keesing, Donald B., 1979, *The Changing Composition of Developing Country Exports*, Washington DC, World Bank (Staff Working Paper no. 314).

Chenery, Hollis B., 1980, Changes in trade shares and economic growth: interaction between industrialization and exports', *American Economic Review*, May, pp. 281–7.

CIA (Central Intelligence Agency), 1979, *The Burgeoning LDC Steel Industry: More Problems for Major Steel Producers*, Washington DC, CIA.

CIRFS (Comité International de la Rayonne et des Fibres Synthétiques), 1979, *A Study of the Evolution of Textile Final Consumption*, Paris, CIRFS (mimeo.).

Cockerill, A., 1974, *The Steel Industry: International Comparisons of Industrial Structure and Performance*, London, Cambridge University Press.

Comptroller-General (USA), 1978, *Adjustment Assistance under the Trade Act of 1974 to Pennsylvania Apparel Workers*, Washington DC, General Accounting Office (Report to Congress by the Comptroller-General of the United States, HRD-78-53).

Conseil Économique et Social, 1979, 'L'Avenir des industries françaises et la nouvelle répartition internationale de la production industrielle', *Journal officiel de la République française*, no. 4, 27 January (Avis et rapports du Conseil Economique et Social, session de 1978).

Council of Economic Advisers, 1981, *Economic Report of the President*, Washington DC, CEA.

Curhan, Joan P., Davidson, William H., and Suri, Rajan, 1977, *Tracing the Multinationals: A Sourcebook on US Based Enterprises*, Cambridge, Mass., Ballinger.

Curzon, Gerard, 1965, *Multilateral Commercial Diplomacy: An Examination of the Impact of the General Agreement on Tariffs and Trade on National Commercial Policies and Techniques*, London, Michael Joseph.

Curzon-Price, Victoria, 1980, 'Capital formation and investment policy', in: J. W. Wheeler (ed.), *Western Economies in Transition: Structural Change and Adjustment Policies in Industrial Countries*, Boulder, Colo., Westview.

Dam, Kenneth W., 1970, *The GATT: Law and International Economic Organization*, Chicago, Ill., University of Chicago Press.

Davignon, Étienne, 1979, 'Strengths and vulnerabilities of the free market in Europe', *Chemistry and Industry*, 1 December pp. 812–14.

Davignon Plan. *See* EC Commission, 1977.

Davignon De Bandt, J., 1979, 'Préférences (nationales) de structure', in: *The European Economic Community and Changes in the International Division of Labour*, Brussels, EC Commission, Directorate-General for Development, January (Paul-Marc Henry Report).

de la Torre, José, 1978, *Corporate Responses to Import Competition in US Apparel Industry*, Atlanta, Ga, Georgia State University (Research Monograph no. 74).

de Miramon, Jacques, and Kleitz, Anthony, 1978, 'Tariff preferences for the developing world: operations and evolution of the Generalized System of Preferences', *OECD Observer*, no. 90, January, pp. 30–7.

Diebold, William, 1980, *Industrial Policy as an International Issue*, New York, NY, McGraw-Hill.

Dunn, Robert M., jun., assisted by Salih N. Neftci, 1980, *Economic Growth Among Industrialized Countries: Why the United States Lags*, Washington DC, Committee on Changing International Realities.

DWIT (Developing World Industry and Technology Inc.), 1978, *Sources of Competitiveness in the Japanese Color Television and Video Tape Recorder Industry*, Washington DC, DWIT (Report prepared for the US Department of Labor).

EC Commission, 1975a, *Guidelines on Iron and Steel Policy*, Brussels, EC Commission (COM(75)701).

EC Commission, 1975b, *(Background Paper no. 2244)*, Brussels, Information Office of the EC Commission, 23 September.

EC Commission, 1976a, *Guidelines on the Iron and Steel Policy*, Brussels, EC Commission (Simonet Plan) (COM(76)543).

EC Commission, 1976b, 'General objectives for steel 1980–85', *Official Journal* (C323).

EC Commission, 1977, 'Community steel policy', *Official Journal* (C303) (Davignon Plan).

EC Commission, 1978a, *Communication to the Council on General Guidelines for a Textiles and Clothing Industry Policy*, Brussels, EC Commission (COM(78)362 final).

EC Commission, 1978b, *Communication to the Council on Sectoral Aid Policy*, Brussels, EC Commission (COM(78)221 final).

EC Commission, 1978c, 'The European Community and the textile arrangements', *Europe Information.*

EC Commission, 1978d, *General Objectives for Steel 1980, 1985 and 1990*, Brussels, EC Commission. (SEC(78)3205 final).

EC Commission, 1978e, *Social Aspects of Steel Policy*, Brussels, EC Commission (SEC(78)2636).

EC Commission, 1978f, *Towards a Community Growth Policy*, Brussels, EC Commission, 6 July (Europe Documents, no. 1011/1012).

EC Commission, 1979a, 'The social aspects of the iron and steel policy', *Official Journal*, 7 June (C142).

EC Commission, 1979b, *The European Economic Community and Changes in the International Division of Labour*, Brussels, EC Commission, Directorate-General for Development (Paul-Marc Henry Report).

EC Commission, 1980, 'Étude: l'industrie de l'habillement', Brussels, EC Commission (III/936/80) (unpublished).

ECSC (European Coal and Steel Community), 1980, *Investment in the Community Coalmining and Iron and Steel Industry*, Luxembourg, European Communities.

Edwards, Anthony, 1979, *The Newly Industrializing Countries and their Impact on Western Manufacturing*, London, Economist Intelligence Unit, 2 vols. (Special Report no. 73).

EECMA (European Electronic Component Manufacturers' Association), 1978, *European Electronics: Critical*, London, EECMA.

EIU (Economist Intelligence Unit), 1974, 1979, *Quarterly Economic Reviews*, London, EIU.

Esser, Josef, 1979, *Konfliktregulierung durch Kartelbildung: Die Stahlkrise an der Saar*, Berlin, Internationales Institut für Management und Verwaltung (Discussion Paper no. 32).

Europa (annual), *The Europa Year Book: A World Survey*, London, Europa.

Eurostat (Statistical Office of the European Communities), statistics on textiles and clothing trade (unpublished).

Eurostat, 1979, *Iron and Steel Year Book*, Luxembourg, Statistical Office of the European Communities.

Farrands, Christopher, 1979, 'Textile diplomacy: the making and implementation of European textile policy 1974–1978', *Journal of Common Market Studies*, vol. XVIII, no. 1, September.

Fei, John C. H., Ranis, Gustav, and Kuo, Shirley W. Y., 1979, *Growth with Equity: The Taiwan Case*, Oxford, Oxford University Press.

Fishlow, Albert, 1975, *Foreign Trade Regimes and Economic Development in Brazil*, New Haven, Conn., Yale University (mimeo.).

Fleischle, G., and Krueper, M. (eds.) 1975, *Investitionslenkung: Überwindung oder Ergänzung der Marktwirtschaft*, Frankfurt a/M, Europäische Verlagsanstalt.

Fleischmann, G., 1976, 'Forschungs- und Technologiepolitik als Strukturpolitik', in: G. Bombach and B. Gahlen (eds.), *Probleme des Strukturwandels und der Strukturpolitik*, Tübingen, Mohr.

Florkoski, E. S., 1980, 'Policy responses for the world steel industry in the 1980s', *OECD Symposium on the Steel Industry in the 1980s*, Paris, OECD, February (paper).

Frank, Charles, 1977, *Foreign Trade and Domestic Aid*, Washington DC, Brookings Institution.

Franko, Lawrence G., 1976, *The European Multinationals*, London, Harper & Row.

Franko, Lawrence G., 1979, *A Survey of the Impact of Manufactured Exports from Industrializing Countries in Asia and Latin America*, Washington DC, National Planning Association.

Franko, Lawrence G., 1980, *European Industrial Policy, Past, Present and Future*, Brussels, Conference Board in Europe.

Franzmeyer, Fritz, 1979, *Industrielle Strukturprobleme und sektorale Strukturpolitik in der Europäischen Gemeinschaft*, Berlin, Dunker & Humblot/ Deutsches Institut für Wirtschaftsforschung (Occasional Paper no. 130).

FRG, Bundesregierung, 1966, 'Grundsätze der regionalen und sektoralen Strukturpolitik', *Bundesanzeiger* (Bonn), no. 219, 24 November.

FRG, Bundesregierung, 1968, 'Grundsätze sektoralen und regionalen Wirtschaftspolitik', *Bundestagsdrucksache* (Bonn), 16 January (V/2469).

FRG, Bundesregierung, 1969, 'Strukturbericht der Bundersregierung', *Bundestagsdrucksache* (Bonn), (V/4564).

FRG, Bundesregierung, 1978, *Jahreswirtschaftsbericht*, Bonn, Bundesregierung.

FRG, Bundestag (alternate years), 'Subventionsberichte', *Bundestagsdrucksachen* (Bonn), 1969 (V/2423), 1971 (VI/391), 1973 (VI/2994), 1975 (VII/4203), 1977 (VIII/1195).

Fröbel, Folker, Heinrichs, Jürgen, and Kreye, Otto, 1977, *Die neue internationale Arbeitsteilung*, Hamburg, Rowohlt.

Fuller, Mark B., and Salter, Malcolm S., 1981, *Profile of the World-Wide Auto Industry* (Harvard Business School, May 1980) as modified in *The US Automobile Industry, 1980: Report to the President from the Secretary of Transportation*, Washington DC, US Department of Transportation, table 4–10, p. 60.

GATT, 1979, *The Tokyo Round of Multilateral Trade Negotiations*, Geneva, GATT.

GATT, 1980a, *Prospects for International Trade*, Geneva, GATT, 9 September (press release).

GATT, 1980b, *Demand, Production and Trade in Textiles and Clothing since 1973*, Geneva, GATT, 3 December (Report by the Secretariat of the Textiles Committee) (COM.Tex/W/84).

GATT, 1980c, *Statistics on Textiles and Clothing*, Geneva, GATT, 29 September (COM.Tex/W/78).

GATT, 1980d, *Textiles and Clothing Production, Employment and Trade Statistics 1973–1979*, Geneva, GATT, 9 October (COM.Tex/W/63).

GATT, 1980e, *International Trade, 1979/1980*, Geneva, GATT.

Geiger, Theodore, and Geiger, Frances M., 1973, *Tales of Two City-States: The Development Progress of Hong Kong and Singapore*, Washington DC, National Planning Association.

Giersch, Herbert, 1978, *The Problems of Adjusting to Imports from Developing Countries*, Kiel, 1978 (mimeo).

Glismann, H. H., and Weiss, F. D., 1980, *On the Political Economy of Protection in Germany*, Washington DC, World Bank (Staff Working Paper no. 427).

Godesberg Programme, 1959, *Grundsatzprogramm der Sozialdemokratischen Partei Deutschlands*, 15 November.

Golt, Sydney, 1978, *Developing Countries in the GATT System*, London, Trade Policy Research Centre.

Golt, Sydney, 1980, 'The new protectionism', in: J. W. Wheeler (ed.), *Western Economies in Transition: Structural Change and Adjustment Policies in Industrial Countries*, Boulder, Colo., Westview.

Gordon, Lincoln, 1979, *Growth Policies and the International Order*, New York, NY, McGraw-Hill.

Hamilton, Carl, 1980, *Effects of Non-Tariff Barriers to Trade on Prices, Employment and Imports: The Case of the Swedish Textile and Clothing Industry*, Washington DC, World Bank (Staff Working Paper no. 429).

Hanabusa, Masamichi, 1979, *Trade Problems between Japan and Western Europe*, Farnborough, Saxon House/Royal Institute of International Affairs.

Hauff, V., and Scharpf, F. W., 1975, *Modernisierung der Volkswirtshaft: Technologiepolitik als Strukturpolitik*, Frankfurt a/M, Europäische Verlagsanstalt.

Helleiner, G. K., 1977, 'Political economy of Canadian tariff structure: an alternative model', *Revue canadienne d'économie*, May.

Helleiner, G. K., 1979, *Transnational Corporations and Trade Structure*, Toronto, University of Toronto (mimeo.).

Henry Report. *See* EC Commission, 1979b.

Hindley, Brian, 1980, 'Voluntary export restraints and the GATT's main escape clause', *World Economy*, vol. 3, no. 3, November, pp. 313–42.

Holmer, Ed. C., 1980, 'The Challenges of the '80s from the perspective of the US chemical industry', *Chemistry and Industry*, 5 January, pp. 18–21.

IMF (International Monetary Fund) (annual), *International Financial Statistics Yearbook*, Washington DC, IMF.

IMF, 1980, *World Economic Outlook: A Survey by the Staff of the Fund*, Washington DC, IMF, May.

IMF, 1981, *World Economic Outlook*, Washington DC, IMF, June (Occasional Paper no. 4).

Interfutures, 1978, *Long-Term Perspectives of the World Car Industries: Intermediate Report*, Paris, OECD, 3 February.

Interfutures, 1979, *Facing the Future: Mastering the Unpredictable*, Paris, OECD.

Jefferson, Edward G., 1979, 'Research and development in the US chemical industry', *Chemistry and Industry*, 2 June, pp. 366–70.

Jones, Daniel T., 1979, *The European Motor Industry and Government Intervention*, Brighton, Sussex, Sussex European Research Centre (mimeo.).

Jones, Daniel T., 1981, *Maturity and Crisis in the European Car Industry: Structural Change and Public Policy*, Brighton, Sussex, Sussex European Research Centre (Industrial Adjustment and Policy: I) (Sussex European Papers no. 8).

Jones, Kent, 1979, 'Forgetfulness of things past: Europe and the steel cartel', *World Economy*, vol. 2, no. 1, January, pp. 139–54.

Keesing, Donald B., 1979a, *World Trade and Output of Manufacturers: Structural Trends and Developing Countries' Exports*, Washington DC, World Bank (Staff Working Paper no. 316).

Keesing, Donald B., 1979b, *Trade Policy for Developing Countries*, Washington DC, World Bank (Staff Working Paper no. 353).

Keesing, Donald B., and Wolf, Martin, 1980, *Textile Quotas against Developing Countries*, London, Trade Policy Research Centre (Thames Essay no. 23).

Kemper, Ria, 1980, *The Tokyo Round: Results and Implications for Developing Countries*, Washington DC, World Bank (Staff Working Paper no. 372).

Kohler, H., 1968, 'Walzstahlkontore – neuartige Organisationsform im Wettbewerb', *Der Volkswirt* (Beiheft zum Eisenhüttentag).

Kono, Tsutomu, 1980, 'Outlook for world steel industry up to 1985: demand, trade and supply capacity', *OECD Symposium on the Steel Industry in the 1980s*, Paris, OECD, February (paper).

Kostecki, Maciej, 1978, *East–West Trade and the GATT System*, Basingstoke, Macmillan.

Krause, Lawrence B., 1981, 'Conference summary', in: Krause and Hong (eds.), q.v.

Krause, Lawrence, and Hong, Wontack (eds.), 1981, *Trade and Growth of Advanced Developing Countries in the New International Economic Order*, Seoul, Korean Development Institute.

Krueger, Anne O., 1978, *Foreign Trade Regimes and Economic Development: Liberalization Attempts and Consequences*, vol. 10, Cambridge, Mass., Ballinger.

Kurth, Wilhelm, 1980, 'Textiles and clothing: a national and international issue', *International Symposium on Industrial Policies for the Eighties*, Madrid, Spanish Ministry of Industry/OECD, May (paper).

Liang, Kuo-shu, and Liang, Chin-ing Hou, 1981, 'Trade strategy and the exchange rate policies of Taiwan', in Krause and Hong (eds.), q.v.

Lin, Tzong-Biau, and Ho, Yin-Ping, 1981, 'Export-oriented growth and industrial diversification in Hong Kong', in Krause and Hong (eds.), q.v.

Magaziner, Ira C., and Hout, M., 1980, *Japanese Industrial Policy*, London, Policy Studies Institute (Paper no. 585).

Malan, Pedro, and Bonelli, Regis, 1977, 'The Brazilian economy in the mid-1970s: old and new developments', *World Development*, vol. 5, no. 1/2.

Maldague Report, 1979, *Changes in Industrial Structure in the European Economies since the Oil Crisis, 1973–1978*, Brussels, EC Commission, July (Report of the Group of Experts on Sectoral Analyses).

Marcus, P. F., 1979, 'A Western world steel supply/demand scenario for the 1980s', in: *World Steel Dynamics*, Washington DC, Paine Webber Mitchell Hutchins Inc., 23 October.

Marks, M. J., 1978, 'Remedies to unfair trade: American action against steel imports', *World Economy*, January, pp. 223–37.

Marsh, Peter, 1980, 'EEC foreign economic policy and the political management of East–West economic relations', *Millennium*, vol. 9, no. 1, Spring, pp. 41–54.

Meltzer, Ronald I., 1979, 'Colour-TV sets and US–Japanese relations: problems of trade-adjustment policy makers', *Orbis*, summer, pp. 421–46.

Merrill Lynch, 1977, *The Japanese Steel Industry: A Comparison with its United States Counterpart*, Washington DC, Merrill Lynch.

Meyer, F. V., 1978, *International Trade Policy*, London, Croom Helm.

Miles, Caroline, 1968, *Lancashire Textiles: A Case Study in Industrial Change*, Cambridge, Cambridge University Press.

Mitteilungen, 1976, 'Überlegungen zu einer aktiven Strukturpolitik', *Mitteilungen*, nos. 10, 11 and 12, October-December. (*Mitteilungen* is the journal of the WSI: the Wirtschafts- und Sozialwissenschaftlichen Institut des Deutschen Gewerkschaftsbundes).

Monnet, Jean, 1978, *Memoirs*, London, Collins.

Morici, Peter, and Megna, Laura (forthcoming), *US Domestic and International Economic Policies Affecting Trade*, Washington DC, National Planning Association.

Morton, Kathryn, and Tulloch, Peter, 1977, *Trade and Developing Countries*, London, Croom Helm.

Mueller, Hans, and Kawahito, K. 1978, *Steel Industry Economics: A Comparative Analysis of Structure, Conduct and Performance*, New York, NY, Japan Steel Information Center.

Mueller, Hans, and Kawahito, K., 1979, *Errors and Biases in the 1978 Putnam, Hayes and Bartlett Study on the Pricing of Imported Steel*, Tennessee, Middle Tennessee State University (Monograph Series no. 17).

Murray, Tracy, 1977, *Trade Preferences for Developing Countries*, London, Macmillan.

Mutti, John, (forthcoming), *Taxes, Subsidies and Competitiveness Internationally*, Washington DC, National Planning Association.

MVMA (Motor Vehicle Manufacturers Association), n.d., *World Motor Vehicle Data* (1980 ed.), Detroit, Mich., MVMA.

Mytelka, Lynn Krieger, 1980, *Crisis and Adjustment in the French Textile Industry*', Northfield, Minn., Carleton University.

Nelson, Douglas R., 1981, *The Political Structure of the New Protectionism*, Washington DC, World Bank.

Nijhawan, B., 1980, 'Global scenario of world steel industry growth, particularly up to 1985', *OECD Symposium on the Steel Industry in the 1980s*, Paris, OECD, February (paper).

Nomura Research Institute, 1979, *Prospects for Japanese Industry to 1985*, 2 vols., London, Financial Times Ltd.

NPA (National Planning Association), 1979, *National Economic Projections*, Washington DC, NPA.

NPA, 1980a, *The Automobile and Parts Industry in Mexico*, Washington DC, NPA (mimeo.).

NPA, 1980b, *The Automobile Industry in Argentina*, Washington DC, NPA (mimeo.).

ODI (Overseas Development Institute), 1980, *Lomé II*, London, ODI (Briefing Paper no. 1).

OECD (annual), *Foreign Trade Statistics*, series C, Paris, OECD.

OECD, (1975), *Trade by Commodities: 1975*, Paris, OECD.

OECD, (1977), *Trade by Commodities: 1977*, Paris, OECD.

OECD, 1978a, *Policies for Adjustment: Some General Orientations*, Paris, 15 May (Council Communiqué, Presse/A(78)23, annex II.

OECD, 1978b, Council Decision Establishing the Steel Committee, Paris, 26 October.

OECD, 1979a, *The Impact of the Newly Industrializing Countries on Production and Trade in Manufactures*, Paris, OECD.

OECD, 1979b, *Positive Adjustment Policies: Some General Issues*, Paris, OECD.

OECD, 1979c, *The Case for Positive Adjustment Policies: A Compendium of OECD Documents*, Paris, OECD.

OECD, 1979d, *Manpower and Employment Measures for Positive Adjustment*, Paris, OECD, (MAS(78)40).

OECD, 1979e, *Report to the Council on Positive Adjustment Policies in the Industry Sector*, Paris, OECD (IND(79)3).

OECD, 1979f, *Economic Outlook*, Paris, OECD, December (no. 26).

OECD, 1980a, *OECD Symposium on the Steel Industry in the 1980s*, Paris, OECD.

OECD, 1980b, *Trade by Commodities 1980*, Paris, OECD.

OECD, 1980c, *The Steel Market, 1979, and Outlook for 1980*, Paris, OECD.

Ohlin, B., 1978, ch. 2 in: *The International Allocation of Economic Activity: Readings of a Nobel Symposium*, London, Macmillan.

Orwell, S., Welte, F., Paterson, P., and Jacobs, E., 1979, *The Approach to Industrial Change in Britain and West Germany*, London, Anglo-German Foundation.

Page, Jean-Pierre, 1980, 'Criteria for assessing trends in OECD countries' industrial structures during the 1980s', *International Symposium on Industrial Policies for the Eighties*, Madrid, Spanish Ministry of Industry/ OECD, May (paper).

Page, Sheila, 1979, 'The management of international trade', in: Robin Major, *Britain's Trade and Exchange Rate Policies*, London, Heinemann, pp. 164–99.

Pavitt, Keith (ed.), 1980, *Technical Innovation and British Economic Performance*, London, Macmillan.

Pincus, J. J. 1975, 'Pressure groups and the pattern of tariffs', *Journal of Political Economy*, vol. 83, no. 4, August, pp. 757–78.

Pinder, John, Hosomi, T., and Diebold, W. 1979, *Industrial Policy and the International Economy*, New York, NY, The Trilateral Commission (Triangle Paper no. 19).

Plässert, G., 1974, in: H. Giersch (ed.), *The International Division of Labour: Problems and Prospects*, Tübingen, Mohr.

Postan, M. M., 1977, 'European economic policy since 1945', in: Michael Watson and R. T. Griffiths (eds.), *Government, Business and Labour in European Capitalism*, London, Europotentials Press.

Preeg, Ernest H., 1970, *Traders and Diplomats: An Analysis of the Kennedy Round of Negotiations under the General Agreement on Tariffs and Trade*, Washington DC, Brookings Institution.

Putnam, Hayes and Bartlett Inc., 1977, *Economics of International Steel Trade*, Newton, Mass., PHB Inc.

Putnam, Hayes and Bartlett Inc., 1978, *The Economic Implications of Foreign Steel Pricing Practices in the US Market*, Washington DC, American Iron and Steel Institute.

Ranis, Gustav, 1980, 'Challenges and opportunities posed by Asia's super-exporters: implications for manufactured exports from Latin America', *NBER/FIPE/BEBR Conference on Trade Prospects among the Americas, 24–26 March 1980, São Paulo, Brazil* (paper).

Ringelstein, Ernst, 1979, *Gewerkschaft Textil-Bekleidung* (paper for Third Sekretärtagung, Düsseldorf, 14–19 October) (mimeo.).

Rothschild, Emma, 1981, 'Reagan and the real America', *New York Review*, 5 February, pp. 12–18.

Shell, 1980, *Chemicals Information Handbook 1979–80*, London, Shell International Chemical Company.

Shepherd, Geoffrey, 1980a, 'New and old industrial countries: industrial strategies in textiles and motor cars', *Sussex European Research Centre Conference on New and Old Industrial Countries, Sussex, 6–8 January* (paper).

Shepherd, Geoffrey, 1980b, 'UK economic policies and their implications for Third World countries: the case of textiles and clothing', in: Riddell, Abby Rubin (ed.), *Adjustment or Protectionism: Challenge to Britain of Third World Industrialization*, London, Catholic Institute of International Relations, pp. 84–110.

Shinohara, Miyohei, 1980, 'Japanese style industrial policy', *International Symposium on Industrial Policies for the Eighties*, Madrid, Spanish Ministry of Industry/OECD, May (paper).

Shonfield, Andrew, 1965, *Modern Capitalism*, London, Oxford University Press.

Silberston, A., 1980, 'Industrial strategy in Britain: fact or fiction?', *International Symposium on Industrial Policies for the Eighties*, Madrid, Spanish Ministry of Industry/OECD, May (paper).

Simonet Plan. *See* EC Commission, 1976a.

Sobeslavsky, V., and Beazley, P., 1980, *The Transfer of Technology to Socialist Countries: The Case of the Soviet Chemical Industry*, Farnborough, Hants, Gower.

Solomon Report, 1978, *Report to the President: A Comprehensive Programme for the Steel Industry*, Washington DC, November.

Stegemann, Klaus, 1976, *Price and Output Adjustment in the European Steel Industry 1954–75*, Tübingen, Mohr.

Stoffaes, Christian, 1978, *La Grande Menace industrielle*, Paris, Calmann-Lévy.

Stoffaes, Christian, 1980, 'The French experience of industrial policy', *International Symposium on Industrial Policies for the Eighties*, Madrid, Spanish Ministry of Industry/OECD, May (paper).

Stout, D. K., 1980, 'Adjustment policies in Europe', *International Symposium on Industrial Policies for the Eighties*, Madrid, Spanish Ministry of Industry/OECD, May (paper).

Suzuki, Kimiro, and Miles, Tudor, 1980, 'The growth of steel making capacity in the 1980s', OECD Symposium on the Steel Industry in the 1980s, Paris, OECD, February (paper).

Taiwan, Council for Economic Planning and Development, 1980, *Taiwan Statistical Data Book 1980*, Taipei, CEPD.

Tharakan, P. K. M., 1980, *The Political Economy of Protection in Belgium*, Washington DC, World Bank (Staff Working Paper no. 431).

Thormählen, G., 1978, *Die Grossunternehmen der westdeutschen Textilindustrie im Strukturwandel*, Hamburg, University of Hamburg (doctoral dissertation).

Thurgpen, Elton, 1978, *International Cotton Market Prospects*, Washington DC, World Bank (Staff Commodity Paper no. 2).

Turner, Louis, and Bedore, James, 1979, *Middle East Industrialisation: Saudi and Iranian Downstream Investments*, London, Teakfield, and New York, NY, Praeger.

Turner, Louis, Bradford, Colin I., Franko, Lawrence G., McMullen, Neil, and Woolcock, Stephen, 1980, *Living with the Newly Industrializing Countries*, London, Royal Institute of International Affairs (Chatham House Paper no. 7).

Tyler, William G., 1980, *Advanced Developing Countries as Competitors in Third World Markets: The Brazilian Experience*, Washington DC, Center for Strategic and International Studies, Georgetown University.

UK, Clothing Economic Development Committee, 1978a, *Progress Report 1978*, London, National Economic Development Council.

UK, Department of Industry, 1978b, *Wool Textile Industry Scheme*, London, Department of Industry.

UK, FCO (Foreign and Commonwealth Office), 1979, *The Newly Industrializing Countries and the Adjustment Problem*, London, FCO, 1979 (Government Economic Service Working Paper no. 18).

UK, House of Commons, 1971–2, *Official Report, Fifth Series, Parliamentary Debates*, vol. 837, cols. 10010.

UK, House of Lords, 1978, *State Aids for Steel*, London, Her Majesty's Stationery Office (11th Report of the Select Committee on the European Communities, Session 1978–9).

UK, House of Lords, 1979, *Textiles*, London, Her Majesty's Stationery Office (16th Report of the Select Committee on the European Communities, Session 1978–9).

UK, NEDO (National Economic Development Office), 1977, *International Price Competitiveness, Non-Price Factors and Export Performance*, London, NEDO.

UN (annual), *Yearbook of International Trade Statistics*, New York, NY, United Nations.

UN (annual), *Yearbook of National Accounts Statistics*, New York, NY, United Nations.

UN, (1978), *Yearbook of International Trade Statistics 1978*, New York, NY, United Nations.

UN, 1979, *Yearbook of Industrial Statistics: General Industrial Statistics 1979*, New York, NY, United Nations.

UN, 1980, *1979 Yearbook of International Trade Statistics*, New York, NY, United Nations.

UNCTAD, 1970, *Liberalization of Non-Tariff Barriers: Adjustment Assistance Measures*, Geneva, UNCTAD, 17 December (Report by the Secretariat, TD/B/C.2/106).

UNCTAD, 1979, *Handbook of International Trade and Development Statistics, 1979*, Geneva, UNCTAD.

UNIDO, 1976, *Draft World-Wide Study of the Iron and Steel Industry 1975–2000*, Vienna, UNIDO, International Centre for Industrial Studies, 15 December (UNIDO/ICIS.25).

UNIDO, 1978a, *The Impact of Trade with Developing Countries on Employment in Developed Countries.* Vienna, UNIDO, International Centre for Industrial Studies (Working Papers on Structural Change no. 3).

UNIDO, 1978b, *Progress Report for the Second Consultation Meeting on the Iron and Steel Industry*, Geneva, UNIDO, 24 October (ID/WG.286/1).

UNIDO, 1978c, *The World Iron and Steel Industry, Second Study*, Vienna, UNIDO, International Centre for Industrial Studies, 20 November (UNIDO/ICIS.89).

UNIDO, 1979a, *World Industry since 1960: Progress and Prospects*, New York, NY, United Nations (Special Issue of the Industrial Development Survey for the Third General Conference of UNIDO).

UNIDO, 1979b, *Industry 2000: New Perspectives*, New York, NY, United Nations.

UNIDO, 1979c, *Report of Second Consultation Meeting on the Iron and Steel Industry*, Vienna, UNIDO (ID/224 (ID/WG.286/7).

USA, Bureau of Labor, 1980, *National Industry Occupation Employment Matrix*, Washington DC, Bureau of Labor.

USA, Comptroller-General. *See* Comptroller-General (USA).

USA, Department of Commerce, 1979, *Long Term Trends in US Steel Con-*

sumption: Implications for Domestic Capacity, Washington DC, Department of Commerce.

USA, Department of Commerce, 1980, *US Industrial Outlook 1980*, Washington DC, Department of Commerce.

USA, Federal Trade Commission, 1977, *The United States Steel Industry and its International Rivals: Trends and Factors Determining International Competitiveness*, Washington DC, Federal Trade Commission (Staff Report to the Bureau of Economics).

Vaupel, J. W., 1971, 'Characteristics of multinational enterprises', Cambridge, Mass., Harvard Business School (unpublished MS, Harvard Multinational Enterprise Project).

Vernon, Raymond (ed.), 1974, *Big Business and the State: Changing Relations in Western Europe*, London, Macmillan.

Verreydt, E., and Waelbroeck, J., 1980, *European Community Protection against Manufactured Imports from Developing Countries: A Case Study of the Political Economy. Protection*, Washington DC, World Bank (Staff Working Paper no. 432).

Waddams, A. Lawrence, 1978, *Chemicals from Petroleum: An Introductory Survey*, London, John Murray.

Walker, W. B., 1980, 'Britain's industrial performance 1850–1950: a failure to adjust', in: Keith Pavitt (ed.), *Technical Innovation and British Economic Performance*, London, Macmillan.

Warnecke, Steven J. (ed.), 1978, *International Trade and Industrial Policies: Government Intervention and an Open World Economy*, London, Macmillan.

Watson, Michael, and Griffiths, R. T. (eds.), 1977, *Government, Business and Labour in European Capitalism*, London, Europotentials Press.

Westphal, Larry E., 1978, 'The Republic of Korea's experience with export-led industrial development', *World Development*, vol. 6, no. 3, pp. 347–82.

Westphal, Larry E., 1979, 'Korea's experience with export-led industrial development', in: *World Bank, Export Promotion Policies*, Washington DC, World Bank.

Westphal, Larry E., and Kim, Kwang Suk, 1977, *Industrial Policy and Development in Korea*, Washington DC, World Bank (Staff Working Paper no. 263).

Wienert, Helmut, 1980, 'World trends in steel consumption and production to 1990', *OECD Symposium on the Steel Industry in the 1980s*, Paris, OECD, February (paper).

Wolf, Martin, 1979, *Adjustment Policies and Problems in Developed Countries*, Washington DC, World Bank (Staff Working Paper no. 349).

Wolter, Frank, 1976, 'Adjusting to imports from developing countries: the evidence from a human capital rich, natural resource poor country', in: H. Giersch (ed.), *Reshaping the World Economy*, Tübingen, Mohr.

Wolter, Frank, 1979, *Industrial Policy in the Federal Republic of Germany*, Kiel (mimeo.).

Woolcock, Stephen, 1980, *Industrial Policy in the European Community*, Edinburgh, University of Edinburgh (M.Phil. thesis).

Woolcock, Stephen, 1981, 'Industrial adjustment: the Community dimension', in: William Wallace (ed.), *Economic Divergence in the European Community*, London, Allen & Unwin.

Woolcock, Stephen, 1982, 'The international politics of trade and production in the steel industry', in: John Pinder (ed.), *National Industrial Strategies and the World Economy*, Totowa, N. J., Allanheld Osman.

World Bank, 1978, *World Development Report 1978*, Washington DC, World Bank.

World Bank, 1979a, *World Development Report 1979*, Washington DC, World Bank.

World Bank, 1979b, *World Trade and Output of Manufactures: Structural Trends and Developing Countries' Exports*, Washington DC, World Bank.

World Bank, 1979c, *The Changing Composition of Developing Country Exports*, Washington DC, World Bank.

World Bank, 1979d, *Mexico: Manufacturing Sector: Situation, Prospects and Policies*, Washington DC, World Bank.

World Bank, 1979e, *Export Promotion Policies*, Washington DC, World Bank.

World Bank, 1979f, *Development Indicators 1979*, Washington DC, World Bank.

World Bank, 1979g, *1979 World Bank Atlas*, Washington DC, World Bank.

World Bank, 1980a, *World Development Report 1980*, New York, NY, World Bank, Oxford University Press.

World Bank, 1980b, *Annual Report 1980*, Washington DC, World Bank.

Zysman, John, 1978, 'The state as trader', *International Affairs*, vol. 54, no. 2, April, pp. 264–81.

Zysman, John, 1980, 'Remarks', *'Towards the 1980s in US/EC Relations'*, Conference Organized by the University Association for Contemporary European Studies, London, 26–27 March.

Index